HIGHWAY 99

The History of California's Main Street

HIGHWAY
99
The History of California's Main Street

Stephen H. Provost

CRAVEN
STREET
B O O K S
Fresno, California

Published by Craven Street Books
An imprint of Linden Publishing
2006 South Mary Street, Fresno, California 93721
(559) 233-6633 / (800) 345-4447
CravenStreetBooks.com

Craven Street Books and Colophon are trademarks of
Linden Publishing, Inc.

ISBN 978-1-61035-296-3

35798642

Printed in the United States of America
on acid-free paper.

Library of Congress Cataloging-in-Publication Data

Names: Provost, Stephen H., author.
Title: Highway 99 : the history of California's Main Street / Stephen H.
    Provost.
Description: Fresno, Calif. : Craven Street Books, 2017. | Includes
    bibliographical references and index.
Identifiers: LCCN 2017035955 | ISBN 9781610352963 (pbk. : alk. paper)
Subjects: LCSH: United States Highway 99--History. | California--Description
    and travel. | California--History, Local. | Automobile
    travel--California--History.
Classification: LCC F866 .P85 2017 | DDC 979.4--dc23
LC record available at https://lccn.loc.gov/2017035955

Contents

ACKNOWLEDGMENTS

Several people were instrumental in helping me make this work possible through their contributions, guidance, and support. Among them:

Deborah Cismowski (now retired) of the Caltrans office in Sacramento graciously allowed me to comb through folder after folder of agency photographs for most of an afternoon, then scanned and emailed them to me for use in this volume. Bonnie Ketterl Kane did the same at the Ridge Route Communities Historical Museum in Frazier Park and pointed me toward a volume she authored titled *A View from the Ridge Route: The Roadways* as a helpful resource. Art Van Rhyn, editorial cartoonist for *The Cambrian* newspaper, where I served as managing editor starting in 2014, even allowed me to use some of his own photos and material he dug up while writing a paper on the Ridge Route several decades ago.

Louie Dewey of Cave Springs Motel in Dunsmuir, Neil Pollard of Pollardville in Stockton, and Ron Perry of the Tulare-based Perry's Coffee Shop chain provided invaluable insights about the roadside culture during the Golden Age of Highway 99.

Several highway experts and historians also provided expertise. Michael J. Semas, author of postcard series books on Fresno and Kings County, graciously supplied a number of photos from his personal collection. Joel Windmiller's background as historian of highways in general and U.S. 99 in particular was greatly appreciated. Historian Michael Ballard also provided insightful information about the history of the highway between the San Fernando Valley and Bakersfield. John Kelley, president of the Ridge Route Preservation Organization, also provided helpful information along with tips on where to look for photos.

I'd also like to thank Kent Sorsky, Jaguar Bennett, and the rest of the team at Linden Publishing/Craven Street Books for their faith in me and in this project, and for their support and professionalism throughout the process of bringing this dream to fruition. I'm also grateful to William B. Secrest Jr. for his thoughtful foreword that perfectly captures the tone and substance of this work. I want to thank my parents, David and Lollie Provost, for driving me up and down the highway between Fresno and Los Angeles too many times to count. Then there was my grandmother, Frances Larsen, who put up with a young boy counting gas stations—and becoming very animated about it at times—as he rode in the backseat with her. Most of all, I'd like to thank my wife and fellow writer, Samaire, who has been unwavering in her faith that I would succeed as an author. Her support and input have been invaluable through this and a series of other projects.

This undated panoramic shot shows the Grapevine area of the Ridge Route. *From the collection of Art Van Rhyn.*

IN LOVING MEMORY OF MY FATHER, DR. DAVID H. PROVOST, WHO INTRODUCED ME TO THE HIGHWAY, ENCOURAGED ME TO WRITE, AND ALWAYS SUPPORTED ME. THIS ONE'S FOR YOU, DAD.

FOREWORD

As a pathway to advance society and civilization, California's Highway 99 rightfully takes its place among history's foremost thoroughfares. Like the Appian Way and the Great Silk Road, it made commerce feasible and reliable over a vast region. Today, it's an essential unit of the world's sixth-largest economy, moving people and tonnage by the millions every year.

Perhaps the greatest testimony to this road's importance lies in the fact that much of it was created long before there was a California. The native populations, recognizing the value of trading foods and materials throughout the region, established lengthy north–south trails that fairly parallel today's Highway 99. They couldn't imagine their world without it—nor can we.

As the route's modern era began, horses, carts, and stages gave way to railroads, and railroads then yielded to today's paved lanes. Thus the Highway 99 we know is a relatively recent creation. Yet in that time, it's become far more than a transportation artery, evolving a distinct culture replete with gateway arches, distinctive hotels, deluxe fruit stands, and vest-pocket amusement parks.

It should surprise everyone that this road has never found a proper biographer—until now. Noticing this glaring gap in the Golden State's story, Stephen Provost assumed the mantle of Highway 99's Boswell, chronicling the rise and fall of landmarks such as J's Coffee Shops, the Richfield beacons, Pollardville, the pretentiously named Emery Whilton Florafaunium, and so much more.

The temptation to dwell on such minutiae is great (in fact, irresistible). To his credit, Steve has seen fit to balance these delectable asides and anecdotes with a traditional narrative, depicting the political and engineering process that gave birth to the road we know, and how California's ever-increasing population required innumerable improvements and adjustments to it. Some phases of this tale—especially the one relating the convoluted Ridge Route's multiyear unkinking—are remarkable additions to the record of major American public works.

Studies of this sort are few. We must salute Steve for understanding how to present this material in a way that will make those living around Highway 99 feel nostalgic, and those unfamiliar with the story, appreciative; and, also, for his exhaustive recourse to hundreds of books, articles, and ephemera necessary to assemble this account. The bibliography demonstrates that the research effort must have been overwhelming. That the author prevailed and crafted such a lucid account, lively on every page, is remarkable in itself.

For the first time, then, we have a full portrait of Highway 99, where its split personality is unveiled to all. It's partly commercial pipeline, partly collection of roadside diversions and relief stations. It conflates the practical, humdrum, and frivolous. While it serves the same purpose as many other roads, there's nothing else like it anywhere. And no matter what you think of the landscape it's created, we must concede it's been absolutely successful at its designated mission.

That being the case, isn't it a lot like California itself?

—William B. Secrest Jr., author of *Greetings from Fresno* and editor of *Garden of the Sun*

The map above depicts the historic path taken by Highway 99 through California, along with some of the many bypasses created through the years.

INTRODUCTION

I grew up on Highway 99—not the old U.S. route, which was decommissioned a year after I was born, but the California freeway with the green shield. My grandparents lived in Southern California, so at least twice a year my parents would load me into the car and we'd head south from our home in Fresno.

My grandmother, who spent summers with us and winters down south, would often head up by bus to be collected at the Greyhound station in downtown Fresno. Even though she never learned to drive, she probably saw more of the old road than the rest of us. At one time, this "Main Street of California" lived up to its name: It passed straight through the cities and farm towns along its path, past storefronts and through major intersections.

By the time I was born, the new freeway had bypassed many of the old stoplights, guardians of what came to be called Business 99 or Golden State Boulevard, fragments of which emerge in places like J and K streets in Tulare or Union Avenue in Bakersfield. As an adult, I remember stopping at the last stoplight on 99, up in Livingston at the Blueberry Hill

Café. Even that last way station became a memory when the Livingston Bypass opened in the middle of 1996; the old café was lost in the bargain, demolished to make way for the new thoroughfare.

But most of my memories of traveling up and down Highway 99 are from my childhood. Like any kid, I passed the time whatever way I could. Maybe you played "Slug Bug" or the alphabet game, trying to find letters of the alphabet in order on billboards or license plates. Or maybe you played Mad Libs and asked your parents every couple of minutes, "Are we there yet?"

Me? When I was young, I lay in the backseat of my parents' blue Pontiac Grand Prix, staring out through the windows at the passing phone poles, billboards, and stands of eucalyptus. When I got older, I kept track of how many gas stations of each brand I could find. Chevron always wound up with the most, followed by Shell and Union 76, but I was always particularly thrilled to find one of the lesser-known stations: a Sunland or a Hancock or a Terrible Herbst.

Cars still travel this stretch of former Highway 99 (Union Avenue) near Greenfield heading to and from Bakersfield.

There were plenty of other sights to see along the way, too. There were fruit stands, coffee shops, roadside attractions, and motels. There were signs announcing the entrance to the next town on the horizon, some bearing catchy slogans and others covered with the symbols of numerous service clubs and churches. There were Good Sam Club stops and other highways that branched out to far-flung destinations. At least they seemed far-flung to a kid.

Many of those places are gone now, boarded up or torn down. Some of their ghosts still haunt the freeway in the form of signs standing over vacant lots and in the memories of those who recall them fondly.

These are the ghosts of the Golden Road, and this is their story.

PART I:
THE STORY OF
OLD 99

1

MAKING THE CONNECTION

The Rincon Road Causeway in Ventura County, seen here in 1912, was the predecessor of U.S. 101. Plank roads and wooden causeways were an early form of roadway that quickly gave way to roads built of sturdier stuff.
McCurry Foto Co., public domain, 1912.

Y ou can't take it with you.

In 1910, "it" was your automobile. Californians were still nearly a generation away from Herbert Hoover's famous (or infamous) campaign promise of "a chicken in every pot and a car in every garage." Still, with the introduction of Henry Ford's trendsetting Model T two years earlier, the age of the automobile was starting to pick up the kind of steam no railway engine had ever mustered. That year, Ford produced more than 32,000 Model T's,

and No. 2 automaker Willys-Overland cranked out more than 18,000. Already, there were more than 450,000 cars on American roads.

But almost all those roads were in the cities. If you wanted to get out of town, chances were good that you still went by rail; there simply was no system of intercity or interstate highways in place to accommodate gasoline-powered vehicles.

The California State Legislature had recognized the problem in 1909, when it passed the first State Highway Bond Act, an $18 million issue that voters approved the following year. (That would amount to more than $426 million in 2014 dollars.)

A RICH HISTORY

Many wax nostalgic about the Lincoln Highway or Route 66, but the road that would become Highway 99 has a history that is just as illustrious as those famed early routes. The Lincoln Highway was the brainchild of Indianapolis Motor Speedway principal Carl Fisher, who promoted the idea of connecting America's two coasts two years *after* California passed its historic bond measure. The idea was to create a paved road all the way from New York to the Bay Area in time for the Panama-Pacific International Exposition in San Francisco in 1915. Unfortunately, there wasn't enough money to complete the project, which emerged as a patchwork of dirt highways interspersed with paved "seedling miles" designed to showcase the contrast between the two surfaces.

Route 66, meanwhile, didn't arrive on the scene until 1926, when the U.S. Highway System replaced a patchwork network of auto trails. "Trails" was the right word for them, too, because they were more dirt—and sometimes mud—than concrete. The Ocean-to-Ocean Highway, established in 1912, was the predecessor to Route 66 and ran more than 3,000 miles from Maryland to California. But by the time it was incorporated into the U.S. Highway System as Route 66, less than one-third of that distance (800 miles) was actually paved.

To make matters worse, many of the early trails were roads to nowhere … or somewhere pretty far out of the way. Cities and businesses paid dues to promote and maintain the roads, so naturally the roads themselves wound up directing traffic to those cities and businesses. In some cases, competing interests promoted different routes between Point A and Point B. Travelers had to guess which was the most direct and best maintained. Often, it was a matter of trial and error—or trial and flat tire, if the chosen roadway proved to be little more than a badly rutted dirt track.

California, with its voter-funded system, provided a contrast. Not only were the highways part of an inte-grated system that predated the national network by more than a decade, they were also clearly marked thanks to the efforts of California's two auto associations, which created uniform road signs by the thousands. These signs, with black lettering on white porcelain backed by steel, stood in marked contrast to the crude markers posted by private trail associations outside the state, some of which were nothing more than hand-painted signs nailed to telephone poles or propped up against barns.

The same year Carl Fisher first floated his plan for the Lincoln Highway, the state of California broke ground on the first contract in its planned statewide network, a portion of what is now State Route 82 in San Mateo County. The date was August 7, 1912. A three-member highway commission oversaw the mammoth project, which ended up costing more than the initial $18 million approved under the 1910 bond act. So five years later, in 1915, voters passed a second bond that allocated $12 million to finish the job, plus $3 million more for an additional 680 miles of roadway.

The initial bond set forth plans for 31 state legislative routes, numbered 1–30 plus a Route 34. The numbers don't correspond to the modern highway numbers, and

In 1916, the road that would become U.S. 99—seen here north of Bakersfield—was little more than a country road still used, at times, by horse and buggy. At the time, it was known as state Legislative Route 4. © *California Department of Transportation, used with permission.*

they were indicated only on maps, not highway signs, but they did set forth a plan that formed the basis for the modern network. Route 4, for instance, was a 359-mile stretch of highway from Sacramento to Los Angeles that later became the backbone of the state and western U.S. highway system: U.S. Route 99. The southern section of what would become U.S. 99 was Route 26 (often referred to as LRN 26, for Legislative Route Number 26), which in 1935 ran from Aliso Street in Los Angeles to Calexico via Monterey Park, Pomona, Colton, and El Centro.

CHOOSING A PATH

When the members of California's Highway Commission decided to carve out a path for the state's new north–south highway, they weren't starting with a blank slate. Even before the advent of the automobile, people had been making long treks up and down the coast on dirt trails cleared for travel on foot, horseback, or, later, via stagecoach. Among the longest of these was the Siskiyou Trail, which began as a series of Native American footpaths and, in the 1820s, became a favored route for trappers and hunters associated with the Hudson's Bay Company.

These traders forged the trail by traveling south from the Hudson's Bay trading post on the Columbia River, across the entire state of Oregon, and southward to Stockton. Alexander McLeod led an expedition to the Sacramento Valley in 1828, creating what some called the Southern Party Trail and others referred to as the California Brigade Trail. If there was any doubt about where the trail lay, it likely disappeared beneath the hooves of 700 head of cattle that trader Ewing Young drove northward from California to Oregon in 1837.

It wasn't long before traders began settling along the route. In 1844, Pierson Reading received a land grant from the Mexican governor around the site that later became the town of Redding. According to some accounts, he pronounced his name "Redding," but this isn't the origin of the town's name. In fact, it was named for railroad man Benjamin Redding after the Southern Pacific laid down track there in 1873. Settlers tried to change the name to Reading in honor of the early pioneer, but the railroad refused to hear of it and the Redding name stuck.

By that time, many more frontiersmen had settled in the area, drawn by the Gold Rush. The railroad route followed the Siskiyou Trail and, farther south through the San Joaquin Valley, blazed a trail of its own that Highway 99 would one day follow. This only made sense: Towns popped up around depots on the rail line, and road builders would lay down highways to connect those towns. Even today, motorists driving the highway between Bakersfield and Fresno find the tracks a near-constant companion.

A section of the Ridge Route near Sandberg shows the original concrete paving and a layer of asphalt used when the road was widened and modernized. The asphalt proved less durable than the concrete, wearing away over time to reveal the road's first surface underneath.

WHAT IN SAM HILL?

At the dawn of the new century, California wasn't alone in its ambition to create a new highway system. Sam Hill, the son-in-law of a major railroad operator, formed the Washington State Good Roads Association in the waning days of the 19th century, a move that eventually led the state to form its own highway department in 1905. A few years later, Hill bought a 7,000-acre ranch near the Columbia River. He originally intended it as the site of a Quaker colony, but it instead came to serve as an immense outdoor laboratory for the nascent road-building industry.

"Good roads are more than my hobby," Hill declared, "they are my religion."

He proved it by spending $100,000 of his own money to build several miles of roads on his ranch, using them to demonstrate various surfacing techniques.

Until this time, many of the best roads were "macadamized," the name for a process created by a Scotsman named John Loudon McAdam in 1820. The technique was relatively simple: Road builders would clear a smooth path, elevated with a slight slope for drainage. As long as the road was kept dry, McAdam reasoned, a layer of small stones would suffice to convey horse and buggy to their destination on a (relatively) smooth surface. Later engineers mixed stone dust with water to fill in the gaps between the stones and provide a still-smoother ride, but when the age of the automobile rolled around, a new problem arose: dust. The new contraptions kicked up a lot more of it than the old buggies had, and road builders adapted by spraying tar on the surface of the roads to keep the dust down. The practice gave rise to the word "tarmac"—from a combination of "tar" and "macadamized"—and paved the way for the asphalt roadways of the future.

Hill explored half a dozen paving techniques on his ranch, building segments in each style to see which would work best:

- concrete
- macadam
- oil-treated crushed rock macadam
- sand and gravel macadam
- decomposed rock macadam
- asphalt macadam

They were the first paved roads in the state, and Hill wanted to be sure they wouldn't be the last, so he paid for the governor and the entire state legislature to visit them and see the future for themselves.

In the meantime, he became involved in the effort to construct a highway from British Columbia to the Mexican border. This grand vision was born in the fall of 1910, when a group of automobile enthusiasts met in Seattle to form the Pacific Highway Association.

The purpose of the group, according to news accounts, was "to construct a trunk line highway from Canada to Mexico." Most of the members came from the Pacific Northwest, but Los Angeles was also represented at that initial meeting, and Hill was a major booster.

Hill himself turned the first shovelful of dirt in breaking ground for the new highway in late November of 1913 south of Ashland, Oregon. The northern stretch of the Canada-to-Mexico highway did, indeed, become known as the Pacific Highway—not to be confused with the Pacific Coast Highway (California State Highway 1), which runs along much of the California coastline. The section of highway that passed through the San Joaquin Valley, however, was generally called the Valley Route until 1927, when a tourist association conducted a formal naming contest.

There was incentive to enter: First prize was a week-long stay for two at Yosemite National Park; second was a free pass, good for a year at any theater in the West Coast Theaters chain; and third was a free quart of Benham's ice cream every Sunday for a year.

Some 10,000 people submitted suggestions, with one Taft resident entering 20 times. But it was James S. Anderson of Fresno who came up with the winner: Golden State Highway. Runners-up were Fremont Highway (presumably in honor of early California governor John C. Fremont), California Highway, Sierra View Highway, and Inland Empire Highway. In the years to come the Golden State name would stick, not only for the valley, but also for the area to the south of the Tehachapi Mountains.

The Long White Line

There, in 1917, the road that would become Highway 99 bore witness to a milestone, sparked by a truck driver's poor navigation.

June McCarroll had moved from Nebraska to Southern California in 1904 after her husband contracted a case of "consumption" (tuberculosis). Fortunately, June was a physician, and she hoped the dry climate would speed her husband's recovery. En route to Los Angeles, the couple stopped at a tuberculosis health camp in the desert town of Indio, which was run by a politician with designs on the Los Angeles mayor's office. He ulti-

June McCarroll, a physician from Indio, painted a white line down the center of Indio Boulevard to keep vehicles from drifting onto the wrong side of the road. Here, a double bridge over the Whitewater River carries westbound out-of-town traffic on Indio Boulevard. The westbound span was built in 1956, a year after the eastbound lanes, built in 1925, were reconfigured for their current use.

mately lost the race, but during the time he spent on the road campaigning, he entrusted the Indio operation to McCarroll and her husband.

Soon McCarroll's practice expanded beyond caring for tuberculosis patients. Her patient load increased significantly in 1908 when the Bureau of Indian Affairs selected her as physician for the Cahuilla tribe, which was spread out over five reservations—all of which lacked electricity and running water. She performed routine surgeries such as tonsillectomies and, in 1908, helped the community endure a measles epidemic.

After McCarroll's husband died in 1914, she eventually cut back on her schedule and remarried. It was three years later, when she was driving home in the lengthening shadows of twilight, that she saw a truck coming straight for her. She swerved and just managed to avoid a collision, running off the road and into the sandy earth so common in the area.

"My Model T Ford and I found ourselves face to face with a truck on the paved highway," she later recalled. "It

did not take me long to choose between a sandy berth on the right and a ten-ton truck on the left!"

The incident must have thrown a scare into her, but McCarroll wasn't the type to back down, so she was soon back behind the wheel again. Not long afterward, she found herself on a different road in the area that had recently been widened to 16 feet—twice its original size. The old and new pavement hadn't fit together perfectly: In the center was a pronounced ridge that clearly separated one from the other. This feature had the unintended consequence of keeping vehicles from straying onto the wrong side of the road … and gave June McCarroll an idea: What if the road builders were to draw a line down the center of the road, clearly distinguishing which side was which? She took her inspiration to the county supervisors, who dismissed it with polite talk and no action.

So McCarroll decided to draw her own line in the sand or, rather, on the pavement. Taking some cake flour, she traipsed out onto the center of Indio Boulevard (later a segment of Old 99), got down on her knees, and painted a white stripe four inches wide in the middle of the road, covering a distance of two miles.

But even this graphic illustration of how to fix the problem failed to convince the local authorities that action was necessary; they simply weren't interested in going to the time or expense of doing anything about it. Still, McCarroll wouldn't quit. With the support of the local women's club and its statewide parent organization, she lobbied the Highway Commission to implement her idea. Seven years after her near collision, the state legislature approved the concept, one that later spread to virtually every mile of public highway in the United States.

The broken white lines, adopted to cut the cost of paint, and the double yellow lines that prohibit passing came later.

Traversing muddy roads that were little more than trails could be challenging even on flat surfaces—and impossible when floods roared through the canyons used by early travelers. Here, a pair of motorists navigates what passes for a road in the Owens Valley around 1907.
Public domain.

Over the Mountains

When it came to building the Pacific/Golden State Highway, the most challenging section of terrain for planners and construction workers was the Tehachapi mountain range that separated the San Joaquin and San Fernando valleys. The name is said to have been derived from *tihachipia*, a word in the Kawaiisu language meaning "hard climb."

It turned out to be appropriate.

There was precedent for crossing the mountains. The Southern Pacific rail line had traversed the mountain range via the Soledad Pass, making its way up through Mojave and Tehachapi, then up across Tejon Pass. The line, completed in 1876, followed what seemed to be the path of least resistance, going around the Tehachapis as much as possible. But it was also the path of least resistance for waters, as the route was subject to frequent and severe washouts during winter storms.

A report in the December 27 edition of the *San Francisco Chronicle* in 1889 stated: "Terrible washouts have occurred in the Soledad canyon. Five miles are under twenty feet of water. Several stretches of 1000 feet each of track are washed out, besides small ones. One iron and many wooden bridges are washed away."

The Highway Commission considered—and rejected—the Soledad Pass option and three other established routes. All three ran roughly parallel to one another from Saugus, at the north end of the San Fernando Valley, northeast through the San Gabriel Mountains. Once drivers reached the Antelope Valley, they would hook back northwest toward the Tejon Pass and follow the path of today's highway north to Bakersfield.

The middle of the three routes, Bouquet Canyon, was out of the question because it suffered from bad drainage. This problem was common along routes that had started out as horse and wagon trails, following paths already set by river canyons. Wherever the waterway changed course, crossing the canyon, the road would have to cross it, creating a muddy, mucky predicament for the wheels of carriages and motorcars alike.

With Bouquet Canyon eliminated from the equation, planners were left with two other possibilities: the longest route, which went through Mint Canyon to the south, and the San Francisquito Canyon route, the option farthest north and west.

A 1907 journey across the mountains by two touring cars, a Reo and a Columbia, illustrated the pitfalls of each route. The Reo went by way of San Francisquito, while the Columbia followed Mint Canyon to the east. Both cars emerged on the other side of the mountains at the same time, but a newspaper account noted that "a great deal of trouble was experienced by the Reo on account of bad roads and grades, and though the route is some 40 miles shorter than the other, it is estimated that more time was lost than gained."

San Francisquito was the older of the two routes and, while more direct, presented early motorists with an obstacle course. In addition to a steep grade that extended over four miles, drivers had to navigate some 60 fords (waterways, not automobiles) in a span of just 11 miles. In winter, the number was more like 100. No wonder the Reo took so long traversing this primitive roadway.

The Mint Canyon alternative, by contrast, presented few if any fords on a route of easy grades interspersed with flat table lands. It was well marked by Automobile Club of Southern California signs and seemed the logical choice, but it was also rejected. Paving such a long stretch of road in concrete was deemed simply too expensive (it eventually became the corridor for State Route 14, the southern end of the Sierra Highway to Lake Tahoe).

Yet another route, through Piru Canyon to the west, wound up being used for the Ridge Route Alternate that opened in 1933, but it was ruled out at the time because plans called for a dam to be built on Piru Creek. Ironically, the dam eventually was built, creating Pyramid Lake and submerging the Ridge Route Alternate (U.S. Highway 99) under 72 billion gallons of water in 1973. The modern Interstate 5 was built nearby to replace it.

After San Francisquito Canyon was eliminated from consideration, a dam was built there, as well—with disastrous consequences, as we shall see later.

As for the path ultimately chosen for the highway over the mountains, it didn't go through any canyon but right over the top of the ridge. Hence the name: the Ridge Route.

②

ON TOP OF THE WORLD

A sign near Sandberg designates the old Ridge Route as "a miracle of modern engineering providing safety with a maximum speed of 15 m.p.h. and a saving of 44 miles over the former road."

The folks mapping out California's roadway system might have wished they'd chosen a different route for its trans-range mountain highway.

I can just picture them saying, "It seemed like a good idea at the time."

The Highway Commission wanted a direct route across the mountains, one designed to avoid both the natural obstacles of the soon-to-be-dam(n)med San Francisquito Canyon and the cost overruns projected for the Mint Canyon option. In 1912, however, there was no such direct route. The highway builders couldn't very well blast their way through such a long stretch of mountainous terrain, so they would simply have to go over the top of it—which is exactly what they did.

They didn't follow any previous road or even any old trail. They blazed a new one. Well, "blazed" isn't exactly the right word.

The most popular car of the day, Ford's Model T, was no speedster, topping out at about 45 mph. But the speed limit over the Ridge Route was only one-third that: 15 mph. That's the same speed required of modern drivers going through a blind intersection.

Why so slow?

These cars were going over the top of the mountains, like children taking stepping-stones across a creek. Drivers had to be careful to avoid going off the narrow road, because it was a long way down, and there were a lot of turns. A lot, as in 697 of them. That's 77 more than the Hana Highway on the island of Maui, where drivers in modern cars need 2½ hours to cover a mere 52 miles. Imagine navigating the equivalent of more than a hundred complete circles in an old Tin Lizzy with a crank starter, no power steering (or power brakes), and a two-gear system. That's what it took to get from Bakersfield to L.A. on the Ridge Route.

A section of highway between Lebec and Grapevine, seen in the early 1930s, provides a glimpse of the beauty described by authors who traveled the road.
© *California Department of Transportation.*

The Automobile Club of Southern California described the road in vivid terms as being "so torturous as to give a backache to a king snake."

Yet despite these drawbacks, the new road, once finished, was hailed as a wonder of modern engineering and a vast improvement over any of the routes that had preceded it. As the road prepared to open in November of 1915, *The Bakersfield Californian* predicted that travelers would be able to leave Bakersfield in the morning and reach L.A. in time for lunch, "and without speeding either."

The editor marveled that "the traveler of the future will not chug his way down sandy canyons and along the edge of desert wastes, through a section dreary to the eye and devoid of interest." Over the Ridge Route, he declared, "each dip of the road over the brow of the mountain, each curve that sweeps around jutting hill from one canyon to the next, opens up a new vista, presents new delights to the eye, the whole constituting a journey through a seeming garden of nature."

The writer concluded: "The authorities in charge of the great task of building the highways of the state have done much splendid work, but they have done nothing that surpasses the Ridge route."

Thomas D. Murphy, author of the book *On Sunset Highways*, was similarly impressed: "No description or picture can give any idea of the stupendous grandeur of the panorama that unrolls before one on this marvelous road," he gushed. "Vast stretches of gigantic hills interspersed with titanic canyons—mostly barren, with reds and browns predominating—outrun the limits of one's vision."

And the Kern County Chamber of Commerce described it as "a paved road on the rim of the world, where the skyline is a highway in the cloud."

Initially, the highway was oil and gravel. The concrete would come later, in 1919.

But even before the road opened, a number of landowners along its path set plans in motion to capitalize on it.

Cornelia Martinez Callahan, who lived near the southern end of the route, deeded some of her land to the state for the project but probably made back whatever money she sacrificed by selling gas and refreshments to passing motorists once the road was open. Her husband had just died, and she ran the place herself, earning the nickname (for whatever reason) "the witch of the Ridge Route."

Nell, as she was known, was just one of several people who set up car service stops along the ridge for travelers whose vehicles had overheated, run out of gas, or otherwise broken down. Driving north, you'd find the Owl Garage, which sold Standard gas and, just a couple of miles up the road, the Ridge Road Garage. Another mile farther on was Martin's, which also dispensed Standard gasoline. While the Ridge Route traversed some remote territory, motorists were never far from an outpost of civilization.

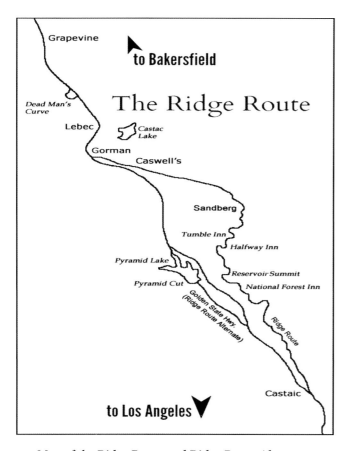

Map of the Ridge Route and Ridge Route Alternate.

If you wanted a room for the night or a bite to eat, you could find those, too. At various points along the way, enterprising souls had built inns, auto cabins, and other accommodations for those too tired or dizzy from the curves to make the trip in a single shot.

Farthest south was the National Forest Inn, where you could rent one of nine heated cottage rooms—complete with running water—for $2 a night in 1926. If you wanted to rough it, you could pay 50 cents to camp. Lunch was available for 75 cents, and you could fill up your tank with General Petroleum, a Southern California company that had more than one distributor along the mountain road. (General Petroleum was sold to Socony—Standard Oil Company of New York—in 1926, which later combined with Vacuum Oil to form Mobil, one-half of ExxonMobil.)

Fred Courtemanche, a French Canadian carpenter who had come to California in 1915, opened the National Forest Inn a year later; he hung a makeshift sign stating "U R WELCOME" over the front entrance, and the business grew from there. It wasn't just a way station for travelers crossing the mountains, it was also a weekend getaway destination for folks from the Newhall-Saugus area. Those so inclined could indulge themselves in a night of dancing or a few games of tennis.

The inn took its name from the Angeles National Forest, from which it leased the land. The area was prone to wildfires, and in 1928, a thousand firefighters

The National Forest Inn was a popular stopping point before it burned to the ground in 1932.
Ridge Route Communities Historical Society

waged what one newspaper called "a frantic battle" against an out-of-control blaze that started nearby. The fire started when a truck carrying provisions to a ranch near the inn toppled over and caught fire, the flames quickly spreading across 5,000 to 10,000 acres. Seven people trying to traverse the Ridge Route were trapped and severely burned, one critically. Fortunately for the inn's owners and guests, the establishment itself escaped damage.

Manuel Martin, who purchased the inn from Courtemanche about the time of the 1928 fire, wasn't as fortunate a few years later. In January of 1932, a fire that started in the garage burned the place to the ground. According to one account, Martin managed to save the cash register from the garage as it burned. Because the new, more direct Ridge Route Alternate diverted most traffic away from the original Ridge Route the following year, Martin never bothered to rebuild. He died five years later at the age of 62.

Kelly's offered three furnished rooms, camp cottages, and lunch. The Mohawk-Hobbs 1926 *Pacific Highway Guide* also noted that it featured a "good small garage with tow car." The accommodations weren't as high-class or extensive as what you'd find at the National Forest Inn, but it was a place to stop. Unlike the National Forest Inn, it survived after the Ridge Route Alternate was built: The owner tore down the buildings, carted off the pieces, and reassembled them at a new location known as Young's Place along the modern three-lane Highway 99, at the intersection with state Highway 138. Later known as the Sky Ranch, it had a lunch counter, tables, and a Mobil service station to fill 'er up.

A couple of miles north of Kelly's on the old Ridge Route was the Tumble Inn, a sprawling complex built in 1921 that offered rooms for $2 (the same price you'd pay at the National Forest Inn), along with a restaurant and Richfield gas station. Like the National Forest Inn, it was built by the Courtemanche family—in this case, Fred

Kelly's Halfway Inn, like many stops along the Ridge Route, offered travelers a place to gas up and a garage in case their vehicles broke down—as they were known to do with some frequency on the road.
Ridge Route Communities Historical Society.

If the National Forest Inn wasn't to your liking or you wanted to make it at least halfway across the mountains before stopping for the night, you could travel another 7½ miles to Kelly's Halfway Inn. To get there, you'd have to navigate Serpentine Drive, one of the most curve-intensive stretches of roadway, and pass through Swede's Cut, created when steam shovels carved a 110-foot-deep passageway straight through a mountain.

Courtemanche's brother Frank, who got a helping hand from his sibling on the project. The pair made extensive use of river rock on the front of the buildings and porch pillars to give the inn a rustic look.

Coincidentally, the inn stood at 4,144 feet, the exact elevation of Tejon Pass on the current Interstate 5, but it was hardly the highest point on the Ridge Route.

The inn closed when the Ridge Route Alternate opened, though it remained standing for two more decades. For a time during World War II, a family leased the inn and lived in the restaurant, using the remote location as a place of refuge in the event of a Japanese attack on the West Coast. They left after the war, and by 1952 the inn had been torn down, leaving only some concrete steps that once led to the establishment and now lead nowhere at all.

Also long gone is the most impressive inn on the Ridge Route, Sandberg's Summit Hotel, which stood about 4 miles north of the Tumble Inn. Norwegian immigrant Harald Sandberg had acquired the land where his hotel would be built two decades earlier as part of three adjoining homesteads approved by the U.S. government in 1897. He and his brother and sister each applied for and received 160 acres, where they established a ranch. Harald bought his two siblings out a few years later and, in 1910, planted an apple orchard on the property.

Sandberg's was the most prestigious inn on the original Ridge Route, catering to tourists, not truckers. This photo shows an early incarnation of the mountain resort. *Ridge Route Communities Historical Society.*

The apples were an immediate hit, and Sandberg's Mountain Apples were soon available across the state. He even sent a box to each president from Woodrow Wilson to Franklin D. Roosevelt as an inauguration gift.

As profitable as the apples were, Harald Sandberg saw something even more lucrative coming down the road: automobiles. And the road in question was the soon-to-

Sandberg's later expanded to include second and third stories. *Ridge Route Communities Historical Society.*

be-built Ridge Route. Knowing that this great highway would soon be meandering right past his front door, Sandberg built a single-story inn, restaurant (Sandberg's Meals), and garage in 1914, then added to it in the 1920s. Eventually, the hotel grew to three stories: A post office shared the first floor with the lobby and dining room, the Sandberg family occupied the second floor, and guests stayed on the third or in one of the cabins out back.

In contrast to the Tumble Inn's river rock construction, Sandberg's Summit used a log cabin theme that was appropriate to the hotel's elevation. Harald Sandberg built it himself, using a sawmill on the property that ran off electricity he generated himself. Surrounded by oak trees, the hotel stood just north of Liebre Summit (the road's highest point at 4,233 feet), and it offered "elevated" accommodations in more ways than one. At $2.50 to $3.50, they cost a little more than a room at the National Forest or Tumble Inn, but all were equipped not only with running water but toilets. The restaurant stayed open all night, and so did the garage, which sold Richfield gas. The hotel even had its own phone booth.

A trip to the dining room might have meant a taste of Marion Sandberg's famous apple pie or apple dumplings, which she baked using fruit from the apple orchard on the property. Dinner was a dollar, or you could just relax and read a good book in front of an impressive stone fireplace.

Sandberg wanted to ensure that his hotel remained a high-class resort, serving tourists rather than truckers seeking a bed for the night. If the higher prices didn't keep the riffraff away, a sign on the property made it explicit: "Truck drivers and dogs not allowed." Vagabonds passing through were either shown the door or given work in the Sandberg's apple orchards.

Little remains at Sandberg to indicate that the once-grand resort ever existed. This stone wall east of the road is among the few remnants of the once-sprawling ranch and resort.

The resort drew an exclusive clientele, including an actress and filmmaker named Ida Lupino, who had a fondness for horseback riding. Lupino, who had once drawn the attentions of Howard Hughes, appeared in 59 films and directed seven others during a career that spanned nearly half a century. Her trip to Sandberg was less successful, however: As she was riding on horseback near the lodge, a wayward tree branch got in her way and knocked her to the ground.

One of the most famous people to ever stay there, however, never left. Ulysses S. Grant Jr., son of the Civil War general and president, was on his way back to his home in San Diego after a trip to Northern California with his wife. A noted attorney and investor, the younger Grant had built the U.S. Grant Hotel in San Diego and at one time ranked as that city's biggest taxpayer. He checked into Sandberg's with his wife in late September of 1929 and proceeded to retire for the evening.

He was found dead in his room the next morning.

Sandberg's weathered the bad publicity, and the hotel made it just fine through other adversity, too. Fire was always a danger in mountains thick with scrub brush, and in July of 1924, a wildfire near Sandberg's threatened not only the hotel but "scores of summer houses and hundreds of ranches along the Ridge Route." The situation was so bad that officials began drawing up tentative plans to forcibly conscript hundreds of men from Los Angeles to fight the fire.

Sandberg's was spared. But three years later, it was threatened again when someone tossed a smoldering cigarette from a car. About 500 firefighters worked frantically to contain the fire as it burned on both sides of the highway from Sandberg's to a distance some 16 miles north. One family from

Van Nuys managed to make it across the mountains despite being told to proceed at their own risk.

The fire had loosened huge boulders and sent them tumbling down the mountainside onto the road, damaging it in several places. The family even reported seeing one boulder careen down the mountain and hit a large car, which was "practically demolished." At Sandberg's, the flames reportedly got within 100 feet of the resort before firefighters beat them back.

An old sign at the intersection of the old Ridge Route and Pine Canyon Road, just north of Sandberg, points the way to Highway 138, Liebre Gulch, and Pine Canyon.

The resort continued to operate after the Ridge Route Alternate opened, but business declined dramatically. When Harald Sandberg died in 1939, his wife, Marion, sold the lease. The person who purchased it, one Larry Brock, sought to reignite interest in the place by reopening it under the name Sandberg Lodge and Dude Ranch, but the concept fizzled and a succession of owners followed. The famed apple orchard was eventually abandoned, and the isolated location of the aging hotel gave rise to ghost stories and tall tales as the years passed.

A rumor got started (no one knows how) that one of the owners, a woman named Lillian Grojean who had done time at Tehachapi State Women's Prison for writing bad checks, was in fact a Nazi spy transmitting secrets to the Germans during World War II. The nature of these secrets was left unsaid, as was the small matter of how a woman in such a remote location would have access to any secrets worth transmitting. In reality, she was just a pottery maker whose ceramics and tableware were sold in Los Angeles department stores.

Walter "Lucky" Stevens, a Hollywood stuntman, made one final attempt to rehabilitate the place in the 1950s after buying it from Grojean for $15,000. His plan was to make repairs and transform the dilapidated resort into a summer camp for underprivileged kids, to be called Sandberg Town for Lucky Children. He refurbished the buildings, collected donations of furniture, and solicited help from various actors and Hollywood connections to make his vision a reality. Then, just before he was scheduled to open the camp, he was burning trash in the old stone fireplace that had warmed so many guests back in the hotel's heyday. Sparks flew up the chimney, landed on the wooden roof, and ignited it.

The old hotel burned to the ground, as did most of the other buildings on the property. The resort that had survived raging forest fires had been destroyed by a chimney fire. Stevens was unable to rebuild and, two years later, in 1963, the Forest Service took back the lease.

WHITEOUT ON THE RIDGE

On the far end of the spectrum from the ever-present fire danger stood another natural threat that came with the territory along the Ridge Route: snow. The state had taken the high road in constructing the Ridge Route in part to avoid dealing with traversing the creeks that cut canyons through the Tehachapis. It saved money on bridges, which could be expensive, and on repairing roads damaged by washouts. But traversing a road at 4,000 feet above sea level—at least during wintertime—could be a chilling experience. There was a reason Harald Sandberg labeled his apple crates "Sandberg's Mountain Apples, Grown in the Snow."

Just how bad could it get? Motorists found out in January of 1922, when the Ridge Route endured a particularly difficult winter.

Traveling the Ridge Route during a snowstorm could be treacherous, and motorists could become stranded for hours. Here, seven years after the disastrous storm of January of 1922, cars wait by the side of the road after heavy snow made the road impassible.
Ridge Route Communities Historical Society.

First came a report in the *Oakland Tribune* that a truck owned by the Busk Bros. company had run into trouble traveling northbound between the Christmas and New Year's holidays. The truck left Los Angeles in the late afternoon and "ran into a heavy snow and winds storm which blew so hard that the driver at times was afraid the van would topple over." The writer went on to report that the driver had passed numerous other trucks stalled out along the side of the road and believed his vehicle was the only one that made it through that night.

It was a portent of things to come.

The worst storm of the season, and for that matter in memory, hit the Tehachapis on January 29.

Suddenly, motorists and passengers in 48 vehicles found themselves trapped on the road, barred from going anywhere by drifting walls of snow. Cars became stalled in whiteout conditions, and their occupants had no choice but to spend the night inside open vehicles. Some found their way to the Tejon Ranger Station but could go no farther: The road north was impassible unless you happened to have a sled. By the time they got there, eight women and several children were suffering from frostbite and exposure.

But it wasn't as though they were safe. A few had managed to make it to Lebec on a rudimentary sled, but the rest were in dire straits. By the time one of them managed to get through by telephone, those who had taken refuge there had enough food for only two more meals and enough wood to keep a fire going a few more hours. They planned to huddle around this single source of heat and wait out the night, hoping help would arrive.

They weren't the only ones stranded. Everything was cut off. Seventeen tourists found themselves trapped in a cabin at Kelly's Halfway Inn, and 50 more were stuck at Sandberg's. One hundred and fifty others were stranded miles away at Randsberg, in the mountains east of Bakersfield. Some of those at Sandberg's, heedless of their own safety, ventured out into the blizzard with a team of horses, carrying blankets for those trapped on the roadway. They only made it a mile before they had to turn back because the horses could go no farther.

When word finally got through to Bakersfield and Los Angeles that so many travelers were stranded, organizers began forming rescue parties. In L.A., the Automobile Club of Southern California prepared to send a tow car northward, together with a truck loaded with supplies. In Bakersfield, a group of 15 civic leaders got together at the American Legion Hall and set out for Lebec with more supplies and tools to break through the snowdrifts.

Time was of the essence.

Alaskan sled dogs were pressed into service, as were men on snowshoes carrying packs of food on their back. One by one, they came upon stalled and snowbound vehicles, helping stranded motorists as soon as they reached them. They reached Kelly's in time to save a baby who was near death after subsisting on nothing more than sugar water for the previous two days. Amazingly, no one had succumbed to the cold and exposure. After 48 to 60 hours without food or fuel, 38 motorists were finally freed from their icy highland prison and taken down the Grapevine grade to Bakersfield.

It wasn't the last time travelers were stranded in the snow going over the Ridge Route. In January of 1930, the Automobile Club of Southern California used a snowplow to free 50 cars marooned on the road near Sandberg's.

Within three years, they'd have an alternative.

3

BYPASSED

You can see three highway alignments running parallel to one another just south of Tejon Pass. In the foreground is a section of the original concrete from the old Ridge Route; farther away is Peace Valley Road, formerly a section of the Ridge Route Alternate (U.S. 99); and in the distance is Interstate 5.

Treasure hunters looking for pieces of old Highway 99 sometimes might imagine they're seeing double, or even triple. Over the years, workers built a road, then rebuilt it, and sometimes rebuilt it yet again. Increased traffic replaced wide-open spaces with bottlenecks, and sleeker motorcars with more horsepower created a demand for roads that could accommodate higher speeds.

The scenic Ridge Route was fine and dandy for a leisurely spring outing, but if you wanted to get across the mountains fast, it wasn't much of an improvement on the speed of an old horse and buggy. Fifteen miles per hour? You can go faster than that through a school zone these days. Imagine being a commercial truck driver plodding along over the Ridge Route with a deadline to meet. It just wasn't the most practical way to go. Heck, if you were hauling fruit, it might spoil by the time you got to the other side. An exaggeration, perhaps, but you get the picture.

Then there were all those stop signs and traffic lights that made the many towns along the way feel like obstacles on a military training course. They were great for roadside merchants, who found a captive audience of motorists impatient to find a bite to eat or a place to rest as they drummed their fingers on the steering wheel, waiting for the light to turn green. But those motorists were none too pleased, especially if they had irritable, impatient kids (or adults) along for the ride.

Old 99 was called the "Main Street of California" for a reason: It really *was* Main Street, or Broadway, or "the boulevard" in many of the cities and towns it passed through. As those towns grew bigger, however, and more local drivers joined highway travelers on increasingly congested roads, it became clear that something would have to give.

Engineers began looking for a way to circumvent the increasing number of driveways and intersections that were making highway beelines look more like spiderwebs.

And just before World War II, they found one: the freeway. The first segment of virtually uninterrupted roadway in the United States, the Arroyo Seco Parkway, opened in 1940 in Southern California. Trumpeted in the press as the "Highway of Tomorrow," the nine-mile section of highway ran alongside Figueroa Street, connecting Pasadena with Los Angeles.

North portal of Figueroa tunnel No. 3 on the Arroyo Seco Parkway, the first freeway in California, as seen in 1938. Known from 1954 to 2010 as the Pasadena Freeway, the highway reverted to its original name as part of a Caltrans effort to enhance its scenic value.
Library of Congress.

This segment of Figueroa was the old Route 66, which intersected Old 99 at San Fernando Boulevard. Now, the new parkway became Route 66, and Figueroa became the alternate route—if anyone wanted to take it.

The Arroyo Seco route was both faster and more fun. It was six lanes wide with a center divider, and 16 bridges carried surface streets and railroad tracks across the parkway, guaranteeing the free flow of traffic long before the era of rush hour and gridlock. Vehicles didn't access the highway via intersections but via "modified cloverleaf arrangements" that allowed cars to merge seamlessly with the flow of traffic.

Later called the Pasadena Freeway and renumbered as State Route 110 after Route 66 was decommissioned, it became the model for bypass routes around the state. New freeways would be built, and the old highways would be paved over or shunted aside, labeled as frontage roads, alternates, or "business" routes through town.

In some cities, bypasses weren't built right away, but traffic was instead routed through town via two parallel one-way streets meant to ease congestion without the expense of building an actual freeway. Before U.S. 101 bypassed San Luis Obispo on the Central Coast, it went straight through town on Marsh and Higuera streets (north- and southbound, respectively). Chico did the same thing when old 99 East passed through its downtown district. And Fresno tried a similar Band-Aid approach by creating a number of one-way streets downtown, paralleling Old 99 and siphoning traffic onto Route 41 toward Yosemite. Fresno and Bakersfield both added traffic circles along Old 99 to control traffic, as well.

In Fresno, a traffic circle 300 feet in diameter was installed at the southwest edge of Roeding Park, at what was then the north end of town. The circle routed southbound traffic downtown via a "subway" underneath the railroad tracks at Belmont Avenue. Alternately, drivers could head west alongside the southern edge of the park. A committee of Fresno engineers reported that the circle was the best way of dealing with traffic congestion north of downtown, and at least one out-of-towner seemed to agree. Philip Paterson of San Francisco took the time to write the editor of *The Fresno Bee*:

> The expansive open view of the park afforded from the new traffic circle appeals to the traveler as an invitation to enter the city and is certainly a vast improvement over the dangerous camel's-hump railroad crossing that existed there several years ago, not to mention the line of frame shacks which have been done away with.

In Bakersfield, motorists heading northward followed the highway along Union Avenue to White Lane, south of town. There, Chester Avenue broke off diagonally from the road, then veered northward on a parallel course and headed straight into downtown. Most drivers ended up taking this route through the city, and, by the 1930s, it had become congested with a mixture of local and highway traffic.

To relieve the gridlock, planners wanted to reroute traffic away from downtown and have it continue north-

The Belmont Circle in Fresno routed traffic from H Street via an underpass onto Motel Drive—both segments of U.S. 99 before they were bypassed by the freeway—and alongside Roeding Park.

water fountain, illuminated by rainbow lights, featuring 124 jets and streams of water rising 75 feet into the air. The $10,000 price tag and maintenance costs proved prohibitive, however, and it wasn't until four years after the circle was complete that a solution was found: The site would be marked by a 22-foot-tall lime-stone statue of Father Francisco Garcés, the first explorer of European descent to cross the Tehachapis into the southern San Joaquin Valley, in 1776. Sculptor John Palo-Kangas created the piece, and it was unveiled in the spring of 1939.

ward along Union, then build a diagonal highway that would eventually meet up with the current freeway route. This new highway would cross Chester north of downtown, and that's where the traffic circle was planned. *The Bakersfield Californian* described the proposal as follows in 1932:

> The "circle," if constructed, would loop the point on North Chester Avenue intersected by the proposed highway. It would cost in the neighborhood of $25,000, and permit traffic to continue straight through the city, or into Chester Avenue, without confusion. Within the road loop will be a circular garden. The loop would be unique, one of the largest in the state, and an outstanding bit of construction work that would cause motorists to remember the city.

How to make the circle memorable was the subject of some debate. When it opened in September of 1933, it ringed a bare-dirt central area distinguished by nothing more than a couple of telephone poles. The city manager proposed construction of a mission-style service station, which would provide a source of income to maintain the circle, but leaders eventually decided this would merely add to the traffic tie-ups the circle was designed to alleviate.

Another possibility was an illuminated oil derrick (as though the oil-rich city didn't have enough of them already). Then there were plans for a 200-foot-wide

Problems on the Ridge Route

One of the most extensive alternate routes of the era was the new route across the Tehachapis. The scenic Ridge Route had been a wonder in its day, but with automobile design improving rapidly, the road was fast becoming obsolete. When the Ridge Route had opened, the industry standard Model T topped out at 45 miles per hour; even then, slowing to the speed limit of 15 over the crest of the mountains required some patience. But when the Model A replaced it as Ford's marquee car in 1927, drivers had a car with twice the horsepower that topped out at 65. Creeping along at 15 must have seemed like it took an eternity.

Speeding was a constant concern for the Los Angeles County Sheriff's Department, which patrolled the road in the days before the CHP came into being. Instead of lying in wait on a secluded turn to catch someone going a little too fast, one officer stationed himself at each end of the Ridge Route and handed a voucher to everyone who started up the road. Each voucher would be marked with the car's time of arrival and checked at the other end; simple mathematics let the officers know when drivers who arrived too soon had been going faster than the prescribed 15 mph limit.

Not only were cars going faster, there were considerably more of them on the road, as traffic counts nearly tripled between 1920 and 1925. By then, nearly 100 cars an hour were traveling the highway, a small number by later Los

Talk about a contrast. A car zips past on Interstate 5, background, just beyond a segment of Dead Man's Curve on the original Ridge Route, still visible north of Lebec.

cated $1.5 million in gasoline tax revenues to improve road conditions in Southern California. *The Van Nuys News* reported that state workers were hard at work in the spring of 1924 "daylighting and widening blind curves, and otherwise improving the road to make it safer." At the Callahan Line Change on a southern stretch of the roadway, workers eliminated seven tight curves and replaced them with one long, sweeping paved arc.

Still, the route was not only tedious but also dangerous.

Highway engineers tried to ease the pain of traveling the original Ridge Route through a practice known as "daylighting": straightening the road as much as possible to reduce the safety hazards of blind curves and hairpin turns. Evidence of daylighting can be seen in this photo, taken south of the Templin Highway on the original Ridge Route. The original concrete, at right, has been bypassed by the more direct asphalt roadway.

Angeles freeway standards, but enough to challenge the capacity of a two-lane mountain road. Perhaps it would have been manageable if cars were the only traffic on the route, but truckers hauling goods and produce north and south relied on it, as well. In 1926, the road accommodated 400 carloads of creamery products, 3,100 loads of perishable fruit, and 42,000 bales of cotton.

Highway engineers tried to keep pace by modifying the Ridge Route. They closed the route for eight months beginning in March of 1919, adding concrete paving to a road that had been, until that point, oil and gravel. More improvements came five years later, when the state dedi-

The white wooden guardrails that guarded some of the curves were neither high enough nor sturdy enough to keep a car on the road if it was heading for the edge. And over the course of the highway's busiest years, it wasn't unusual to open the newspaper and learn that some unfortunate soul had lost control and gone over the side. The results were seldom pleasant.

An Oregon man who fell asleep at the wheel while driving the Ridge Route in August of 1922 never woke up. Instead, his car plunged over a 150-foot cliff and he was crushed to death beneath it (two youths riding with him were, amazingly, only slightly injured).

On Christmas Eve, 1927, two Santa Barbara men were riding in a new sedan when it skidded off an icy road and fell 215 feet into a canyon. Both were killed.

In April of 1928, a boxing promoter named E.O. Rosencrance of Los Angeles was forced off the road by another motorist. His car careened 150 feet down the side of a rocky canyon, and sheriff's personnel went to retrieve the body. Unable to find it in the charred wreckage, they returned to find none other than Rosencrance himself, alive and well, on a stage. He told authorities that he had jumped from the car just as it went over the ledge and had seen the vehicle burst into flames below.

Later that same year, near Sandberg's, three travelers on their way back from checking out some oil land in Bakersfield missed a turn and went off a 1,000-foot precipice. None of the three survived.

A pulley is used to recover a car that went off the road along the Ridge Route in Los Angeles County, 1920. Often, such recovery efforts proved too much trouble, and the vehicles were left to rust in the canyon below. Other drivers, unable to get their cars going again after they stalled or overheated, would actually push them over the side to be rid of them.
California State Archives/public domain.

Drivers wanted to go faster, but sometimes they couldn't. All too often, they found themselves stuck at a speed that would make them cast an envious eye at modern rush-hour traffic. The tight turns and steep grades—especially the Grapevine Grade from the north base of the Tehachapis to Tejon Pass—slowed traffic to a crawl interrupted by overheating engines and trucks struggling uphill at barely one-third the posted speed limit. One driver recalled it might take an hour to get from the bottom of the hill to Fort Tejon if you got stuck behind a slow-moving truck. Hot weather posed a particular challenge for truckers, whose floorboards became so overheated that they risked burning their feet. In order to keep going, they'd put one foot on the gas pedal while half-standing on the running board beside the car, a precarious position that required both balance and gumption. But then, as now, truckers facing deadlines had little choice but to complete the trip any way they could.

A Ridge Route Alternate

Trucks weren't the only road hazards other travelers faced along the route. Sometimes, when cars stalled, drivers would hop out and wedge a large rock under one of the rear tires to keep their vehicles from rolling backward. If they were able to get the machines moving again, they'd be too worried about stalling out again to go back and remove the rocks, which created an obstacle course for drivers who came along after them.

If they avoided the trucks, skirted the rocks, and managed to keep from overheating, drivers had to brave yet another concern as they traversed the Ridge Route: highway robbery. Because cars moved at such a leisurely pace, it was a simple matter for bandits hiding by the roadside to run up alongside them, hop on the running board, and demand that the travelers "give up the goods."

In the winter of 1923, the *Newhall Signal* newspaper reported that such holdups had become so common between Sandberg's and Bakersfield that police had been forced to take drastic action to curb the practice. Still, they weren't always there when you needed them, and drivers were occasionally forced to take matters into their own hands. One fellow driving down the ridge in a Marmon—an upscale passenger car of the day—proved to be a tempting target for two bandits. But the driver wasn't about to let himself get robbed. Instead of stopping, he floored the accelerator and actually ran over one of the highwaymen. According to the newspaper account, "he did not wait to see how badly the man was injured but continued on his way."

By 1927, officials were starting to wonder whether the road was adequate in the face of faster cars and the ever-increasing volume of traffic. Cars were backing up in the

Saugus-Newhall area at the southern end of the route as traffic slowed to head up the hill. In October of that year, the state director of public works ordered a survey to assess the road's conditions and determine whether any improvements would be enough to keep it viable as the primary road across the mountains. The director "declared the feasibility of constructing a new road as a means of affording necessary relief from congested conditions will be considered if the situation cannot be improved by radical changes in alignment."

Straightening the road through Piru Gorge, March of 1934. © *California Department of Transportation.*

Feasibility would become reality within six short years. In 1929, survey teams started staking out the course of the highway that would become known as the Ridge Route Alternate. It wasn't intended to become the main road over the Tehachapis, merely an alternative that would relieve congestion on the venerable mountaintop highway. Builders assumed that the casual motorist would still prefer the leisurely drive across the scenic crest, while truck drivers and others in a hurry would choose the Alternate.

The path they chose for construction, interestingly enough, was one they had avoided when deciding on the original highway's course: the Piru Canyon route. This course had been bypassed back in the early 1910s because the canyon had been considered as the possible future site of a dam. The St. Francis Dam disaster, which took place close to the same time the state was starting to formulate plans for the new highway, may have put to rest any talk of a new dam along Piru Creek. But whatever the reason, the state decided that the Piru route was perfect for the Alternate and chose to go full speed ahead on the project.

Speed would indeed be a consideration. In contrast to the original Ridge Route, the new highway would offer a relatively straight shot through the mountains, allowing speeds far greater than the pokey 15 mph limit on the high road. Curves on the new road would have a minimum radius of 1,000 feet, compared to 70 feet on the old Ridge Route, shaving nearly 10 miles off the journey from one end to the other. And not only would the new road be straighter, it would also be wider: 38 feet as opposed to 21–24 feet for the original highway. The extra width enabled builders to add a third lane in the center, a passing lane available from both directions. At times, this arrangement could yield explosive results, and it wasn't long before the head-on collisions that occurred there earned it the nickname "suicide lane."

The Ridge Route Alternate (U.S. 99) generally followed the future course of modern Interstate 5, slightly to the west. It dipped down into Piru Canyon, where four steel-reinforced concrete bridges carried it across Piru Creek. Officially dedicated on October 29, 1933, it quickly became not the alternate but the main road across the mountains. Shaving a full hour off the time it took to get over the Tehachapis was just too tantalizing for

This section of the Ridge Route Alternate through Piru Gorge, just south of Pyramid Lake, remained accessible by foot or bicycle in 2015, though a gate two miles south of the lake blocked access to all motorized traffic except official vehicles.

most drivers to resist. Soon the road over the top of the mountains became an afterthought. The service stations, diners, and auto courts that had sprung up in a matter of months to serve the old route closed down just as quickly when motorists forsook it for the faster alternative.

The new 27-mile road was built at a cost of $2.9 million using California gas tax dollars on the equivalent of 100 million gallons of petroleum. It rejoined the old Ridge Route around Gorman, where portions of the old Ridge Route, the Alternate, and the newest highway alignment, Interstate 5, are all visible.

At the south end of Gorman Post Road, where it meets the Lancaster Freeway, you can still see a dead-end spur of Ridge Route concrete, about the length of a football field, jutting eastward. At the north end of the same road—another dead end—lies a rare three-lane segment of old U.S. 99, now appearing to be nothing more than an extra-wide road, with the old concrete hidden beneath asphalt.

Across Interstate 5 to the west lies another segment of the Alternate, called Peace Valley Road, and if you climb a ridge just to the west of it, you'll find a crumbling section of concrete from the original Ridge Route just north of Tejon Pass, the highest point along the highway. On the old Ridge Route, the pass stood at 4,230 feet, but engineers shaved several feet off the elevation (reducing it to 4,183) when they graded the Alternate, and lowered it further to 4,144 feet when they laid a course for the interstate.

After the short climb up from Peace Valley Road, you can walk a few hundred yards along slabs of concrete that remain from the old Ridge Route, though they're cracked, crumbling, and beset by weeds. You'll notice that the hill has given way to some extent beneath the pavement, sending small bits and larger chunks of concrete sliding down toward the newer highway. Only in one short portion at the north end of the segment do two lanes of concrete remain intact. From that vantage point, you can see all three generations of highway at once: the original Ridge Route beneath your feet, Peace Valley Road just to the right, and Interstate 5 as it curls its way past the Frazier Park exit just to the north.

Other concrete remnants of the oldest road can be found a few miles farther on at Lebec, near the site of the opulent but long-vanished Hotel Lebec, and then again to the east of I-5 at Tejon Ranch. There, two well-preserved segments are clearly visible beside the school—where one serves as a bus loading lane—and a little to the south behind a locked gate.

The latter segment became a dead end when the Alternate bisected its predecessor's winding path by taking a much straighter shot down the mountain.

You can access another section of the Alternate from the south, where it follows a canyon course well below the level of both the old Ridge Route and the newer Interstate 5. To reach this segment, take the Templin Highway exit west, then turn north onto the cracked asphalt of the Alternate, which will carry you north for several miles parallel to I-5 toward Piru Canyon. If you gaze up, you'll be able to see the traffic on I-5 whizzing past several hundred feet above you. But you can't get all the way through to Gorman from here. That's because the road comes to an end a few miles short of there, blocked by a towering embankment that holds back a large body of water called Pyramid Lake. Actually, the Alternate doesn't really end; you just can't drive any farther on it—unless you have a submersible car, that is. The road's actually still there; it's just underneath the man-made lake.

Remember those plans for the dam that were shelved when the highway was originally built? They were eventually resurrected, and the dam was completed in 1970, flooding Piru Canyon and leaving Old 99 under more than 7.2 million gallons of water. Those bridges they built over Piru Creek are under there, too, along with the rest of the road. Pyramid Lake got its name from a cut in the side of a mountain that engineers carved to make way for the highway; they left a sheer face in the shape of a pyramid that's clearly visible from the newest version of the highway, Interstate 5. On the north end of the lake, the old highway emerges again (it's now a boat ramp for recreational use) and continues northward for a short way, paralleling the current freeway.

A chunk of concrete from the original Ridge Route broke off and slid down the hill, coming to rest just west of Peace Valley Road—the Ridge Route Alternate (background)—a couple of miles south of Interstate 5's Frazier Park exit.

ALL BUSINESS

As time went on, more and more freeways were built to bypass more and more congested city streets. As with the Ridge Route Alternate, speed was preferred to a leisurely Sunday drive, at least by the vast majority of motorists, most of whom welcomed the bypasses. In some cases, the new freeways were laid right on top of the old highways they replaced; in others, however, the older roads remained as surface streets still used today. Some are labeled "business" routes, while others carry signage designating them sections of "historic" highways. Still others aren't labeled at all, and it takes some detective work to rediscover them.

The old highway here looks a lot different today than it did in its glory days. Gone are most of the motels and service stations that used to line the road; in their place is a mix of liquor stores, garages, abandoned buildings, and industrial sites. Drivers have to slow down in San Fernando and Burbank, where the road narrows considerably as it passes through downtown retail districts.

Past Griffith Park, San Fernando Road eventually ends at the Arroyo Seco Parkway, where the old alignment veers briefly southwest across the Los Angeles River toward downtown. In the space of just a few miles

This section of three-lane highway, originally part of the Ridge Route Alternate, can be seen north of Gorman: It dead-ends where the road is cut off by Interstate 5. Unfortunately, the clearly marked three lanes of concrete pavement seen here are no longer visible, having been paved over by asphalt in recent years.
Ridge Route Communities Historical Society.

Oops

Before Interstate 5 made its grand entrance, efforts were made to improve U.S. 99 through Piru Gorge. With cars and trucks slamming head-on into one another at an alarming rate, it became clear that the "suicide lane" would have to go, and plans to widen the road were drawn up around 1940. Unfortunately, those plans were put on hold when World War II intervened, only to become more pressing once the war ended: With the 35 mph wartime speed limit lifted and gasoline no longer rationed, America hit the accelerator. The year the war ended, 1945, produced more traffic deaths per mile traveled than any year since.

Within a few years, highway workers were out in force, working in earnest to clear a wider path through the canyon for that all-important fourth lane.

A February day in 1951 started out as a routine day at the outdoor office for the dynamite-wielding crews working for the contractor, A. Treichert and Sons, but it ended up as something far more memorable—for all the wrong reasons. One of the workers later recalled:

> Pyramid cut was very hard shale rock, and we had to stake it hanging from ropes like mountain climbers, 300 or so feet above the highway. Most of the earlier blasts had been big ones, and when the newspaper photographers came out to take the pictures, we were pressed into service to drag them back from the falling rock.

On this particular day, the shot was small, and we didn't even go to see it. We called it a "firecracker." Traffic was stopped during all of these blasts, and allowed through only after the road had been cleaned up, usually about 30 minutes. We heard the blast and went on working, but soon noticed that traffic (still) wasn't moving. We crawled down off the hill, and went up to the Pyramid cut, and there she was . . . the bridge was right down in Piru Creek.

Two sections of a 180-foot span over Piru Creek had collapsed under a rockslide. More than 3,000 vehicles were stalled—all of which had to be rerouted through Lancaster to the east. Apparently the blast, which was detonated about 40 feet from the bridge, had been the straw that broke the bridge's back: Engineers said later that the span had been weakened by previous dynamiting in the area.

Pavement from the Ridge Route Alternate, foreground, once continued past the iconic Pyramid Cut. Today, this is as far as you can go on this segment of the road. To the north, beside the cut, the concrete is submerged beneath man-made Pyramid Lake.

The Old Road looking north from Magic Mountain Parkway in 2014.

it reaches a junction with U.S. 101 affectionately known as the Four Level or the Stack. Built in 1953, it was the first interchange of its kind and soon became the standard, replacing the older cloverleaf mode as the design of choice.

The Stack redirects traffic on the old 99 alignment, sending it eastward and away from downtown. Motorists following the old highway cross back over the river, then follow Main Street for a short distance to Lincoln Park. There, the road's name changes to Valley Boulevard, which sends motorists eastward toward Pomona, where it becomes Holt Avenue.

A newer alignment was created in the early 1930s, with the new highway route running slightly to the south along Ramona Boulevard and, farther east, Garvey Avenue. It shaved three miles off the Valley Boulevard route from Los Angeles to Pomona, resulting in an estimated savings for drivers of 4 cents a mile. At that rate, the state calculated, the project would pay for itself in less than two and a half years. A six-mile segment between Los Angeles and Monterey Park was entirely free of grade crossings and offered a straight shot out of (or into) the city along what builders termed the Ramona "Airline" Highway.

Motorists leaving L.A. in those days were already contending with increased traffic—an estimated 20,000 cars a day—that threatened to ruin an otherwise pleasant ride out past citrus groves and orchards. Not only would the new highway provide drivers with a shorter distance

between two points, it would also circumvent "a maze of heavily traveled intersecting streets and railroad crossings in the industrial district, with the consequent hazard and delay in traffic," the state declared. Estimated time saved: 20 minutes.

The new roadway was a mixture of broad straightaways and gently sloping curves, a marked contrast to its predecessor.

Even with such highly touted projects as the "Airline" highway, however, planners and road builders ultimately were unable to keep pace with urban sprawl and the growth of traffic in the region. The orchards and citrus groves of the 1930s are long gone; today, the most visible landmarks are strip malls and seemingly endless subdivisions, creeping by slowly when viewed from amid a sea of bumper-to-bumper traffic. The current freeway, known as Interstate 5 or the San Bernardino Freeway, closely follows the old Ramona alignment as it moves from the L.A. metro area toward what's known as the Inland Empire. Originally called the Ramona Parkway, it was largely built on top of the older highway route, though the latter could still be seen in a few places.

Other remnants of Old 99 can be found to the north of Los Angeles County, bypassed by other sections of newer freeway.

Heading north on the current 99 alignment into the San Joaquin Valley, the Union Avenue exit to Greenfield serves as the gateway to a lengthy stretch of Old 99. Travelers can't help but notice the numerous palm and eucalyptus trees that line both sides of the road along this stretch of highway. The vision of a tree-lined thoroughfare serving as a gateway to the city dates back to before the dawn of the automobile age. In the 1890s, a developer named Will Houghton joined forces with a local land company to plant 1,000 eucalyptus trees.

In the 1920s and the two decades following, more trees were planted along Old 99 south of town. Palm and eucalyptus were chosen in part because their roots

Crossing from Los Angeles County into Kern County, heading north. *From the collection of the Ridge Route Communities Historical Society.*

poplars, Chinese pistache, and oriental plane trees. The plan for "unbroken rows of shade trees" was ambitious, to say the least.

Today's driver will pass long stretches along the highway with nary a tree in sight, especially north of Bakersfield. At one time, motorists would drive through a nearly unbroken corridor of eucalyptus between Goshen and Kingsburg and see a portion of the tree-planters' vision. But even along that stretch of highway, the trees are thinner than they once were, with more empty spaces than branches beside the road. Still, thick clusters of the trees have survived around Gateway Avenue in northern

sought out the water that could accumulate under the pavement, siphoning it away before it could cause cracking, potholes, and other road wear. The shade of the eucalyptus, meanwhile, protected the pavement from the scorching summer sun.

The trees were so effective that in the mid-1930s, highway officials decided to extend the planting project up and down the length of the roadway throughout the southern San Joaquin Valley. The winning bid for the project went to a Bakersfield nursery, which set about growing more than 3,000 young trees. According to a newspaper report, the beautification effort, "when completed, will see the Golden State highway from the Tejon pass to Fresno bordered with unbroken rows of shade trees."

Nearly two-thirds of the trees dedicated to the project were eucalyptus (four kinds), but the collection also included more than 300 oaks in three varieties and nearly 400 oleander, along with lesser numbers of elm,

Eucalyptus trees line both sides of the road near the Blue Gum Motel along the western alignment of Highway 99 near Willows in Northern California.

Madera, near Ashlan and Olive avenues in Fresno, and elsewhere. And perhaps the thickest grove of eucalyptus along the old road is far to the north along 99 West near Willows, where the Blue Gum Motel takes its name from a slang term for the eucalyptus tree.

Oleanders, with their pink blossoms, remain common sights in the medians of 99, as they are on 101 and other highways. The plants require minimal watering and work well as hedges, shielding north- and southbound lanes from each other. They can be found on both the newer stretches of freeway and the older, bypassed sections.

North of Bakersfield, the old highway makes limited-run showings through several small towns bypassed by the freeway. Old 99 makes an appearance along High Street in Delano between Woollomes Avenue and County Line Road. In Earlimart, the old highway is known as Front Street; in Pixley, it's Main Street.

A rare left exit from the freeway led drivers into Tulare along the older alignment, now designated the business route, in this photo dated March 1, 1956. © *California Department of Transportation.*

The bypass in Tulare was unusual: For many years, northbound drivers from the new freeway could access the bypassed old road via a left-lane exit onto K Street. The exit bridge was torn down a few years ago, but drivers can still find their way to the old highway, which follows K Street toward town before jogging west slightly toward the railroad tracks and following J Street the rest of the way. Motorists on this route drive past such landmarks as the county fairgrounds (across from the old Virginia Lodge motel) and the iconic creamy white Adohr Farms statue of a milkmaid and cow, just north of the Cross Street intersection. Although Tulare County is a major dairy producer, the statue itself was a late arrival to the city. One of several such statues created in the 1920s to promote Adohr products, it originally stood at the company headquarters in Tarzana, a tribute to "the largest Guernsey herd in the world." Only in 1966, when the dairy was sold, did the maid and her cow find a new home in Tulare. Though neglected for several years, a renovation effort restored it to its former glory.

Old 99 picks up again on the other side of the current freeway, to the east, about 26 miles farther north in Kingsburg. Golden State Boulevard, as it's called these days, runs parallel to the current freeway through the towns of Selma and Fowler before merging with it at the southern edge of Fresno. Another segment of Golden State Boulevard began just south of Fresno's Roeding Park and continued northward past the former highway communities of Highway City and Herndon, now both absorbed into the fringes of the growing central state metropolis. The new high-speed rail project, under construction as of this date, has eclipsed part of this historic corridor.

The old highway is Gateway Drive in Madera and 16th Street in Merced. It's Atwater Boulevard in Atwater and Golden State Boulevard again through Turlock—where the road has much the same character as the old highway in the Fresno area. In Modesto, it follows Ninth Street through what is largely an industrial area and past the historic Modesto arch. In each case, the original alignment is west of the newer freeway.

Reaching the original route through Stockton, which is on the west side of the freeway, is a little more complicated. Traveling north, exit on Mariposa and take Mariposa to Martin Luther King Boulevard (which becomes Charter Way after a couple of blocks). Then, turn north on Wilson Way, which follows the old route through the center of town.

The freeway was also built east of the old road in Lodi, where it's called Cherokee Lane, a shaded, divided highway that offers some of the most picturesque in-town scenery to be seen along the old road.

In Chico, it's Park Avenue south of town and Esplanade to the north. Downtown, it splits into a pair of one-way streets directing traffic in opposite directions: Main and Broadway. The Redding bypass is some 14 miles long, and the old highway diverges from the freeway at Anderson and continues all the way to Redding, where it's known as Market and California streets, renumbered as Route 273.

This kind of divided thoroughfare through town was, in a few cases, an intermediate step to ease traffic before construction of a freeway. Downtown Fresno's streets provide another example of this strategy. Constructed as one-way streets before the city's freeway system was complete, they remain so decades later, even after the construction of new bypasses that have alleviated congestion through town.

Railroaded

The highway began its life as the little brother of the railroad, following its elder sibling just about everywhere. It made sense, considering the number of cities and towns that had sprung up along rail lines and sidings during the second half of the 19th century. Those few towns that had preceded the railroad's arrival often lured the iron horse to their vicinity by their mere existence as natural way stations and shipping points. Los Angeles comes to mind.

But as the little brother grew and his elder sibling became longer in the tooth, problems arose. Most often, they took the same tack, running parallel to each other for miles on end. Where they crossed paths, however, they weren't always the most congenial of kinfolk. There were places where, for various reasons, the tracks crossed over the highway to run along the opposite side, and because they generally ran in the same direction, many of those crossings were at snakelike S curves rather than the more usual perpendicular intersection.

Such meeting places could turn into graveyards—most often for those on the highway, whose jalopies could hardly match the size or velocity of the iron horses

that rode the rails. As highway traffic increased, so did the danger.

If you travel down 99 near Delano, you'll come to a spot where the freeway descends to pass beneath the rail line as it crosses the road.

It wasn't always that way.

Before the railroad overcrossing was built in 1936, railroad and highway intersected at one of those S curves, where drivers had to crane their necks and look back over their right shoulders to make sure trains weren't approaching. This was before the widespread use of crossing arms. Many railroad crossings then were marked only with the familiar "crossbuck" signs, sometimes accompanied by flashing red lights, but it was still a case of "cross at your own risk."

With highway traffic increasing by the month, crossing arms could be problematic for another reason: Long freight trains, such as those that commonly traverse the Central Valley, could (and still do in places) back up traffic as effectively as rush hour in Los Angeles. The overpass/underpass solution might have seemed like a luxury at first, but it was fast becoming a necessity in places such as Delano and Fresno, where another overpass project in 1947 required the removal of an entire neighborhood.

In the crosshairs at Fresno: 67 houses, a gas station, grocery store, beer wholesaler, shoe store, and restaurant-bar, along with a charitable institute for immigrants. The most impressive structure in the affected area was the German Lutheran Cross Church, a sturdy brick edifice built in 1914 and measuring more than 8,000 square feet. Stained-glass windows adorned its walls, and a bell tower rose to a height of 88 feet above its colonnaded entrance. Inside, a congregation of more than 2,000 met every Sunday, many of them descendants of Volga Germans who had settled in the neighborhood and founded the church in its original location—a wooden building down the street—two decades before it had moved to the larger site.

For members of the church, taking a wrecking ball to the building that served as both their spiritual home and crowning achievement simply wasn't an option.

But what alternatives were there?

The German Lutheran Cross Church in Fresno had to be moved—all 1,800 tons of it—to make way for a new freeway alignment.

The structure weighed a whopping 1,800 tons (yes, that's *tons*), so moving it wouldn't be a matter of simply placing it on a moving truck with a "Wide Load" sign on the back and hauling it down the road. Such a move would require a Herculean effort, especially for a building made entirely of (unreinforced) brick. A basement complicated matters further. But the church members were determined, and the California Highways Department was willing to undertake the task.

A new location was chosen one block west and a block south, requiring a move of 300 yards and a 90-degree turn. To accomplish their purpose, highway workers used more than 15,000 timber blocks, a dozen steel H beams, steel rollers, and 60-pound railroad rails. It took them more than a month just to prepare for the move. Once they finally got under way, officials reported that it moved "quite easily." But once they reached the intersection, they had to put the entire structure on jacks while they turned the rails at right angles to the direction they'd been going, then turned the structure before setting it back down again.

The last 15 feet were perhaps the slowest, because workers had to be sure they were placing the structure directly over the new foundation. All this took place under the watchful eyes of "a large number of elderly spectators and 'sidewalk superintendents,'" many of whom were church members with a direct stake in the project's success.

In the end, the amount of care taken with the move paid off, and the project was a rousing success. The Highways Department gave itself a well-earned pat on the back in its subsequent report, contained in the winter edition of *California Highways and Public Works.*

"There was considerable skepticism among the 'sideliners' as to the feasibility of completing the job successfully," Associate Highway Engineer L.S. Van Voorhis wrote. "However, they were quite obvious in displaying their satisfaction in seeing the job finished, and it was a pleasure to observe. The statement was made that, 20 years hence, a person would have a difficult time convincing anyone the church had not always rested in its present location, but was two blocks distant."

Those 20 years hadn't passed, however, before the congregation decided to sell the building and move north to a new facility. By 2009, its membership had declined to 130 members and the building it had once occupied—now included on Fresno's Local Register of Historic Resources—was being used by the Fresno Temple Church of God in Christ.

THE ULTIMATE BYPASS

When it was commissioned in 1926 as a crucial link in the federal highway system, few would have guessed that the lifespan of U.S. 99 would be less than half a century. In fact, just three decades after it was founded, the federal highway system would begin to yield its place as the nation's primary road system. With the stroke of a pen, President Dwight Eisenhower authorized the creation of a new, more modern network of roads called the interstate highway system.

The interstate system didn't come into being full-blown overnight, and—although it was sometimes referred to as the Eisenhower Interstate Highway System—it wasn't even the president's idea. The concept had been kicking around since at least 1938, when President Franklin Roosevelt began pushing the idea of a national network of toll roads. The year saw an economic downturn within the already protracted Great Depression. Manufacturing entered a slump, and as unemployment rose from 14.3 percent to 19 percent, Roosevelt saw construction of a new highway system as a means of putting people to work.

Soon the Bureau of Public Roads was studying the idea of creating a six-route network of national toll roads, and a year later, an exhibit at the New York World's Fair called Futurama fired the public imagination by showing what a national network of highways might look like in 1960. Its designer, Norman Bel Geddes, presented the concept as "a large-scale model representing almost every type of terrain in America and illustrating how a motorway system may be laid over the entire country." Broad freeways passed through a metropolis of skyscrapers with plenty of open spaces. Such a system, the designer posited, could be laid out while "never deviating from a direct course and always adhering to the four basic principles of highway design: safety, comfort, speed, and economy."

Nearly 10 million people saw the Futurama exhibit, and doubtless came away impressed, but it was one thing to create models of the future and quite another to bring them to fruition. Still, there was no arguing that the expanding number of cars or the road made it necessary to address what Bel Geddes called "the complex tangle of American roadways."

In 1944, Congress passed legislation that authorized the creation of a "National System of Interstate Highways" covering 40,000 miles, and Los Angeles lost little time in formulating a plan for an extensive system of parkways, aka freeways.

Planners in Los Angeles, which opened the nation's first freeway—the Arroyo Seco Parkway—in 1940, realized that the city would soon need more of the same if it

The freeway bypass between Fresno and Kingsburg is seen at left, with the older alignment at right, in this photo taken September 23, 1964. © *California Department of Transportation.*

were to keep traffic moving through the region. In 1946, they produced a report titled *Interregional, Regional, Metropolitan Parkways*, which concluded that "the existing streets are not designed to meet the needs of modern automotive traffic." As a solution, it envisioned a series of parkways, thoroughfares portrayed in terms that sound a lot like a modern freeway:

Traffic can enter only at specially designed connections with major streets, varying from ¼ to ½ mile apart. Individual roadways, separated by a continuous dividing strip, are provided for each direction of travel. Crossings and left turns at grade are eliminated by bridges and ramps, thus making traffic signals and stops unnecessary.

The report mentioned five highways that it foresaw as components of the still-to-be-built federal interstate system:

- the Ramona Parkway (future San Bernardino Freeway, I-10)
- the Ventura-Hollywood Parkway (the freeways of the same name, U.S. 101)

- the Santa Ana Parkway (I-5 from L.A. through Orange County)
- the Santa Monica Parkway (roughly corresponding to Santa Monica Boulevard)
- the San Fernando-Riverside Freeway

This last corresponded with U.S. 99 and the future Interstate 5 through the San Fernando Valley and south past Griffith Park. The "Riverside" in the name wasn't the city of Riverside, more than 50 miles to the east, but referred instead to the Los Angeles River, which paralleled the highway for some distance.

The report included 11 other proposed state parkways, as well as 27 locally funded routes with the parkway designation. The resulting blueprint, which would undergo several revisions over the next decade, laid out a comprehensive network of parkways for Southern California. Some came to fruition, some were abandoned, and still others were built under entirely different names.

The Colorado Freeway, for example, did not go all the way to Colorado, or even nearly so; instead, it followed the route of Colorado Boulevard out to Pasadena. Planning documents also referred to it as the San Bernardino Freeway, a name that would instead come to be associated with a different highway a few miles to the south, the one referred to in the same documents as the Ramona Freeway (the future Interstate 10).

A long stretch of road called the Los Coyotes Parkway, which would have extended from Orange County northeast to connect with the Colorado Freeway, was never built. Neither was the Reseda Freeway, an extension of the Antelope Valley Freeway that was to have run down through the San Fernando Valley, ending in Santa Monica.

Perhaps the most ambitious project left on the drawing board was the Whitnall Parkway (sometimes referred to as the Whitnall Super Highway), which would have bisected the San Fernando Valley from northwest to southeast before veering south through a tunnel more than two miles long that would have run under the Hollywood Hills near Griffith Park. It was to have connected with another never-built highway, the Normandie Parkway, on the other side of the mountains.

The Whitnall was unique in that it was named for a living individual: Gordon Whitnall founded the Los

This short stretch of road in Burbank is nearly all the physical evidence there is of the Whitnall Highway. Most of the highway's designated right-of-way is taken up by a wide median park used as a corridor for power lines. The "highway" itself consists of two lanes in a residential neighborhood on either side of the median.

Angeles Planning Department and served as its director for a decade starting in 1920. Under his direction, the city purchased the right-of-way necessary to build the highway and actually broke ground on it in June of 1927. Three hundred people attended an opening ceremony at Cahuenga Boulevard, about two miles from Universal City, where Whitnall himself spoke about its benefits: It would shave 45 minutes off the time it took to reach Los Angeles via the "inland route" (U.S. 99). In 1930, he touted plans for the tunnel and compared the highway to "the trunk of a tree, and all the existing Valley highways to the branches of that tree."

The tunnel would have been the longest of its kind in California and, nearly a century later, it would still rank as the third longest in the United States. Engineers conducted a survey of the tunnel plans, and the *Los Angeles Times* published a map showing how the subterranean highway would connect with "existing boulevards."

It never did.

Whitnall left his planning post in 1930, and the project languished, probably because the exorbitant cost of such an endeavor made it impractical in the midst of the Great Depression. The trunk of his envisioned tree of highways never grew beyond a stump, and the branches were left to fend for themselves. As to the tunnel, it remained on the drawing board for years, but nothing ever came of it. The right-of-way for the Whitnall Parkway is still visible from the air today, following the path of power lines that run along its wide, grassy median. In places, there's even a street there called the Whitnall Highway, but it's not a freeway by any stretch of the imagination; it's just an overly broad residential street that hiccups its way in fits and starts across a few small segments of the valley floor.

In 2002, a portion of it served as the site for a new endeavor: the Whitnall Off-Leash Dog Park.

The parkway's demise left U.S. 99 as the major route for traffic from the San Fernando Valley into Los Angeles. Would it have alleviated some of the gridlock that wound up plaguing the Greater Los Angeles area, or would the tunnel have instead become a major bottleneck? It's impossible to know.

Either way, however, the Whitnall Super Highway was a false start in the drive toward a network of superhighways, not just for Southern California but for the nation: the interstate highway system.

The new roads would be wider, free of cross traffic, and would follow a strict set of standards designed to speed traffic along as quickly and efficiently as possible. Interchanges such as the Stack would proliferate, with on- and off-ramps replacing stoplights and intersections. Blue shields with red accents and white lettering would substantially replace the black-on-white scheme that had become so familiar on highway signs across the country.

Despite the road designers' best efforts to maintain consistency, those signs could be confusing, to put it mildly. Federal highways that ran north and south were supposed to carry odd numbers, while east–west thoroughfares bore even numbers. That worked fine in theory, but it failed to account for two spurs off 99—highways 199 and 299 in the far north end of the state—that ran mostly east to west despite their odd-number designations. It also didn't explain the fact that U.S. 101 ran east to west for nearly 120 miles from North Hollywood to

beyond Santa Barbara. At some freeway on-ramps in the San Fernando Valley, drivers are likely to find directions to "101 north," even though the asphalt clearly headed west. Other on-ramps are signed as both north *and* west, giving rise to even more head-scratching.

In other places, drivers confronted not one but two federal highways bearing the same number. Beginning around 1933, the 99 split at Sacramento into a pair of highways dubbed 99W and 99E. The western route followed the path eventually chosen for Interstate 5, passing through Davis, Woodland, and Willows. Meanwhile, the eastern road (current State Route 99) passed through Roseville, Marysville, Yuba City, and Chico. The split highways merged again at Red Bluff.

Originally, the western route, previously numbered State Highway 7, was to carry the designation U.S. 99, while the eastern route, State Highway 3, was to be called the 99 Alternate. The east-siders, however, would hear none of this second-class nonsense and insisted on equal status. According to one newspaper account, "the issue became rather heated" until the east–west compromise was finally reached. That didn't end the rivalry between the two roads, however, as the East Side Highway Association commissioned 30 billboards encouraging drivers heading south from Oregon to "turn left at Red Bluff." Each of the signs was to be 20 feet long by 10 feet high and bear a cutout image of the state capitol's dome, emblematic of the route's designation as the Capitol Highway. To drive home the message, a representative of the association was to be stationed at Red Bluff to distribute literature touting the eastside route.

This wasn't the only place where the highway split: A second split between 99W and 99E was instituted farther to the north, in Oregon.

Similarly, an old map of Southern California shows U.S. 101 similarly following two distinct routes: The "alternate" western course follows the Pacific Coast Highway in Orange County, then runs northward along Sepulveda Boulevard, while the main eastern alignment follows the present I-5 alignment.

As if all this weren't confusing enough, some roads carried signs that marked them as more than one highway in the federal system. Highway 99 shared the road with 101 for a short stretch in Los Angeles, with U.S. 6 in the

San Fernando Valley, and with not one but two federal highways (U.S. 60 and U.S. 70) east of Los Angeles. Talk about a numerical nightmare of split-personality signage. It was hard for drivers to know whether they were coming or going.

Interstate 5 simplified things, at least somewhat, and in the process created the ultimate bypass, particularly through the San Joaquin Valley, where it was meant to serve as a more direct route between Los Angeles and San Francisco—although it did not actually stretch all the way to the Bay Area. The West Side Freeway, as it was dubbed, skirted Bakersfield, Fresno, Modesto, and all the smaller towns in between, covering a vast expanse of undeveloped and largely uninhabited land on the western edge of the valley. Rolling hills on one side, seemingly endless fields on the other, and signs that warn "Next Gas 31 Miles." Not much to look at, but that was the idea. The interstate was the antithesis of the grand old Ridge Route, sacrificing scenic beauty and historic character for a faster way to get there. To turn the familiar saying on its head, it was all about (getting to) the destination, not the journey.

As time passed, however, it would attract opportunistic merchants, just as the Ridge Route and U.S. 99 through the valley had. This time, however, they were in the form of modern truck stops and artificial retail "towns" consisting of little more than multiple gas stations, truck stops, convenience stores, and fast-food outlets just off the highway. Such outposts rise above the west valley flatlands near Buttonwillow, Lost Hills, Kettleman City, Santa Nella, and Patterson. But there isn't much else around them. They are creatures of the freeway, pure and simple, built in recognition of the reality that no matter

This sign points the way to on-ramps for north and south Interstate 5 at Grapevine.

how rushed motorists are to get from here to there, they still have to eat and they still have to fill their tanks.

Through the Los Angeles area, the interstate diverges from the old 99 route and follows the path carved out by U.S. 101 instead. Old U.S. 99, which skirted the southern portion of the burgeoning L.A. metroplex to the east, made its way south instead by way of the Salton Sea to its terminus at Calexico. I-5 follows the primary 101 alignment through Orange County, while the former 101 Alternate down Sepulveda Boulevard gave way to a parallel freeway in the interstate system numbered 405, the San Diego Freeway, which as of 2008 had established itself as the busiest freeway in the entire United States.

4

POINTING THE WAY

Foster & Kleiser billboards seemed to be everywhere on California highways throughout much of the 20th century. Dorothea Lange photographed this one along Highway 99 in March 1937. *Library of Congress/public domain.*

Signs are almost as much a part of the highway as the road itself. From the familiar highway shields and exit signs to the neon-lit standards of motels and service stations, you can't get far without being told how far it is to the next town or what services are available at the next turnoff. Even back in the horse-and-buggy days, merchants were putting up signs directing travelers to stop at their inns, saloons and general stores. Roadside billboards first appeared on the East Coast in the first half of the 19th century, and billboard space was leased for the first time in 1867.

Billboards built by companies such as Foster & Kleiser—founded in 1901 in the Pacific Northwest—began popping up and soon became ubiquitous. Foster & Kleiser's billboards were familiar sights along Old 99, often featuring latticework beneath the main horizontal image and light standards jutting out from the top to illuminate the message.

Palmolive might point out that "Gentlemen prefer ... a schoolgirl complexion" on one sign. The Southern Pacific Railroad, conscious that it was losing potential customers to the highways, erected signs that read

"Next time try the train," alongside images of a passenger reclining in a plush seat and a teenage boy, eyes closed and smiling with his head against a pillow. Public service ads proclaimed, in the midst of the Depression, "There's no way like the American Way," and touted the "world's highest standard of living" alongside a picture of a happy family of four on an outing in their automobile. (Another in the same series boasted of the "world's shortest working hours.")

Foster & Kleiser's owners eventually sold the company, which became known as Clear Channel Outdoor.

In 1925, brushless shaving cream manufacturer Burma-Shave began placing sequential billboards at regular intervals along highways. A series of a half-dozen signs would appear, one after another, with a message that kept travelers alert to see what came next. There were some 600 different rhyming messages, both promotional and humorous, and each series typically ended with the company name on the final sign.

A few examples:

> The wolf
> is shaved
> so neat and trim
> Red Riding Hood
> is chasing him

> Nobody likes
> to snuggle
> or dine
> accompanied by
> a porcupine

> Saw the train and
> tried to duck it
> kicked first the gas
> and then
> the bucket

> Don't lose
> your head
> to gain a minute
> you need your head
> your brains are in it

This billboard along Highway 99 advertised United States Tires c. 1920 and carried a bit of information about the city of Fresno, which was 11 miles away: "Fresno, the dried fruit center of the world, founded in 1862, is the gateway to Yosemite and the General Grant Parks, known for their giant sequoias, Huntington Lake and Kings River." The company posted similar signs in or near various cities across the nation. *Collection of Michael J. Semas.*

> It's best for
> one who hits
> the bottle
> to let another
> use the throttle

Burma-Shave's campaign began in Minneapolis and proved so successful that the company expanded its reach nationwide, putting up signs in 44 of the then-48 states (the exceptions were Arizona, Massachusetts, Nevada, and New Mexico). The company owners wrote the earliest slogans, then solicited others in annual contests that paid out a $100 prize. Sales continued to rise until just after World War II, by which point Burma-Shave was the nation's No. 2 brand. They began to falter as cities grew and drivers began spending more time commuting in urban areas than traveling the rural highways where the signs were typically placed.

They disappeared after 1963, when Gillette bought the company.

SHIELDS AND SYMBOLS

If you were familiar with the road, it was simple enough to know where you were based on landmarks such as billboards and merchant signs beside motels or service stations. But if you were new to the area, you needed signs that were more specific about where you were and where you wanted to go.

In 1906, when the newfangled motorcar was still less common on the roadway than the horse and carriage, the Automobile Club of Southern California began erecting porcelain road signs in the state's 13 southern-most counties. Four years after it began the project, it had already erected 2,400 signs. It also put up signs in Arizona, southern Nevada, and Baja California, a task it continued to perform for half a century.

The California State Automobile Association (CSAA) followed suit for the northern 45 counties, starting in 1914 and continuing until 1969, planting signposts along Highway 99 in addition to U.S. routes 40, 50, and 101. Diamond-shaped yellow signs with blue arrows and lettering displayed the directions and mileage to important destinations. The blue-and-yellow diamond remained the auto club's symbol decades after it stopped posting signs in this style.

Diamond-shaped signs placed by the Automobile Club of Southern California marked Tejon Pass on the original Ridge Route, elevation 4,213. *Collection of Joel Windmiller.*

The club replaced most of them after 1926, when the federal highway system adopted a scheme that featured black lettering on a white background. Highway designators were in the form of a shield signified by five points across the top and a single point at the bottom. Some had argued that the signs should carry a yellow background for improved visibility in snowy conditions, but that color was already widely in use for road hazard signs. (Even stop signs were originally yellow—except in California, which pioneered use of the red sign that was ultimately adopted nationwide in 1954.)

Although they rejected the idea of yellow route signs, designers of the new federal highway shield recognized that visibility was important, so they added a black border to help the signs stand out against a snow-covered landscape. A black stripe separated the "crown" or top section, above which the state's name was written, from the rest of the shield; below the crossbar were the letters "U.S." and, in larger print, the route number. Designers rejected an alternative form, which would have carried the letters "T.C." for "trans-continental" instead.

In 1948, a new shield design was unveiled that did away with the old, blocky font, replacing it with smoother, curved numbers and lettering. An alternative form, used in urban areas, dropped the lettering and crossbar altogether, placing the white shield against a rectangular black background. Signs along U.S. 101 in California, however, retain a variation on the vintage look today: Although lacking the crossbar and state name, they still bear the "US" designation (without periods) and a slim black outline that traces the shape of the sign. There's no black rectangle as a backdrop.

At the state level, a sign shaped like a miner's spade replaced the old triangles. Like the federal sign scheme, it utilized black lettering on a white background, featured the route number most prominently, and showed a reverse, white-on-black strip reading "STATE HIGHWAY" at the bottom. Adding to the sign's distinctive flavor was a small black silhouette of the state symbol, a grizzly bear, above the route number.

Rectangular mileage signs along roadsides also featured black lettering on a white background (along with directional arrows as warranted). So did elevation signs, which the CSAA installed at intervals of 1,000 feet in elevation, beginning in 1929. When the state added overhead highway mileage signs in urban areas during

A freeway entrance for U.S. 101 at the northern edge of San Luis Obispo shows a variation on the original federal highway shield design.

until a given exit. For instance, the figure 3^2 would indicate three and two-tenths miles; 1^6 would mean one and six-tenths mile, and so on.

The white-on-black signs didn't last long. The state adopted a new, universal green background (with white lettering) for its road signs in the 1960s, even reworking the iconic miner's spade signs. The spade's shape changed slightly, with "CALIFORNIA" appearing in an arc across the top to replace the grizzly bear symbol and the words "STATE HIGHWAY" at the bottom disappearing.

It was this green spade symbol that appeared on portions of 99 when it was decommissioned as a federal highway and the state took over in the 1960s.

By this time, the state was posting its own signs rather than contracting with the two auto clubs that had begun the process. By 1937, the CSAA had put up an astonishing 135,000 signs in Northern and Central California, but a decade later the state decided to take direct responsibility for road signs along its highways. The Southern California auto club continued to post signs along city- and county-maintained roadways until 1956, and the CSAA did so for 13 years after that, finally calling it quits on the operation in 1969.

Welcome to . . .

Road builders and merchants weren't alone in providing information along Old 99 and other highways. Municipalities, too, sought to welcome motorists as they approached their city limits, touting themselves with slogans such as "Raisin Capital of the World" (Selma) and "The Heartbeat of Agriculture" (McFarland). Small towns built signs with wooden panels dedicated

the 1950s, it adopted the reverse color scheme: white lettering on a black background. An interesting early variation: Distances to upcoming exits were broken down in tenths of a mile, rather than the quarter- and half-mile increments familiar today. A small, underlined number indicated how many tenths of a mile remained

An overhead sign bearing the 99 shield is seen at the Ashlan Avenue exit in Fresno on June 14, 1969.
© *California Department of Transportation.*

to various service clubs and churches. Larger towns built bigger signs, and some even went so far as to build arches across the road itself.

Lodi, a city of barely 2,000 people, had just been incorporated when it dedicated the Lodi Arch in 1907. The structure, which predated Old 99, wound up being a little west of the highway on Pine Street and was built at a cost of $500 to celebrate the city's first Tokay and Wine Festival. Considering the structure's durability, the price was a bargain: As of 2014, it was believed to be the oldest welcome arch in the state, looking almost exactly the way it did when it was built. A sturdy structure of concrete, masonry,

Looking west through the Lodi Arch into the city's historic downtown.

and stucco built over an iron frame, it had a span of 80 feet and rose 40 feet above the earth. Its most distinctive feature was a row of three portals, each containing a mission bell (two smaller ones flanking the largest, at the center). A year after it was built, the name of the town was added just underneath the bells, and a statue of a California golden bear was placed at its apex.

It stayed that way until 1956, when an extensive restoration project ensured the arch would continue to welcome visitors to the city.

Most visitors, anyway.

In 1918, during World War I, city trustees ordered an electric sign added with a message that not everyone was welcome: "Lodi for 100 Per Cent Americans," it was to read. According to the *San Francisco Chronicle*, a certain Glenn West came up with the idea in order to "serve notice on pro-Germans that they are not welcome as visitors and if now in the city, are not wanted as guests." No word on how long the message remained there.

Modesto, about 40 miles to the south, got a sign of its own a few years later courtesy of the Business Men's Association that welcomed visitors with the phrase "Water, Wealth, Contentment, Health." In 1912, this phrase won a civic contest. Well, it didn't exactly win. In truth, the phrase came in second to "Nobody's Got Modesto's Goat," which may have reflected the community's sarcastic sense of humor or an epidemic of goat thievery in the region. Regardless, town leaders thought better of it and chose the second-place option, instead.

Other signs went up across or near the highway in the Northern California towns of Orland, Weed, Williams, and Yreka, to name a few. Most of the highway signs and arches fit into one of two categories: steel signs straddling the road or stucco arches. A few hung from wires

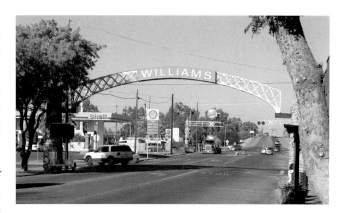

The Williams Arch, looking west, a couple of blocks from 99W.

stretched across the highway from the upper stories of buildings in business districts. Two examples of the latter were set up in Pixley, whose sign is long since gone, and Clovis (about 10 miles east of the highway), whose neon-lit "Gateway to the Sierras" sign remains in place.

The concrete-and-stucco Orland arch was built in the summer of 1926, just a few months before the highway became designated as U.S. 99, with the interior opening designed to look like the top of a covered wagon. It still stands over Sixth Street, aka U.S. 99W, south of Red Bluff.

Weed put up a concrete arch of its own in 1922, but the city grew nervous when cracks started to appear four decades later. Because no blueprints were known to exist, there was no way to tell whether the structure was safe or whether it might come crashing down at any moment. The decision was made to demolish it, but the task turned out to be more difficult than workers had envisioned: Once they fired up their blowtorches, they discovered that the concrete exterior was supported by steel railroad

track. In the end, they needed more than three weeks to bring it down. The current steel arch, featuring pine trees and a depiction of Mount Shasta surrounding the city's name as its centerpiece, went up in 1989.

Yreka's arch, which spells out the town's name in capital letters, was moved from the roadway to a concrete island just off the highway, where it stands over a more recent sculpture of a prospector, with his mule, panning for gold.

Merced put up an impressive sign across U.S. 99 that consisted of two pillars in the shape of thick sequoia tree trunks supporting a wooden crossbeam perhaps 40 feet overhead. Emblazoned on the face of it was the town's name surmounting the slogan "Gateway to Yosemite."

Fresno commissioned its own sign in 1915, choosing a more permanent structure to welcome motorists traveling down what was then still Legislative Route 4. The impressive terra-cotta-and-stucco arch was flanked on either side by a pair of 14-foot-tall Doric columns. Its

Fresno's arch was saved from the scrap heap in the 1950s, but the city grew northward, away from it, and the newer freeway alignment bypassed it, consigning it to what became a seldom-used industrial area south of town.

total height was 35 feet, and it measured 54 feet wide: more than three times the width of the highway itself at the time. It lit up automatically at night, making it visible from two miles down the road. There was never any doubt that you were approaching the Fresno city limits.

Unfortunately, you can't see the arch today. The $3,000 structure burned down less than a decade after it was constructed, to be replaced in 1929 by the more modest gateway over the entrance to Van Ness Avenue: a steel truss arch supported by a single pillar on either side. The sign reads "FRESNO" in large capital letters above the arch, with the words "VAN NESS AVE" slightly smaller across the face of it.

But even that sign isn't on Highway 99 anymore. The highway alignment has shifted westward—not once but twice—since the sign was erected. Around 1950, the two-lane road that used to be Highway 99 at the south end of Fresno is now simply Railroad Avenue, a forlorn-looking strip of asphalt at the edge of an industrial area dominated by warehouses, railroad crossings, and a few scattered businesses. By the second half of the 20th century, the sign, like the rest of the area, had fallen into a state of rust and disrepair along with the rest of the neighborhood.

At one point, in 1952, it was nearly torn down and used for scrap, but historical preservationists cried foul. They managed to save the sign, but nothing was done to restore it to its former glory until the owner of some nearby property got a permit to do so—complete with working neon—more than a quarter-century later. It was then that the slogan "Best Little City in the U.S.A." was added beneath the city's name on the side of the sign facing Railroad Avenue. On the reverse side, motorists heading out of town were notified that "You Are Now Leaving the Best Little City in the U.S.A."

Bakersfield might have disputed that. For years, the two largest cities in the San Joaquin Valley have been engaged in a friendly (and at times not-so-friendly) civic rivalry. The Kern County oil town had an iconic sign of its own for many years across Old 99, otherwise known as Union Avenue.

The Streets of Bakersfield

The Bakersfield Inn had opened in 1929 and quickly became a hit. Some accounts say Oscar Tomerlin, who owned the inn with his brother, coined the word "motel" by fusing "motor" and "hotel" (though Arthur Heineman is also credited with having invented the word when he opened his Milestone Mo-Tel in San Luis Obispo a few years earlier). For a time, the Bakersfield establishment was called the Motel Inn. It was, however, a good deal fancier than most modern motels.

The venture was such a success that the business expanded several times, growing from "a cluster of 26 tourist cottages in 1930 to a deluxe system of 167 rooms" a decade later, according to an account in *The Bakersfield Californian*. The inn's hacienda-style theme featured tile roofing, adobe walls, and fountains on grounds that covered two city blocks. It had four banquet rooms, a beauty parlor, and a barbershop in a complex that seemed far more like a luxury hotel than a roadside auto court. The patio was enlarged in 1940 with the addition of 100 grand palm trees. Then, that same year, the owners opened their most extravagant feature yet: a sumptuous 3,300-square-foot ballroom known (appropriately) as the Palm Room, complete with gold drapes, a stairway, a mezzanine, and a wood-inlaid floor.

The green-hued walls and cooling system offered guests a welcome contrast as they sought shelter from the triple-digit heat of the South Valley.

And once inside, they were entertained.

Big-band leaders Harry James and Duke Ellington were among the acts that performed at the Palm Room during its heyday. Dancer/actress Ann Miller, who appeared in musicals such as *Easter Parade* and *Kiss Me Kate*, was the guest of honor at a ball held there in the summer of '44. Other celebrities seen on the premises at one time or another included Clark Gable, oil tycoon J. Paul Getty, Jimmy Durante, Stan Kenton, Fred MacMurray, and Lionel Hampton. The hotel played host to political events, dances, weddings, and fashion shows.

It grew so popular that in 1949 its owners decided to build an annex on the east side of the road. To save guests the difficulty of dodging in and out of traffic while attempting to cross the busy four-lane highway, they built an elevated walkway supported by steel columns

The letters from the iconic Bakersfield sign were saved and installed on a replica outside Buck Owens' Crystal Palace museum and nightclub. Unlike the original, you can't walk across it.

and a network of steel webbing. Across the front was the city's name, written in big, blue capital letters.

Suddenly, Bakersfield had a welcome sign as iconic as any along the highway—perhaps more so.

But in 1963, the new freeway diverted many of the cars that had stopped at the inn over the years, and patronage began to decline. Union Avenue was no longer Highway 99; it was just Union Avenue, still a busy thoroughfare but one used more by locals than out-of-towners looking for a place to spend the night. A year later, when the owners were in the midst of remodeling, a fire started in a kitchen electric panel and spread to the coffee shop, cocktail lounge, and upstairs party rooms by way of painters' material left on-site. The flames were extinguished before they reached any of the guest rooms, but the fire did $400,000 worth of damage.

The inn's owners rebuilt, but it never again attained its former glory. Scenes from Clint Eastwood's movie *Any Which Way You Can* and the miniseries *Roots II* were filmed there, and the sign was featured in the 1987 Buck Owens–Dwight Yoakam video for *Streets of Bakersfield*. But the sign fell into disrepair and, by the mid-1990s, the state began to worry that an earthquake could send it crashing onto the street below.

It was Owens who came to the rescue, dedicating $175,000 to salvaging the letters from the sign and putting up a replica in front of his Crystal Palace museum and nightclub. There was no elevated walkway this time: The new arch didn't lead from or to anywhere; it just acted as an entryway.

"Each time I would come back to Bakersfield I would always see the famous sign," Owens said. "It had a great warmth to it. It became an old friend."

After the state bypassed Bakersfield with a new freeway east of Union Avenue, civic leaders decided they needed another sign to let motorists know the city was up ahead. The new highway still passed through a portion of Bakersfield, but only what was then its western edge. So in 1966, the city decided to put up something a little more impressive than an arch or a billboard welcoming travelers. In case there was any doubt the city lay ahead, it was erased by a pair of massive signs (one at each end of town) that towered 49 feet above the earth and stretched 60 feet wide. The city's name all but screamed out at passing motorists in capital letters some 10 feet high on a central nameplate.

Above were the words, set against four colorful circles, "sun. fun. stay. play." Then, beneath the city's name was a marquee designed to tell visitors what was going on in the city. The entire thing was supported by five big columns.

The signs, as impressive as they were, didn't last too long. They were removed in 1983.

WATER TOWERS AND GREEN ACRES

The Kingsburg water tower's coffeepot design is relatively recent. Though the 122-foot-tall tower went up in 1911, it didn't assume its most recognizable shape until 1985.

Tulare, perhaps taking a bit of inspiration from Kingsburg, modified its water tower to look like a glass of milk, complete with a "flex" straw sticking out of the top. It would take a mighty big giant to take a sip of that milk, though Tulare's dairy industry doubtless has enough cows to fill the tower to capacity with milk should the city ever care to do so.

Tulare's water tower has been decorated to resemble a glass of milk, complete with straw.

But perhaps the most famous water tower along 99 is in Pixley, an unincorporated town of some 3,000 people about 18 miles south of Tulare. Its water tower doesn't look like a coffeepot or a glass of milk. It looks like … well … a water tower, pretty nondescript—except for the fact that it made an appearance every now and then on national television. The CBS comedy *Petticoat Junction*, which ran from 1963 to 1970, was set in a hotel not too far from a fictional town called Pixley whose very real water tower could be seen from Highway 99.

Petticoat Junction was a spinoff of the immensely successful comedy *The Beverly Hillbillies*, where actress Bea Benadaret had a recurring role. Benadaret (who also provided the voice for *The Flintstones'* Betty Rubble) was cast as the widowed owner of a hotel in the middle of nowhere whose three daughters helped run the place.

The fictional version of Pixley was several miles from the hotel, which was dubbed the Shady Rest. This Pixley was a lot more cosmopolitan than the real one, boasting an international airport, its own TV station, a secretarial school, supermarket, and other modern amenities that distinguished it from the more backwater town of Hooterville. For the record, the real Pixley does have an airport called Harmon Field, but it's about as far from "international" as you can get. The town on 99 also has a market or two, but nothing you'd call super in the sense of a Ralph's or a Safeway.

The real Pixley's main street is also a segment of the old Highway 99 that was bypassed when the freeway came along. It runs parallel to the tracks of the Southern Pacific, which once had its own depot along that north–south rail line. A rail line figured prominently in *Petticoat Junction*, too. A steam train called the Hooterville Cannonball rode the rails of the C&FW Railroad, which provided service to the Shady Rest and had Pixley as its terminus. *Petticoat Junction* even aired an episode titled "Last Train to Pixley."

Just as the show itself was spun off from *The Beverly Hillbillies*, it eventually spawned a spinoff of its own. The new show was called *Green Acres*, and it also featured references to Pixley, including an episode titled "How to Get from Hooterville to Pixley Without Moving." *Green Acres* starred Eddie Albert and Eva Gabor as Oliver and Lisa Douglas, a lawyer and his wife who leave New York City for the "charm" of a rural life they haven't the slightest clue how to navigate. It ran from 1965 to 1971 and featured some of the same characters seen in *Petticoat Junction*, including Sam Drucker, proprietor of the general store in Hooterville.

If Pixley was based on a Tulare County town, what about Hooterville? Get out a map and trace your finger roughly 25 miles to the east, and it'll land on a town with the similar-sounding name Porterville.

And what about *Green Acres*? There are a couple of possibilities. If you head south from Pixley on the 99 and veer west on the 58 in Bakersfield, you'll hit the town of Greenacres off the Rosedale Highway. It's a small, unincorporated community founded in 1930, and it's less

The Pixley water tower was a familiar image in the TV series *Petticoat Junction*, **where it represented a fictional (and somewhat larger) town of the same name.**

than an hour away from Pixley's water tower. Or you could keep your map open and find Visalia, a town just a half-hour away from Pixley. It shouldn't take you long to locate Green Acres Drive and Green Acres Middle School. As a matter of fact, the entire neighborhood where both are found shares the name of the TV show. It's an older, upscale area of attractive homes just an errant tee shot away from the Visalia Country Club—a place where the Douglases would doubtless have felt quite at home.

In Visalia, Green Acres was the place to be.

5

THE LONG, HARD ROAD

A homeless family walks along U.S. 99 near Brawley in February of 1939. They were traveling from Phoenix to San Diego, where the father hoped to get on relief. *Dorothea Lange, Library of Congress/public domain.*

They came west from Oklahoma, from Arkansas, from Kansas and the great plains, a region devastated by dust storms and extreme poverty. The twin scourges of drought and Depression spurred them forward. Some rode the rails; others packed up all they owned and piled it in heaps on top of old jalopies they hoped wouldn't break down along the way. Mattresses, old chairs, clothes, and blankets weighed down cars as they rumbled along on old Route 66 toward California during the 1930s.

Many came from cotton fields turned to dust, searching for a place to settle and a piece of Hollywood-style hope.

Hollywood, and the rest of California, didn't want any part of them. The city of Los Angeles sent police officers to the state line in 1936, where they formed a "bum blockade" to keep the migrants out.

It didn't work.

The refugees were too many, too desperate, and too resourceful. They had already traveled more than a thousand miles on what John Steinbeck called the "Mother Road," passing through Amarillo, Albuquerque, and Flagstaff in an informal convoy that stretched across not only miles but years as it traversed the nation's great southwestern expanse. They bought gas at a string of discount Whiting Bros. stations, where they could save a few pennies off the name-brand price and, during summer, a bag of free ice when they filled up. Some of the 30-plus stations along the route also offered groceries.

Route 66 crossed the Arizona state line into California at Needles, roughly following the road that replaced it, Interstate 40, all the way to Barstow.

Once there, the refugees had a decision to make. They could continue along 66 as it turned southward toward Los Angeles, or they could head northwest along Route 466, across the high desert toward Mojave and Tehachapi. About twice as many took that route as headed for the City of the Angels, and even some of those who went south changed their minds. When 66 hit San Bernardino, it turned westward again—and it kept going roughly in that direction until it reached the Santa Monica Pier.

From San Bernardino to Pasadena, Route 66 followed Foothill Boulevard, a broad surface street running alongside the 210 or Foothill Freeway that replaced it. The old U.S. 99, meanwhile, ran parallel to the 66 just a few miles south, roughly along the route traveled by the modern Interstate 10 (San Bernardino Freeway). The two legendary highways met in Los Angeles, not far from Dodger Stadium. Route 66 turned southwest at Pasadena and followed Figueroa Boulevard until it intersected San Fernando Road—Old 99.

From there, travelers could continue on the 66 into Hollywood and Beverly Hills, or they could choose to follow the 99 in either direction. The highway acted as the spine not only for the state itself, but also for its most fertile agricultural regions. Travelers could double-back and find work in the citrus groves of Ontario, picking dates in Indio or working the lettuce and alfalfa fields near Brawley. This southern branch of U.S. 99 still exists, though it has been renumbered as State Route 86.

Northbound 99 ran roughly along modern Interstate 5, up over the Tehachapis. By the time many of the Dust Bowl refugees were arriving, travelers no longer had to rely on the curvy Ridge Route to convey them northward but could travel instead through Piru Gorge along the much more direct Ridge Route Alternate, which opened in 1933. On the other side of the mountains lay more farms, yielding citrus, raisin grapes, cotton, and other crops.

Agriculture was what many of the refugees knew, and they found jobs in agriculture—at pauper's wages—waiting for them there. The road to opportunity they'd seen advertised in magazines and newspapers was, for most, a dead-end highway. As the earliest waves of Dust Bowl refugees made their way into the great Central Valley, they found the land of milk and honey they'd come in search of was shriveling on the vine. The Depression had made its mark here, just as it had everywhere else.

Dorothea Lange photographed the route over the Tehachapis many migrants took to reach the San Joaquin Valley via U.S. 99. This photo was taken in February of 1939. The billboard up ahead advertises the "Grapevine air cooled café." *Dorothea Lange, Library of Congress/public domain.*

Most of their experience in agriculture had come in the cotton fields, which had been laid low by the drought and the sky-high walls of dust that had swept across the plains in its wake. Drought wasn't a problem in California, but there were other hardships to contend with. The refugees arrived to find themselves in competition with an established group of laborers who had come up from Mexico to work the fields. Worse, they arrived just as wages hit rock bottom. In 1929, pickers had been paid $1.40 for every hundred pounds of cotton they'd picked; three years later, the wage had plummeted to 40 cents.

Dell and Lillian Dunn were among that first wave of refugees. The couple had moved west from Oklahoma to New Mexico, where Lillian opened a café in Roswell with a partner before heading back out onto the highway

for California. They had family there: Lillian's mother, brother, and sister had found employment harvesting oranges on a ranch in Tipton, just south of Tulare.

But the Dunns' new life was hardly what they'd envisioned. Just six months after they arrived, their 17-month-old son, Donald, bit into a piece of rotten fruit that their employer had provided as part of the family's wages. When the boy grew ill, his parents took him to the hospital, only to be told that the doctors there wouldn't treat him because he wasn't a California resident. He died a few days later.

That was in 1931, and conditions only got worse from there. Wages continued to fall, and by 1933 the laborers had reached the end of their rope. In the summer, peach pickers went on strike in Tulare, along with citrus and other field laborers up and down the valley. And in

Relief clients line up early in the morning for federal distribution of surplus sugar, oranges, apples, and dry beans one mile south of Tulare in April of 1940. *Dorothea Lange, National Archives/public domain.*

October, 12,000 cotton pickers walked off the job state-wide, demanding higher wages—and the growers who paid those wages responded with a vengeance. The local sheriff deputized some of the growers, who proceeded to confiscate strikers' pickets and evict them. Some were told not only to get off company property, but to leave the area altogether, and pressure was put on community members to make sure they were shown the door.

An ad that appeared in the *Tulare Advance-Register* on October 9 made the growers' sentiments plain: "We, the farmers of your community, whom you are dependent upon for support, feel that you have nursed too long the viper at our door. These communist agitators must be driven from town by you, and your harboring them further will prove to us your non-cooperation with us, and make it necessary for us to give our support and trade to another town that will support and cooperate with us."

That same day, 200 strikers in Kern County were forcibly removed from their dwellings.

Growers, fearing the strikers would try to damage their crops, formed vigilante committees to drive them from the fields. Tensions built into what one newspaper account labeled "a smoldering volcano of unrest and hatred" until, on October 11, it finally erupted in Pixley. It was there that a group of cars carrying armed ranchers arrived to interrupt a protest by several hundred farm laborers.

Shots were fired, and two women in their 50s lay dead. Eight other people were injured.

"It all started when one of the farmers took a shot at someone in our crowd," striker Billy Thomas told the United Press. "Then there was a volley of shots. It was soon over. When the growers and the strikers saw the bodies and realized what happened, most of them ran away. Two of us were dead."

The same story related word of another outbreak in Arvin, where one man was reported slain and at least 20 others injured.

Lillian Dunn was among those who witnessed the Pixley shootings, after which seven strike organizers were arrested. They were ultimately acquitted, but the "communist" stigma—rein-

forced during court proceedings—lingered. A year later, a worker at a food distribution center in Pixley denied Lillian Dunn her share of aid, calling her a communist. Dunn (who was pregnant at the time) stood her ground, and the supervisor eventually saw to it that she received her food … but officers arrested her that night on charges of instigating a riot. She wound up spending two weeks in jail, even as the *Visalia Times-Delta* ran a headline convicting her in print: "Communists lead attack on Pixley food depot."

Although wages rose somewhat in the ensuing years, life didn't get easier for the Dust Bowl refugees. More and more kept arriving in the fields that flanked Old 99, with the migration reaching its peak in the mid- to late '30s. Many wound up in squatters encampments of anywhere from a handful to a few hundred migrants, finding shelter wherever they could: beside irrigation ditches, behind highway billboards, or, if they were lucky, in abandoned barns.

Those who found jobs in the fields were the lucky ones. Many others failed to find employment and wound up applying for government relief, which got those who had already settled the cities along Old 99 even more riled

Three families built a makeshift shelter behind this billboard on Highway 99 in Kern County during November of 1938. *Dorothea Lange, Library of Congress/public domain.*

View of the Arvin Federal Government Camp, also known as the Weedpatch Camp, as seen in 1936.
Dorothea Lange, Library of Congress/public domain.

up. Not only were the squatters camps an eyesore, they were a burden on the honest taxpaying citizen, or so the argument went.

When Congressman John H. Tolan of Berkeley proposed a relief bill to help the migrants, he met stiff opposition from the likes of the California Citizens Association. The association fired off a letter criticizing Tolan's proposal, arguing that there were six workers for every agricultural job in California and that the prospect of federal relief would only attract more.

"More than 1,000,0000 people are already living on public assistance of one kind or another in California," the letter stated. "Hundreds of thousands of these people are without jobs or prospect of jobs. California cannot absorb any more on relief and the people coming into the state cannot expect to get jobs unless they take them away from the local residents."

Even in the face of such resistance, the federal government did what it could. The Farm Security Administration (FSA) set up a chain of labor camps, many of them roughly following the course of Highway 99 through the state's agricultural heartland. The first and perhaps most famous of these was in Weedpatch, about seven miles east of 99. It was here that author John Steinbeck found his inspiration for his novel *The Grapes of Wrath*.

Shelter was basic: Laborers lived in tents along dirt roads, surrounding a central community building. If you wanted to take a shower, you had to visit one of three utility buildings, which also contained sinks, toilets, and a place to do laundry. When the camp was built in 1935, the Weedpatch tents were pitched directly on the ground, and rainwater invariably found its way inside, turning the "floor" into a muddy soup. Occupants laid down cardboard, but this quickly became sopping wet, as well, until the FSA installed raised wooden platforms nearly a year after the camp opened.

Families could pay a dollar a week to stay in the camp or, if they didn't have the money, they could work there in exchange for a place to stay. What they couldn't buy was respect. The newcomers were labeled as dirty and slow-witted, unfit to mingle in so-called polite society. Their distinctive accents identified them to many as illiterate "country bumpkins," bums, drifters, and poor white trash.

The attacks didn't stop there: The state Chamber of Commerce accused them of lacking any moral standards whatsoever, declaring, "There is so much unmorality among them—not immorality; they just don't know any better." The article in the August 1938 issue of the chamber's magazine, *California*, went on to report the arrest of a certain man for molesting his own daughter. At his court appearance, his wife reportedly stood up in his behalf and declared, "They oughtn't to send paw to jail for that. She's his own property and he can do what he pleases with her."

This particular story, whether accurate, manufactured, or embellished, was just one example of widespread efforts to stigmatize the laborers. Ironically, most of the newcomers were Bible-believing Christians whose code of ethics expressly forbade such behavior.

"We like the camp rules here," a woman named Mrs. Jenkins said in an interview with *The Bakersfield Californian* in the summer of 1939. "We're law abidin' and we allus expect to be. They was a family drove up here this morning when I happened to be down by the gate. When they read the rules, they didn't want to come. Well, me for one, am glad they weren't let in."

Jenkins was a resident of the FSA camp in Shafter, about 20 miles northwest of Bakersfield. "We was so glad to get into this camp," she said. "The camp nurse examined us, and we ain't got no disease."

Those found to be suffering from an infectious disease were placed in an isolation ward at the rear of a medical clinic on the grounds. It was a far cry from the conditions found at makeshift squatters camps of just a couple of years earlier, when an estimated 30,000 migrants could be found living in squalor along the ditch banks and byways in Kern County alone. By 1939, just 50 or so were found to be there.

It was a noticeable improvement.

Sam Jenkins, his wife, and their three children had arrived at the Shafter camp from Oklahoma with an old, black washtub tied to the rear of their 1931 jalopy. It's no wonder his wife was delighted to find a place with running water and electricity that powered something she'd never seen before: a washing machine. "One of the ladies here promised to show me how to run it," she said. "It's almost a pleasure to git yore clothes dirty just to wash 'em in that. It shore is hard to keep three kids cleaned up."

Sanitation was a problem in the unregulated camps, and health problems were common, especially among

Women do laundry at a common building in the Weedpatch Camp, in February of 1936. *Dorothea Lange, Library of Congress/ public domain.*

young children. Illness accounted for just a part of the problem; some of it could be traced to malnutrition. In early 1938, a federal worker assigned to investigate the problem, Dr. Omer Mills, reported that two children were dying every day in Tulare County—home to thousands of migrant laborers. Twenty-seven of 30 children examined in the Farmersville area were found to be undernourished, and children accounted for a whopping nine out of every 10 deaths countywide. Upon visiting one of the county's squatter camps, Mills found a family of nine virtually without food and the youngest child dressed in a flour sack. The camp, he said, consisted of "dirty, torn tents and makeshift shacks in a sea of mud."

That winter was a particularly difficult one for the refugees, whose numbers had reached their peak just as a season of heavy rains inundated the camps. When the rains hit in late winter, they submerged Highway 99 under nearly a foot of water near Madera, making it impossible to reach Fresno from the north. By March 4, no railroad trains were moving as the Chowchilla and Fresno rivers rose past flood stage.

Fresno, Anaheim, and Los Angeles were among the cities where roads were underwater, and the Los Angeles River that ran parallel to U.S. 99 burst its banks in several places.

Tulare Lake, once the most expansive lake west of the Mississippi, had dried up entirely since farmers had begun diverting water from its tributaries to irrigate their crops. But in 1938, it suddenly sprang to life anew. Landowners scrambled to shore up levees against the onslaught of water, but they were no match for nature's fury. Runoff from snowmelt in the Sierra piggybacked on the initial heavy rains, and by early June nothing more could be done. Growers got their heavy equipment out of harm's way and watched as water rushed out onto some 49 square miles of lakebed that had been reclaimed for cropland. Cotton, wheat, and barley were laid waste.

Not only were crops valued at up to a million dollars lost, the laborers who had worked the now-submerged fields found themselves without homes. Some of the camps in which they had lived were flooded out, as well, and others were isolated by waters that washed out roads and left the surrounding land a mucky swamp. More than a thousand laborers found themselves marooned in the Mendota area for more than two months, and heavy trucks were the only vehicles equipped to get in or out. To make matters worse, many squatters had set up camp beside rivers that had breached their banks, washing away what little the migrants owned.

Tulare County experienced a rash of smallpox cases, and there was another outbreak near Madera.

The extent of the health problem had been clear even before the floods. Dr. R.C. Williams of the U.S. Public Health Service had noted at the outset of 1938 that "while a large number of those in these camps come from the Dust Bowl, conditions here are much worse than anything we find in the Dust Bowl area. . . . In some cases, (laborers) are forced to live in a condition of indescribable squalor."

In many ways, however, 1938 marked a turning point in the history of the Dust Bowl refugees. At Williams' urging, the FSA set aside $150,000 to improve health care for laborers. Meanwhile, migration from the Southwest to California began, gradually, to taper off and conditions on the ground began to improve, if only marginally. The wage per hundred pounds of cotton picked was 75 cents in 1938, up from the 40-cent level that had triggered the strikes of five years earlier. And many of the FSA camps were upgraded, as well, with sturdier and more permanent structures.

Disease became less prevalent: Typhoid fever was "almost non-existent" in the camps, the state public health director reported in 1938. More than 20,000 migrants had been vaccinated against both typhoid and

A nurse tends to a sick baby at the Tulare County Farm Security Administration migrant camp in May of 1939. Squalid conditions in the migrant camps made disease a constant threat. *Dorothea Lange, Library of Congress/public domain.*

smallpox, and tuberculosis rates were no higher among the laborers than in the general population.

Yet even as conditions improved, the popular perception remained the same: Labor camps were still assumed to be breeding grounds for everything from smallpox to typhoid fever, offering a handy excuse to ostracize those who lived there. Even when the facts no longer supported it, however, that excuse remained, as intractable as those who employed it. A sign at a Bakersfield movie theater read "Niggers and Okies upstairs."

Children from refugee families weren't welcome in city schools, where their peers teased them for their accents and tattered clothing, while teachers forced them to sit at the back of the classrooms. There was no use trying to educate them, anyway, some said; they were bound to end up just like their parents—shiftless, dirty, and barely literate. In truth, members of the established community didn't *want* to believe the refugee children could learn, because then they'd have to integrate them—to admit that they, themselves, were no better than the "Okies" and "Arkies" they were condemning.

HIGHWAY OF FAME

John Steinbeck would win the National Book Award and a Pulitzer Prize for *The Grapes of Wrath*, the novel he wrote based in large measure on what he saw at the Weedpatch FSA camp. The plaudits, however, were far from universal—especially among ranchers along the U.S. 99 corridor. Kern County's library system refused to carry the book, which of course made it even more popular for the curiosity factor.

In 1936, Steinbeck had written another work titled *In Dubious Battle*, based on the peach and cotton strikes of 1933. Names like Merritt and Tagus, which dot the highway between Bakersfield and Fresno, were familiar to the ears of those involved in those struggles.

Hulett C. Merritt gave his name to a street that runs east to west in Tulare: The eastern end of Merritt Avenue is an on-ramp to southbound 99. In 1912, he had founded a 7,000-acre spread of farmland called Tagus Ranch along 99 just north of Tulare. Merritt Peaches were served at New York's Waldorf Astoria Hotel, and the farm—billed as the largest fruit ranch in the world—produced a variety of other crops, including grapes and prunes. Then there was cotton, which was king in the San Joaquin Valley for much of the 20th century. The Tagus land not only gave rise to row upon row of cotton, but it even had its own cotton gin to process the crop.

Merritt was a millionaire by the time he was 18 and at one point was the richest man in California, having accumulated much of his wealth as a partner with John D. Rockefeller in the iron mining business and as 1 of 10 principal owners of U.S. Steel. He built a million-dollar mansion in Pasadena before he bought his land near Tulare, and he also had an estate in Santa Barbara. The Pasadena mansion would be featured in the opening scenes of the 1950s television series *The Millionaire*, which aired fictional stories of people who received $1 million from a mysterious benefactor.

Merritt, who owned another impressive estate in Tulare called The Oaks, was not nearly so lavish with his employees. More than 2,000 laborers worked his fields at Tagus for 15 cents an hour, many of them living in tents and toiling under the oversight of the owner's son, ranch manager H.C. Merritt Jr. When peach pickers went on strike in the summer of 1933, the younger Merritt was anything but sympathetic. He called upon California Governor James "Sunny Jim" Rolph to put down the strike by sending out the National Guard, contending that it was the work of professional union agitators.

A vineyard is seen during pruning in Tulare County, photographed in February of 1939. *Dorothea Lange, Library of Congress/public domain.*

"Those who are picking on the farmers of California are not interested in economics but in the political angles," he declared.

In the end, he wound up raising his laborers' wages to 25 cents an hour.

Tagus was not only a working ranch but a community in its own right. Even though it was just five miles north of downtown Tulare, it had its own post office, general store, school, bank, and church. It also became a popular stop along Highway 99, serving motorists with a restaurant, a motel, and a service station.

In later years, Tagus Ranch would be known for its "world famous" country theater, which was owned by

The Tagus Country Theatre sign couldn't be missed just north of Tulare on Highway 99 until it was torn down in December of 2014, along with the building itself, which had fallen prey to vandals and graffiti taggers after having been closed for many years.

Rick Nelson of *Ozzie and Harriet* fame for a brief time in the early 1980s before closing its doors and becoming a magnet for vandals and graffiti.

Other famous names passed through Tagus, as well. Tagus served as the inspiration for Hooper Ranch in *The Grapes of Wrath*, and Leonard Slye worked the fields at Tagus before he moved south to make a name for himself in Hollywood as a singing cowboy named Roy Rogers. Simeon "Sim" Iness, an Olympic gold medalist in 1952 who became the first man to throw a discuss more than 190 feet, came to Tulare at the age of 4 when his family moved from Oklahoma, where his family had been sharecroppers. They wound up working at Tagus, too.

Actor Richard Deacon was a bartender at Tagus before moving on to the small screen, where he could be seen weekly on such shows as *Leave It to Beaver* (in the role of Fred Rutherford) and *The Dick Van Dyke Show* (as producer Mel Cooley).

Other famous transplants from the Southwest during the Dust Bowl era included a healthy dose of country-western, hillbilly, folk, and western swing musicians. Among them were:

- Bob Wills, a Texas native and pioneer of the western swing style who formed a band called the Texas Playboys and settled in Fresno for a few years in the 1940s.
- Spade Cooley, the "King of Western Swing," who was born in Oklahoma and had a top-rated television show for several years in the early '50s; he was convicted of killing his wife on their Kern County ranch in the early '60s after his career took a downward turn.
- Folk-protest singer Woody Guthrie, known for such compositions as "This Land Is Your Land" and for being a key influence on songwriters including Bob Dylan, Pete Seeger, and Bruce Springsteen.
- Merle Haggard, who proclaimed himself proud to be an Okie from Muskogee, even though he was born in 1937 in a converted boxcar in Oildale (his parents had moved out west from Checotah, Oklahoma, after their barn burned three years earlier).

Buck Owens, who at one point topped the charts with a string of 15 consecutive No. 1 country hits, built his Crystal Palace museum and nightclub in Bakersfield in 1996. He died 10 years later, shortly after performing a show there. This sign is visible from Highway 99.

Buck Owens was born in Texas but became known for pioneering what came to be known as the Bakersfield Sound.

Owens moved with his family to Arizona in 1937, but he didn't settle in California until 14 years later. He'd gotten a job as a truck driver and heard from a friend that Bakersfield had a thriving country music scene. In a few short years, the music the Dust Bowl refugees had brought west with them had taken hold. Plenty of clubs in Bakersfield played Owens' brand of music, so he packed up his belongings and headed to Kern County. His parents followed him that same year. In his autobiography, Owens called it "the most important move I've ever made."

It wasn't long before Bakersfield became known as Nashville West, the center of country music west of the Mississippi. Places like the Big Fresno Barn west of Fresno packed in as many as 2,000 people for western swing barn dances, and the culture that had been on the outs a few years earlier was not only becoming mainstream, it was

coming to dominate the region. The Dust Bowl refugees were moving out of the fields and into jobs as bankers, business owners, and big-time entertainers.

Owens was foremost among them. He produced 21 chart-topping country hits and signed on as co-host of the syndicated *Hee Haw* television series in 1969, where he stayed for nearly two decades. In 1963, he even popularized a song later recorded by the Beatles, "Act Naturally" (his first No. 1 country hit).

Buck and his band, the Buckeroos, became Bakersfield institutions. In 1966, Owens bought radio station KUZZ, which featured a logo designed to look like the singer's distinctive red, white, and blue guitar. Travelers and truckers passing through Bakersfield on 99 often tuned their dials to the station as they made their way north or south. In 1996, he built a music hall called the Crystal Palace just off 99 on Pierce Road, which was renamed Buck Owens Boulevard two years after that. Owens died there in 2006, a few hours after performing his final show.

His final chart-topper was, fittingly, a duet with Dwight Yoakam titled "Streets of Bakersfield."

Mexican migrants stop by the side of the road near Bakersfield on their way to harvest Imperial Valley peas in November of 1936. *Dorothea Lange/Library of Congress.*

6

DISASTER AREAS

A collapsed highway overpass blocks then-recently rechristened Interstate 5 at State Route 14 in February of 1971 following the 6.6-magnitude San Fernando earthquake. The quake was one of many tragedies and full-scale disasters to take place along the Golden State Highway. *U.S. Geological Survey/public domain.*

During my early teens, I lived in the foothills of the Santa Monica Mountains, at the western end of the San Fernando Valley. Within walking distance of my front door, down a steep grade, lay a road called Mulholland Highway. I never gave much thought to the road, beyond the fact that my parents did their shopping at an Alpha Beta supermarket on the corner of its intersection with Mulholland Drive.

Whoever this Mulholland was, he must have been someone important, but it was many years before I bothered to look into it.

What I found was that William Mulholland was a self-taught engineer from Ireland who had begun his career as a ditch cleaner. His chief accomplishment was diverting water from the Owens River in eastern California to Los Angeles via an aqueduct hundreds of miles long. A hero to water-starved Southern Californians, Mulholland was reviled by many Owens Valley residents for acquiring rights to their irrigation water under false pretenses.

It was a huge letdown for ranchers and farmers in an area that had showed considerable promise as a new agricultural heartland. Shortly after the turn of the 20th century, the Federal Bureau of Reclamation was looking at Owens Valley as one of eight candidates for an irrigation project. Engineer J.C. Clausen, who surveyed the area for the bureau in 1894, reported that it had "many peculiar merits to favor it" for such a project, including "an abundance of water, power, fertile soil, (a) genial climate, nearby markets for agricultural products . . . and a possible outlet to Los Angeles in the near future."

It was this final point, however, that proved to be the project's undoing.

Fred Eaton, the mayor of Los Angeles, concocted a scheme to separate the Owens Valley farmers from their precious H_2O and send it south before the irrigation project had a chance to work its magic. Eaton went undercover, posing variously as a bureau representative and a cattleman who intended to establish a large ranching operation there. It helped that he had a friendly contact within the Bureau of Reclamation: its local manager, J.B. Lipincott.

Mulholland, meanwhile, built support for the project by depicting it as a matter of survival for Los Angeles residents. Could their rapidly growing metropolis, where the population had just surpassed 100,000, continue to survive on the limited supplies in its own watershed? Mulholland argued that it could not. In reality, however, a huge quantity of the water brought in from the valley wasn't sent to homes at all, but was instead used to irrigate land in the San Fernando Valley—much of it owned by wealthy friends of Eaton and Mulholland. (No wonder those two major thoroughfares on the edge of this same valley, Mulholland Drive and Mulholland Highway, were named for the man from Ireland.)

Before the Owens Valley farmers knew what hit them, Eaton had secured the rights to their water and the reclamation project had been canceled. The aqueduct, on the other hand, went full speed ahead. Mulholland was put in charge of overseeing the project, which the city of Los Angeles financed by passing a $23 million bond measure in 1907.

Construction went forward, but not everything went smoothly. In May of 1913, a few short months before the project's completion, there was a "disastrous break" in the aqueduct at Sand Canyon near Mojave: An earthen tunnel gave way near the point where steel piping had been inserted to carry the water. As a result, the tunnel was abandoned and steel pipe had to be used across the entire length of the canyon. The cost of the failure was estimated at $80,000, but it was neither the most costly nor the most embarrassing failure on a Mulholland project. That was still years away.

The tunnel's collapse didn't stop the aqueduct, which was completed on November 5, 1913. On that date at 1:15 p.m., Mulholland gave the order to release the first drops of a torrent from the gates of the 233-mile aqueduct into the San Fernando Reservoir. The windfall for Los Angeles was 260 million gallons a day. "There it is. Take it," Mulholland told a crowd of 40,000 people who gathered to watch history in the making.

The Jawbone Siphon under construction in Owens Valley, 1913. Water was propelled through the 233-mile Los Angeles Aqueduct system by gravity, and this was the most severe incline along the route, at Jawbone Canyon in the western Mojave Desert. *Public domain.*

THE OWENS WATER WAR

But Mulholland wasn't finished—not by a long shot. Ten years later, he embarked on another project, the construction of a dam in San Francisquito Canyon. The dam was designed to provide storage for the aqueduct system, which itself was still under attack from Owens Valley interests. Literally.

Between 1900 and 1920, the population of Los Angeles had grown from just over 100,000 to more than half a million, straining the aqueduct system and bleeding Owens Valley dry. To make matters worse, the region was in the midst of a severe drought that was taxing both areas. The tug-of-war over water became even more intense as Owens Lake, a catch basin for runoff from the Sierra Nevada that provided the area with its water, dried up and left the area desolate. In its stead, it left nothing more than salt flats that gave rise to blinding dust storms.

The people of the once-fertile Owens Valley were livid,

Authorities inspect dynamite found in Owens Valley amid a series of sabotage incidents along the aqueduct (around 1924).
Los Angeles Times archive/public domain (copyright not renewed).

and they focused their wrath on the aqueduct. In the 1920s, protesters targeted it more than a dozen times with dynamite. In the spring of 1924, they targeted a section of the canal in Inyo County with explosives that left cracks 100 feet long in the concrete. It was no small-scale operation. Dozens of residents were implicated in the attack, and a $10,000 reward was posted. But it wasn't enough to persuade area residents to turn in their neighbors.

In November, the Owens Valley contingent struck again, this time taking control of the aqueduct 50 miles south of Bishop and opening the gates so that the water streamed back into the Owens River. The sheriff arrived with two armed deputies, but the ranchers stood firm, setting up a camp with as many as 150 men beside the aqueduct. They said they wouldn't budge unless the situation was resolved to their satisfaction, and the sheriff in turn refused to act, instead calling upon the governor to intervene. Only the appearance of state troops, he cautioned, would be enough to prevent actual bloodshed.

The governor, however, didn't send in troops, and the standoff continued for five full days.

It was only when an influential Inyo County banker wired a telegram to the ranchers that the trouble was defused. "If the object of the crowd at the spillway is to bring their wrongs to the attention of the citizens of Los Angeles, then they have done so 100 per cent," W.W. Watterson wrote, "and further defiance of law would only injure the Valley's cause beyond all possibility of remedy."

Why did the ranchers listen to Watterson? Because he had credibility: He and his brother Mark had led much of the opposition to the aqueduct, arguing that the city of Los Angeles should pay reparations for business lost to Owens Valley since the water diversion had begun. W.W. Watterson's assurances that Los Angeles was ready to listen placated the ranchers for the moment, but the trouble wasn't over. L.A. continued to grow, as did its insatiable thirst for water, and as time went on, the Owens Valley landowners saw little being done to protect their interests.

In the spring of 1927, nearly three years to the day after the 1924 occupation, a group of armed men decided they had waited long enough: They ambushed guards stationed at the aqueduct and held them at gunpoint as they touched off an explosive charge that tore away a 300-foot section of pipe.

Mulholland, who had received death threats over the project, was anything but sympathetic to the plight of the ranchers. His disdain was such that he "half-regretted the demise of so many of the valley's orchard trees, because now there were no longer enough trees to hang all the troublemakers who live there." What should be done about them? Mulholland responded to the ranchers' latest provocation by sending out mounted patrols of men armed with machine guns, ordering them to use deadly force against anyone who tried to sabotage the aqueduct.

The Owens Valley protesters were undeterred. In early June, they formed a unit of "minute men" armed with rifles and sawed-off shotguns and charged them to "protect the valley from the attacks of Los Angeles city detectives." Other so-called riot squads were reportedly in the works, and the leaders of this armed resistance movement said they would ask the Inyo County sheriff or U.S. marshals to deputize them.

Later in the month, a gun battle erupted between guards stationed along the aqueduct and unnamed intruders. Then, in July, the aqueduct was dynamited twice in a span of just 12 hours. The first explosion, via a floating barge, destroyed a 14-foot section of concrete wall, while the second wrecked some control gates and left a gaping 40-foot opening.

The water war was beginning to look like it would be a protracted affair, with dynamite attacks coming at regular intervals and the guards stationed along the aqueduct hard-pressed to stop them.

Then, suddenly, it was all over. Out of the blue in the first week of August, customers of all five banks in Owens Valley arrived to find themselves locked out and notes posted on doors with the following message: "We find it necessary to close all of our banks in Owens Valley. This result has been brought about by the last four years of destructive work carried on by the city of Los Angeles."

The notes, signed by the Watterson brothers, might have served as a call to escalate the fight against the L.A. water interests. But then a routine audit turned up a discrepancy in the books of the banks' operations. This wasn't just a matter of a few pennies or even a few hundred dollars: State banking officials charged that a whopping $880,000 was missing. Barely a week after the banks closed, the two brothers were arrested on 36 charges of embezzlement. In one fell swoop, opponents of the aqueduct had lost not only the leaders of their movement but thousands upon thousands of dollars.

The Wattersons were ultimately convicted, attacks on the aqueduct stopped, and Mulholland could relax.

Or could he?

Just a few months in the future lay an event that would make the Owens Valley water wars look like a picnic. It would leave hundreds of people dead, roads and buildings destroyed, and Mulholland's reputation in ruins.

It would be the second-worst disaster in California history.

THE DAM BREAKS

The St. Francis Dam was to be William Mulholland's crowning achievement. Built across San Francisquito Canyon at a location Mulholland chose himself, it rose to a majestic height of 205 feet when it was completed in 1926. The idea was to provide a reserve of water for the L.A. area in case the water wars escalated to the point that service from the aqueduct was interrupted for an extended period—or in the event of a natural disaster such as an earthquake.

A disaster was, indeed, in the dam's future, but contrary to reports at the time, it had nothing to do with an earthquake.

It had everything to do with an earthquake *fault*.

William Mulholland was a self-taught engineer who probably had little if any understanding of plate tectonics and who certainly was concerned about making (and saving) a buck. He had originally wanted to build the dam on Big Tujunga Canyon above the community of

The view south-southeast along the Los Angeles Aqueduct, looking toward the filtration plant and L.A. Reservoir, in 2001. *Jet Lowe, Historic American Engineering Record, U.S. Geological Survey/public domain.*

The St. Francis Dam in San Francisquito Canyon was considered an engineering marvel and one of William Mulholland's greatest triumphs when it was completed. This photo shows some of what remains of it nearly a century later, resting with various other debris in the canyon bed.

Sunland but dropped the idea because it would have been too expensive to buy the necessary land from private owners. The San Francisquito site, by contrast, was on public land in the Angeles National Forest; he wouldn't need to buy any public land, merely obtain a use permit, which was much less costly.

Unfortunately for Mulholland, an earthquake fault ran smack down the middle of the public land in question.

But that wasn't the only problem. Construction began in 1924 on a dam originally designed to be 185 feet tall and 700 feet wide. That wasn't good enough for Mulholland, however, who worried that the resulting capacity of 9.8 billion gallons wouldn't be enough to serve the growing L.A. basin. So he raised the height by 10 feet, then raised it by 10 more, effectively increasing the reservoir's volume by more than one-quarter. But while raising the height, he neglected to widen the base, setting up what amounted to a top-heavy dam with much less stability than provided under the original plan.

To make matters worse, the base wound up being 20 feet thinner than the original drawings indicated, further destabilizing the structure.

There was no steel reinforcement, and the dam had only 10 drainage wells—vertical shafts designed to intercept seepage. All 10 were in the central portion of the dam, the only thing that would be left standing a mere two years after its completion. The eastern end of the dam may have been destined to give way, no matter what. It had been built against an ancient landslide, where the earth appeared solid but was nonetheless still moving, gradually and imperceptibly.

Mulholland was nonetheless so pleased with his work that a year after it opened he proclaimed it "the driest dam of its size that I ever saw." Whether he was oblivious, delusional, or trying to hide something is unclear. What is clear, however, is that warning signs were apparent soon after the reservoir behind the dam began to fill. Cracks began to appear in the concrete almost immediately (though they were dismissed as being acceptable for a dam the size of the St. Francis), and some seepage was noted under the abutments.

The reservoir continued to fill until it reached just 3 inches below the top of the spillway on March 7, 1928. It was only then that Mulholland personally gave the order that no more water be allowed behind the dam.

Most of the time, Mulholland wasn't out inspecting the dam himself; he had someone else to do that for him. Tony Harnischfeger, a father of two young children, had come from Antelope Valley to assume the position of dam keeper at St. Francis.

Harnischfeger's marriage had recently come to a messy end, and he had brought his young son, Coder, with him when he arrived to take up his new position (his daughter, still a toddler, remained with her mother). Harnischfeger spent part of his time in Saugus with his new girlfriend, Leona Johnson, and part of his time in a cottage at the base of the dam.

On the morning of March 12, Harnischfeger was inspecting the structure's western abutment when he noticed muddy water was leaking from the site. Leaks near the abutment weren't unusual at the St. Francis (which in itself indicated a problem), but this one worried the dam keeper because he thought the murky content might indicate something more ominous: erosion of the dam's foundation. Alarmed, he got on the horn to

The ruins of the Santa Clara Bridge are still visible if you hike through a few yards of undergrowth just east of Six Flags Magic Mountain in Valencia. The bridge was destroyed in the St. Francis Dam disaster.

Mulholland, who went out with top assistant Harvey Van Norman to have a look.

The leak was not inconsiderable: as much as 22 gallons per second. Still, after a couple of hours poking around the dam, Mulholland and Van Norman were satisfied that the dam remained structurally sound and that any repairs could wait until later. He turned around and headed back to Los Angeles, leaving Harnischfeger to stand watch over the dam, which continued leaking throughout the day. Harnischfeger himself must not have been too concerned, because he remained in the cottage at the base of the dam with his son and his girl-friend into the evening.

It was a quiet evening, except for the sound of a motor-cycle that broke through the silence a few minutes before midnight. The owner of the motorcycle, a carpenter at an electrical powerhouse up the road, passed the dam and continued on his way another mile or so before he heard something else that pierced the silence. It wasn't

his motorcycle, or the sound of an engine. It sounded like a landslide. Pulling off beside the road to listen for a moment, he heard the sound again, growing fainter. Concluding that it was, indeed, a rockslide, he got back on his bike and rode on.

Less than three minutes before midnight, Tony Harnischfeger, Coder Harnischfeger, and Leona Johnson were swept away along with the little cottage at the bottom of the dam—or, rather, the place where the dam used to be. A tidal wave 180 feet high broke through both sides of the failed barrier, barreling down the canyon at 70 miles per hour. It picked up broken pieces of concrete and tossed them aside as though they were feathers, though some weighed as much as 10,000 tons. Then it hurtled down the canyon, uprooting trees and felling homes as it morphed into a morass of debris and destruction.

One of the canyon's two power stations was reduced to a single turbine; 84 of the people working there were

One small section of the St. Francis Dam rears its head above the ruins in this 1928 photo taken after the dam burst, sending a torrent of water down the canyon all the way to the sea at Ventura. *Public domain.*

killed. Many of those who survived had the clothes ripped off their backs or were flung bodily into trees.

Harry Ferguson, who was living in a shanty at the foot of the dam, was carried on his bed for more than two miles on the crest of the unnatural wave before he was able to jump onto the bank of the newly re-formed river.

L.M. Hall, chief at the Southern California Edison power station, managed to escape with his wife and children. "I heard a noise that sounded like a terrific blast about midnight," he recalled. "I saw men running down the road and saw flashes on the power lines. . . . As the water rose, my son and I climbed a telephone pole and clung to it until the waters receded. My wife and daughter were rescued by two employees at the power house, who had seized a log drifting by, and the four made a temporary float of it."

Highway 99 was deluged by the wall of water that submerged it for a four-mile stretch. The Santa Clara Bridge, a sturdy metal-truss span barely a decade old, was washed out and ruined beyond repair. Nine other bridges met the same fate. And still the water kept going, pouring down San Francisquito Creek into the Santa Clara River and onward. In fact, it kept going all the way to the Pacific Ocean in Ventura County, where the early death toll stood at 70 in Fillmore, 52 in Santa Paula, and 12 each along the coast in Oxnard and Ventura.

"Thousands of people and automobiles are slushing through the debris, looking for their dead," one journalist reported in the aftermath of the catastrophe. "Bodies have been washed into the isolated canyons. I saw one alive, stuck in the mud (up) to his neck."

At final count, the dead and missing numbered somewhere between 450 and 600. Leona Johnson's body was recovered, but the bodies of Tony and Coder Harnischfeger—along with many others—were never found.

Almost as soon as the dust settled, fingers were being pointed at Mulholland and the city of Los Angeles. C.C. Teague, president of the Santa Clara Conservation District, accused the city of negligence. One survivor, having lost her husband and children to the flood, erected a sign with a simple message in red letters: "KILL MULHOLLAND."

At an inquest nine days later, the 72-year-old engineer appeared visibly shaken.

"Apparently, we overlooked something," he said in answer to the coroner's questioning. "It is very painful for me to say it. And the only ones I envy now are those who died in the flood."

Alternately chagrined and remorseful, Mulholland declared, "I have more experience in building dams than any man I know." He recounted his own visit to the dam mere hours before it gave way, admitting that he had seen a new leak. "All dams seep," he said matter-of-factly. "St. Francis was the driest dam I ever saw."

Still, when it came down to accepting responsibility for the collapse, Mulholland made no attempt to shift the blame. Instead, he broke down sobbing: "If the dam was at fault, I am at fault, and the blame is mine," he declared.

If given a chance to do things differently, Mulholland testified, he would not have built the dam in the same place.

When asked why, he stated the obvious.

"It failed."

Eight months later, Mulholland resigned his post as chief engineer of the city waterworks bureau in November of 1928.

The man who replaced him?

Harvey Van Norman, the man who inspected the dam alongside him 12 hours before it failed. Van Norman had a dam of his own named after him, and it nearly failed, too.

PARADISE AND ROTTEN EGGS

"If you build it, they will come."

That line from the movie *Field of Dreams* has inspired legions of builders and dreamers over the years.

Sometimes, however, the inspiration is misunderstood (the original quote, for the record, is "If you build it, he will come"). And sometimes, it's misplaced. Sometimes, they don't come . . . even if it's along a major highway like Old 99. This is especially true if you build whatever "it" is amid all the ambience of dead fish, triple-digit heat, and the smell of rotten eggs. Sounds like just the place to spend a holiday, doesn't it?

To be fair, the stench and the rotting aquatic life forms weren't there in the beginning, and the heat—while oppressive—hadn't yet been augmented by the onset of global warming when the idea for the place was conceived beside an accidental ocean. Not an ocean, really. But it was an expansive body of heavily saline water that really wasn't supposed to be there, the result of humans making a mistake and nature taking its course.

The mistake involved digging irrigation canals from the Colorado River to a basin east of San Diego that had once been home to a large prehistoric body of water called Lake Cahuilla. A report by the U.S. Bureau of Soils in 1902 warned of the land's high alkali content, lamenting the fate of "prospective settlers, many of whom talk of planting crops which it will be absolutely impossible to grow."

The California Development Company (CDC) had other ideas. The company christened the area the "Imperial Valley" and set about providing water to those brave enough to defy the government's warnings.

Plenty of farmers were, indeed, brave enough, and they came by the hundreds, proving the government naysayers wrong. All they needed was water to irrigate their crops, and the CDC was all too willing to provide it the form of the Colorado River. Attempts to divert water from the river into irrigation ditches, however, kept running into the same problem: Silt and sediment from the river were clogging up the ditches, blocking the water from reaching the crops. Unfortunately, so much silt was entering the channels that it was clogging them faster than the CDC could dredge it away.

The flood of 1906 inundated the Southern Pacific rail line, seen here, and the tracks had to be moved to higher ground. The disaster ended up costing the railroad millions. *Salton Sea History Museum.*

The company was faced with a conundrum: If it failed to act, the farmers would lose their crops and the company, in consequence, would lose its customers. Unfortunately, the company didn't have the resources to dredge the silt out of the existing canal. It was more economical to simply dig a new canal that would require much less dredging (slightly more than a half-mile as compared to four miles through the existing channel).

Water started flowing to the farmland again, but the company hadn't counted on heavy rains that raised the river to dangerous levels. The additional water increased the risk of flooding, and the CDC suddenly found itself facing the task of closing the channel it had just created, lest the entire river break through and inundate the basin. Workers hurriedly tried to block the intake by throwing up a mixture of sandbags, brush, and whatever else they could scrounge together, but the combination was no match for the Colorado, which did what rivers naturally do: It flowed downhill. Along the way, it obliterated

the sides of the channel that had been dug for it, raging ahead over newly formed waterfalls up to 80 feet high and carving out a channel as much as 1,000 feet wide.

Farmers watched helplessly as the water that was to have been their salvation instead inundated and destroyed acre upon acre of crops. Inexorably, the entire basin began to fill. For a time, it appeared as though the entire Colorado River might empty into it, re-creating the ancient Lake Cahuilla.

When it appeared things couldn't get any worse, another massive flood in 1906 drove a 10-mile-wide liquid bulldozer careening toward the mistake of a lake.

"At the present moment, every drop of water in the Colorado River is flowing into the Salton Sea," federal immigration inspector J.B. Bryan remarked upon visiting the area in the summer of 1906. "And while I may be a poor judge of the situation, having spent only one day there, I do not believe they will ever turn the river back to the old bed."

More storms stirred up huge waves that made the lake seem more like an ocean. Such a scene, according to one newspaper account, had never before been witnessed anywhere inland.

"Colorado River On a Rampage," read one headline.

"Breakers on Salton Sea," read another.

"Salton Sea Is Menace To Many."

Five times, workers tried to stem the tide by closing off the river's path to the basin. Five times, they failed. Telegraph poles were knocked down, and before long, the growing inland sea laid siege to the nearby Southern Pacific rail line that followed much the same path as the future U.S. 99.

The railroad now had a direct stake in the matter, having seen the raging waters wash out its tracks in two places in the spring of 1905. It set up a temporary bypass that quickly proved inadequate, so they tore it up and moved the track to still higher ground. Then, when the waters engulfed that line, the tracks were moved again. The problem quickly proved too big for the CDC to handle, and the railroad was all too willing to step in and help—even at the cost of three-quarters of a million dollars.

It ended up costing more than that, with expenses surpassing $2 million, then closing in on $3 million. It wasn't until 1907 that Southern Pacific was able to cut off the flow, recruiting 2,000 laborers from six Native American tribes, area residents, and across the border in Mexico to move 3,000 rail cars full of gravel, rock, and clay into place. The river's flow was finally stopped, but the story doesn't end there.

This satellite view produced using a Thermal Infrared Sensor Instrument shows the Salton Sea as it appeared on March 24, 2013. *NASA/public domain.*

LEMONADE OUT OF (SALTY) LEMONS

Deprived of its river source, the Salton Sea might have gradually dried up had it been left to its own devices. But some of the farmers who had been drawn to the region stuck around, and the runoff from their irrigation efforts naturally sought out the lowest point in the region: the Salton Sea basin.

The lake wasn't going away. In fact, it was the largest lake in the state of California at 45 miles long and 20 miles across. It was just a matter of figuring out what to do with the water and the 120 miles of shoreline that surrounded it.

Two activities immediately came to mind: fishing and boating. Early developer Gus Eilers saw the sea as a great place to go boating and bought some land on the lake's north shore from Southern Pacific in 1926, with the intention of building an Egyptian-themed resort called Date Palm Beach. Those plans evaporated amid the stock market crash three years later, but Eilers did manage to build a 200-foot pier and a couple of guest houses, then marketed the site as a destination for motorboat enthusiasts.

The three-day Salton Sea Regatta became a major event from at least 1931 onward, attracting competitors from across the country eager to test the waters in their quest for new speed records. Heading into 1948, no fewer than 26 standing speed records had been set on the lake, far more than at any other site.

Among the lake's most famous patrons was Guy Lombardo.

Most people remember Lombardo as the bandleader whose New Year's Eve performances became an annual tradition for radio listeners and, later, television viewers. But Lombardo also had a passion for speedboat racing, and one of the places he pursued that passion was on the Salton Sea.

In March of 1946, Lombardo brought his speedboat the *Tempo IV* down to the sea for an assault on a world speed record. He reached a speed of 113 miles per hour over the course of a mile, the best ever for a boat in his class but short of the overall mark (124 mph). Lombardo tried again less than two months later and improved his speed to 117 mph, though he still failed to eclipse the top record.

Speedboat racing was a major draw on the Salton Sea in the 1940s. Morlan Visel's *Hurricane IV*, seen here, veered into the path of Guy Lombardo's *Tempo VI* at the start of the 1948 Gold Cup race in Detroit, causing an accident that left Lombardo with a broken arm. Lombardo later described it as "a big humpbacked affair that seemed perpetually airborne." *Salton Sea History Museum.*

Other celebrities were drawn to the Salton Sea, as well. It served as a stand-in for the Pacific Ocean in the 1942 film *Wake Island*, and Claudette Colbert starred in another war movie filmed there a year later, *What So Proudly We Hail*. Those who enjoyed lighter fare could catch the lake playing a supporting role to Bud Abbott and Lou Costello in *Pardon My Sarong*, also from 1942.

But many, like Lombardo, went for play rather than work. Jerry Lewis and Frank Sinatra joined him for some fun in the sun there. The Marx Brothers visited, as did Sonny Bono.

Sinatra even announced plans for a major development on the lake in November of 1948. Sure, it was hot in the area, but people were making desert destinations out of Palm Springs and Las Vegas, and the Salton Sea had

The North Shore Yacht Club was the focal point of a development by Ray Ryan on the Salton Sea.
Salton Sea History Museum.

something neither of those places did: water. Proclaiming that Palm Springs had become too crowded, Sinatra announced that he and his investment partners planned to build a $2 million Riviera-style resort near the town of Mecca on the sea's north shore. The development would include a golf course, tennis courts, swimming pools, and a landing strip for aircraft.

Less than a week later, however, those plans had fallen through. It seems the folks in Palm Springs weren't too happy about their town being labeled overcrowded, and Sinatra's press agent had released word of the singer's plans too soon. But even if Sinatra wasn't interested

in spending $2 million to turn the Salton Sea into the American Riviera, others were. In 1958, an oilman named Ray Ryan partnered with fellow Palm Springs businessman Trav Rogers in a scheme to develop a major resort on the north shore.

Ryan had the sort of outsize personality that made him a lot of friends. Among them were many residents of Palm Springs, for which Ryan was a tireless booster. A former mayor of the town called him "a one-man chamber of commerce," promoting the city as a sort of desert Hollywood annex. He once bought a home there for Clark Gable in an attempt to lure other movie stars to the area, and he was among a group of investors who spent $5 million to renovate the historic El Mirador Hotel, an early destination for Hollywood stars that had fallen on hard times. Later, he built the Bermuda Dunes course that hosted the Bob Hope Desert Classic, one of pro golf's premiere events, for more than half a century.

But Ryan also made his share of enemies—dangerous enemies. He liked to gamble, and he was good at it. He once won a quarter of a million dollars from fellow oilman H.L. Hunt (father of sports entrepreneur Lamar Hunt, who coined the name "Super Bowl") in a high-stakes gin rummy game. Ryan liked to play poker, too, and like a growing number of gamblers, he enjoyed visiting Las Vegas, which was becoming a center for organized crime.

In 1949, he visited the new Thunderbird Hotel on the Strip to play a weeklong lowball poker series against professional cardman Nick Dandolos. Nick "The Greek," as he was known, had played with various crime bosses, including the likes of Legs Diamond and Al Capone. That same year (1949), he also played a five-month poker marathon against Johnny Moss in a promotion that helped inspire the World Series of Poker.

Dandolos reportedly lost more than $2 million to Moss, and he lost to Ryan, too, leaving the Thunderbird match $550,000 poorer than when he had arrived. (Their match reportedly served as the inspiration for a scene from Ian Fleming's James Bond novel *Goldfinger* and the subsequent movie of the same title.) Shortly after the encounter, however, someone told him that Ryan had been cheating. The oilman was accused of fielding discrete signals via shortwave radio from associates who were using binoculars to keep tabs on the game. Dandolos demanded his money back, but Ryan denied the charge and refused. Considering The Greek's gangland connections, it was a dangerous thing to do.

Wisely, Ryan hired protection. On one occasion, an employee of a Palm Springs magazine went to the El Mirador to collect some money Ryan owed for advertising. She was directed to Ryan's cottage, but he didn't answer the door. A mountain-size man holding a gun did. Ryan was sitting at a table inside, surrounded by several other gentlemen who looked very much the part of bodyguards. He retrieved a wad of cash, sepa-

rated out 50 hundred-dollar bills, and handed them to her, announcing, "Now we're even." The woman left and asked her boss not to send her on any more errands to the El Mirador.

He never did.

Ryan could be impulsive. He once went on safari in Africa with actor William Holden. While staying at a hotel in Kenya, Ryan complained to Holden about the service. The actor's response? Why not take care of the problem by buying the hotel himself? Ryan responded by doing just that, getting Holden to join him in the venture and renaming the hotel the Mount Kenya Safari Club.

About the same time, Ryan embarked on his next big gamble: a resort on the north shore of the Salton Sea. The centerpiece of the project was the North Shore Yacht Club and Marina, which had space for as many as 400 boats, to be built alongside a luxury hotel and homes. Postcards billed North Shore Beach as the "Glamour Capital of Salton Sea." The Beach Boys weren't named for this particular beach, but they did play there. Ryan and his partner, Rogers, announced plans for the development in 1958 and opened it to a flurry of excitement four years later. It proved so popular that at one point in the '60s it attracted more visitors than Yosemite National Park.

The area attracted other entrepreneurs, as well. The company behind Salton Sea Vista on the western shore marketed the development as "an investor's dream." A brochure promised that "Salton Sea Vista will grow . . . and your investment will grow along with it. Perhaps you were born fifty years too late to catch the Gold Rush . . . the Uranium cache, Newport, Palm Springs . . . or even Wilshire and La Brea! But there's no reason NOW for you to miss this opportunity . . . and it doesn't take a 'bundle' to do it."

M. Penn Phillips also chose a spot on the western shores of the inland sea, close to U.S. 99, as the site for Salton City. There's no question Phillips was serious about the idea. He subdivided his development into 25,000 residential lots and installed the infrastructure necessary to support it: electricity, water, and sewer services, along with 250 miles of paved roads. Phillips enlisted Albert Frey, the architect who had designed the

A family checks out a sign for Kate and Ed Ainsworth's Palm Island Estates on the north shore of the Salton Sea. In 1962, the Ainsworths were offering lots of 10,000 square feet and up for 15 percent down ($2,750 to $2,995) plus a $400 premium for water. Ed Ainsworth was a *Los Angeles Times* **columnist, and the pair co-authored a biography of Junipero Serra,** *In the Shade of the Juniper Tree. Salton Sea History Museum.*

North Shore Yacht Club and the Tramway Gas Station in Palm Springs, to do the planning. There would be a business district, schools, a golf course, a luxury hotel, and, of course, a yacht club alongside the largest lakeside marina in California.

Former heavyweight champ Jack Dempsey was on hand to celebrate the opening day of sales in 1958, but Phillips was the one celebrating. On that first day alone, he sold lots of 1.25 acres and smaller for down payments of $200 on a $3,500 purchase price. Phillips himself had paid just a dollar or two for each of these same lots, so even with the investment he'd made in the community infrastructure, he made a killing.

The idea so effectively captured the imagination of prospective buyers that they gobbled it up. More than 20,000 people put money down or signed contracts to purchase land on Phillips' planned "Salton Riviera," but Phillips sold his interest in Salton City to another development company just two years after his grand opening extravaganza. The early buzz soon subsided, and only a few hundred homes were ever built. A 10-month reces-

sion in 1960 and '61 may have had an effect, but many of the buyers never had any intention of building on the seashore. They were investors and speculators who hoped to turn a profit. But with many of the lots left vacant, no one was interested in buying. Before it was ever a real town, Salton City became a ghost town, a grid of streets lined with empty lots and unfulfilled promise.

Meanwhile, the sea itself was changing, morphing from an oasis into something closer to a sewer. For years, it had attracted not only boaters but also anglers who found its waters teeming with fish. When all that water from the Colorado River had flooded the basin, it had brought with it thousands upon thousands of freshwater fish. The lake's salt content was initially low, reflecting that of the river, but as time passed, salinity levels increased. As irrigation water from the surrounding area drained into the lake, it inevitably brought with it sediments from the region's highly alkaline soils.

By 1930, most of the freshwater fish had perished, and by the mid-'50s, the water was 10 times as salty as it had been a half-century earlier, rivaling the Pacific Ocean in

An abandoned gas station stands alongside other deserted businesses along West Access Road in the community of North Shore. Envisioned as a resort community, North Shore has become all but a ghost town.

terms of salinity. Still, anglers adapted. In the early 1950s, state Fish and Game officials introduced 30 species of fish from the Gulf of California, and they continued to thrive in the 1960s and '70s. But as the sea's salinity continued to rise, with 4 million tons of salt introduced into the water each year, it became more difficult even for saltwater species to survive.

The sea's salt content was 1¼ times that of the ocean by 1994, not only threatening the fish, which began to die (helping to produce a putrid stench), but also causing problems for migratory birds that had come to depend on the sea as a stop along the Pacific Flyway. Some 400 species of birds have been sighted using the place to rest and refuel as they travel north to south and back again. Pelicans, loons, ducks, hawks, flamingos, storks, ibises, jays, starlings, sandpipers, cranes, plovers . . . the list continues.

Waterfowl by far outnumber the tourists and the human residents along the Salton Sea these days, and the dreamers who sought to lure vacationers to the now shuttered and abandoned resorts are long gone, too. Floods in the 1970s and '80s damaged many of the buildings and sent most of those who had clung to the idea of

A collapsed structure at Salton Sea Beach is one of many abandoned buildings and trailers that litter the area. This section on the west shore is covered with graffiti and strewn with decaying furniture, discarded tires, and trash.

allegedly crooked poker victory over their friend. One of them tried to extort $60,000 from Ryan in 1963, ostensibly on behalf of Dandolos, but Ryan wasn't about to be blackmailed. "They tried it once before," he told a newspaper. "It didn't work then, and it never will work. They won't get anything out of me." So saying, Ryan turned the tables by reporting the incident to the FBI, and the two people behind the extortion plot wound up serving five-and 10-year prison sentences.

They were still behind bars when Dandolos died in 1966, broke at the age of 83.

Ryan himself died 11 years later at the age of 73, when a bomb planted underneath his car exploded outside a health club in his adopted hometown of Evansville, Indiana. Parts of the car were found 150 feet away from the blast; Ryan was rushed to the hospital, where he was pronounced dead.

Though suspicion immediately fell on the two men who had been convicted of extortion years earlier—and had since been released from prison—no one was ever arrested in the case.

INUNDATED

The floods that created the Salton Sea and killed hundreds after the St. Francis Dam failure were accidents, but a couple of floods along U.S. 99 happened very much on purpose. One created Pyramid Lake and buried a section of the Ridge Route Alternate under millions of gallons of water.

You can still drive a part of the old highway known as Pyramid Lake Road down to the lakeside from the north. You can also reach the dam from the south via another truncated segment of Old 99, which runs alongside Piru Creek. Those who want to see the dam have to travel the last couple of miles on foot or bicycle, as a gate bars motor vehicles beyond a certain point (though the road is still in decent shape). In addition to a view of the dam, the rewards of the walk include encounters with a couple of old highway bridges and a look at iconic Pyramid Rock, once a key landmark along 99. Walking north, gaze up to the right for a glimpse of traffic making its way along Interstate 5 high above; you'll get a sense of just how much difference there is between the two highway alignments in terms of elevation.

An old television set sits discarded in a cinder-block building in Salton Sea Beach, just north of Salton City, near a faded sign that identifies at least a portion of the complex as the "Park Estates Office." Above the gutted TV, someone has scrawled the apt message, "Hope has left."

an oasis resort scurrying for the comfort of the cities and towns whence they had come.

Ray Ryan's North Shore Yacht Club closed for good in 1984 and was left to the devices of graffiti artists and the elements. (It was restored for use as a museum in 2010, but the museum was moved to another location two years later, leaving the space available only for occasional community functions.)

Ryan himself fared even worse. It seems Nick Dandolos' syndicate friends never forgave him for his

A view of Pyramid Lake shows Pyramid Cut, carved out to make way for the Ridge Route Alternate, in the background, beyond the lake waters that inundated the highway. For a view of the old highway just south of the lake, see Chapter 3.

The waters of Pyramid Lake buried plenty of history, but little else of consequence beyond the asphalt of the old highway. The area was isolated and largely unpopulated when the dam went up, so little was lost when the waters started to rise. The same, however, can't be said in the case of a different dam project in 1928, three decades earlier—one that submerged another section of Old 99, this one in the northern part of the state. The project was so large that it was more than a decade in the planning and required 16 miles of new highway and 37 miles of new rail line to replace the sections that would end up underwater.

By contrast, the towns and settlements along the old routes, likewise submerged beneath the waters of the new-formed lake, would never be replaced.

Driving up I-5 beside the placid waters of Shasta Lake today, it's impossible to tell that towns like Delamar,

Copper City, and Kennett even existed. All were mining towns that now lie beneath the surface of those waters, submerged like some Old West Atlantis—along with a section of the old highway—when dam builders created Shasta Lake. In the early 20th century, Delamar was a prosperous town with a thriving business district that included four hotels, six saloons, a livery stable, and a butcher shop. It was even big enough to have its own suburb, called Sallee.

Copper City, near the site of the Bully Hill copper mine, was just four miles away.

Kennett was the biggest boomtown of the bunch, a bustling city that at one time boasted a population of some 10,000 people. It had an opera house, hotels, a school, a hospital, retail shops, and as many as 40 saloons.

Why so many drinking establishments?

The Kennett Railroad Depot is pictured in this photograph from 1910 (note the deviant spelling of the town name as "Kennet"). The town, once one of the largest in Northern California, lies buried under the waters of Shasta Lake.
Meriam Library, CSU Chico.

Because Kennett was a mining town, and miners developed quite a thirst working under the mountains.

Like many towns in Northern California, Kennett was the creation of those twin economic engines, the railroad and the mining industry. But it wasn't gold that made Kennett prosper, it was copper. The metal was first discovered in the area in 1857, and the Mountain Copper Company built the county's first copper smelter at Kennett around the turn of the century. Soon, business was booming. A *San Francisco Chronicle* article in the spring of 1901 estimated that one mine could produce as much as 9 million tons of ore, and reported that a 2,000-ton smelter was being erected in Kennett to process it. Soon, the Mammoth and Golinsky mines were churning out such huge quantities of pure copper ore that Shasta County produced more of it than any other U.S. county in 1906 and '07.

Victor "Slim" Warrens saw the boom coming and, in 1905, opened the Diamond Saloon and Hotel, which was reputed to be the finest (or perhaps bawdiest) establishment of its type between San Francisco and Portland. It had everything a hard-drinking miner might want. Its redwood bar was long enough, at 150 feet, to accommodate the throngs of customers who came in looking for a stiff shot 24 hours a day. Warrens distilled and bottled his own whiskey, then served it up in a bar that featured Tiffany chandeliers, mirrors with beveled glass, and paintings—on both the wall and the ceiling—of scantily clad women.

But while Warrens and the town raked in profits hand over fist, they were doing so at great cost to the environment. Lumberjacks cut down thousands of trees for use in the smelting process, and thousands more to build the town and hold up the mines' earthen walls. The trees

The Mammoth Mine smelter was the economic engine that brought prosperity to Kennett . . . and the environmental nightmare that poisoned the landscape for miles around. *Meriam Library, CSU Chico.*

that weren't cut down met with an even worse fate: The smelting process produced smoke so toxic with sulfur dioxide and other chemicals that it killed whatever it touched. Trees. Flowers. Shrubs. The damage was such that the five copper smelters operating in Kennett left a landscape barren of living vegetation within a 15-mile radius of the town. Wherever the wind blew the chemicals spewed forth by the smelters' smokestacks, it left an environmental nightmare in its wake. At times, the town was enveloped in a sickly blue haze, while the surrounding area looked like it had gone through a nuclear winter.

Not only were the fumes harmful to vegetation, they could affect animals, as well. A lawsuit brought by two Montana ranchers against a copper mining company in 1905 had alleged that smoke from smelters in Butte was killing livestock and causing the value of their land to plummet. The pair claimed to have suffered combined damages of more than $367,000.

Similar complaints weren't long in coming to Kennett. In 1907, a board of arbitration awarded an orchard owner $200 for damage done to his trees by the Mammoth Copper Company smelter. Other farmers soon began to protest, as well, and the company began to recognize that unless it did something, its entire operation would be in peril. So in 1909, it announced plans to reduce pollution by way of a concrete filtering device called a baghouse to be installed at a cost of $200,000.

The farmers, however, were not so easily placated. Contending that the copper processors hadn't gone far

The old Pit River Bridge, seen here, was replaced by a higher span when the waters rose with the construction of Shasta Dam. The new steel-truss bridge is a double-deck design, and Interstate 5 ran over the top deck and a rail line on the lower deck. The original concrete bridge in this photograph was replaced in 1942. The signs at lower left read "Texaco Gasoline Motor Oil" and "Buffalo Lager Beer." *Meriam Library, CSU Chico.*

enough to reduce pollution, they refused an offer from the Balakala mining company to set up a $250,000 indemnity fund against damage to their crops and instead took the Mammoth company to court. They were rebuffed, however, when a judge conducted a personal inspection of the region and endorsed Mammoth's baghouse system.

The smelter continued to operate. At least for the time being.

What ultimately doomed Kennett's economy wasn't a lawsuit but a labor dispute. The plant's machinists, railroad workers, and boilermakers went out on strike after Mammoth Copper refused their demands for a 50-cent wage increase and a half-day off on Saturdays. The walkout was intended to put pressure on the company, but it had the opposite effect: Instead of capitulating, Mammoth pulled the plug. The general manager, citing a reduction in demand for copper brought about in part by the end of World War I, shut down the plant and said he had no intention of starting up again until it saw a decided improvement in the market. He forecast an extended period of inactivity, and about 600 men were suddenly thrown out of a job.

As the smelter went, so went the town.

Less than a month after the smelter shut down in the spring of 1919, Kennett was well on its way to becoming a ghost town. In that short period of time, every seat on the school board became vacant as all the members moved away. The weekly *Kennett Outlook* newspaper, which hadn't missed an issue in almost 14 years, announced it was ceasing publication until the smelter could be restarted. All but three of the streetlights were turned off to save money, and of the town's 12 remaining saloons, the vast majority said they planned to be out of business within the month.

Mammoth did fire up the smelter again in 1923, bringing a flurry of new activity to the area, but the town's revival was short-lived, as the company called it quits for good at the site within a couple of years.

By 1930, Kennett was on its last legs, and the few residents left there seemed to recognize it. The city hadn't collected any taxes in two years, and its treasury contained a paltry $150. Only 36 registered voters remained within the city limits, and 27 of the 35 who went to the polls in April of that year voted to disincorporate.

As a municipality, Kennett ceased to exist.

The following year, junk dealers bought up the parts to the Mammoth Copper mining and smelter works—which had been built for $2 million—at the bargain basement price of $97,000. Meanwhile, plans for what was then to be called the Kennett Dam, already on the drawing board for many years, remained there as the Depression took hold and dragged on. Work on the project (renamed Shasta Dam in a final indignity against the once-proud town) began at last in the late summer of 1937, and the waters of the newly forming Shasta Lake began to consume the town in 1944.

A section of highway overpass lies fallen, blocking the lanes of the freeway below it in February of 1971 following the San Fernando (Saugus) earthquake. The scene here is at the interchange of Interstate 5 and State Route 14.
U.S. Geological Survey/public domain.

If you're looking for Kennett today, you won't find it. In drought years, the lake's water level drops significantly, exposing some segments of the old highway, and a stretch of U.S. 99 is still above water at the north end of the lake, where it's called Lakeshore Drive. One such segment, the Pollock Bridge, has been used as an extended boat ramp and is visible rising from the waters near the old settlement of Pollock. Also visible nearby when the waters get low is the top of an old railroad trestle, an abandoned train tunnel, and fragments of old highway infrastructure. Pollock, a small community with a post office and a Shell gas station, was founded in 1918 along the highway at the eastern end of the bridge but was, like the bridge, submerged when the dam was built.

Also submerged was much of the land scarred by the toxic fumes of the smelters. Much of what one newspaper report described as "the greatest man-made scar there is in the state" was replaced by the blue waters of the newborn lake.

It's unlikely the waters will ever recede far enough for anyone to get a look at the remains of Kennett, which are 400 feet underwater at the deepest part of the lake, less than a mile north of the dam. Many of the town's buildings were dismantled and carted away before the lake filled up, but many others were left there, including the school and the Diamond Saloon.

One of the last references in print to Kennett as a contemporary town appeared in January of 1943 at the end of a story in *The Bakersfield Californian*. It proved a sad but somehow appropriate epitaph for the soon-to-be-submerged town: "Snow collapsed a bridge at Kennett, north of Redding, marooning the five known residents of the little town, which will be submerged with the completion of Shasta dam."

Before long, the bridge itself would be underwater, along with the town and an extended segment of Old 99.

SHAKEN

It's the stuff of nightmares. You're driving along on an empty highway in the cool, quiet hours before sunrise. The midwinter air carries the crisp bite familiar to those who drive the mountain passes, and the streetlights cast their dull glow on the asphalt. Up ahead stands a gently sloping bridge; a familiar sight, you've crossed it a hundred times. You drive onward and then, all of a sudden, you realize the bridge isn't there anymore. It's just gone. Before you know it, you're tumbling through empty space, abandoned by fate to the forces of gravity, falling into some nameless abyss.

Death reaches out for you.

You wake up in a cold sweat. It was just a dream.

But for a motorcycle cop with the Los Angeles Police Department, it constituted the last few seconds of his 46 years on planet Earth. A violent tremor had jolted

Damage to a steel-reinforced concrete support at the Interstate 5–State Route 14 interchange is seen in February of 1971, following the San Fernando earthquake. *U.S. Geological Survey/public domain.*

This photo shows damage to Lower Van Norman Dam caused by the '71 quake. The dam is named for Harvey Van Norman, assistant chief engineer on the St. Francis Dam, which failed catastrophically nearly a half-century earlier, leaving hundreds dead in the resulting flood.
U.S. Geological Survey/public domain.

Clarence Wayne Dean awake in his Lancaster home on the morning of January 17, 1994, and he knew something was wrong. An earthquake—a strong one—had hit Southern California, so he got on his motorcycle and headed southwest toward the city, taking the Antelope Valley Freeway toward his station, in Van Nuys. Time was of the essence, so he activated his flashing blue light and sped onward to the bridge that spanned Interstate 5.

Then, he saw it. The earthquake he'd felt earlier had not only damaged the bridge, it had brought a huge section of it crashing down, leaving a gap between where Dean was riding and where he was going . . . or would have gone. Dean tried to stop, but it was too late. He and his bike went flying 75 feet through the air before landing on the ground 30 or 40 feet below.

Clarence Dean did not survive the fall.

"He was not your typical hero, dying in a blazing shootout," his best friend and fellow officer Bill Harkness said at his memorial. "But he died a hero just the same. He was on his way to help people. He gave his life for others."

Dean was not the only victim of the Northridge quake, a 6.7-magnitude shaker that rose up from 11 miles underneath the town of Reseda to leave a trail of destruction across the San Fernando Valley and beyond. Palm trees caught fire, burning across the suburban skyline like grotesque, oversize tiki torches. Apartment buildings buckled in pancake fashion. A 64-car train derailed, windows shattered, and more than 9,000 people were injured. Fifty-seven of them died.

Peter Criss, former drummer of the rock band KISS, wrote in his autobiography that he was so shaken he put a gun in his mouth and seriously considered pulling the trigger. He didn't, but his feeling of desperation and hopelessness wasn't unique. It permeated a region where 90,000 homes were damaged or destroyed and more than 100,000 people were put out on the streets, at least temporarily.

Other bridges failed, too—200 of them in all sustained at least some damage from the quake, which held the sad distinction of remaining the most expensive natural disaster in U.S. history for more than a decade, before it was eclipsed by Hurricane Katrina.

Perhaps even more tragic for Clarence Wayne Dean is the fact that the bridge he was crossing that morning should have been safe. It had been laid low once before, in an earthquake nearly a quarter of a century earlier, only to be rebuilt, reinforced, and reopened to the public. The state had even launched a retrofitting program to guard against damage from future earthquakes, with the goal of making the new overpass and others like it capable of surviving another quake of similar magnitude.

Tragically, it failed to meet that goal.

I remember riding in the back of my parents' car to Southern California when my father took a job there in 1972. Driving down Interstate 5—which most people from the San Joaquin Valley still knew as the 99 at that point—my father took us through the Sylmar area where the Antelope Valley Freeway bridge crossed the north–

Massive damage is evident in this photo (taken February 10, 1971) of a collapsed overpass connecting Foothill Boulevard and the Golden State Freeway after the San Fernando quake. *R.E. Wallace, U.S. Geological Survey/public domain.*

A freeway overpass collapsed in the 1994 Northridge earthquake, stirring memories of the San Fernando earthquake less than a quarter-century earlier. *U.S. Geological Survey/public domain.*

south highway . . . or partially crossed it. It hadn't even opened to traffic when the Sylmar–San Fernando quake of 1971 hit, bringing the entire structure crashing down on the freeway below. A year later, as we passed beneath this half-wrecked bridge to nowhere, I remember asking my parents what had happened. It looked like something out of a postapocalyptic novel: soaring overpasses ending in midair and columns sticking up toward the sky, supporting absolutely nothing.

My parents told me that there had been an earthquake and that this desolate scene was the result. The highway builders were working to rebuild it, but it would take awhile, they said. They didn't tell me that more than 64 people had died in the disaster, including 47 at a veterans hospital and two men in a pickup who were crushed beneath a fallen overpass—just one of a dozen that came crashing down onto freeways below.

It could have been a whole lot worse.

The St. Francis Dam disaster of 1928 very nearly repeated itself just a few miles away with the near failure of the Lower Van Norman Dam. The dam dated to 1918, six years before work began on the St. Francis, and used a different technique called hydraulic fill, in which earthen materials are washed into place.

Had the reservoir behind the dam been full, it would have almost certainly meant a catastrophe far worse than the St. Francis disaster. In the roughly four decades since the St. Francis had failed, Los Angeles had grown from a city of 1.2 million people to a megalopolis of 2.8 million, with large numbers of residents fleeing north to the burgeoning suburbs of the San Fernando Valley. Many of those suburbs were now directly in the path of a potential tsunami that would be unleashed if the Lower Van Norman Dam were to fail.

The St. Francis disaster had left as many as 600 people dead. Had the Van Norman failed, experts later estimated, the resulting torrent could have killed as many as 123,000 people.

It came perilously close to doing just that.

Earthen dams are particularly vulnerable to seismic activity, and the Van Norman was no exception. In absorbing the tremors that jolted the area that morning, it underwent a process known as liquefaction, losing cohesion and becoming malleable, like quicksand.

The crest of the dam sagged as the quake jarred a huge section of the embankment loose; it tumbled to the floor of the reservoir, taking the concrete lining with it and raising the level of the water precariously close to overflowing. Two cracks formed in the dam, measuring 20 feet long and a foot and a half wide. The entire dam actually moved six feet. A year earlier, when the reservoir had held 6.5 billion gallons of water, the dam would have certainly collapsed altogether. But on the morning the temblor hit, the structure was holding back "only" 3.6 billion gallons—half the reservoir's capacity.

On the morning of February 9, the water was a healthy 36 feet below the top of the dam. It should have been plenty of room to spare, but it turned out to be just enough. The top 31 feet seemed to melt away, leaving just six feet between the dam's summit and the waters, roiled into spasms by the still-moving ground. With every aftershock (and there were many), a little more of the earth crumbled away. No one knew when the shaking would resume or how bad it would be; over the course of the day, a dozen aftershocks of magnitude 4.5 or higher shook the site, including two of 5.8 within just two minutes of the initial jolt.

Fearing the worst, officials evacuated 80,000 people from a 20-square-mile area in the bedroom communities of Granada Hills, Northridge, Mission Hills, Reseda, and Van Nuys, just east of Interstate 5. Meanwhile, workers scrambled to lower the reservoir's water level by boring a 24-inch hole in a pipe and creating a second hole in the face of the dam. The water level fell by about three feet the first day and three more feet the second. It wasn't until three days after the quake that the evacuees were allowed back home.

The temblor had been the first strong quake in the San Fernando Valley since a 5.7-magnitude jolt had hit Newhall in 1893. A slightly stronger quake (6.4) in Huntington Beach to the south had left 120 people dead in 1933, but since that time the fault lines south of the Tehachapis had been relatively stable and the region had been lulled into a false sense of security. When the region's tectonic plates rumbled to life again in the Sylmar quake, it awakened a curiosity among southlanders as to what the heck was going on.

Dr. William Kaufmann, director of the Griffith Park Observatory, concluded that a total eclipse of the moon was "more than coincidental" and "quite probably triggered" the quake. Kaufmann theorized that the alignment of the earth between the sun and the moon had caused the disaster, with the gravitational pull of the two heavenly bodies tugging the earth simultaneously in two different directions.

Some scientists were clearly still fumbling about in the dark to some extent when it came to explaining the movement of the earth.

Whatever the cause, however, the most pressing need was picking up the pieces and putting them back together. Buildings and freeway overpasses would have to be rebuilt, but they would also need to be capable of withstanding another quake the size of the one that had laid them low. The state created a retrofit program, and engineers set about resurrecting the fallen overpasses. It took two and a half years before the Foothill Freeway interchange with Interstate 5 was ready to reopen, and longer still before the Antelope Valley Freeway overpass was restored.

But as time passed and the Sylmar quake faded from the headlines, the commitment to upgrade the new bridges seemed to fade away, as well. With the earth seemingly quiet once again, the sense of urgency that had existed in the aftermath of the quake soon disappeared. Instead of undertaking a complete retrofit, workers simply used cables to tie the overpasses more firmly to their supporting pillars. One official lamented that "it was just a stopgap measure, but even that ran into money problems."

Money was, in fact, a major issue. Instead of $30 million a year, the seismic retrofit program was receiving as little as $2 million and, as of 1988, the state was spending three times more money on highway landscaping than it was on reinforcing bridges. The first phase of an expansive three-phase retrofit project took 15 years to complete, the work receiving only "intermittent attention as time permitted," a state report acknowledged. The second phase wasn't scheduled for completion until 2000.

When a double-decker bridge in Oakland collapsed in pancake fashion during the 1989 Loma Prieta earthquake, it should have been a wake-up call for the state

to accelerate work on reinforcing the bridges rebuilt after the Sylmar quake. Sadly, however, California was in the midst of a budget crisis, and precious time was lost deciding which of the 12,000 highway overpasses would receive priority.

Lightning, as the saying goes, seldom strikes twice in the same place. In contrast, however, the earth tends to move along the same fault lines. When the Northridge quake shook Southern California in 1994, it struck just eight miles from the epicenter of the Sylmar quake. And the Antelope Valley Freeway overpass across Interstate 5 that had fallen in 1971 crumpled and crumbled once again.

Clarence Wayne Dean died as a result.

Five other bridges failed, as well, and four others were severely damaged. The irony: At the time the earthquake hit, two of those bridges were scheduled to be strengthened as part of the state's retrofitting program.

Work was set to begin on one of those projects the following month.

In a Fog

"Slow down, you move too fast."

The Simon & Garfunkel tune "Feelin' Groovy" might be a good selection for drivers barreling down the midsection of Highway 99 late at night or early in the morning during late fall and early winter. That's when the San Joaquin Valley's infamous Tule fog arrives, cutting visibility to a few hundred feet—or less. Drivers will try to stay close enough to see the taillights ahead of them to provide some sense of depth perception, without getting so close they risk a rear-end collision if those taillights turn into brake lights.

The fog can creep in and hover over the roadway all along the San Joaquin–Sacramento Valley corridor, anywhere from south of Bakersfield all the way north to Red Bluff. The Fresno area sits at the epicenter of fog country, with the lowest-lying farmland between Delano and Merced particularly vulnerable. The Kings River area about 20 miles to the south can be particularly troublesome, as the river water itself fuels the mists that roll low across its surface where it runs beneath the highway. You won't see it above the low foothills of the mountain ranges that ring the valley, forming a bowl to contain what's often referred to as "pea soup."

Tule fog tends to form in the wake of rainstorms that pass over the region, soaking the ground and forming a low-hanging canopy when the mercury dips to meet the dew point. In the still air of the nights following a storm, it hovers like the white-shrouded ghost of the rain that left it behind. If you're driving through a particularly nasty patch, you're likely to see a Highway Patrol pace car moving just a little faster than a snail's pace, making sure everyone else on the road stays off the accelerator. The state also set up cameras, microwave sensors, and nearly 40 electronic messaging signs that can be used to warn drivers of looming fog, accidents, detours, and other road conditions.

Such precautions are anything but overkill, considering the treacherous history of the highway when and where it meets the fog. The area just south of Fresno has seen more than its share of accidents. In February of 1991, three people were killed in three separate crashes involving more than 100 vehicles over a span of just 15 miles between Fresno and Fowler. Another chain-reaction crash in 2002 involved 81 cars and six tractor-trailers in the space of less than two minutes. Amazingly, only two people were killed. And perhaps even more amazingly, it wasn't the worst fog-related crash to occur on that particular stretch of road.

Five years later, on a morning in early November, conditions were ripe for another massive pileup. The fog that day was patchy, covering just 10 percent of the valley floor, but it was in the wrong place at the wrong time: along the 99 corridor a few miles south of Fresno. Within the space of a few short minutes, 108 vehicles—including 18 big rigs—became tangled up in a chain reaction between Fresno and Fowler. Two vehicles caught fire, and by the time it was over, northbound 99 looked more like an auto parts graveyard than a highway, as cars and trucks were strewn across all three lanes, their frames marred in varying degrees by twisted metal and broken glass. Spilled cargo lay on the highway, as well. Ambulances and fire engines rushed to the scene.

They were too late to save two victims: A young boy and a 26-year-old man lost their lives, while three dozen others went to the hospital.

The good news for drivers is that the heavy fog has become less common over the past three decades. As of 1980, the Fresno area suffered through an average of 37 foggy days annually, and during one stretch in 1985, Tule fog settled over the ground for more than two weeks without a break. By 2014, however, the average had dipped to 22 days a year, and just two foggy days were reported that year. Warmer winters, periods of drought, and a reduction in agricultural burning are possible causes (fog forms by clinging to microscopic particles in the air—just like the kind formed by burning).

7

FULL SERVICE

Dorothea Lange captured this image of a Texaco station (with gas selling for 13.9 cents a gallon) in May of 1939, noting that "small independent gas stations litter the highway." *Dorothea Lange, Library of Congress.*

Once you start traveling beyond your own city limits, you need a way to know where you are. Maps can be helpful, and in the first part of the 20th century, filling stations (as they were called back then) started producing those old-fashioned foldout paper maps and guidebooks that were so popular before GPS came along.

Not only did these maps help drivers get their bearings, they also helped direct customers to the next of the many Standard or Richfield or Hancock gas stops, all of which were prominently displayed on the Standard or Richfield or Hancock map.

Gas stations were an integral part of any traveler's trip up or down Old 99, and before major consolidations started in the 1960s, you had plenty of choices. The first half of the 20th century was a boom era for oil companies, as big oil derricks churned up gushers in places like Bakersfield, Coalinga, Signal Hill, and Summerland. It's hard to imagine now, but those derricks rose above the landscape in the heart of many Central and Southern California cities.

Soon after oil was found at Signal Hill near Long Beach, oil companies build 100 derricks there. It became known as "Porcupine Hill." Derricks lined the seaside at Huntington Beach and in Santa Barbara County. You could see them along 99, as well, across a swath of land stretching down from the Kern River Oil Field northeast of Bakersfield into the Fruitvale Oil Field that falls partly within the city limits. The area was so closely associated with oil production that an area just north of town became known as Oildale and Bakersfield High School adopted the nickname "Drillers." An ad in the school's 1960 yearbook even shows students relaxing in a public pool just off the Old 99 (Union Avenue) and a line of oil towers stretching skyward in the background.

It might seem hard to fathom in an era of environmental consciousness, but one oil company even used the derricks as a model to increase its visibility—substantially—along U.S. 99 and elsewhere in California, Oregon, and Washington.

Richfield Oil opened its first service station in 1905 in Los Angeles and grew quickly from there. Before long, it had stations up and down Highway 99 and elsewhere across the western states. Flush with success in the midst of the "Roaring Twenties," the company hit on an idea: What if it could create an icon that linked it to both the burgeoning automotive travel industry and the nascent aviation industry?

That's what the company set out to develop with its Richfield Beacons, towers shaped like slimmed-down

Traffic passes a Richfield Beacon station between the Yolo Causeway and Vallejo—probably in Vacaville—on Nov. 20, 1953. The portion of that highway (now Interstate 80) between Sacramento and Davis was signed then as U.S. 99W. © *California Department of Transportation.*

oil derricks that rose 125 feet above the earth. Richfield would place one of these towers alongside more than 30 new service stations up and down the West Coast. The Richfield company name would be spelled out in big, red neon letters vertically, descending from the top of each structure. At its apex would be a 24-inch directional beacon designed by the Sperry Gyroscope Company, emitting a beam of light measured at 8 million candlepower.

The towers would be placed near airports to guide aircraft traveling north and south along the coast. Richfield promoted the program in the 1928 issue of *Touring Topics* magazine, produced by the Automobile Club of Southern California, as an "effort to lessen the hazards of night flying as part of its general aviation program." Richfield announced that the towers would be placed at intervals of about 50 miles, "furnishing a brilliant guide light to help make night flying both safe and practical."

Night flights bearing airmail were becoming more common, and Richfield was eager to be seen as doing a public service.

The towers, however, were anything but selfless.

Two years before Beacon announced its project, in 1926, Standard Oil of California had erected two towers of its own. One was in Montebello, east of Los Angeles and just south of the newly minted U.S. 99, and the other rose atop Mount Diablo in the Bay Area. Standard was the No. 1 oil company in the state at the time, but Richfield was a fast-growing company intent on challenging the industry leader. What better way than by putting up towers of its own?

Richfield was uniquely positioned to do just that. Company President James Talbot also ran Western Air Express, the forerunner of Western Airlines. WAE started out transporting airmail between Los Angeles and Salt Lake City after Congress opened the skies to private delivery contractors in 1925. A year later, it was carrying passengers, too, becoming the first airline to do so.

These planes were, naturally, powered by Richfield gasoline, giving the product a level of visibility that made other players in the nascent air industry sit up and take notice. Soon, others were flying on Richfield, as well. In fact, its popularity was such that, at one point, the company provided fuel for 4 out of every 10 airline miles

This adobe structure in Willows is one of the few Richfield Beacon stations still standing, though it no longer dispenses gasoline. As of 2014, it was being used as an office for a storage yard. It was among the northernmost of the Spanish mission-style stations.

flown in the United States. In short order, Talbot became a very wealthy man, worth an estimated $20 million (nearly half a billion in 2015 dollars).

In this booming climate, the Beacon towers were a natural next step in tying together the company's two main moneymakers: air travel and motor fuel.

The towers weren't just aimed at fliers. Motorists couldn't miss them. If you knew another station was coming up in less than 50 miles, you could plan ahead and figure out when it would be time to fill 'er up: "At the base of each tower will be an artistically designed Richfield service station for the comfort and convenience of our motorists."

The resulting network of service stations was built in the late 1920s at a cost of $10 million, creating what was called the "Great White Way." When the company moved into its new Los Angeles headquarters in 1928, it placed one of the towers at its zenith. In Merced, the company actually bought the entire airport—the first investment of its kind by an oil company—where it planned to invest $100,000 in improvements that included a new hangar and roadside cabins for auto travelers.

The purchase pointed up the fact that Richfield's plan went far beyond gas stations. The company planned to establish a series of mini-villages that foreshadowed the later "travel centers."

In addition to a full-service gas station, each site would eventually include a Beacon Café and a Beacon Tavern—the company's name for its motor inns. (An

actual tavern was out of the question, since Prohibition was still in effect.) The architecture was to be Spanish mission-style for the southern beacons, whereas beacons in Mount Shasta City and points north were to be built in English-Norman style. The latter looked something like Swiss chalets.

The company went all out in building the stations, each of which featured two gas pumps—one for "regular" and the other for "ethyl" gas—enclosed in thick concrete or

The chalet-type design was used in the Pacific Northwest, including this station in Mount Shasta City.

adobe-style casings; the former was surmounted by a sculpted miniature race car, and the latter topped by a similar model of an airplane. Another plane, this one in the form of a weathervane, rose from the roof of the station itself.

All of beacons in the Pacific Northwest were installed along U.S. 99, as were the majority in California, turning the highway into a "Lane of Lights."

In California, two roughly parallel lines of beacons were installed, branching off at Los Angeles and running north along U.S. highways 99 and 101, while individual stations were built along Route 66 in Barstow, U.S. 40 in Vacaville, and U.S. 48 in Livermore. Most of the Beacon towers followed a familiar pattern: 125 feet tall, they measured 6 feet across at their apex and three times that width at their base. Each was three-sided, like an Egyptian pyramid, and the company name rose vertically on at least two and sometimes all three sides. In the early years, those letters were illuminated in red neon; later, they glowed bright blue.

Amid the uniformity, there were a few variations. Two large, distinct letters were placed near the top of each tower, in each case identifying the beacon with a specific location—PR for Paso Robles, BF for Bakersfield, etc.—so aviators could tell from a distance precisely where they were. (The MS atop one of the two remaining beacons, in Mount Shasta City, could still be seen as of this writing in 2015.)

The beacon atop the company's Los Angeles headquarters was four-sided instead of three and had no affiliated service station. Instead of a beacon, the toll gate to the San Francisco Bay Bridge featured two 135-foot towers bearing Richfield signs. And Portland had the distinction of getting what was billed as the largest electric sign in the world: a series of 60-foot-tall neon letters spelling out the company name on the crest of a hill in Healy Heights. It was like the Hollywood sign in Southern California, only brighter—a lot brighter—and was reportedly visible at a distance of 100 miles.

Mayor George Luis Baker threw the switch lighting up the great sign for the first time on September 30, 1928, declaring, "Hereafter, when you see this great sign's lights nightly, remember that it is building the destinies of the government's great air mail service and our ever-increasing travel by night."

It was a grand beginning.

The first six actual beacons lit up on December 17, 1928, the 25th anniversary of the Wright brothers' first flight, and a Navy admiral in the San Diego suburb of Palm City did the honors. When he hit the switch, the lights went on in Palm City, Beaumont, Capistrano, Livermore, Merced, and Santa Rosa. Then, a couple of months later, three more came online at Castaic, El Centro, and Visalia.

An ad by Sperry Gyroscope touted the company's technology, which was used in Richfield Beacons up and down the West Coast. A map detailing station locations appears at the left of the ad.
Public domain.

Richfield Beacons in California

U.S. 99 (SOUTH TO NORTH)

Imperial Valley (IV)—At airport in El Centro; southwest corner of Imperial Avenue (U.S. 99) and Airport Road

Beaumont (BM)—2.5 miles east of town; north side of Ramsey Boulevard (U.S. 99)

Alhambra (AR)—At airport 1.25 miles south of town; just south of Valley Boulevard (U.S. 99) between Garfield and New avenues

Castaic (CT)—4 miles south of town; Castaic junction by the Santa Clara River, just northwest of Magic Mountain

Bakersfield (BF)—At airport 3 miles northwest of town; may have been located at the north end of State Road, from Olive Drive exit; apparently moved in 1934 to a location near the south end of State Road

Visalia (VS)—At airport; east of 99 and just south of SR 198

Fresno (FO)—At airport 8 miles north of town*; on the west side of Golden State Boulevard (U.S. 99) at Barstow Avenue

Merced (MD)—At airport; northeast of 16th Street (U.S. 99) and west of Snelling Highway, north of Bear Creek

Willows (WL)—North end of town on 99W, also known as Tehama Street**

Redding (RD)—6.5 miles south of town*; at curve of Market Street (U.S. 99), halfway between Anderson and Redding

Mount Shasta City (MS)—1.75 miles south of town**; on east side of Mount Shasta Boulevard (U.S. 99)

U.S. 101 (SOUTH TO NORTH)

Palm City (PC)—5 miles north of Mexican border; near Coronado Avenue exit in the San Diego metropolitan area

Capistrano Beach (CB)—In Dana Point on SR 1; an ARCO station still operates at the site of this beacon, on the Pacific Coast Highway west of I-5, on the north side of the road just before Del Obispo Street; the beacon light is preserved at the Dana Point Heritage Museum

Santa Barbara (SB)—10 miles south of town*; actually closer to Carpinteria; apparently at south end of Santa Claus Lane

Santa Maria (SM)—2 miles south of Hancock Field; southeast corner of Betteravia and Broadway (U.S. 101)

Paso Robles (PR)—1.5 miles south of town***; west of highway just south of SR 46 on Theatre Drive, used as bus stop

Chualar (CL)—12 miles south of Salinas; east side of freeway at south end of small community along Grant Street (U.S. 101)

San Francisco (SF)—Center of town; Van Ness Avenue (U.S. 101) at Market Street, east side of intersection

Santa Rosa (SR)—2 miles northwest of town at municipal airport; dedicated in May of 1929 and closed by the end of WWII, the airport was under lease to Richfield Oil; on west side of highway, just north of Mendocino overcrossing

OTHER LOCATIONS

Barstow (BS)—North side of town along Route 66****; on the southeast corner of Main Street (U.S. 66) and 7th Avenue

Los Angeles—Atop Richfield Building*; Flower Street at 5th Avenue

Livermore (LM)—U.S. 50, 1 mile west of town; site of old Livermore Intermediate Field, about a mile east of the current airport, on the south side of Portola Avenue, west of Rincon Avenue

Vacaville (VV)—U.S. 40; northeast of town; possibly north of the highway at Quinn and Leisure Town roads, or farther northeast on the south side near Vacavalley Raceway

* Beacon only; no service station
** Tower and building still stand
*** Building still stands
**** Site of Beacon tavern

The massive project generated plenty of excitement. *The Bakersfield Californian* crowed: "Bakersfield's place on the map is assured. That is the airway map through the western United States from the Canadian to the Mexican borders, and on which Bakersfield is marked by a great 8,000,000 candlepower beacon—one of 32 established by the Richfield Oil Company on its 'great white way,' as the coastal airway has been named."

The project was to be built in stages, the towers and the service stations going in first, followed by the cafés and then the "taverns." Grocers and snack shops were also envisioned, and the towers were built a few miles outside established cities so communities of their own could grow up around them. The company built the first Beacon Café and Tavern along Route 66 in Barstow, near the airport and the junction with highways 91 and 466. The $180,000 inn featured tile roofs, adobe-style archways, colorful floor tiles, and Spanish-themed furniture in each of its 50 rooms.

You could rent one for $3 to $6 a night, and many people did, including celebrities such as Clark Gable, Mickey Rooney, and F. Scott Fitzgerald. The Tavern opened to the public on June 27, 1930, with a Mexican-themed celebration that heralded big things to come for the nascent avenue of lights. A couple of months later, plans were announced for Taverns to be built in San Juan Capistrano, Santa Maria, and Visalia.

Meanwhile, Richfield went about publicizing its great venture with press releases and publicity stunts that promoted not only the beacons but also the company's core products: gasoline and oil. Above all else, the firm touted its success in air races and record-breaking stunts. It took out a newspaper ad in September of 1930 that bragged of Richfield's success in the 1930 National Air Races:

> "The world's greatest air meet! And Richfield wins the lion's share of the awards ... 42 victories out of 67 events! *More than all other gasolines combined*!!

QUEEN OF THE AIR

One of the faces of Richfield during the summer of 1930 was a 25-year-old aviator named Ruth Alexander.

A Kansas native like her contemporary, Amelia Earhart, Alexander had always wanted to fly. She had grown up around her father's machine shop, and at the age of 7 she had experimented with the concept by jumping off the top of a barn while holding an umbrella. When a barnstorming pilot landed in a nearby field for a Fourth of July exhibition in 1925, she paid $5 for a flight in his plane and was hooked.

Alexander had been looking for direction in her life for a few years. After graduating from high school in the spring of 1923, she had enrolled in college but hadn't stayed long. Instead, she had taken a job at a general store and within a year had earned enough money to buy a beauty parlor in Olathe, just outside Kansas City. In 1926, she married and settled down, but two years later she came down with a bad case of pneumonia and was diagnosed with tuberculosis. Her doctors said she wouldn't live, but she survived and decided it was time for a change.

Ruth Alexander poses for a photo atop her Barling NB-3 in San Diego, where she was a member of the Anne Lindbergh Flyers. The aviatrix set altitude records and survived a harrowing flight, reportedly with help from the Richfield Beacons. *San Diego Air and Space Museum/public domain.*

In need of a better climate to maintain her health, Alexander separated from her husband and hitched a ride to San Diego with a family member who needed a driver. Using money she had saved up from her beauty parlor, she paid for an apartment on Coronado Island and began working 16 hours a day at two jobs—at a soda fountain and a beauty shop—so she could earn enough money to pursue her pilot's license.

As luck would have it, a local newspaper was sponsoring a contest that offered flying lessons to the winner. "Queen of the Air" it was called. Alexander caught wind of it and entered, and though she placed second, she impressed Earl Prudden at the T.C. Ryan Flying School enough that he offered her a scholarship: She would receive 195 hours of navigation and meteorology, in addition to 22 hours of flight instruction.

More good fortune followed: A wealthy Coronado couple actually gave her a plane.

Alexander earned her wings in near-record time, soloing for the first time just six weeks after enrolling in flight school and obtaining her pilot's license shortly after that. Mission accomplished? Hardly. Alexander knew she was destined for greater heights, and she was determined to reach them.

On November 19, 1929, she took off in a 90-horsepower biplane and did just that, soaring 15,500 feet above San Diego and setting an altitude world record for women flying light planes. It could be argued that this was no great feat, considering she was one of just 65 women to have earned a pilot's license, but Alexander had bigger things planned. She earned a license to fly gliders and, later, became a glider instructor. She also joined the San Diego–based Anne Lindbergh Flyers, organized by the wife of famed aviator Charles Lindbergh.

Then, in July, she celebrated Independence Day (and a two-week-old marriage to her second husband, flying instructor Robert Elliott) by breaking her own altitude mark, piloting her monoplane to 20,000 feet—nearly four miles high.

And still, she wasn't done.

A week later, determined to go even higher, Alexander went up again, this time equipped with oxygen and a breathing tube. Flying in an open cockpit, she was dressed warmly, but the human body can only go so high without being affected. Peter Hackett, a physician specializing in high-altitude medicine, has noted that health will start to deteriorate above 17,000 and that anything above 26,000 is called the "Death Zone" because at that point it's simply impossible to adapt.

That's how high Alexander got.

Taking off from Lindbergh Field in San Diego, she kept track of her progress in a flight log. Twenty minutes into the flight, she hit 10,000 feet and reported she could see the bottom of the bay. Then, a half-hour in, she started to feel colder and put on her heavy gloves.

Subsequent entries documented her progress—and her physical deterioration:

14,000 feet—Altimeter doesn't seem right. Getting colder.

15,000 feet —Oxygen tank leaking.

17,000 feet—Feet cold.

18,000 feet—Sleepy. Better use oxygen.

19,000 feet—Cold. Ground hazy. Feel better with oxygen.

20,000 feet—Head aches.

Then she wrote in large, shaky letters across the face of the card, "Cold … sleepy."

The temperature had dropped to 20 below.

Alexander later recalled: "The engine had begun to labor. I tried to push the plane higher and did succeed for a while. Then it stalled and seemed to settle back after each climb. I didn't realize the oxygen was gone. Then, I fainted."

Alexander was apparently out cold for several minutes, during which time the plane started to descend:

The next thing I knew, I was 4,000 or 5,000 feet lower, fighting for air. I was gasping, my head felt groggy and my chest hurt. I felt terrible. . . . I put the plane into a steep dive and came down fast in a series of circles until I reached 7,000 feet. I was still gasping for breath and very tired. My arms, legs and my brain all functioned like they had dead weights on them. . . . I was still groggy when I hit the ground.

Groggy but alive. Not only had Alexander broken her own altitude record for a woman flying a light aircraft, she'd gone higher than anyone—man or woman—ever had in a small plane. She'd done the equivalent of climbing Mount Everest, something that wouldn't be accomplished for nearly a quarter of a century.

"Girl Faints In Setting New Altitude Record," the *Springfield Leader* of Missouri announced.

"Girl Flyer Loses Senses But Sets Altitude Record," the *Alton Evening Telegraph* told Illinois.

Perhaps at last satisfied she could go no higher, Alexander turned her attention to a different sort of aviation feat. Her accomplishments had brought her fame across the nation and had, by this time, attracted the attention of various sponsors. After her first altitude record, the Great Lakes Company of Cleveland, whose biplane she had flown in the attempt, had rewarded her with a surprise check for $100.

"I was all over the newspapers," Alexander would recall. "People looked at me like I was something in a zoo."

Before long, other sponsors started to approach her. Among them was the Richfield Oil Company, which was expanding its footprint in aviation—not just by buying the Merced airport, but also by purchasing a controlling interest in the Fokker Aircraft Corporation of America in 1928. Richfield helped promote Alexander's next attempt at making history: a nonstop flight along the Pacific coast from Vancouver, Canada, to Baja California. The endpoint of the journey was Agua Caliente, a hot new resort complex in Tijuana that featured a casino, a race-track, a hotel, and a golf course that would draw the likes of Charlie Chaplin and Rita Hayworth.

The resort had opened just two years earlier, and Alexander's flight was the perfect opportunity to publicize it; the resort, along with Richfield, signed on to sponsor her. A shield on the side of her plane touted Richlube Aviation Motor Oil, with the message "Agua Caliente. Canada to Mexico with Richfield" emblazoned on the aircraft.

Flying up and down the West Coast was the perfect opportunity to test out Richfield's new network of beacons, and Alexander got some practice in before her historic attempt. On a flight north in August, the beacon

The Willows Beacon may have been one Ruth Alexander used to guide her in her flight along the West Coast.

towers came in handy. As she approached Mount Shasta, flying at 9,000 feet "over the most rugged country you ever saw," Alexander found herself blinded by smoke from three wildfires. She descended, looking for a place to land, but got too low and almost crashed into the trees.

It was dusk, and the light was fading quickly from the sky. Alexander came upon a valley and caught sight of a rail line heading northeast. "I followed it, and after a while, I saw a Richfield air beacon, then another and another, and from then on the beacons just unfolded, one after the other," she recalled. "Within an hour, they led me to Portland. It's a mighty lucky thing for me."

From a map, it appears that Alexander saw the beacons that had been placed in Grant's Pass, Roseburg, Eugene, and Salem, Oregon, leading up to Portland. Alexander's trip back south, her so-called three-flag nonstop flight from British Columbia to Agua Caliente, was a great success. She averaged 91 miles per hour, using 117 gallons of fuel to complete the trip without a hitch in just under 16 hours. She left Vancouver at 3:25 a.m. and landed at the Agua Caliente airstrip at 7:15 p.m.

Flush with the feeling of accomplishment from her latest flight, Alexander laid plans for an even more ambitious journey: a cross-country flight from San Diego to Roosevelt Field on Long Island, where Charles Lindbergh had embarked on his historic transatlantic flight. It would take three days, with a single stop in Wichita, Kansas, for refueling, and she planned several overnight stops on the way home, including a visit to her hometown.

Alexander initially hoped to start her flight from Agua Caliente, but weather conditions there forced her to fly up the coast and begin the trip from her familiar home airstrip of Lindbergh Field in San Diego. There, too, she was met with inclement weather, a blanket of fog that limited visibility on the day of her scheduled flight. She believed she could navigate despite the fog and assured her friends that she wouldn't bank east until she had gained enough altitude. If the weather proved to be too great a challenge, she'd fly out over the ocean, dump her gasoline, and return to Lindbergh.

A friend of hers, airplane designer T. Claude Ryan, warned that she was carrying 650 pounds more than the plane was designed to carry.

"I'm not afraid of it," she told him. "That's exactly the load I carried from Vancouver."

The plane took off at 3:28 in the morning and disappeared into the mists. Ruth Alexander was never seen alive again. A few minutes after takeoff, her plane fell into a spin and crashed into a hillside at Point Loma,

Ruth Alexander in the cockpit. Alexander died in a crash shortly after taking off on a planned cross-country flight from Lindbergh Field in San Diego. *San Diego Air and Space Museum/public domain.*

only a few miles from her point of departure. Her heavy payload was ruled the cause of the crash. One final note of mystery surrounded her death: Before she departed, Alexander left her wedding ring behind in her hotel room, along with a note to her husband:

> To my husband, Bob:
>
> Life is strange, honey. If I have preceded you do not grieve for me, but be content. Finish your work down here and make me proud of you, as I ever will be by your side.
>
> And when you come I will welcome you. Always I will love and wait for you. And, sweetheart, keep my pretty wedding ring always with you. Ruth.

THE BEACONS' DEMISE

Not long after the 25-year-old aviator's life came to a tragic end, so did Richfield's plan for its "Great White Way." After the stock market crash of 1929, such extravagant projects simply weren't in the cards. It wasn't as though people didn't want Richfield's product. In fact, the company's advertising campaigns were such a success that more drivers than ever were pulling into Richfield stations, even amid the economic downturn.

The company had built its reputation on powerful, antiknock fuel, having attained a then-lofty octane rating of 75 that powered the majority of top Indy 500 finishers during the "Roaring Twenties." Now, however, that reputation began to crumble. Unable to produce enough gasoline to meet the demand, the company began making purchases from lesser-quality producers, which alienated some motorists. Meanwhile, the high cost of lighting and maintaining the beacon towers drained Richfield's accounts further.

In 1931, the company was forced to file for bankruptcy and Richfield was placed in receivership.

James Talbot, the high-flying multimillionaire company president, resigned and in 1932 was convicted of fraud and misappropriating company funds. Sentenced to San Quentin State Prison, he was released three years later, only to die scarcely 12 months later of heart failure at age 56.

The beacon project, which had lasted only a couple of years, ground to a halt.

Four plots of land designated for Richfield beacon stations never were developed. At seven other sites, the towers stood as lonely sentinels over vacant lots after the company ran out of money to build stations alongside them. As for the more expansive developments Richfield had envisioned around each of the beacons, these remained almost entirely a pipe dream. The Barstow Tavern was the only one ever built, while plans announced for San Juan Capistrano, Santa Maria, and Visalia never came to fruition.

By the time Richfield exited bankruptcy, the towers and the stations themselves were starting to become obsolete. Because traffic was on the rise, two gas pumps were no longer enough to meet the demand of drivers in a hurry to fill their tanks, and the stations' design made it difficult or impossible to add any more. As for the towers, radio communications rendered the visual aids they provided unnecessary.

All but a handful of the beacons atop California's impressive towers had ceased to operate a mere two years after the system's inauguration. The San Francisco beacon operated for only a few months before going dark with the new year in 1930. In April 1931, the *Air Commerce Bulletin* listed only Beaumont, Capistrano, and El Centro as "recertified," while the rest had been "discontinued."

Within a few years, many of the towers themselves started to come down:

It took some detective work and hunting to find these three concrete bases, which once anchored a Richfield Beacon tower off Golden State Boulevard (old Highway 99) in northwest Fresno near Barstow Avenue.

- In 1931, the tower in Salem, Oregon, came crashing down, severing 55 telephone wires. Only a light breeze was blowing at the time, according to the *Oregon Statesman*, which blamed the collapse on the "removal six weeks ago of a nut from one of the three foundation bolts." Traffic on U.S. 99 was delayed for more than two hours.

- The tower at Siskiyou Summit, just north of the California state line in Oregon, gave up the ghost in 1939 when the road was widened.

- The Roseburg, Oregon, tower was removed in 1942.

- At Castaic Junction, the tower was purchased and moved to a new site, where an antenna was affixed to it for use as a broadcasting station.

- The Livermore tower was torn down in 1943 amid concerns that it posed a hazard for student fliers.

- The tower atop the Richfield building in Los Angeles got a facelift in 1955 before the entire structure was demolished in 1969 to make way for a more modern building.

- Barstow's Beacon Tavern remained popular as a way station between Los Angeles and Las Vegas until it was bypassed by Interstate 15 in 1957;

the tower served as a sign for a bowling alley for several years before it was finally scrapped in 1970.

- The Capistrano tower was removed in 1971 when the state of California widened the Pacific Coast Highway.
- The Santa Maria tower came down on March 2 of that same year.
- The tower in Roseburg, Oregon, was purchased in 1942, dismantled, and moved to a mountain near Elkton, Oregon, where it was reassembled to serve as a fire lookout. The tower was damaged in a storm in 1962 and sold for scrap in 1978.
- The Richfield Beacon station three miles south of Paso Robles on Highway 101 was advertised for lease in 1953, but the beacon remained in place for four more decades. It was used to advertise a swap meet before it was finally removed in 1995, but the station itself remained as of 2015, when the closed building was being used as a bus stop.
- Only two of the original beacon towers remained standing into the new millennium, both along Old 99: in Willows and at Mount Shasta.

Roar with Gilmore

Richfield wasn't the only oil company seeking to ride the coattails—or contrails—of the aviation revolution into an era of increased sales and profits. Add the Gilmore Oil Company to that list.

Gilmore was one of the largest California-based independent oil companies during the first half of the 20th century, and it was also one of the most flamboyant. Company founder Arthur Gilmore started out as a dairy owner. He bought a small piece of land from the Hancock family (more on them later) west of downtown Los Angeles before the turn of the century. He turned out to be sitting smack-dab on top of an oil field. One day, when he was digging for water for his dairy herd, he struck oil instead.

Recognizing a good opportunity when he saw it, Gilmore began building derricks on the property and transformed his dairy farm into an oil company. "Someday you will own a horseless carriage. Our gasoline will run it," the company declared brashly in 1913, and for many California motorists it turned out to be right.

Gilmore's son, E.B. Gilmore, took over the company five years later and proceeded to make it a household name through his use of innovative promotions. The company served up "Blu-Green" gasoline, and it put transparent glass globes on the top of its pumps so customers could see the colorful concoction. It built up a network of 3,500 independent service stations, all of which proudly displayed the Gilmore red lion logo. Customers were invited to "roar with Gilmore," and the fierce-looking lion may have inspired Louis B. Mayer to adopt the iconic roaring lion as the symbol of MGM. (A side view of the lion looks very similar to the logo adopted by the Detroit Lions of the NFL.)

Just as Richfield enlisted the services of Ruth Alexander to promote its product, Gilmore sought out famed barnstorming aviator Roscoe Turner to lend a hand with publicity. Turner, who sported a stylish waxed moustache and had dabbled in acting, set a speed record between Los Angeles and New York in 1929. He also won a series of air races, and his colorful personality made him the perfect pitchman for Gilmore.

An old Gilmore station on the southwest corner of Highland and Willoughby avenues in Los Angeles was refurbished and reopened in 2015 as a Starbucks drive-through.

Roscoe Turner waves with Gilmore the Lion Cub from the cockpit in 1930. *Public domain.*

It was actually Turner's idea to have Gilmore buy a Lockheed Air Express, which he proceeded to fly all over the West Coast, and he didn't go alone. He bought a lion cub, dubbed it "Gilmore," and had it ride right up in the cockpit with him. When the SPCA protested, Turner outfitted the cub with a parachute and a leather flying cap.

Wherever Turner and his cub went, they would draw crowds of curious onlookers and generate a lion's share of publicity for Gilmore.

Other (caged) lions also made the rounds, stopping at various Gilmore stations, accompanied by circus clowns who would hand out candy and comic books to the children. And to reinforce this carnival atmosphere, Gilmore began airing a Friday evening radio show called the *Gilmore Circus Radio Program*. Listener participation was encouraged. One element of the show involved an invitation to call in and add goofy lyrics to jingles such as "That Funny Red Lion Song." Those whose lyrics were used on the air each week received a $5 coupon book, and a $100 prize was awarded each month. It was an ingenious strategy that kept listeners singing along to the company's tunes until those tunes got stuck in their heads . . . as they headed straight to the Gilmore gas pumps.

While Turner was setting speed records in the air, Gilmore-sponsored drivers were doing likewise on the ground. The company sponsored drivers at the Indy 500, including Kelly Petillo, who won in 1935 driving the Gilmore Speedway Special, and Wilbur Shaw, who took the checkered flag three times in four years, starting in 1937. He designed and built his Gilmore-sponsored car, christened the Shaw-Gilmore Special.

Then there was John Cobb of Great Britain, who piloted the Railton Red Lion to a land speed record of 369.74 miles per hour on Utah's Bonneville Salt Flats in 1939. The record, set in a vehicle that looked like a flying saucer on wheels, stood until Cobb broke it himself more than eight years later at the same location.

E.B. Gilmore was a pioneer in other areas, as well. In 1934, he built Gilmore Stadium, an 18,000-seat stadium that hosted auto racing, baseball, pro football, and other athletic pursuits. It was the home of the Los Angeles Bulldogs, the first major-league football team to play its games in the city and one of just four teams ever to go undefeated for an entire season. The team was awarded a "probationary franchise" in the NFL for the 1937 season, but it was revoked when the league's owners decided the travel costs of sending its teams to play on the West Coast were simply too great.

Instead, the Cleveland Rams of the upstart American Football League were awarded entry into the NFL, and in a dose of irony, the L.A. Bulldogs replaced them in the upstart league. The Bulldogs then proceeded to demolish the competition, winning all eight of their games and rolling to the league championship. They also drew the largest crowds: about 14,000 a game came to Gilmore Stadium, but the rest of the league did so poorly that it folded.

Two years later, in 1939, the Bulldogs joined another national league, the American Professional Football Association, and again ended up posting the best record at 7–1. After that season, however, they jumped to the regional Pacific Coast Football League and spent the next decade there, winning titles in 1940 and 1946.

A bicycle rack fronts a mural showing five attendants at the Gilmore gas-a-teria, an early self-service station in Los Angeles where motorists could save 5 cents a gallon by pumping gas themselves. The mural is in front of Peet's Coffeehouse and across the street from the Farmers Market at 3rd and Fairfax in Los Angeles.

that time, Gilmore was out of the petroleum business, with E.B. Gilmore having sold his company to Mobil in the early 1940s. One of his last promotions was an innovation that presaged the future: a gas-a-teria on Beverly Boulevard in Los Angeles, where customers could save 5 cents a gallon by pumping their own gas. Who would have guessed that by a half-century later, everyone would be doing it?

Meet Axelrod

You could get a tiger in your tank with Enco, or you could roar with Gilmore, but not all service stations had big cats as their mascots. Hancock had a rooster, Mobilgas had Pegasus, Richfield had an eagle, Sinclair had a dinosaur, Polly Gas had a parrot, and Flying A had a dog named Axelrod.

You might not remember Flying A, but the chain had a major presence along Highway 99 and across the West Coast up through the mid-1960s. One of its stations in Fresno even had a derrick-style sign reminiscent of the old Richfield beacons. The 110-foot sign at Princeton Avenue presided over a Flying A flat-top station: an early truck stop that featured a truck lube pit, public scale, and free shower rooms for truckers. Long after most of the Richfield towers were torn down, the Flying A derrick continued to stand tall beside 99, minus the company's winged A logo at the top.

Meanwhile, in a second bit of irony, the Cleveland team that had beaten them out for membership in the NFL relocated in 1945—to Los Angeles.

While the Bulldogs were playing football at Gilmore Stadium during the fall and winter months, the Hollywood Stars baseball team was playing just down the street at 13,000-seat Gilmore Field. The Stars were actually owned in part by real Hollywood stars, such as Gene Autry (who later owned the Los Angeles Angels), Gary Cooper, Bing Crosby, Barbara Stanwyck, and William Frawley of *I Love Lucy* fame.

Gilmore Stadium closed in 1952, and Gilmore Field followed in 1957, a year before the Brooklyn Dodgers' move to Los Angeles rendered the Stars expendable. By

The "A" was short for "Associated," but the wings that extended from the logo were meant to provide the same sort of link to aviation that Gilmore's flying lion and Richfield's Great White Way had offered. Airplanes were trendy. They were fast. And Flying A advertising emphasized the kind of "aero-type" speed and performance that an early company slogan said "Makes Airways Out of Highways."

Mobilgas (formerly Socony-Vacuum and later just plain Mobil) did the same thing with its red Pegasus logo and its accompanying slogan, "Flying Horsepower."

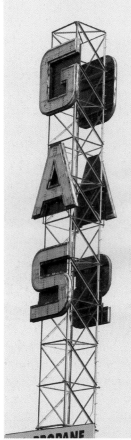

Still operating as a gas station in Fresno as of 2015, this Valero-branded stop off the west side of 99 on Princeton Avenue opened in 1952 as a "Flying A Flat-top" station on eight acres, with public scales, showers, and other truck-stop amenities. The sign in this photo, originally surmounted by a 37-foot winged A symbol, stands 110 feet high.

Wings were also incorporated into Chevron's early logo, which featured a flying V at its center, and Douglas Oil, whose symbol was a flying heart.

Years before Enco urged customers to put a tiger in their tanks, Flying A was inviting drivers to live on the wild side. "For new thrills on hills, unleash the extra Tiger Power of today's Flying 'A' Ethyl in your car," one newspaper ad read, boasting that Flying A's fuel was "richer than ever in 'tiger stocks' … special power-packed gasoline molecules that make modern motors eager for action."

To further associate itself with action and performance, Flying A pursued partnerships with major college athletic programs. As part of the grand opening of its Fresno truck stop in 1952, the company showed anyone who stopped by film highlights from four top Pacific Coast Conference football games played the previous year. It was all part of the "Play ball with Flying A" ad campaign, and the company carried it even further by sponsoring scoreboard and public address systems at many major college arenas and stadiums along the West Coast. (Union 76, another West Coast brand, had a similar tie-in with Dodger Stadium in Los Angeles, not far from Old 99, where the familiar orange 76 circles topped both outfield scoreboards for decades.)

Before Enco (later Exxon) began using a tiger as its symbol for high-performance gasoline, Flying A was urging drivers to "TREAT your car to TIGER POWER" with "the most potent motor fuel ingredient ever refined."

As a new era dawned in the 1960s, however, Flying A chose to downplay the high-performance angle in favor of a new ad campaign focusing on service and dependability. It dropped the tiger references and adopted as its mascot a cute but forlorn-looking basset hound named Axelrod. In print advertisements, the droopy-eyed pup was seen poking his head out of an A-shaped doghouse labeled "the house that worry built."

Axelrod became the face of Flying A, illustrating its new slogan, "When it comes to your car … Ooooh, do we worry!" Plush stuffed animals, piggy banks, trinkets, and decks of playing cards were produced in the likeness of poor, worried Axelrod, while many ads featured Flying A attendants wearing similar concerned expressions. One ad read:

> This is the face of worry … the face of Axelrod, Flying A worry dog. Constant reminder to Flying A service men that worry, extra worry about customers' cars is our business. We've got motor worriers, crankcase worriers, spark plug worriers. Worriers who worry about parts you didn't know you had to worry about. So if you're looking for dedicated worriers … men who worry a little bit more about your car than anyone else … Flying A is your kind of service station. Drive in. We're waiting to worry for you … all of us, Axelrod, too!

The house that worry built

Axelrod mopes about in "The house that worry built," part of a 1965 ad campaign. The text reads, in part: "Who'd pick a worried-looking dog like Axelrod as a mascot? The world's champion worriers at Flying A … that's who! Extra worry about your car is our job."

As it turned out, Flying A had reason to worry, but not just about its customers' cars. A year after that ad ran, Axelrod had been sent to the doghouse for good. In 1966 (appropriately), Phillips Petroleum purchased the entire chain of Flying A stations and set about rebranding them as Phillips 66 stations.

INDEPENDENT OPERATORS

There was a time when a seemingly endless variety of service stations greeted customers with ringing bells and smiling attendants up and down Old 99. They were ready to wipe your windows, check your oil, make sure you had enough air in your tires, and send you on your way with a helpful road map.

You could trust your car to the man who wore the big, bright Texaco star, or you could stop in and fill 'er up with Super Shell. Some companies even drilled for oil or refined it only a few miles from the "Main Street of California." Many readers will remember seeing oil derricks alongside the road in Kern County, and some drilling rigs, shaped almost like the dinosaurs whose remains they're extracting, still bob their metal heads up and down methodically by the side of the road in the South Valley.

Mohawk operated a refinery on the Kern River in Bakersfield for nearly four decades, starting in 1932, and other small- to medium-size independents had a presence in the San Joaquin Valley, as well. Beacon, which ran a refinery in Hanford, had several stations up and down 99. Sunland gasoline started out based in Fresno, then moved to Bakersfield; it had a station on 99 near the Kings River for many years.

There were others, too.

Terrible Herbst had a station in Selma, across 99 from a World station whose huge sign with five separate lighted letters was impossible to miss for years. Terrible's, as it was called, boasted stops up and down Old 99 in such places as Atwater, Bakersfield, Ceres, and Turlock. The company pulled out of Central California a few years after the oil crisis of the 1970s, and a company called Gas-N-Save bought up most of the stations along 99, keeping the distinctive signs with their swirling arrows.

The Herbst family, meanwhile, refocused its attention on the Las Vegas area, adding slot machines to

Terrible Herbst had stations up and down Highway 99 in the San Joaquin Valley, many of which were later purchased by Gas-N-Save, including this one on Union Avenue, the old 99 alignment through the heart of Bakersfield.

their convenience stores and eventually becoming Nevada's biggest non-casino operator of the one-armed bandits. (As of 2014, the company had nearly 100 stations in the Las Vegas–Henderson metro area.) The Herbsts eventually opened some casinos of their own and purchased others. As of 2014, the company's presence in California was negligible, consisting of no more than two or three convenience stores, all co-branded with Chevron stations.

From its name, one might have guessed that the Wilshire Oil Company started in Los Angeles, like so many others. Wilshire Boulevard runs directly across the Salt Lake Oil Field, which in turn lies buried right underneath the city of Los Angeles. That, however, is not the case. Wilshire Oil actually started out in Texas, but stations carrying the Wilshire name and its associated Polly Gas brand (complete with parrot mascot) could be found along 99, including one south of Fresno.

That station later became a Red Triangle outlet, part of a small San Joaquin Valley chain that operated for several years in the 1970s and '80s.

Hancock, which also had stations along 99, owed its name to George Hancock, owner of the Rancho La Brea Oil Company. He had inherited a piece of land in central Los Angeles from his father and, in the first decade of the 20th century, began to drill for oil there. By 1907, Hancock's company had more than 70 wells producing more than 300 barrels of oil a day. But in addition to the oil, he found something else: bones. Big bones. They turned out to be the remains of prehistoric animals, and in 1913 Hancock gave the county of Los Angeles exclusive rights to excavate what became known as the La Brea Tar Pits.

(Yes, this is the same Hancock family that sold a small piece of the property to Arthur Gilmore for his dairy—the property where he, too, struck it rich with oil.)

George Hancock eventually deeded the tar pits and some surrounding acreage to the county, while using the profits from his oil business to develop a high-end

A photo from the 1957 Roosevelt High School yearbook in Fresno shows the Wilshire station at 2874 Highway 99, later a Red Triangle site.

neighborhood called Hancock Park nearby. Hancock gas stations could be found at various points along Highway 99, with their orange-and-black color scheme and distinctive strutting mascot, the "Cock o' the Walk"—also known as the "Mileage-Booster Rooster." Signal Oil acquired the stations in 1958 but retained their brand identity, doing the same with a California company called Norwalk that also had a presence along the highway.

Signal, in turn, was purchased by Humble Oil (which was affiliated with Enco and Esso) in 1965; the Hancock and Norwalk brands disappeared in the early 1970s, about the same time Humble's parent company consolidated its brand identity under a single name: Exxon. Lerner Oil, Urich, Hudson, and others also had stations along Old 99.

GAS WARS

At its height, the era of independents gave rise to a phenomenon drivers came to love: the gas war. In a game of "Can you top this?," a station on one corner would lower its price a few pennies, only to be undercut by a station across the way. A third operator at the same intersection might lower the price still further, kicking off a downward spiral.

A Hudson gas station started just such a cycle in Bakersfield during the winter of 1955, dropping its price to 22.9 cents a gallon at its station along Old 99 at Third Street. General Petroleum (Mobil) countered by cutting its price to 20.9 cents at two other highway locations. Douglas, Hancock, and Texaco followed by lowering their prices, but several downtown service stations simply couldn't afford to follow suit. As a result, prices in Bakersfield ranged from a low of 20.9 cents all the way up to 30.6 in early February.

"This happens every year or so when one independent company wants to attract more business by lower prices," one dealer explained. "When the low price is met, then the prices readjust to normal levels again."

Sometimes, it happened more often than that. In 1965–66, Fresno experienced no fewer than nine price wars in the course of a year.

In the summer of 1971, an independent called U-Save posted bargain-basement prices in Modesto and sold 350,000 gallons in a month—nearly half the amount normally sold by 27 stations in the area.

The gas wars caused such a furor that the Federal Trade Commission convened hearings on the matter in the spring of 1965. George F. Getty II of the Tidewater Oil Company, owner of the Flying A chain, called for greater federal oversight, accusing major chains of lowering prices in one section of the country while raising them elsewhere to make up the difference. Such "predatory gasoline pricing practices," he charged, amounted to "competitive cannibalism."

Indeed, the mid-'60s were a time of consolidation in the industry, as many large chains bought up midsize and regional groups.

Some independents were able to stay in business by using self-service to undercut the big boys. It cost a few cents more per gallon to dress attendants up in those spiffy white uniforms and pay them to look under the hood, wash your windows, and check your tires. Some smaller stations dropped their prices even further and took a loss at the pump temporarily as the price of attracting new customers, who might make up the difference by picking up a carton of cigarettes or a roll of candy during their visit. The major chains had no choice but to counter the independents' reduced prices by offering affiliated dealers a subsidy so they could compete. Once prices were stabilized again, the subsidy was revoked.

A short editorial in *The Bakersfield Californian* explained the phenomenon: "By pricing their products several cents a gallon below the major brands, the independents patrolled

Red & Jacks Service Station was at Selma and 3rd in Chico, one block off the old alignment of U.S. 99E (Broadway). *Meriam Library, CSU Chico.*

A Shell station on the Esplanade, the old alignment of 99E through Chico, around 1945. *Meriam Library, CSU Chico.*

the market place, keeping downward pressure on prices. Gas wars often were touched off when independent stations cut prices or when major dealers lowered prices in an effort to recapture customers lost to smaller markets."

The OPEC oil embargo of 1973 helped to shift the dynamic, as the price for a barrel of oil on the world market quadrupled. Cars lined up around the block to fill up, and the federal government imposed a national speed limit of 55 mph to conserve fuel. Gasoline became so scarce that rationing was instituted, and cars with license plates ending in odd numbers were allowed to buy gas only on odd-numbered dates; those with even-numbered license plates, meanwhile, could fill up only on even-numbered days.

The embargo gave motorists a massive jolt of sticker shock from which they never really recovered. Prices spiked dramatically, then kept on rising even after the flow of Middle Eastern oil was restored, hitting $1 a gallon in 1980, with no end in sight. It had taken roughly six decades for the price to quadruple from a quarter a gallon in 1919, but it took less than a third of that time to quadruple again, hitting $4 a gallon in 2008.

As consumers suddenly became more focused on price, the old-fashioned service and incentives went out the window. Large chains began to offer a self-service option at more stations and, within a few years, had phased out full service altogether. Gas was already so expensive that only a few customers were willing to pay extra to have their windows washed, and lines often formed at the self-service pumps while their full-serve alternatives stood vacant.

Soon, the familiar bell that had once greeted all motorists as they drove into a station, alerting attendants of a new customer's arrival, fell silent. Stations stopped offering the free drinking glasses, road maps, and S&H Green Stamps that had once lured customers by the thousands, and many stations dropped the old-fashioned mechanics' bays, replacing them with convenience stores to boost revenues. Suddenly, the big chains looked a lot like the independents, and many of the latter were forced out of business.

By 1985, the number of gasoline stations had fallen from 220,000 in 1970 to just 130,000 nationwide. As *The New York Times* put it: "Free maps and clean windshields are out; self-service and price cutting are the vogue."

Only the strong survived as the oil industry began a contraction that undid much of what had been accomplished in 1911, when the U.S. Supreme Court broke up the massive Standard Oil monopoly, splitting it into 34 pieces. Over time, most of the independents went out of business or were gobbled up by bigger operators, many of which were, in turn, absorbed by still bigger companies. Richfield merged with Atlantic, and BP bought the resulting combination (ARCO). Chevron bought out Texaco and part of Union Oil, Phillips 66 taking the other portion. Exxon and Mobil, which had started out as two of

This Richfield station between Tulare and Fresno featured a steeply gabled roof. It offered the "Finest Non Premium Gasoline" and "Double Money Back" in 1939. *Dorothea Lange, Library of Congress/public domain.*

the original Standard Oil offshoots, undid part of what the Supreme Court had done by merging again.

The length of Highway 99 became littered with old, rusty signs rising up beside abandoned stations and vacant fields, tombstones in a long and winding graveyard path from years and decades past.

⑧ REFRESHMENTS

Perry's Ranch House Café, one of several coffee shops "Hoot" Perry operated in the Tulare area, was open from 1962 to 1982 at the Avenue 200 exit off Highway 99. *From the collection of Ron Perry.*

In the mid-'20s, an idea began to take shape in Frank "Pop" Pohl's head. It was the shape of an orange, to be exact—a big orange.

Frank opened the original Giant Orange roadside stand on Tracy's 11th Street in 1926, part of the old Lincoln Highway that brought traffic to the Bay Area from points eastward. The stand offered everything from (of course) orange juice and orangeade to lemonade and grapefruit juice. Once Prohibition ended, cold keg beer was added to the menu.

The business featured a service window in a 10-foot-high stand shaped like an orange, but it wasn't just the eye-catching shape and color that made it effective. Orange juice and lemonade were just the right medicine for overheated travelers driving overheated cars—without air conditioning—through sweltering Central California in the middle of summer.

Pohl's idea wasn't entirely new. He actually started out in the roadside refreshment business the way a lot of kids do: with a lemonade stand—but in this case, it was shaped like (you guessed it) a giant lemon.

Down in Southern California, there was a Giant Lemon or Big Lemon along the old Ridge Route, a few miles southeast of Gorman near Quail Lake. A pair of stepsisters owned the establishment, which had begun as a lemonade and takeout stand in a 15-by-20-foot yellow building next to the owners' home. The "dining room" was a grove of shade trees out back, where visitors could cool off with orange juice or lemonade, or wake up with a cup of coffee.

By the early 1930s, the thriving business had morphed into a full-fledged 24-hour diner serving up full chicken and steak dinners. Improvements continued, and the Giant Lemon Ranch (as it became known) added a volcanic rock fireplace and U-shaped counter, along with a Chevron garage on the premises that qualified it to advertise as a "truck stop." When the Ridge Route Alternate replaced the old road, the owners moved just up the road, closer to the new highway.

The Giant Lemon was in business for more than three decades, still operating in the early 1960s when it placed ads for "waitresses, cooks (and) dishwashers" in the Bakersfield newspaper down the road. But it never expanded beyond that single location.

The same couldn't be said for Frank Pohl's operation, which multiplied up and down the highway. Initially, he had one or two outlets for his own lemony endeavor, including one in Menlo Park called the Jumbo Lemon Stand. The orange shape, however, proved more lucrative. The Tracy business had just one window when it opened, but Pohl added two more to keep eager customers from waiting too long in the hot sun for his cold liquid nectar. A shaded overhang helped shield them from the unforgiving summer heat.

In fact, the business was so popular, Pohl opened a second one less than five miles away in Banta. A third location followed, also in Tracy, but Pohl's giant oranges made their most lasting impression along Highway 99. Pohl franchised the concept, charging something like $25 a year, and Giant Oranges started popping up at regular intervals along 99 and other highways across the northern half of the state.

As with any good moneymaking idea, the Giant Oranges spawned imitators who built their own juice stands in the shape of the citrus fruit. When a similar business called the Orange Basket opened next to Tracy High School, just down the road from Pohl's Giant Orange in 1934, Pohl cried foul. He filed a lawsuit, accusing the owner of stealing his idea, but a judge dismissed the suit on the grounds that Pohl couldn't claim exclusive use of the word "orange."

More juice stands followed, with names like Big Boy Orange, Great Orange, and Whoa Boy Orange, and Pohl continued to fight the wannabes. In 1941, he was back in court in Stanislaus County, where he succeeded in obtaining an injunction against two other imitators—who were thenceforth restrained from operating such copycat stands. The judge also awarded Pohl damages as part of his ruling.

The big Oranges themselves, which were actually service windows for larger, more traditional buildings, weren't cheap. Ed Power, who owned the Nut Tree restaurant in Vacaville, manufactured them for $1,000 to $1,500 apiece from steel and plaster. Flexible pine

The Orange Zone advertises "Fresh Fruits in Season" and "Ice Cold Orange & Grape Fruit Juice" south of Orland on old U.S. 99W.

was used to create curved "ribs," and stucco was applied to the outside to mimic the look of a genuine orange. The structure was basic: shelving and a rear door on the inside, three service windows, and a floor drain.

At its peak in the 1950s, the chain numbered between 16 and 24 locations scattered across Northern and Central California. By that time, two stands in the Solano County city of Dixon alone were squeezing 12,000 oranges a week. Pohl's son-in-law Arnet Ballenger operated those stands from 1939 until the last one closed. "You would never get rich," Ballenger said, "but you'd make a good living."

During the 1930s, Pohl's stands brought a couple of truckloads of oranges in from the San Fernando Valley every other day to ensure they had enough on hand. The chain expanded rapidly, as locations popped up in Bakersfield, Chowchilla, El Dorado, Galt, Lodi, Madera, Merced, Modesto, Patterson, Placerville, Roseville, Sacramento, Shasta Lake, Tulare, Turlock, and Williams. Many were operated by members of the Pohl family, although Frank Pohl himself retired in 1944.

Business began to drop off in the 1960s, following the advent of freeway bypasses that made access to the stands more difficult and air-conditioned cars that made their product less essential. It was one thing to chug along at 45 miles per hour with open windows your only defense against triple-digit heat; it was quite another to zoom along at 60 or 70, comfortably insulated in a compartment cooled by Freon. A blast of air-conditioned air was a lot more immediate and just as refreshing as a long swig of orange juice.

The business tried to adapt to the changing times. In 1947, after U.S. Highway 40 was realigned through Dixon, Ballenger placed two stands on opposite sides of the road so drivers traveling in either direction could have easy access.

Mammoth Orange in rural Fairmead, about 10 miles north of Madera on Highway 99, had the same idea. Originally located in nearby Chowchilla when it opened around 1948, the business moved six years later to a prime spot on the highway: just south of the junction with State Route 152, which carried Bay Area–bound travelers eastward toward the Pacheco Pass.

At first, the wood, aluminum, and stucco stand offered a simple menu: orange juice, lemonade, and hot dogs. Then, as fast-food outlets came on the scene, the offerings were expanded to keep up with the competition.

All that's left of the old Mammoth Orange in Fairmead is this dilapidated orange structure, which sits in a field outside the Fossil Discovery Center in Chowchilla.

In addition to the juices, workers started offering up such delicacies as Alaska-size burgers and Texas-sized fries. (The burgers were originally Texas-size, too, but as the highway's traffic counts grew larger, so did the name.) The large lettering spelling out "HAMBURGERS" over the aluminum overhang were even more visible than the orange itself.

Over the years, the place developed quite a reputation. Well-known celebrities ranging from Bob Hope and Kenny Rogers to the shah of Iran were said to have stopped by. Barbara Eden of *I Dream of Jeannie* fame even reportedly popped out of her bottle for a visit. The stand was featured on the cover of a 1984 album titled *Big Orange* by Bobby Volare, alter ego of Fresno deejay Dean Opperman.

A second stand was built on the west side of the highway to attract southbound travelers, almost directly across from the original, but it wasn't as profitable because it was too close to the 152 junction. Drivers would whiz past by the time they caught sight of it, and owners Doris and Jim Stiggins eventually sold it while retaining title to the eastern "twin." At some point, the western Orange received a distinctive paint job—blue and white with stars and a red stripe down the middle—and became known as Fast Eddie's Mammoth Orange. It was demolished in the late 1990s, but the Stigginses' stand lasted awhile longer. It was only when a highway expansion project pushed through in 2007 that the old orange was displaced and, ironically, carted back to its original home in Chowchilla after the city purchased it.

In 2012, the city sold it to the San Joaquin Valley Paleontology Foundation for just over $2,000. The foundation moved it to the Fossil Discovery Center, where it was supposed serve as an on-site concession stand, doubtless on the theory that one good mammoth deserves another. As of 2014, however, it stood unused and in disrepair at the edge of the center's parking lot, covered in cobwebs and graffiti.

Mammoth Orange lasted a lot longer than Giant Orange did. Most of the big oranges were torn down long ago, though a few managed to survive. Joe's Giant Orange, a restaurant in Shasta Lake, was built around an orange stand that opened in 1946. One of the Dixon Giant Oranges survived as a Mexican Restaurant; another Orange, built in 1936, became a San Jose hot dog stand 11 years later.

Even before the end came for the Giant Orange chain, the oranges themselves had become nothing more than eye-catching roadside fixtures. By 1963, all the business was being done out of the main buildings. The oranges themselves, Arnet Ballenger said, "were getting too small to work in, and the health departments were complaining that too much dirt was coming in the open windows."

Ten years later, the last Giant Orange—one of the original pair Ballenger had opened in Dixon—closed for business.

"There's no way to continue," Ballenger, then 68, told the *Solano Reporter*. "Nobody's going to get off the freeway and drive down an access road a mile for a glass of orange juice. . . . There are a lot of people who like fresh orange juice, and they won't be able to get it anymore … We make it fresh when they ordered it, and when we're closed, there won't be anyone else doing it."

A Thrill in Livingston

Sometimes, travelers wanted something more substantial than a glass of orange juice or a hot dog. Truckers driving through the Central Valley tended to develop an appetite, and they'd be on the lookout for a place that could serve up a full, hearty meal.

One such place was the Blueberry Hill Café in Livingston, whose name had more to do with the jukebox than actual blueberries. The story goes like this: Ray Pratt built the place in 1957 and didn't know what to call it. Just then, a customer punched up a particular song on the jukebox. The song in question, titled "Blueberry Hill," had been recorded by the likes of Gene Krupa and Glenn Miller before the war, but Fats Domino had reworked it as a rhythm-and-blues tune a year before Pratt opened his café. Domino's version had rocketed to number one, spending eight weeks at the top of Billboard's R&B Best Sellers chart. It would become an early rock 'n' roll standard, later receiving prominent play on the nostalgia-driven TV show *Happy Days* in the '70s.

It would also inspire Pratt in the naming of his new restaurant, with its flagstone floors and Old West décor.

At least part of its success was its prime location. For years, the Blueberry Hill Café stood at the only stoplight intersection left on 99 in California. It was a natural place for truckers and travelers to stop smack-dab in the middle of the valley and grab a bite or two or three to energize them for the rest of their journey.

It was almost as if time had stood still at that corner. That lone stoplight stood watch over a place where you could get enough meat-and-potatoes comfort food to fill your belly and clog your arteries, all in one sitting. No guilt, no health-food specials, just down-home, friendly service. You could get steak and eggs in the morning for under seven bucks, or you could grab a dessert of blueberry pie or an ice-creamy blueberry shake.

You couldn't miss the Blueberry Hill on the highway, with its river-stone walls and huge parking lot. It had one of those distinctive roadside signs as tall as a big rig was

The Blueberry Hill Café was a Livingston landmark along Highway 99 for four decades before it was demolished to make way for a freeway bypass. This photo shows it from the air in 1966. © *Copyright Vintage Aerial 2010-2015. All rights reserved.*

long and, for part of its history, a billboard bearing its name that ran the length and breadth of the building. A fire in the early '60s led the owner to revamp the place. And at some point, the billboard was replaced by a wood-shingle roof probably 10 to 15 feet tall. At its apex, a bigger-than-life-size statue of a horse reared up, beckoning passing motorists to give the place a try.

Even if you didn't see the café driving up Old 99, you probably knew about it—especially if you were a trucker listening to the radio late at night. Blueberry Hill's radio spots aired regularly across the valley on Fresno-based KMJ radio, a 50,000-watt station that could be heard as far north as San Francisco and as far south as Valencia. The commercials were like a beacon to truckers at all points in between who listened to newscasts on the hour in 1964 or, nine years later, a late-night music show called *24th Hour.*

Country music station KRAK in Sacramento, another 50,000-watt blowtorch, drew in listeners from even farther north, and people as far away as Alaska, Nova Scotia, and the Pitcairn Islands, more than halfway across the Pacific, reported hearing about the Blueberry Hill. It was the voice of Frieda Vilas, a rancher in her 60s, that crackled out over the car speakers in the cabs of Mack trucks and Mustangs across half the Northern Hemisphere. Vilas, who served as president of local women's clubs and was a member of the state Republican Committee, had a radio show sponsored by Blueberry Hill. She returned the favor by writing commercial spots for the restaurant, flavoring them with the same sort of personal touch its patrons had come to expect.

"Hello out there, you truckers. Tired? Hungry? Ready for a break after a hard day's driving? Why not take a break at the Blueberry Hill Café?" she said in one of her ads. In another: "Now and again, it helps to do something as simple as taking a little drive at the end of a hectic day and having dinner along the way at some nice spot like the Blueberry Hill Café."

Ultimately, one of Blueberry Hill's advantages—its location—proved to be its undoing. The stoplight might have been

A postcard image shows the Blueberry Hill Café in its prime.

Hill, the iconic restaurant was one of them. The new northbound freeway lanes joined the existing highway south of the Merced River, in the precise spot where the café had stood for 40 years.

It wasn't exactly the day the music died, but when the old restaurant was demolished, a bit of history went with it. On one occasion, Fats Domino himself heard one of Frieda Vilas' commercials

a blessing for business at the restaurant, but all too often it was a curse for drivers passing through the area. So many accidents occurred there, it earned the nickname "Blood Alley." Whether bleary-eyed and unprepared for the stoplight or disoriented by the Tule fog that blanketed the area in late autumn, drivers who weren't paying close attention often ended their journey prematurely.

Some permanently.

A concrete underpass, built in 1939, that guided motorists beneath a rail line near the stoplight didn't help matters. Neither did a curve right before the intersection for southbound drivers.

Since a couple of years after the Blueberry Hill was built, the state had been promising to build a bypass. One of the first sections of freeway on 99 had been laid down north of Livingston in 1953, and the other two remaining stoplights—in Denair and Keyes—were removed during the 1980s.

In all, more than 40 people died in accidents near the traffic light from the 1960s until it was finally removed in 1996, and many more were injured in crashes. (The stoplight found a new home at the Livingston Historical Museum, where it sits outside, greeting visitors.) About 40 businesses were demolished, along with more than 64 homes, to make way for the new freeway bypass, and unfortunately for longtime customers of Blueberry

when he was passing through the valley and pulled off the highway to grab a sandwich and some coffee. It was then that he learned that the restaurant had been named after his hit recording in 1956, whereupon he reportedly quipped, "Blueberry Hill has been good to both of us."

EAT AT J'S

J's Coffee Shops were a fixture for a time along Highway 99, from Newhall in the south to Modesto in the North.

My parents and I often stopped for lunch at the J's off White Lane in Bakersfield during the '70s. You could get a freshly baked strawberry pie with whipped cream for just 75 cents. Or, if you had a heartier appetite, you could order the Saturday night special: steak kabob, baked potato, green salad, and garlic bread, all for a mere $2.95. Being a preteen with a discriminating (read: finicky) appetite, I usually opted for a sandwich or a burger and fries.

The White Lane restaurant flagged down passing motorists with scores of lightbulbs illuminating the giant J's on a sign that was a good 27 feet tall. It was so big and bright that you could see it when you were coming down the Grapevine grade at night. The restaurant itself was far less impressive: a typical coffee shop with a slightly angled roof and those bland orange-yellow-brown colors that seemed so pervasive among roadside diners of the era. My parents tended to eat

Selma, as well as three in Bakersfield. In addition to the White Lane restaurant, J's had two other Bakersfield locations: farther north on 99 at 24th Street and at Weedpatch Highway and Highway 58.

The majority were right off 99. That's where Farmer John's Pancake House got its start, alongside the old highway when it still followed Union Avenue through downtown Bakersfield. The landmark restaurant with its huge red-and-white sign stood right at the curve where Union Avenue morphed into the Golden State Highway. If you missed Farmer John's, you could always catch a bite up the road at the Golden Key, its sister pancake house, near where Golden State met the new freeway. Or if you wanted to wait, you could spend a couple more hours on the road and eat at the Farmer John's at 99 and Cleveland Avenue in Madera.

Joseph Mooney (the Mooney in May-Mooney) opened Farmer John's in 1951 as a burger place called Mooney's Drive-in, then converted it into a pancake house a few

This sign remained on the west side of Highway 99 at County Line Road in Delano long after the coffee shop itself had been torn down. Only recently was the sign also removed. *Photo by Robby Virus.*

there on trips between Fresno and Los Angeles because, at the time, it was either J's or Denny's, and my mom didn't care for Denny's.

In the long run, Denny's survived and J's didn't, which wasn't too surprising. The J's chain wasn't nearly as large, and it was locally based, operated by a company called May-Mooney Inc. of Visalia and Bakersfield. The J's in Modesto, featuring much the same design as the Bakersfield diner, was the first restaurant to open along the new freeway stretch of U.S. 99 when it came to Modesto in 1965, the same year the chain filed incorporation papers.

The Modesto restaurant cost a mere $50,000.

At one time or another, J's had restaurants in Atwater, Delano, Kettleman, Lost Hills, Madera, Merced, and

A dual newspaper ad from the mid-'60s touts a 79-cent beef patty breakfast at Farmer John's and a 69-cent Thursday combination breakfast special at J's, on White Lane and the "New 99 Freeway."

years later. He eventually built a chain of several restaurants, including one that served Mexican food, a steakhouse, the Golden Key, and half a dozen self-service hamburger stands.

Does the thought of two farm-fresh eggs and three buttermilk pancakes get your mouth watering? That was Wednesday's special at Farmer John's in 1966, and you could get it for the bargain-basement price of 59 cents. Whatever you ordered, you got pancakes along with it. It also served sizzling steaks, fried chicken, red chile, carne asada, fries … you name it. Farmer John's catered to the highway traveler as well as the local resident: The sign out front proudly proclaimed "Charter buses welcome."

It lasted a lot longer than J's. Mooney was 82 years old and still running the place in 1998, still proclaiming his pancake recipe the best in the state. Unfortunately, a fire hit the iconic restaurant the following year, and it was eventually torn down, as was the sign.

The same couldn't be said for the J's sign on the north edge of Delano, which was nothing if not durable. Nearly three decades after the chain went out of business in the '80s, it remained standing sentinel at the County Line Road exit from Highway 99. The restaurant it had advertised was long gone, but the sign itself continued to watch over a relatively lonesome stretch of roadway just north of town, a rusted relic in orange and white with oddly mismatching letters spelling out "coffee shop" (in different-style lettering) on either side. They finally tore it down sometime around 2012.

The Newhall Incident

Unfortunately, J's was perhaps best known as the scene of the most brutal officer-involved shootout in California history.

It began in the spring of 1970, when a couple of ex-cons drove a red 1964 Pontiac down from Northern California, looking for a big score. Jack Twinning, 34, and Bobby Davis, 27, were former prison mates who had hooked up in Houston after Twinning's release from the federal penitentiary in Tallahassee, Florida. Unable to find work in Texas, where Davis was on parole, they headed for Sacramento, where they planned a bank heist that never happened.

Instead, they decided to try their luck farther south, loading up their car with heavy artillery and hopping on the freeway toward Los Angeles. After finding a place to stay in Long Beach, Twinning and Davis caught sight of an armored car entering Santa Anita Racetrack in Arcadia. No doubt figuring the car would contain a significant haul, they decided to trace its route and set up a robbery on a freeway ramp.

What they needed for the job was a mass of explosives.

On their initial trip across the Tehachapis, the pair had noticed an area of heavy construction south of Gorman. So late on the night of April 5, they returned to the area, intent on stealing some explosives from the road crew.

Upon reaching the site, they pulled up behind a family stranded on the side of the road with an overheated radiator. Davis remained in the car, while Twinning got out and started hunting for explosives. But the family with the broken-down car kept looking at Davis and he got anxious, flipping a sudden U-turn onto southbound 99, where his Pontiac cut in front of a car driven by Ivory Jack Tidwell.

Tidwell's wife, Pamela, had been sleeping in the front seat, but as the car swerved suddenly to avoid a collision she came awake with a start.

Tidwell, a 22-year-old sailor on his way to Port Hueneme, was none too pleased at nearly being run off the road. He started following the Pontiac, flashing his high beams as his wife took down the license number. Then, the irate sailor pulled up alongside the Pontiac and began shouting at the man behind the wheel. Both cars pulled off to the side of the road, and Tidwell asked his wife to roll down the window so he could have a few more words with the jerk who had nearly hit him. But before Tidwell could say much, he found himself face-to-face with the open end of a 2-inch revolver. Thinking quickly, the sailor managed to persuade Davis that Highway Patrol officers were in the area, and Davis told him to drive on.

While there may not have been any CHP vehicles in the area at the time, Tidwell was determined to make sure that there would be. Soon. He pulled away and floored the accelerator, driving about 15 minutes before he found a service station. Once there, he got out, phoned police, and reported the incident, along with the Pontiac's license number.

Davis, meanwhile, returned to pick up Twinning, and they headed back south toward the San Fernando Valley. They'd gotten as far as Newhall when they caught the attention of CHP officers Walt Frago and Roger Gore, who began tailing them while radioing for backup. Two other Highway Patrolmen, driving north at Lyons Avenue in Valencia, picked up the call and headed up to meet them. Meanwhile, Davis and Twinning turned off the freeway at what would later be called Magic Mountain Parkway (the amusement park would open for business a little more than a year later). The two ex-cons immediately pulled into a parking lot shared by the J's Coffee Shop and a Standard Gas Station on Old Highway 99.

Gore and Frago turned on their lights and, when the Pontiac came to a stop, got out of the car and approached the suspect vehicle.

It was five minutes before midnight.

J's was busy, packed with an array of customers, including a church choir group that had stopped for a bite to eat.

Outside, Gore and Frago assessed the situation. At first, it seemed like a routine traffic stop, and the pair didn't wait for their backup to arrive. Instead, they ordered the Pontiac's occupants to get out, and, after some delay, Davis complied, stepping to the front of the car, where Gore patted him down while Frago covered him with a shotgun. For a moment, however, both officers seem to have taken their eyes off the second man, and that moment was all Jack Twinning would need. Stepping out of the car while the two lawmen were preoccupied with his partner, Twinning aimed a Smith & Wesson revolver at Frago and pulled the trigger.

Gore drew his own handgun and returned fire, but lost track of Davis in the meantime. As it turned out, Davis still had a .38 Special tucked in his waistband, which he pulled it out and fired twice at point-blank range, hitting Gore with both shots.

Within moments, the backup CHP vehicle had arrived. George Alleyn and James Pence pulled into the parking lot to find their two fellow officers lying on the pavement—and themselves suddenly the targets of a volley of bullets from Davis and Twinning.

They sent an urgent radio message to the CHP dispatch: "Newhall, 78-12! 11-99! Shots fired. J's Restaurant parking lot."

The two ex-cons, meanwhile, kept firing. They quickly exhausted the ammunition in their handguns, but it didn't matter: They had plenty more where that came from. Having loaded up their car with weapons, the two reached into the Pontiac and pulled out a sawed-off shotgun (Davis) and a Colt. 45 (Twinning). When the Colt jammed, Twinning merely tossed it aside and grabbed another out of the car.

Alleyn ran out of bullets after grazing Twinning in the head, but Davis responded with several rounds from his shotgun, two of which hit Alleyn in the face and chest. He fell to the pavement, leaving only Pence to fend off the two gunmen. According to one witness, the 24-year-old patrolman made a valiant stand: "The remaining cop held off these two guys for about five minutes by himself. Finally, one fellow went round to the front of the Highway Patrol car and shot this young cop in the face."

Three of the four officers had already fallen by the time a former U.S. Marine named Gary Kness arrived on the scene. The Palmdale resident was en route to work and could have easily continued on his way, but instead pulled into the parking lot, opened his car door, and sprinted 70 yards across the asphalt. "My brain said to get out of the way," he would recall, "but my feet went the wrong way."

A moment later, Kness was beside Alleyn's fallen form, trying to use the officer's gun belt to drag him to safety. The officer, however, was too heavy, and as the seconds passed, Kness could feel his time was running out: Davis had picked up Frago's shotgun and had Kness in his sights.

The gun misfired, and Davis tossed it aside in favor of Frago's revolver.

This gave Kness the opportunity he needed. Picking up Alleyn's shotgun, he aimed it at Davis and pulled the trigger.

Click.

It was empty.

Following his adversary's lead, he discarded the shotgun and grabbed Alleyn's handgun, which he trained on Davis.

He fired.

The bullet ricocheted off the patrol car and ploughed into Davis' shoulder. Though not seriously wounded, he was stunned enough to retreat, even as Twinning was unleashing the shot that would end Pence's life. Having already hit him with several shots, he walked up to him and put one last bullet through his skull, execution style.

"I got you now, you son of a bitch," Kness would recall hearing him say.

In all, about 100 shots were fired in the exchange. Alleyn, the last remaining officer alive, died on his way to the hospital. Four wives lost their husbands that day, and seven young children lost their fathers: James Pence, George Alleyn, and Walt Frago each left behind two kids; Roger Gore, who had attended the police academy with Frago less than two years earlier, left one. None of the officers was older than 24 years of age.

And still, it wasn't over.

A third CHP unit arrived and took fire before Davis and Twinning, perhaps sensing that they would soon be outgunned, jumped in the Pontiac and put the pedal to the floor—only to find their lone avenue of escape cut off. Realizing their only chance was to abandon the car, they jumped out and made a run for it, fleeing the glare of the coffee shop's lights and disappearing into the dark of night.

They split up, and Davis immediately started looking for a vehicle in which to escape the area. A little over three hours later, he came upon a camper truck parked in San Francisquito Canyon, about 12 miles from the scene of the shootout. The occupant, a 40-year-old man named Daniel Schwarz, was awakened by the sound of Davis at his door, ordering him to come out of the camper and threatening to kill him if he refused.

Schwarz was having none of it, so Davis—who was still carrying Frago's revolver—fired a shot into the camper that missed Schwarz's head by about an inch. Unfortunately for Davis, however, Schwarz was armed with a revolver of his own, and he returned fire, hitting Davis in the shoulder. Still, Davis had one more trick up his sleeve. He finally managed to persuade the other man to leave the vehicle by threatening to target the gas tank and blow it up. Schwarz, unwilling to risk being inciner-ated, stepped outside, whereupon he was promptly pistol whipped by Davis.

The intruder relieved Schwarz of his gun, hit him twice more in the head for good measure, and left when he was sure his victim was out cold.

Except he wasn't.

Schwarz, though badly hurt, was only pretending to be unconscious and, when he heard Davis drive off, he got up and started hiking toward a power station a couple of miles away. Once there, he called the sheriff's office in Newhall to report the assault. Two deputies were nearby and, upon being alerted, only had to stop their patrol car and wait until the lights of the camper appeared on the road ahead.

Davis had no choice but to stop.

"Come out of the car with your hands up slowly, or I'll blow your head off," Deputy Fred Thatcher shouted.

This time, Davis surrendered without a fight.

Maybe it was something in Thatcher's voice. Describing the scene later in court, the deputy made it clear he wasn't about to take anything more from Davis, who had to be warned to spread his arms and legs upon surrendering.

"Did you say anything else to him?" the district attorney asked Thatcher in court a little more than six months later.

"I reiterated what I would do if he didn't," Thatcher replied.

"What was that?"

"That I would blow the top of his head off if he didn't."

"Did you mean it?" asked the attorney.

"Yes, sir," came the answer.

"Did he comply?"

"Yes, sir," said the deputy.

In the meantime, however, Twinning was still at large, armed with a shotgun and a pistol. Less than an hour after Davis was arrested, he came upon a red, three-bedroom house on property overlooking the freeway about three miles from the J's parking lot. It was still pitch black, and everything was quiet. Twinning, wounded during the shootout, was tired from walking and climbing all the way from J's, so he stopped to dip his head in a horse trough.

In that moment, the silence of the night was broken. A dog heard Twinning and started barking, waking Betty Hoag, who was asleep inside the house along with her husband, Steve, and 17-year-old son, Jeffrey. It was a quarter after 4 in the morning.

Betty Hoag had enough time to phone the CHP and, after Twinning entered the home, was able to collect her son and slip out the back. Steve Hoag, however, wasn't as fortunate. Twinning confronted the cement truck driver and, holding Hoag at gunpoint, demanded that he make breakfast. Hoag complied. As he served Twinning "about nine gallons of coffee," he noticed the fugitive still had a pellet sticking out of the side of his head where he had been shot outside J's.

Meanwhile, law enforcement officers were responding to Betty Hoag's call. Three helicopters arrived and began to circle overhead while an armed force of more than 250 sheriff's deputies and CHP officers moved in to surround the house.

Inside, the phone rang.

"You coming out?" The voice on the other end belonged to Deputy Rudy Vasquez.

"I thought about it," Twinning said.

"Going to blow yourself up?"

"That's what I want to do."

After a brief exchange, Twinning ended the conversation: "Catch you later."

A few tense moments followed before Steve Hoag walked out of the house unharmed. "He was 41 this morning. He's 85 now," Betty Hoag said after being reunited with her husband. "Mondays are always lousy, but wow."

Authorities gave Twinning until 10 a.m. to give himself up. Shortly before the deadline, the phone rang again. It was a reporter named Don Chamberlain from an Oakland radio station, trying to persuade Twinning to surrender. He told him no one had been executed in California for several years, and that his chances of avoiding the death penalty were good.

"No one has killed four highway patrolmen in a very long time, either," Twinning told him. "I've been in jail already [and] I don't want to go back. If I tried to give up, the cops would pop me. I figure it's better to do it myself."

When the deadline arrived, officers shot tear gas into the home, and seven heavily armed men rushed the door. At the moment they broke in, they heard a single shot from somewhere inside. One of the officers related what happened: Twinning "blew his head off just about the time our men hit the door. Plaster was still falling from the wall."

So ended the deadliest night in the history of the California Highway Patrol.

Davis was convicted and sentenced to four life terms in prison. He had served 39 years behind bars when, on August 16, 2009, his lifeless body was found hanging in his cell at Kern Valley State Prison. The maximum-security institution in Delano stands barely 5 miles from Highway 99—the same highway where he and Jack Twinning had taken the lives of four young fathers in front of J's Coffee Shop in Newhall all those years ago.

Tip's at the Top of the Mountain

J's had been operating in Newhall for only about a year when those four CHP officers were shot to death in the parking lot.

Before that, the restaurant had been known as Tip's, a popular "last chance" eatery for motorists heading up over the mountains from the Santa Clarita Valley. It may have been just that for one budding movie star.

Tip Jardine opened his first eponymous restaurant in the 1940s, then added another nearby. Both were in the Santa Clarita Valley, and one was later remodeled to become J's. As with many roadside restaurants of the period, Tip's offered a varied menu of breakfast, lunch, and dinner items, along with an array of beverages from coffee to hard liquor.

In the latter department, Jardine had an important ally, a bartender named Valerio Batugo, who had come to the United States from the Philippines at age 20 in 1926 and got a job working for Charlie Chaplin in a restaurant called Henry's. Chaplin couldn't pronounce Batugo's first name, so he had the staff choose a new name for him: Bobby.

Six years after arriving in the States, Bobby Batugo landed a job tending bar at a speakeasy. Prohibition was still in effect, and Batugo was technically the 1932 equivalent of a drug dealer … but only for a year. When Prohibition was repealed, his profession became legitimate, and it wasn't long before his talent was recognized as top shelf, landing him a job at a favorite Hollywood star hangout called Sardi's. Positions at other high-profile clubs followed before Jardine recruited him to work out in what were then the boondocks at Tip's.

Why would Batugo leave the limelight for the headlights along 99?

It was simple, really. Those high-end places all had policies limiting how much a bartender could spend on the tools of his trade: his liquor. Without a little variety, things could get boring pretty quickly. Batugo wanted to be free to use his imagination and be as creative as that imagination allowed. It didn't matter if he was working at a place with a star-studded clientele or at a diner with Formica tables and brown vinyl booths. What mattered was his freedom to explore the limits of the craft called "mixology." Jardine offered him that freedom.

Batugo was so good at his craft that he won three national championships, more than any other bartender, and represented the U.S. Bartenders' Guild a record four times at the International Cocktail Competition. He won in 1973 with a drink he called The Icy Sea that incorporated rum, Amaretto, gin, triple sec, and grenadine along with a selection of tropical fruit juices. Midori, not included in that particular concoction, was among his favorite ingredients.

The word got out, and Tip's attracted a lot of customers. On a late-September day in 1955, one customer was particularly notable. He wasn't there for the drinks, though. It was too early for that. The young man in his mid-20s with a thick head of golden brown hair strode through the front door of Tip's Coffee Shop (the future site of J's) about 3 p.m. and caught the eye of a waitress named Althea McGuinness. He looked like a movie star, but he was dressed casually that day, wearing a white V-neck T-shirt and a pair of light blue jeans.

He came in with another guy, but it was the first man's face that McGuinness recognized.

A road sign at the junction of State Routes 41 and 46 marks the general vicinity where James Dean died in a crash on September 30, 1955.

Others knew who he was, too. Carmen Cummings, the manager on duty, told *The Newhall Signal* newspaper 30 years later that the young man sat at the counter and "we all recognized him." One of the waitresses said she served him apple pie and a glass of milk, before he and the other gentleman went on their way.

They were traveling north in a brand-new 550 Spyder with barely 300 miles on it that the man with the movie-star looks had bought while filming his second movie. The man with him, Rolf Weutherich, was his mechanic. The pair were bound for Salinas, where they planned to put the new car to the test on the racetrack.

The driver of the Porsche didn't have to be behind the wheel that day: A buddy in a station wagon right behind him was hauling a trailer intended to carry the silver speedster. But Weutherich, the mechanic, had suggested it might be a good idea to break the car in before they tried it out in a race.

That's exactly what they did. Anyone who has driven Highway 99 coming down out of the mountains at Grapevine knows what a temptation it is to hit the accelerator. It's hard enough staying under the speed limit on the steep downgrade as you approach the bottom, but once you get there the freeway flattens out into a near-perfect straightaway called the 17-mile tangent, sloping gently as it stretches northward toward the horizon.

A memorial stands at the Jack Ranch Cafe in Cholame, near the Highway 41/46 "Y," the site where actor James Dean was killed in a car crash after being cited for speeding on Highway 99.

Imagine what that temptation must have felt like to a man with a penchant for fast driving, behind the wheel of a car that was built for speed.

A few miles north of the Grapevine grade, they hit a place called Mettler. It's not much more than a frontage road with a few small businesses and scarcely 100 inhabitants. But on that late-September day in 1955, it was notable as the place where CHP officer Otie Hunter caught sight of that Porsche heading north on 99. It was midafternoon, and the car was doing 10 or 15 mph over the posted speed limit of 55. The station wagon, meanwhile, was having trouble keeping up and was running over the speed limit, too.

Hunter pulled the Porsche over, and the station wagon pulled in behind him. The driver of the sportscar admitted he'd been speeding, but he said the car wouldn't run well at lower speeds. It was new, and he was trying to loosen it up.

For Hunter, that was no excuse. He presented the man behind the wheel with a ticket, along with a few more words of friendly advice, then wrote a ticket for the driver of the station wagon, as well (he had been doing 65, which was 20 miles over the limit for vehicles

with trailers). Then, Hunter sent both drivers on their way, having obtained their word that they'd keep it under the limit.

They didn't.

Heading up 99, they cut over on Highway 46 and headed west toward the coast. A little more than two hours later, the driver of the Porsche was dead, killed in a head-on collision at 85 mph on a highway about 90 miles northwest of Mettler.

The signature on the ticket that was never paid belonged to a man named James Dean.

WAFFLES AND THOROUGHBREDS

In the heyday of roadside restaurants, there wasn't a lot of specialization. Even if a restaurant was known for a certain specialty, chances are you could find a varied selection of dishes. Tip Jardine opened his third eatery, for example, with the promise of "food to please any palate." The sign on the roof drove home the message, advertising "thick steaks" and "thin pancakes."

With a clientele that ranged from truck drivers to tourists, from commuters to CHP officers, it just made sense to diversify. Most places weren't Mexican or Italian, steakhouses or breakfast joints. They were any number of those things, all rolled into one, often under a sign that read in large, eye-catching letters "EAT."

Accompanying many of these signs was a neon martini glass, sometimes tilted to one side and nearly always containing the popular green olive at the end of a toothpick. These weren't just places to fill one's tummy—they offered the warming comfort of hard liquor, to boot. Many were built alongside motels, where the weary and sometimes slightly inebriated traveler might find a pillow on which to rest his head.

Tiny's Waffle Shop, for example, operated one of its locations in conjunction with Motel Fresno on Old 99.

Milt's in Bakersfield has been around since 1964, an era in which numerous roadside signs such as this one invited motorists to "EAT" at their establishments.

Despite its name, Tiny's wasn't just a waffle shop. A 1942 menu from its Sacramento restaurant shows an array of dishes, including french-fried Eastern oysters, prime rib, veal, potato salad, a Monte Cristo sandwich, melba peaches, and even Southern-fried young rabbit. One of his signature dishes was "Chicken in the Rough." The menu was anything but tiny, and so was the restaurant's owner: At 6-foot-3 and about 350 pounds, William W. "Tiny" Naylor was described in one press account as "bigger than Man Mountain Dean," an early professional wrestler who also played briefly in the nascent National Football League.

Naylor opened his first eatery in Fresno around the age of 30 and soon added locations up and down Highway 99 in such towns as Merced, Modesto, and Bakersfield. Other locations sprang up in places like Eureka, Los Banos, Oakland, Sacramento, Salinas, San Francisco, San Jose (where Naylor installed an electrical play-by-play scoreboard to create a prototypical sports bar), and even Reno, Nevada.

By 1939, Naylor's establishments were serving between 10,000 and 12,000 people a day. And by 1946, the chain numbered 32 restaurants up and down the state. Meanwhile, Naylor—sometimes known as the "Waffle Man"—was adding other brands to his portfolio: a chain of diners called Biff's, named for his son, as well as a Tiny Naylor's restaurant just off Highway 99 in Newhall, just a few miles south of Tip's. There was also an iconic Hollywood drive-in, built in Googie-style architecture, at Sunset Boulevard and La Brea.

All this success made Naylor wealthy, and he used his new liquid assets to invest in another passion of his: horse racing. Naylor began building a stable of thoroughbreds, which he raced at tracks like Bay Meadows and Santa Anita. His horses won a series of high-profile races, and at one time he was considered the No. 2 breeder in the state. Naylor owned a 660-acre ranch near Riverside, where at one point he considered building a golf course in partnership with famed jockeys Eddie Arcaro and Johnny Longdon, but he sold the spread in 1955 and retired from the business due to poor health.

He was also associated with another famous jockey, George "The Iceman" Woolf. Perhaps best known as the jockey who rode Seabiscuit to an upset victory over War Admiral in 1938, Woolf also won the Preakness and 720 other races during his career. He was, like Naylor, a restaurateur, having founded the Derby near the Santa Anita racetrack northeast of Los Angeles, where he had often visited the winner's circle.

But it became the scene of a tragedy in 1946 when Woolf was riding Naylor's horse Please Me. Woolf had enjoyed a record season, with 14 stakes wins, two years earlier, but had ridden less frequently since then and reportedly was planning to retire. Unlike many of the races Naylor's horses entered, it was a relatively small-time affair: an allowance race with a purse of just $3,500.

Jockey George Woolf with Seabiscuit, whom he rode to victory in a famed 1938 match race with War Admiral. Woolf was riding a horse owned by restaurateur Tiny Naylor in 1946 when tragedy struck. *Seabiscuit Heritage Foundation/public domain photo.*

Please Me was running in the clear, trailing five other horses at the clubhouse turn, when he appeared to stumble and Woolf went flying over the horse's head.

"Woolf had a tight hold on Please Me coming around the turn," race official Herman Sharpe said afterward. "The horse stumbled and jerked Woolfe over his head."

Please Me, now riderless, went on to sprint past the rest of the horses in the field and cross the finish line first as Woolf lay prone on the track. He was rushed to the hospital but never regained consciousness; his death was ruled the result of a fractured skull and brain injuries.

Three years later, a statue of Woolf was unveiled at Santa Anita. It was paid for in large measure by Tiny Naylor, who donated the proceeds from the sale of one of his horses.

PERRY'S IN TULARE

Tiny's Waffle Shop wasn't the only place to offer comfort food and a cup o' joe to travelers along 99.

Motorists passing through Madera could stop at the Fruit Basket off Old 99 (Gateway Drive), which lasted for nearly four decades and served what one customer described as "without a doubt, the best chicken fried steak ever." Other items on the menu included meatloaf, fried chicken, and taco soup.

Farther south, Hoot Perry of Tulare built up a mini-chain of diners and coffee shops that were anything but Starbuck's. No $3 lattes or $4 iced coffee served here. In fact, Perry put on a promotion at his Tulare Inn Coffee Shop and Chuck Wagon Restaurant in Tulare where you could buy a cup of java for a nickel back in 1977—including refills (the previous price was a whopping 20 cents). The reduced price wasn't just good for business, it was good for the waitresses, too.

"Now people come up and tell me they feel guilty laying just a nickel on the counter," Perry said at the time. "But the girls' tips have increased considerably."

Hoot Perry's son, Ron, was the merchandising manager and came up with other promotions, such as a TV give-away and "wooden nickels" that could be exchanged for a cup of coffee. Sambo's ran a similar promotion, which may or may not have been a coincidence considering Ron Perry majored in hotel and restaurant management at San Francisco City College, where he shared classes with Sambo's co-founder, Sam Battistone. Perry doesn't remember who thought up the idea first.

The Perrys weren't new to the business at that point. In fact, Hoot Perry had owned the Chuck Wagon for three decades. Like many San Joaquin Valley businessmen, he'd come from Oklahoma during the Dust Bowl years, leaving home at the age of 18 on an eight-wheel coal car and riding the rails out to California. He wound up in Long Beach, where he got his first job in the restaurant business. The year was 1934.

"It wasn't long before I became a baker's helper, then a cook's helper, and finally cook," he said in a 1970 interview. "When I started, I was earning $11 a week and got one day off every other week."

A billboard along U.S. 99 advertises Perry's Ranch House Café, using its familiar chef logo/mascot.
From the collection of Ron Perry.

Perry joined the Navy in 1942 and was a cook in Honolulu. Starting in 1945, after his discharge, he and his mother spent two years running a lunch counter and fountain operation at a drugstore in Shafter.

Two years later, Perry started scouting around for business opportunities and ended up buying a drive-in restaurant in Tulare. It was on J Street—then the alignment of U.S. 99—near Pleasant Street on the north end of town. There, Perry faced an unusual task for a businessman: He had to actually get rid of customers.

"Perry's Drive-In became the 'it' place for the young crowd, and dad had to call the sheriff many times because of some rowdy teens," said Ron Perry, Hoot Perry's son. The younger Perry started out washing glasses at the drive-in when he was 8 or 9 years old and eventually became a partner with his father in their Fresno restaurant, Perry's Ranch House Chuck Wagon.

"With the drive-in, we had a real good business, but we liked to have good business inside, too," he wrote. "On Friday and Saturday nights, lots of times, the girls would have as high as 200 or 300 cars in the drive-in lot—that was throughout the whole night. It was always 3 o'clock by the time I got home in bed on Friday and Saturday.

"We had a lot of people on Saturday night when the dances were through. When the Murphy's Thunderbowl,

where they had the midget car races, quit, we had a huge crowd come in from that. Some of the midget drivers went on to become world famous, as one of them won the Indianapolis 500. His son later on has driven in it two or three times also. He was just a little boy when they came in. I can't think of their name. I can remember it was a Russian name, Vakovitch."

Perry had the name almost right. The driver he had in mind was Bill Vukovich of Fresno, who won the Indy 500 in 1953 and '54 and was leading the following year when he was killed in a chain-reaction crash on the 57th lap.

"Dad really wanted it to be more of a family restaurant, and most of the time, it was," Ron Perry said. "Oh, the neatest thing: He had an ice cream machine and made his own ice cream. Health law stated it had to be in a separate enclosed area, so Dad built a cubicle with glass windows so people could see the machine and ice cream being made. He also had a Chicken in the Rough franchise. Oh, and of course, a jukebox. Awning was added all around, and it looked like the typical '50s drive-in of *American Graffiti.*"

Perry also had a contract to feed the braceros (Mexican field workers in the United States under a temporary arrangement).

Hoot Perry (right) was a cook in the U.S. Navy from 1941 to 1945. This photo was probably taken at the Royal Hawaiian in Honolulu, site of the Officers Club during World War II. *From the collection of Ron Perry.*

"Dad fenced the back area of the drive-in with chicken wire and made a backdoor to the men's bathroom," Ron Perry recalled. "They came in one door of the restaurant and went to the back of the café, where we sold them sandwiches, milk, and fruit."

Perry's drive-in proved so popular he soon expanded, adding a second restaurant in the city as well as one in Bakersfield he dubbed Hoot Perry's Salad Bowl. In the late 1960s, he bought the Ranch Kitchen in Fresno and opened another restaurant by the same name just south of Tulare in Tipton. Those who stopped in for a bite at his restaurants included Efrem Zimbalist Jr., Fred MacMurray of *My Three Sons* fame, Gene Autry, Roy Rogers, Dale Evans, and comedian Pat Paulson.

Perry chose the locations for his restaurants by design, with the two Tulare stops situated on opposite sides of 99 just south of town. The first, which he built in 1954, was Perry's Sky Ranch Café at Avenue 200 just west of 99. Perry realized the 99 Tulare bypass would open the following year, and he wanted a location that would draw travelers off the new freeway. With the Sky Ranch Motel on the same property, Perry would be able to count on drivers stopping for more than just a cup of coffee: They might pull off the road for dinner, spend the night in the motel, and visit his café again for breakfast the following day.

The biggest days for business were Friday nights and Saturday mornings, when traffic would come through from Los Angeles.

"He was well aware of the traffic and what places could be seen, and easy access," Ron Perry said. "The drive-in north of Tulare was his first in 1947, but the freeway went around Tulare [in the] early 1950s, and Dad found a location just south of Tulare before the freeway went around—at the Tulare Air Park. The Sky Ranch Motel had just opened, and the owner was looking for a person to put a café in on the corner, so Dad invested everything and built there. It really paid off."

The elder Perry, however, knew of an even better location just across the freeway and a couple of miles north at Paige Avenue, where six members of the Tulare Baptist Church had purchased property to build the Tulare Inn Motel. Perry signed on as the seventh member of the partnership, which spent $418,000 to build a 32-room

Perry's Tulare Inn was on the east side of the freeway in Tulare at Paige Avenue. It's seen here during the 1980s.
From the collection of Ron Perry.

motel alongside Perry's Tulare Inn Coffee Shop & Chuck Wagon. This was, according to Ron Perry, "where he really built his reputation."

It remained open for the next four decades, serving its signature dishes, fried chicken and fried sea bass, along with homemade potato salad, macaroni salad, pies, cakes, and pastries. A full-time baker at the Chuck Wagon made more than 100 pies a day and supplied them to all of Perry's Tulare-area restaurants. "I think he was the first to popularize the all-you-can-eat buffet that began in the 1950s," Ron Perry said of his father.

Meanwhile, the Sky Ranch Café and motel eventually changed hands; the neon Sky Ranch sign with its iconic arrow was changed to read "Mom's Motel," and the rusting sign remained visible from Highway 99 long after the structure itself had been demolished. (The café

Interior view of Perry's Ranch Kitchen Café in Tipton, off U.S. 99 at Avenue 152. *From the collection of Ron Perry.*

itself continued to operate under different ownership as of 2014, when it was doing business as T-Bones Ranch House.)

All these businesses were located alongside a major highway, guaranteeing strong business. The Fresno location, which Perry leased from 1969 through 1971, was along Highway 41, and the Bakersfield stop operated on Old 99—Union Avenue—at Highway 58 for nearly a decade and a half starting in 1968.

Perry's coffee shop locations roughly halfway between Fresno and Bakersfield made them ideal for truck

drivers in need of a quick pick-me-up and families who wanted a sandwich or a slice of pie. Perry opened a new restaurant, the Ranch Kitchen Café, in 1962 just a few hundred yards north of the Sky Ranch site at the same intersection.

Another restaurant, Perry's Ranch Kitchen, opened in 1967 about 10 miles south of Tulare in Tipton, at Avenue 152. It was operated by Perry's nephew, Mel Boyd, who later changed the name to Banjo Café.

"Dad always tried to promote the highway cafés as a stopping point for gas and going to visit Yosemite or

Sequoia," Ron Perry said. "We had guests who would stay at the Tulare Inn motel and visit the parks. One family returned every year for 10 years or more to stay at the motel because they enjoyed our hot summers."

During the 1960s and '70s, Hoot Perry was one of the top 10 employers in Tulare, with more than 100 people on the payroll at his three restaurants. Perry used to joke that half of the city worked for him at one time or another, and the other half were his customers. Even though an estimated 40 percent of Perry's business was local, highway traffic still brought in the lion's share of his customers, Ron Perry said.

"We did our best business at the Tulare Inn during the 1960s and '70s. But by the time I-5 opened, it took a big chunk of traffic from the 99. Also, during the 1970s, fast-food franchises expanded rapidly and America's eating habits changed."

The last Perry's restaurant to remain open, the Tulare Inn Coffee Shop, closed in 1999, ending a long run of success for the small chain.

Hoot Perry summed it up: "The San Joaquin Valley and its people have been good to me, my wife, and my children."

THE TORCH RUN

One of Ron Perry's most vivid memories on Highway 99 wasn't made at any of the family restaurants but rather on the road itself.

The year was 1960 and the occasion was the soon-to-be-held Winter Olympic Games at Squaw Valley, just west of Lake Tahoe. With the Olympics right here in California, organizers saw a golden opportunity to get the entire state into the Olympic spirit by organizing a relay to transport the torch north from Los Angeles, site of the 1932 Olympics. It wasn't the first event of its kind—the tradition dated back to the Summer Games of '36 in Berlin—but it was, to that point, the longest torch relay ever undertaken in advance of a Winter Olympics.

Ron Perry carries the Olympic torch in as part of the 1960 relay. *From the collection of Ron Perry.*

Instead of merely flying the torch in from Norway to Reno and bearing it thence on the relatively short jaunt west to Tahoe, organizers plotted a course from L.A. up Highway 99 that would cover 600 miles in 19 days. The torch was to be flown into Los Angeles International Airport, and taken by helicopter to the Los Angeles Memorial Coliseum. From there, it would make its way up the spine of California along the historic highway, passing through Glendale and Burbank (where runners persevered despite a downpour), then to Gorman and Tejon Pass on the third day.

The relay continued through Bakersfield, Delano, Fresno, Modesto, and Roseville, all locations along U.S. 99. Memorable stops included the ninth day in the inland port city of Stockton, where the torch was taken aboard the yacht *Adventuress* of San Francisco's Great Golden Fleet for a side trip to San Francisco, as well as a ceremony presided over by Governor Edmund G. "Pat" Brown on the capitol steps. Tulare was a noteworthy site, as well: The city had produced two-time decathlon gold medalist Bob Mathias, as well as his Tulare Union High School classmate Sim Iness, who claimed gold in the discus at the '52 Summer Games and was the first man ever to hurl the disc more than 190 feet.

For the task of carrying the torch up the highway, organizers enlisted more than 700 high school athletes to join several medalists in the traditional torch relay. Among them were members of San Joaquin Valley cross-country teams, including the squad from Tulare Union, where Ron Perry was a 16-year-old junior.

"Our coach, Ernie Lambert, arranged for me to carry the torch one mile from just south of the Elk Bayou bridge on the 99 freeway to the K Street exit just north of the Tulare Airport, running past Perry's Sky Ranch Café—our family restaurant," Perry recalled.

(You won't find the K Street exit there today. One of the highway's few left-lane exits, carrying traffic onto the older business alignment of U.S. 99, it was removed a few years ago.)

Donning special "torch relay" T-shirts and running shorts, Perry and his Tulare Union teammates set out on February 4, 1960, a morning draped in the Tule fog that was typical of the valley on a winter's morn. They were dropped off at their designated spots along the highway, and the sky began to brighten a bit. The fog was lifting, an encouraging sign.

The relay participants were ready, having prepared for the task of running a mile with the torch by carrying an 8-pound shot during practice. But there was one thing Ron Perry hadn't prepared for.

"After waiting about an hour, I saw the Highway Patrol car lights, followed by Donnie Manro, my teammate, and the official car—a French Renault—behind the runner," he remembered. "As Donnie handed me the torch, he said two words: 'No flame.' I looked, and sure enough, there was no flame in the torch."

Concerned, Perry slowed his stride and yelled back toward the official car, repeating his teammate's words, "No flame!"

"They yelled back, 'Keep going!' so I picked up my pace and headed north."

When he had completed his one-mile leg of the relay, Perry handed the torch off to Tulare Union's top runner, Larry Grimes, who in turn would pass it on to Mathias and Iness. Apparently, however, the organizers didn't care for the idea of the famed gold medalists carrying an extinguished torch (so much for the idea of the "eternal" Olympic flame).

"Larry took the torch and was ready to give his all running when the officials in the Renault told him to stop," Perry said. "The officials then took out a Bic lighter and relit the flame so he could hand it off to Bob and Sim, and they would light a special large torch on the corner of K and Kern Street in a special ceremony in downtown Tulare."

That special torch remains in Tulare today, on display outside Bob Mathias Stadium at Tulare Union High School. Perry and his teammates were treated to a VIP banquet that evening, and each received a commemorative pin and certificate for taking part in the relay. Perry later misplaced both but kept the T-shirt in which he ran that memorable mile.

"I guess that was my 15 minutes of fame … but no flame," he quipped.

9

ACCOMMODATIONS

The Highland Lodge's imposing sign survived into the new century south of Bakersfield along Union Avenue, the old U.S. 99 alignment.

Most people associate tents and cabins with the wilderness, not the highway, but there was a time when most highways stretched through miles and miles of wilderness. Some still do. Travelers on 99 complain, even today, that there's "nothing to see" along the flat, relatively straight asphalt river that bisects the Golden State. (Perhaps they just don't know where to look.) But imagine what it must have been like in the early years of the 20th century.

Thomas D. Murphy, who produced the first edition of his book *On Sunset Highways* in 1915, noted that a trip from Fresno to Bakersfield meant "a day on rotten roads (with) hardly a decent mile between two towns." He followed the Southern Pacific rail line for a full day "over a neglected, sandy trail, with occasional broken-up oiled stretches."

Murphy even went so far as to declare the land "as barren and uncompromising as the Sahara," although his revised version of the same book, released a scant six years later, acknowledged a great improvement in the state of the road. By 1928, the U.S. Department of Agriculture was hailing it as the longest continuously improved highway in the country. Just two years earlier, the road had been incorporated into the fledgling U.S. highway system, becoming a charter member of a club that included the likes of Route 66 and Highway 101.

Still, it was a mere hint of what it would soon become: the bustling Main Street of California. Few cities rose above the level plane of the horizon, and those that did were hardly great urban centers. In 1926, Tulare's population was a mere 6,000, Merced's was just 7,000, and Modesto's stood at 17,000. What passed for a metropolis south of Sacramento? Well, Bakersfield had 30,000 people, Stockton with its busy inland port boasted 50,000, and Fresno topped the list at 75,000.

In between, the road bisected fields and farmland, where plenty of oil derricks reached toward the sky across the southern half of Kern County.

If you needed to stop for the night, your options were limited. Larger cities such as Fresno and Bakersfield had fancy hotels, but what if you couldn't afford the luxury they offered (or just didn't want to tip a bellhop)? What would you do if your eyelids started to feel heavy miles away from any such accommodations?

In the early days of road tripping, the answer was easy: You'd bring along your own tent, bedding, and supplies, and you'd camp out by the side of the road. By the 1920s, the practice of camping at the roadside had become all the rage. A newspaper article from the summer of 1921 documented the trend: "Within the last three or four years, there has been a growing up among motor car

Auto camps such as this one in Tulare County, photographed in 1936 by Dorothea Lange, started out attracting camping adventurers. But as roadside lodging became more sophisticated, they increasingly drew migrant laborers and indigents. *Library of Congress/public domain.*

owners that amounts to a cult, which we may call the fraternity of the motor car gypsies. . . . An increasing number of motorists are discovering the delights of combining motoring with camping. The freedom from convention that such a life brings, the opportunity to travel as far and stay as long as one may happen to desire, satisfies the wanderlust that lies in each of us."

Tents started at about $15 and were available in materials such as balloon silk and khaki, some of them specially made so they attached to the side of your car. Special cots were available to fit in automobiles, and sleeping trailers were available for $100 and up. Soon, camping stoves hit the market, as well, and travelers brought pots, pans, and eating utensils for use at mealtimes. There was a reason folks called them "tin can tourists."

As one might imagine, not everyone took kindly to the practice of motorists just pulling off at some random spot by the side of the road and pitching camp for the night. Sometimes, travelers found themselves chased off for trespassing on private property; on other occasions, pulling off the paved roadway meant getting stuck in the mud, especially in a car weighed down by all that heavy camping gear.

Sometimes, these highway adventurers were mistaken for homeless vagabonds "whose ramshackle, home-made trailer or house-car was to be avoided on the road or shooed out of the pasture lot if it came to rest there." The U.S. Forest Service, meanwhile, lamented that some campers neglected to clean up after themselves. A public service announcement issued in 1926 decried "tin cans and rubbish-befouled camp grounds," despairing that "smouldering fires which result in blackened hillsides are all too common monuments to the American tourist's discourtesy. The 'tin can tourist' is becoming a disgrace to our outdoors."

In response to such concerns, communities started setting up designated spots for overnight stays. The idea was to provide a secure place for these "tin can tourists" to spend the night for a modest fee. Auto camps, as they were called, benefited the communities, as well. Their locations on the outskirts of town helped local retailers win back customers they had lost at the outset of the gypsy craze, when travelers had become enthralled with the idea of packing everything they needed for the trip

ahead of time. If they forgot something, it was much easier to run into town for supplies from a nearby auto camp than it was from the open highway in the middle of nowhere.

As early as 1920, some 300 cities nationwide had set up municipal campsites, and the practice of "gypsying" became so popular that, in 1928, the Associated Oil Company printed a free booklet (available at its service stations) listing more than a thousand auto camps up and down the Pacific coast. Nine years later, California alone had 1,440 of them, and that same year saw the release of *Back to Nature*, one of 17 films in a series of low-budget comedies that featured the fictional Jones Family. In this, the third installment, they were cast as "Tin-Can Tourists in a Trailer."

Sacramento operated one such municipal camp off Highway 99 in 1926. One travel guide proclaimed that the site had "all the conveniences" and a good reputation: "No shade or cabins, but (it) has many shelter booths with tables and ovens; supplies." A night's stay would set you back 50 cents.

Other camps had a little more to offer. By the mid-'20s, several had started to add more permanent structures referred to in the guides as cabins or cottages. Kingsburg offered a place called the Welcome Inn, where you could camp free for the night in a space that offered "shade and

Cabins were an early form of permanent roadside accommodation, forerunners of the motel that endured through the 1930s. Dorothea Lange photographed these in March of 1939 on U.S. 99 between Tulare and Fresno.
Library of Congress/public domain.

Some early motel cabins survived and continued to operate into the new millennium, such as these at Cynthia's Motel on Gateway Drive (Business 99) in Madera.

between as adventure started taking a backseat to convenience. No longer known as auto camps, the evolving roadside rest sites were more often referred to as auto courts or motor courts by the 1930s. The "court" referred to a U-shaped court-yard that was a common feature of many such establishments, some of which offered attached carports next to their cabins.

These places weren't luxury hotels by any stretch of the imagination. This was long before the days of in-room HBO, microwaves, and continental breakfasts. Most accommodations were small, sparsely furnished one-room cabins. You might find a bed and linens inside, or you might not—or you might be able to obtain one for an added fee. (A 1933 touring guide featured a photo of Anderson's Motor Inn in Merced off 99, whose sign advertised "furnished rooms," implying that competing courts might not offer the same luxury.) Moreover, you could count on sharing the "facilities" with other overnight guests. One writer, reminiscing in *The Daily Courier* newspaper in Connellsville, Pennsylvania, described the old auto courts as having "linoleum floors, creaky bed springs, faded

grass." Use of the kitchen or shower, however, would cost you 15 cents, and you could upgrade to a cabin for $1.50. In Bateman's Camp at McFarland, you could get a cabin for $1, but linens would cost you a quarter extra. The fees were modest, but they were enough to keep away squatters, vagrants, and other "undesirables."

As the municipal camps started drawing more customers, it was only a matter of time before entrepreneurs began wanting in on the action. Before long, most of the roadside stops were for-profit enterprises offering their guests permanent or at least semipermanent structures for overnight guests, often alongside a café, a garage, or a service station. Pure campsites became fewer and farther

3-D's Motel in Madera, just down the road from Cynthia's, features the kind of carports that were common for motor courts of the era.

curtains, and towels you wouldn't want to use—let alone steal."

Most of the motor courts were mom-and-pop operations that sprang up by the side of the road as farmers and other landowners came to recognize the potential for profit.

BROWN'S AUTO CAMP

A select few remain in business today, having adapted to changes in the travel industry that range from timeshares to online reservations. One such establishment, the Cave Springs Resort, sits nestled among a grove of Redwoods along Old 99, beside the Sacramento River in Dunsmuir. The "mom-and-pop" label fits perfectly at Cave Springs, where owner Louie Dewey was born a year after his mother and father bought what was then Brown's Modern Motor Lodge from another couple, Clint and Ida May Brown.

Clint Brown had considered buying the Castle Crags Resort beside the rail line a few miles to the south, but his wife talked him out of it and they leased the place instead. The year was 1916. That same year, the new highway bridge went up, accelerating the shift from railway to roadway. It wasn't long before the auto camping craze set in, and the Browns were poised to capitalize. Instead of staking their future on Castle Crags, they paid $2,500 for a piece of land motorists were already using as an informal roadside camp. The only building there at the time was an old Native American shack at a place called Cave Springs, a reference to the soda water springs bubbling up from a cave down by the river.

You can still spend the night in cabins dating from 1922 at Brown's Auto Camp, now known as Cave Springs Resort, in Dunsmuir.

The Browns installed toilets and showers to serve the auto campers in 1922, and three years later built the first six cabins along a low bluff overlooking the river. They called their venture Brown's Auto Camp, later changing the name to Brown's Auto Park. Dewey's parents, Bob and Lois, bought the establishment in partnership with another couple in 1946. None of them had any experience in the business, and they didn't expect it to become a long-term endeavor: "People don't buy a motel and stay in it for generations," Louie Dewey said. "It was right after the war, and everyone was traveling. The idea was to build a motel, make some money, and buy a bigger one in a couple of years and then move on."

The new owners began upgrading the old auto park in 1950, and another couple bought a small diner across the driveway from the Cave Springs office called the Koffie Kup, changing the name slightly to Ma Green's Koffee Kup. The modest eatery and soda fountain could fit eight customers in its two booths, six more at the counter and a few more on benches outside. Lisa Green served homemade pies, burgers, and chicken-fried steak there until she passed away in 1965.

The Deweys' original partners, meanwhile, sold out to them in 1955. The cabins from the days of Brown's Auto Park continued to attract weary travelers, fishermen, and other vacationers, but as times changed, so did the business. The new interstate bypassed the old highway, and the owners had to adapt.

"The business changed," Louie Dewey said. "That prompted my father to convert empty spaces into mobile home spaces, because there were a number of construction workers who came to work on the new highway."

A few years later, the couple added the final piece of the puzzle: a motel. "My mom wanted a new house, and my dad said, 'Let's have a whole new motel, and then we can have a new house.'" The motel phase actually incorporated the Deweys' new home, complete with a custom living room designed to Lois Dewey's specifications, a kitchen, and other living quarters. The Deweys began planning the motel phase in the 1950s and completed it in 1967. By this time, it was clear they weren't going anywhere.

Louie Dewey and his wife, Belinda, continued to operate Cave Springs as of 2014, maintaining the 16 original cabins with "all the amenities of 1923," along with the motel and vacation rentals. A few celebrities have stayed there, Dewey said, declining to name them in order to protect his clients' privacy: "We've got five generations, six generations of people coming back."

NETWORKING

Family-owned-and-operated motels such as Cave Springs, where the owners live on site, have become increasingly rare over the years now that large chains account for a higher percentage of available rooms.

The process of industry consolidation started in the early 1930s, when motor courts and inns began forming networks, referring customers to an overnight stop up the road in exchange for a good word from its proprietor to travelers heading the opposite direction. The loose networks that resulted from such recommendations became more formalized with the advent of associations such as United Motor Courts, founded by a group of independent court owners based in Santa Barbara. Being part of such an association amounted to a seal of approval, guaranteeing travelers that accommodations would meet a certain standard.

"Be assured of restful comfort in any one of these United Motor Courts," a guidebook published in 1933 proclaimed. "While one United Motor Court may be Spanish, another Old English, and another Rustic in design—thus giving you that variety which makes travel interesting and memorable—the interior accommodations are almost identical, and all planned with one

Motels like the Tropics Motor Hotel along Indio Boulevard in Indio marked a step away from the era of cabins and motor courts.

thought: The comfort and well-being of you, your family, and your friends."

United Motor Courts could be found up and down Old 99, making it easy to plan your trip to include stopovers at member locations. Starting down south in Pomona, you could stay at the Big Oak Court along the highway, then perhaps spend a night at the Gypsy Trail or Clark's Motor Lodge, about six miles north of the freeway (off closely parallel Route 66) in Pasadena. In the San Joaquin Valley, you could rest your head at the Merced Motor Tavern in Merced. Or, if you wanted to drive a little farther, Modesto offered Hammer's Tourist Cottages and Sacramento beckoned with the Victoria Motor Lodge and its distinctive pyramid-shaped roofs. Traveling on to Redding, you'd find the A-1 Motor Court in the heart of the city, along with a bonus treat to beat the heat: a milkshake stand right there in the driveway.

The advent of the motor court marked the beginning of a divergence in styles for highway travelers. As time went on, one group graduated from tents to increasingly sophisticated campers and trailers (Winnebago, anyone?), which they parked for the night at the successors to the auto camps: places like the Good Sam Club and KOA campgrounds. The other group preferred the motor courts and their successors, the motor hotel. Or motel.

Motels were another step up from the motor courts, falling somewhere between the auto camps and hotels in terms of amenities. Unlike a hotel, which often rose several stories above the heart

The Astro was at the far north end of Fresno's motel row, separated from most of the other motor inns farther south along the section of U.S. 99 known as Motel Drive.

North of Fresno's Roeding Park, travelers encountered Motel Drive, where a series of motor inns point the way toward downtown.

To distinguish their establishments from one another, owners often adopted unique themes and erected colorful neon signs. The Wigwam Village motels took a unique approach, creating cabins in the shape of Native American dwellings. Three of the seven original wigwam clusters were still standing as of 2014, including the last one, which was built in 1949 along old Route 66 in San Bernardino. It features 19 wood-frame dwellings fortified by concrete and covered in stucco, each rising to a height of 30 feet.

In the community of Sun Valley, along San Fernando Road, you can find the Pink Motel, which looks like something out of an old *Happy Days*

of a major city, motels retained the low-slung look of a motor court while offering a wider array of comforts. Usually one or two stories tall, travelers could find them along 99, often clustered in "motel rows" on the edge of towns large and small.

In fact, drivers became accustomed to seeing a line of motels along the roadside as they approached the next city on their route. Redding had what it called the "Miracle Mile," featuring such stops as the 99, Manhattan, Monterey, and Casa Blanca motels. As you approached Bakersfield from the south, you'd pass through a similar motel row, though many of the old places are now gone.

episode. In fact, it has been used in several film shoots as a stand-in for various fictional '50s locations. The motel, built in 1946, was the brainchild of Pennsylvania transplant Joseph Thomulka, who chose a location along what was then U.S. 99. Thomulka opened his flamingo-hued hostel with 20 rooms in an area that, at the time, was populated by walnut groves. Thomulka gave the property a tropical feel by planting palm trees and put in some citrus fruit trees in the motel's courtyard. A couple of years later, he added the Pink Café (later renamed Cadillac Jack's) next door. Adding to the atmosphere was the motel's fish-shaped swimming pool, lately emptied of water and transformed into a popular spot for skateboarders to ply their trade.

The Pink Motel is one of the few motor inns remaining along the long, straight strip of asphalt that once served as motel row for the Los Angeles area. When Interstate 5 went in parallel to Old 99, replacing the venerable highway as the main artery connecting the valley with downtown L.A., most of the roadside motels closed their doors. The Pink Motel, however, found new life as a set for movies, television shows, and music videos, while staying open as a unique destination for nostalgia-loving vacationers.

Sammy Davis Jr. did some acting there. So did Bruce Willis. If you rent a copy of *The Whole Ten Yards*, a 2004 comedy-adventure featuring Willis and Matthew Perry, you'll recognize the distinctive motel, which also makes an appearance in the 2003 film *House of Sand and Fog*. TV series that have used the Pink as a backdrop include *MacGyver*, *The Rockford Files*, *Dexter*, and *The O.C.* And the Mavericks filmed a music video for their 1999 hit "Here Comes My Baby" there.

The Pink Motel, like many of its contemporaries, drew bleary-eyed midnight motorists with a neon standard that stood out against the velvet sky. Such distinctive signs towered above the highway, lighting up the night in an exotic (or garish, depending on one's point of view) hues. The Highland Lodge south of Bakersfield, for example, still boasted a towering, sea-blue and pink sign as of 2014, though the establishment itself was far less impressive. The Fresno Motel's sign featured the image of a bikini-clad woman in a bathing cap doing a swan dive into a pool of wavy blue water, an effective way of shouting to the world, "We have a pool!" It was one of several you'd see along U.S. 99 just north of town if you drove in from the north on a road trip.

The Pink Motel is one of the few remaining motor inns along San Fernando Road, formerly U.S. 99, now a largely industrial area in the Sun Valley neighborhood of the San Fernando Valley.

At the far north end of Fresno's strip was the Astro, separated from most of the other motels in the area by a mile or two and featuring a star set in a circle atop an ascending spire, all lit up in red neon.

RISE OF THE MEGA MOTEL

Motel strips such as Fresno's inspired the ultimate strip—in Las Vegas. Contrary to the legend that has grown up around mobster Bugsy Siegel's ownership of the Flamingo in the mid-'40s, he wasn't the first resort owner on the strip. That honor belonged to Tom Hull, who purchased a series of movie theaters before getting out of that business and jumping into the lodging industry with both feet. In 1932, he bought up a number of metropolitan hotels, including the Hotel Senator in Sacramento, the Roosevelt in Hollywood, the Mayfair in Los Angeles, and the Californian in Fresno.

The Depression, however, was taking a toll on the hotel industry, which served as many as three-quarters of traveling lodgers the year of the crash (1929). In the ensuing decade, that figure plummeted to just one-third, as many consumers chose instead to lodge at roadside motels. They were cheaper, and you could drive right up to the door without tipping a valet to park your vehicle or a bellhop to carry your bags to the 10th floor.

Hull's vision was to take the convenience of a motel and add the amenities of a big-city hotel, creating a roadside resort: "Superb hotel accommodations in bungalow form," as one postcard put it. He brought this vision to fruition in the form of El Rancho hotels, which he built in cities such as Fresno and Sacramento, where he already had a presence as a hotelier. The Fresno motel, just across the street from the city's major park along 99, featured hacienda-style architecture: white-walled, red-tiled cottages arrayed in a broad semicircle around a landscaped central courtyard. Rows of palm trees lined three large grassy areas. The pool, at the center of the

courtyard, was shielded from the road by a building that housed the front office. A distinctive towering windmill, the chain's signature piece, rose from the top of it.

A western theme dominated the El Rancho, right down to the Wagon Wheel Tavern, where travelers could unwind after hours behind the wheel. Hotel-style amenities also included air-conditioned rooms, private baths and showers, a coffee shop, and a dining room.

The Fresno location opened in 1939, and it wasn't long before Hull sought to reproduce his vision in another western city. As the story goes, he was traveling on Highway 91 when one of his tires went flat just outside Las Vegas. A companion headed into town to seek help, while Hull passed the time counting cars as they passed on the highway. By the time the tire was repaired, Hull

The El Rancho Vegas, seen in this 1940 postcard, featured the chain's trademark windmill, just like the one along U.S. 99 in Fresno. *Burton Frasher/public domain.*

was so impressed with the number of travelers whizzing past that he decided Vegas would be a perfect place to build the next El Rancho.

Hull bought 33 acres off the highway just south of town, at San Francisco (later renamed Sahara) Avenue. The price was a mere $5,000. Then he set about building his resort, teaming up with the same architect who had designed the El Ranchos in Fresno and Sacramento. Wayne McAllister had also designed the Agua Caliente resort in Tijuana, and he lent the same sort of flavor to the El Rancho chain. As with the California sites, the new Rancho Vegas featured the distinctive windmill tower as its centerpiece. Lit up in pink-and-white neon, it rose 50 feet above the main building. It had a Wagon Wheel Tavern, just like the one in Fresno, with the rooms laid out in the same semicircular pattern.

It was bigger, though, as everything in Vegas would be, from the hotels themselves to the massive neon signs out front. Originally consisting of 63 bungalows, the Rancho Vegas eventually grew to include 220 rooms. The hotel was different from others in the chain in one important respect: It had gambling. Modest by later standards, its casino included a couple of blackjack tables, a roulette wheel, a craps table, and 70 slot machines. It also kicked off an enduring Las Vegas tradition with its Chuck Wagon buffet, the first all-you-can-eat operation in the city and, according to some accounts, anywhere in the United States.

Hull didn't own the Vegas property for long, selling it a year after it opened. In the "bigger is better" tradition of the city, other resorts soon surpassed it in terms of hype and glitz, including Siegel's Flamingo, which opened five years later and is often credited (erroneously) with being the first resort on the Strip. The El Rancho continued to attract big names in entertainment, however. The likes of Milton Berle, Jackie Gleason, Jerry Lewis, and Sammy Davis Jr. all performed there, and comedian Joe E. Lewis was the regular act. Joanne Woodward and Paul Newman even got married at the El Rancho in 1958. And on the night of June 17, 1960, Betty Grable and her bandleader husband Harry James were performing there when a fire broke out and burned the El Rancho to the ground. It was never rebuilt.

Newer showrooms, hotels, and casinos were left to carry on the tradition, including Siegel's Flamingo. The mobster, however, was long dead by that time. In a note of irony, a group of investors teamed up to buy the Flamingo in 1955.

One of those investors was a man named Thomas Everett Hull.

LUXURY BY THE ROADSIDE

Another motel on Fresno's motel strip, The Sands, shared its name with a famed Las Vegas resort. So did the Hacienda, which also had the same owner as its Sin City counterpart. There were four Hacienda resorts—including three in California—and Fresno's Hacienda actually opened in 1952, four years before the Vegas location. Each one sported the same neon figure of a cowboy waving from the top of a horse reared up on its hind legs.

The Sands was one of several hotels along Fresno's motel row on 99 that shared their names with early Las Vegas resorts.

The Hacienda, like the Bakersfield Inn, was in many ways more like a hotel than a motel. Sure, it was right along 99, but it had enough amenities to qualify as a resort. A newspaper ad printed shortly before it opened promised "something new in motels"—a large-scale establishment that would come to feature 350 rooms, along with a restaurant, performance stage, and two swimming pools. Some guests might choose to lounge around in the sun at poolside and wait for the Barmobile (a canopied bar on wheels) to swing by and wet their whistle. Others preferred to head indoors to the sunken Mermaid Room, order a martini, and gaze through a window behind the bartender that offered a view of submerged swimmers frolicking beyond the glass.

eventually released as part of a posthumous album called *Coast to Coast Live*. Singer-actress Della Reese headlined a New Year's Eve party there in 1965, and Frankie Avalon rang in 1970 with a similar celebration. Ol' Blue Eyes himself, Frank Sinatra, made an appearance there in the spring of '66.

Down the highway in Bakersfield, the El Adobe Motel and its sister nightclub, the Crystal Inn, brought in some big names of their own, including the Three Stooges and the Marx Brothers. An Italian immigrant named Gere Restituto built the El Adobe in 1936 using adobe bricks baked on the 20-acre site along Union Avenue (Old 99). The motel had 31 guest rooms, but Restituto put just as much effort into making it a showplace for up-and-

Fresno's Hacienda was a step or two up from your typical motel. After it closed, it reopened as a senior living facility, later operating as a transitional home for women dealing with drug, alcohol, and mental health issues.

A decade after it opened, the Hacienda spent $750,000 to add a showroom and convention hall called the Las Vegas Room that, during its heyday, attracted the same sort of first-class acts who frequented showrooms on the casino strip. In anticipation of its opening in 1964, six convention groups canceled plans to gather elsewhere and scheduled their events at the Hacienda instead. In September of that year, Nat King Cole booked a 10-day engagement at the Hacienda, a recording of which was

coming talent. Three years after it opened, he added a bar, a cocktail lounge, a coffee shop, and three themed dining rooms. There was even a wine cellar.

The El Adobe was brimming with that commodity called character. One of the dining rooms featured a rock grotto packed with enough ferns and other greenery to make it look like a set from a Tarzan movie, complete with a wishing well fed by a pair of waterfalls. A staircase at the motel featured a pair of statues: a crouching lion cub halfway up and a life-size replica of the Venus de Milo—complete with arms! With that kind of ambience, it's no wonder that stars arrived at the El Adobe to visit as well as to perform. The husband-and-wife acting team of Clark Gable and Carole Lombard came calling, as did Frank Morgan, best known for playing the title role in *The Wizard of Oz*.

A decade after the El Adobe opened, Restituto opened the Crystal Inn farther to the south on 99, which featured various local and breakout nightclub acts along with a fish tank with a "mermaid" inside who swam around to entertain bar patrons. Might she have been the inspiration behind the Mermaid Room at Fresno's Hacienda?

The sign at the entrance to the Hacienda.

It's possible. What is known for sure is that Restituto sold the Crystal Inn four years after it opened and shut down the El Adobe in 1955 amid a divorce from his wife.

The business that replaced it on the site? None other than the Bakersfield location in the Hacienda chain.

Even more lavish in its day was the Hotel Durant in Lebec, along the Ridge Route some 40 miles south of Bakersfield. An ad in the *San Francisco Chronicle* announced its opening in May of 1921. With "80 rooms, all with bath, steam heat and electricity [and a] telephone in every room," the resort on the shores of Lake Castaic featured "boating, bathing, tennis, golf, hiking over mountain trails, shooting and fishing in season."

Celebrities including Buster Keaton and Charles Lindbergh stayed there, as did Clark Gable and Carole Lombard. In 1922, famed comedian Roscoe "Fatty" Arbuckle and his wife stopped at the hotel on their way back from his second manslaughter trial in San Francisco. Arbuckle, accused in the death of actress Virginia Rappe, had managed to escape with a mistrial after two of the 12 jurors refused to convict him. He vowed to beat the rap at his third trial—and did so, winning acquittal later that year. Still, the scandal ruined Arbuckle. His wife filed for divorce a year later, and filmmakers refused to hire him.

Bugsy Siegel, the noted mobster, also stayed in Lebec. One has to wonder whether Siegel got any ideas for his future Las Vegas ventures from staying at the hotel, which according to one account was a "complete gambling joint" during the late 1920s, when Bakersfield saloon-keeper Thomas O'Brien operated it as the Hotel Lebec. O'Brien, who also operated casinos in Las Vegas and Reno at the time, was involved in the project from the beginning. He had moved to the Lebec area around 1914 and, when the Ridge Route opened, he had built some modest roadside accommodations to serve travelers along the new road. O'Brien's Hotel Lebec was similar to several other Ridge Route stops, offering a garage, gas station, general store, and eatery on the same site. You could buy "Tejon Natural Gasoline" for 20 cents and enjoy "a Sunday dinner in the Tejon Mountains." An ad proclaimed that the lunchroom served meals and sandwiches at all hours from noon to 8 p.m.

Cliff Durant was one of the satisfied customers who visited Hotel Lebec, whereupon he struck up a conversation with O'Brien about the possibility of building a far more lavish establishment. Durant was the son of General Motors co-founder Billy Durant, and he had access to the money that could make it happen. O'Brien agreed and, with Durant's father providing most of the capital, they built a grand two-story hotel that featured two wings of 30 two-room suites apiece (each with a private bath), a dining room that could seat as many as 400 people, and a billiard room upstairs. Designed to resemble a French château, it cost a whopping $225,000 to build, and some 300 guests, including heavyweight champ Jack Dempsey, checked into the new hotel when it opened in 1921.

But trouble soon followed this auspicious beginning, as Durant's father—recently ousted from the board of

Cliff Durant is at the wheel of a new Chevrolet in this 1911 photo. *Public domain.*

General Motors—ran into financial troubles as he sought to establish a new company called Durant Motors. In the midst of all this, he pulled his support from the hotel. This left the younger Durant in a bind, so he negotiated the hotel's sale in the summer of 1922 to a man named Foster Curry. O'Brien, who still owned the 22 acres on which the hotel stood, sold to Curry, as well.

The Curry name might ring a bell if you've visited Yosemite, where Foster Curry's parents—a pair of schoolteachers from Indiana—founded Camp Curry with a dining center and about a dozen tents in 1899. Over the next two decades, the Currys' business prospered, as they added cabins, bungalows, and a dance hall; eventually, the business grew into a massive profit-making machine called the Curry Company, which was responsible for concessions within the national park and raked in $80 million a year.

Foster Curry, who had helped his parents run the increasingly prosperous company, changed the name of Hotel Durant to Curry's Lebec Lodge and kicked off the new era with an elaborate dinner dance on Halloween of 1922. But his involvement in the hotel turned out to

be a lot more trick than treat. Barely a year after Curry took over the business, a grease fire in the restaurant's flue became an inferno that burned down the restaurant, general store, and garage (all part of O'Brien's original development), in addition to some nearby houses. The hotel itself was spared, but the damage to the property as a whole was significant, estimated at $60,000.

Curry had yet to make all his payments on the hotel, and Durant still held a series of promissory notes. Despairing of the new owner's ability to pay, given the damage to his business, Durant sued Curry, claiming first lien on an insurance payoff of $7,000. Not so fast, O'Brien countered. Curry still owed him money for the property, and O'Brien asserted his own claim to the lien superseded Durant's. After all, the buildings that had burned down were the ones he had built.

Eventually, the court actions came down to a contest between Curry, who claimed he was on time with his payments, and O'Brien, who asserted he was in arrears. The ruling ultimately went in favor of O'Brien who, with Durant out of the picture, took full ownership of the hotel and the land. He constructed a new stone structure to replace the buildings destroyed in the fire, reasoning that stone wouldn't burn. O'Brien made other improvements to the hotel, which he rechristened as Hotel Lebec and ran for the next few years until the Depression forced him into financial hardship. Fortunately, he had connections.

In need of capital to keep the hotel open, he approached a man named Mark Fuller for a loan. Fuller had started out as O'Brien's bookkeeper and, since leaving his employ, had risen to become president of Richfield Oil. With significant funds at his disposal, he agreed to advance O'Brien the cash he needed. As it turned out,

ings, which left him so chagrined that he told a business associate to throw the hotel keys across the table at Richfield's lawyers.

Richfield, which by this time was itself in receivership, thus took possession of the hotel. O'Brien's luck ran out at his casinos, as well. He had to sell his Las Vegas property to pay off a jackpot a customer won in Reno; then the Reno operation itself failed when a harsh winter put a damper on business there.

O'Brien died in 1942 at the age of 72, but Hotel Lebec housed a gambling operation long after his death. One employee said it became known as a "party place" for

Hotel Lebec, aka Hotel Durant and Lebec Lodge, was a grand destination in its heyday, as seen here, drawing celebrity guests such as Charles Lindbergh and Clark Gable. But it gradually deteriorated over time and was closed in 1969, two years before it burned down. *From the collection of Michael J. Semas.*

however, that cash didn't belong to him, but the corporation. Fuller resigned and was subsequently convicted of misappropriating company funds. Richfield (which, ironically, had a gas station on O'Brien's property) then came after O'Brien for the cash he'd borrowed from Fuller. Richfield put additional pressure on O'Brien by setting up foreclosure signs around the hotel and other build-

the rich and famous from Southern California during the 1930s: "They had gambling and all the things that go with it."

In 1953, police raided the hotel and made their way up to what press reports described as the second-floor gambling salon, where a state attorney general's spokesmen said they found about a dozen customers standing "foolishly idle in a large room appointed with a roulette table, two craps tables, a blackjack table, and four card tables." The operation, he said, was as plush "as anything in Nevada."

Nevertheless, they had to get a search warrant before they could confiscate the gambling paraphernalia, and by the time they returned, the room had been cleaned out.

Not only was hotel owner Harry Burk Jr. accused of running an illicit gambling operation there, he also found himself under investigation for allegedly running three houses of prostitution. In an attempt to keep the police from shutting him down, he offered a Kern County undersheriff $500 a week to look the other way. When he made the first payment of ten $50 bills, however, police officers emerged from hiding and arrested him; he was convicted a few months later, in December of 1954.

The scandal didn't end there. Burk had leased the hotel to a couple named Frank and Barbara Cotter, who claimed that its value dropped because he (Burk) insisted on continuing to run a gambling room there. They further alleged, in a $53,000 lawsuit, that Attorney General Edmund G. Brown—the future governor and father of another—had received a bribe to look the other way. Brown denied the allegations, which never went anywhere, and in some ways the scandal proved to be the beginning of the end for the venerable lodge.

The Hotel Lebec went through a series of owners over the years and gradually fell into disrepair. At one point, it was called the Hotel Lebec and Dude Ranch, and later owners adopted the Lebec Lodge name again sometime during the 1950s. The hotel eventually closed down in 1969, and the Kern County Health Department condemned it as unsafe. The owner of the property burned it down two years later to clear the land.

Motel Chains

Motels remained largely independent operations through the 1930s and '40s, although the loose motor court associations that surfaced during the Depression gradually became more tightly knit. Best Western started the same way United Motor Courts did, as a group of independent owners referring travelers to other motels in the network. Later, chain motels began to pop up along the roadside. One of the first was TraveLodge, founded in 1940 in San Diego. The chain's mascot, a sleepwalking bear in pajamas and a nightcap, became a common sight along Highway 99 and across the West.

Nashville was home to Holiday Inn Hotel Courts, a motel built in 1952 whose name paid tribute to the Bing Crosby holiday film of the same name. It blossomed into an international chain of more than 3,000 hotels and motels.

For those who wanted a bargain, the first Motel 6 opened its doors, charging a meager $6.60 a night, in 1962. Based in Santa Barbara, the same city that had spawned United Trailer Courts, Motel 6 offered a no-frills experience: even the in-room television was coin-operated. A large number of its early locations were along Highway 99, and the road is still home to many of them. The original price tag from which it took its name has long since fallen by the wayside, but the concept of an inexpensive place to spend the night hasn't gone out of style. Motel 6 grew to more than 1,000 locations and helped inspire similar bargain motels such as Super 8 (which charged $8.88 a night when it opened in 1972) and Econo Lodge.

The rise of the chains marked a decline in the mom-and-pop motels that had dominated the highway for decades from the 1920s onward. Many early motels were the lemonade stands of the lodging industry. Built in a hurry and on a shoestring, they popped up along the roadside quickly to flag down passing tourists with their gaudy signs and neon promises of "vacancy." When they grew worn and weathered, many stopped attracting tourists and were either torn down or converted into low-income housing, where tenants could pay by the month.

Some of these can still be found along Old 99, a few of them retaining vestiges of their initial charm, while others have fallen into varying degrees of disrepair but continue to operate, even though the "no" in front of that "vacancy" sign is seldom, if ever, lit. Cottages connected by carports in the old style can be found in Madera at 3-D's Motel at the southern end of Gateway Boulevard, aka Old 99. Tulare has the Virginia Motor Lodge and the Moto Rest, next door to each other and across from the fairgrounds on what's now the business route.

The Moto Rest Motel, from the era of cabins and motor courts, attracted visitors who drove through the heart of town on K Street, part of the old alignment of U.S. 99 (seen at left).

Once, motor inns lined these sections of the old road for blocks. But freeway bypasses put most of them out of business. What was left of some motel rows became red-light districts, frequented by drug dealers and street-walkers. The terms "fleabag motel," "no-tell motel," and "hot pillow inn" were coined to describe them. Fresno's motel row provided an ironic contrast, aging but still imposing neon signs (seldom lit up at night anymore) towered over rundown buildings, some of which rented room by the hour or the month to whoever was willing to lay down a few bills on the counter.

Fresno's motel row, however, wasn't long for this world: In 2014, they tore down the old Hollywood Inn bar, the first step in a plan to demolish the strip and replace it with multibillion-dollar bullet train project. The road that had replaced the railroad as the preferred mode of transportation was itself being replaced by a rail line.

Things had come full circle.

10
AMUSEMENTS

Pollard's Chicken Kitchen was originally on the west side of U.S. 99 before expanding and moving to the highway's eastern flank, where it became Pollardville. *From the collection of Neil Pollard.*

When Burl Ives won an Academy Award for Best Supporting Actor in the epic 1958 Western *The Big Country*, he could scarcely have guessed what would happen to some of the buildings used in that film.

The movie, which featured the likes of Gregory Peck, Carroll Baker, Jean Simmons, and Charlton Heston, was a big hit for United Artists, but after director William Wyler wrapped production, it had no more use for the buildings.

A couple in Stockton did.

Ray and Ruth Pollard had come to the area in the mid-'40s from Castro Valley, where they had sold chickens to local restaurants from a modest ranch off Highway 50. At some point, they got the idea to market their product directly, selling eggs and poultry from a shack they put up along the highway. "When all of the turkeys didn't sell one year, Ruth Pollard started making turkey sandwiches, and when the turkeys were gone, she changed it to chicken sandwiches," said Neil Pollard, who with his wife Tracy later took over the business from his father. "The little business was such a success that they decided to buy some equipment and add a secret family recipe for frying chicken that Ruth Pollard came up with. And Chicken on a Bun was born with a quarter piece of fried chicken, french fries, and a hamburger bun that started one of the first 'to go' restaurants."

In some ways, the Pollard's roadside stand was to chicken what the Giant Orange was to juice. But instead of building a bunch of chicken shacks up and down the highway, the Pollards decided to go a different direction: east. Two years after the family started its business, they moved it to Stockton (after a brief stop in Tracy) and set up shop on the west side of Highway 99, where you could buy Chicken on a Bun for 65 cents or a full chicken dinner for $1.40. For those who didn't like chicken, there were burgers starting at 30 cents and sandwiches starting at 35. You could take home frozen fresh liver or gizzards, as well as ice cream.

That first version of the Pollard's Chicken Kitchen had just three tables, a lunch counter, and a takeout window—enough room for 18 patrons.

"When we were on the west side of the highway, we were just a little restaurant between Lodi and Stockton, and that was just a two-lane highway back then," recalled Neil Pollard, who was 15 when he started working in the business founded by his father. "One of the first things he did was he bought a buggy from a guy in Galt and put a couple of dummies in it. He set that right there in front of the restaurant, and people would see it when they passed by. It was an attraction."

That buggy was just the beginning. Over the next several years, Ray Pollard began to acquire a collection of antiques.

"We had over 25 nickelodeons and player pianos of other types," Neil Pollard said, along with walking canes, phonographs, and other items. Meanwhile, the Chicken Kitchen itself was expanding, with three new dining rooms added one by one over the course of a decade to accommodate a growing clientele. The restaurant eventually had room to seat more than 100 customers, but it still wasn't big enough, and there wasn't enough room to expand any further on the one-acre leased site. Besides, Ray Pollard had even bigger plans.

As the collection of antiques grew, Neil Pollard said, "you had so much stuff, you needed a town to put it in."

So Ray Pollard set about the task of creating one.

He bought 13 acres on the other side of the highway, about a quarter-mile down the road, and settled into that location for the next half-century.

One of the first things Pollard did was purchase an old cannery building and haul it in from Thornton, a few miles to the west. The 50-by-250-foot building would house his growing assortment of antiques (it was growing in size as well as in number: Pollard acquired several vehicles, including a fire engine and a car dating from 1901). And before long, it became the foundation for a ghost town theme park patterned after the Old West.

The Pollards started out by purchasing the Mountain Ranch Post Office from Calaveras County, a wooden shack that dated back to the 1920s and was hailed as "the smallest post office in the United States." Another historic building on the site was a branch building for the Tuolumne County Jail, which was built in 1897 and taken apart brick-by-brick to be reassembled on the Pollards' site.

The biggest acquisition, however, came from Hollywood.

"My dad bought the whole movie set of *The Big Country*," Neil Pollard said. "He contracted with this guy to move the whole town. I laid out where it should go; I tried to lay it out the way they did it in the movie."

The collection included a firehouse, stable, smithy, schoolhouse, hotel, and livery from the movie. But as with most movie sets, they weren't complete structures, but façades designed to look the part. The hotel appeared to be a two-story building, but "the only thing that held it up was two telephone poles, and they tied the walls to them," Neil Pollard said. "We rebuilt everything gradually and were eventually able to use them."

Pollard added to the atmosphere by sprinkling in the antiques he had collected from the period. The town had everything from liquor bottles to newspapers and shaving mugs. Pollard even built a small wood-and-plaster "mountain" to house a full-fledged mining operation (with authentic equipment) and a mill. Cost of the entire project in 1965 dollars: a cool $200,000.

It paid off. During the first half of that year, 15,000 people had already visited what had become a major

Pollardville from the air, with U.S. 99 in the foreground. *From the collection of Neil Pollard.*

roadside attraction: "A great place for a boy to become a man and a man to become a boy—again." It was used as the backdrop for scenes from *Back to the Future III*, the sixth-highest-grossing film of 1990.

There was plenty to see and do in the ghost town.

You could have your picture taken with gunslingers or watch them shoot it out in mock gunfights that were staged every hour. You could ride the Pollardville Locomotive, a replica of a train from the 1880s. You might even be treated to a bit of unintentional comedy. Neil Pollard remembered the time when "our burro, Toby, got loose from his corral and wandered into the ghost town and locked himself into the jail. We found

him a couple of days later, and he had eaten the guest-book."

One of the main attractions at Pollardville was the melodrama and vaudeville theater. It was originally called the Pollardville Palace, but Neil Pollard had an idea to make it into something a little more distinctive. Drawing upon his love of riverboats, he remade the façade completely to look like something out of a Mark Twain novel, complete with twin smokestacks on the top.

You could stop in at the theater and see shows with titles like *Sherlock Meets the Phantom* and *Seven Wives of Dracula*. Ray Rustigian and show business partner Phil DeAngelo were booked for the second show at the theater and wound up staying for three decades. Rustigian served as emcee, directed melodramas, and sometimes played the part of the villain. He also served as a mentor to up-and-coming actors, some of whom later made the big time, including Grant Lee Phillips, Jeremy Renner, and Fairuza Balk.

"The theater seated 280 people for dinner, and we'd run a show for six months," Pollard said. "We brought

The Pollardville Palace was transformed into the Palace Showboat Dinner Theatre, with seating for 280 people and vaudeville entertainment.
From the collection of Neil Pollard.

in people from 60 miles away. They came from Oakland, they came from Fresno, they came from San Jose. We brought them in by buses, and we had a trailer park where they could park for free, spend the night, and leave the next day."

Pollardville offered tours to schoolchildren, who loved to run around the grounds playing cowboy and learn to pan for gold, and who enjoyed annual events such as a haunted ghost town at Halloween and (of course) a chicken festival. Just driving by the place, you could marvel at the 8-foot-tall fiberglass rooster perched atop an 80-foot tower. Its cousin, another giant rooster, took up residence in the town itself.

Traffic patterns changed when the freeway replaced that old two-lane highway in 1964 and again when Interstate 5 opened, siphoning off business to the east a few years later.

"The highway changes made some difference," Neil Pollard said. "When they opened up Highway 5, we lost some of the long travelers from Canada and Oregon and Southern California. We lost some of that because they would just zip past."

Pollardville faced perhaps its biggest challenge on a foggy night just before Christmas in 1984, when a fire broke out in the restaurant and burned it to the ground. But the Pollards persevered. They purchased a Polynesian-themed restaurant in town that had closed recently after years as a major Stockton nightspot, dismantled it, then moved it to their site and put it back together. After remodeling, it opened as the new location of the Pollards' signature chicken eatery in 1987.

When the restaurant and park finally closed in 2007, it wasn't for lack of business. In fact, Neil Pollard said, an increase in big banquets and company picnics had made the business more profitable than ever.

"We had picnics that would be 1,000 people, and this was in later years. My wife and I said, 'Why didn't we do this earlier?'" Pollard said.

The larger-than-life rooster atop the Pollardville tower was impossible to miss if you were a motorist traveling U.S. 99. *From the collection of Neil Pollard.*

But the Pollards were getting older. "We were wearing out," Pollard said. "I was 75 when we finally quit. The last two years in business were our best ever, but it just came time to move on, and the property became more valuable than the business."

After Pollardville closed, some of the historic buildings were returned to their points of origin: The Jamestown Jail went back to Jamestown, and the post office was moved back to Mountain Ranch. Developers purchased the land as a site for a gated community and shopping center, but as of 2014, all that could be seen there was a vacant lot and the old Pollardville tower, minus the distinctive rooster on the top.

Where's that rooster now?

It's been completely restored and is sitting at the Pollards' home in Calaveras County.

IT WAS MAGIC

Down the road about three hours was an even bigger attraction, where guests were greeted by a bunny instead of a chicken, then turned upside down and inside out over the course of a daylong joyride. Magic Mountain opened in 1971 just off 99 in Valencia. It was the perfect location for a new amusement park built as an alternative to Disneyland for suburbanites in the booming San Fernando Valley. The bunny in question was Bugs, who cut the ceremonial ribbon on the park when it opened just to the west of the new Interstate 5. A portion of the decommissioned U.S. 99, rechristened The Old Road, ran virtually right by the front door.

The $20 million project started out as a gleam in the eye of Sea World, the San Diego–based amusement park whose star attraction was neither a bunny nor a chicken but an orca named Shamu. Officials there found a willing partner in the Newhall Land and Farming Company, which had created the planned settlement of Valencia in 1967 as a bedroom community for Los Angeles. The owners of a massive tract of farmland called Newhall Ranch were looking for ways to develop it, while at the same time reducing their property tax burden and creating a new residential subdivision market. One architect who submitted a plan for the project described it as "a new city concept emerging out of the chaos of Los Angeles (that) replaces the endless confusion of sameness with the heightened sense of a new and different place."

Even as it created this new community of housing for the affluent, with its expansive, tree-lined boulevards and office parks, the Newhall Land company still had plenty of land at its disposal. The question was what to do with it. As it sought ways to draw attention to this new community in the northern hinterlands of the L.A. metro area, an amusement park just made sense. It would provide a focal point for the family atmosphere the developers wanted to create, and it would attract visitors from outside the Santa Clarita Valley who might just like what they saw there and choose to relocate.

Six Flags California opened in 1971 as Magic Mountain. This sign greets visitors passing Magic Mountain Parkway on Interstate 5.

would give you unlimited access to a park that featured 33 rides, many of them designed by the same company that built the rides at Disneyland. The cost of admission would include entertainment, as well.

"Magic Mountain will cater to all ages," Sea World President George Millay said the summer before the amusement park opened. "It will feature a variety of 'white knuckler' thrill rides, three live music dance pavilions, a 300-seat Talent Showcase amphitheater, children's circus tent, restaurants, shows, and a host of other family attractions."

The park would have more than 50,000 plants and 7,000 trees that landscape architect George DeVault said would help create a "total aesthetic experience." Plans called for a sky tram, bumper boats, a monorail, and a historic carousel built in 1912 that was shipped in from an amusement park in Connecticut.

The park would become the center of what they hoped would be the next frontier of development in Southern California. And it turned out to be just that: By 1987, Valencia had banded together with the nearby communities of Saugus, Newhall, and Canyon Country to incorporate as Santa Clarita, one of the five largest cities in Los Angeles County.

A special page dedicated to Valencia in *The Valley News* crowed: "Remember what Disneyland did for property values in and around Anaheim? Sent 'em way up. You should be living here when the Mountain comes to Valencia in the spring of 1971. The value of your home should be all uphill from there."

Magic Mountain would produce 500 new jobs and become a magnet for business at nearby restaurants, motels, and service stations. Admission would be affordable: $5 for adults and $3.50 for kids 12 and younger

At the center of it all was a Sky Tower that rose 300 feet above the valley floor, offering a panoramic view of the rolling hills surrounding it as well as a focal point for motorists on the nearby freeway. "What's that?" the kids might ask, and demand that their parents get off to investigate. A daylong visit to the park would likely follow. In future years, the sky tower was joined by other, even more exciting attractions that were visible from the highway: roller coasters such as the corkscrew-infested Viper and the three-dimensional tumbler called X2.

While Disneyland drew younger kids with electrical parades, Small World, and Mickey Mouse, Magic Mountain would make its name with its roller coasters.

While Disney went after the younger set, Magic Mountain targeted teens with its roller coasters, which were anything but "Mickey Mouse."

In time, it came to have 18 of them, more than any other amusement park on the planet. With that in mind, it may be hard to believe that when it opened, it had just one: the Gold Rusher, a $1.2 million steel coaster that topped out at 35 miles per hour and was still in operation four decades later.

The shift from a Disneyland-style focus to thrill rides was a gradual one. In the beginning, the park placed a lot more emphasis on entertainment. Operators bought the rights to use Bugs Bunny and the Looney Tunes gang as its mascots—taking a cue from Mickey and Donald down in Anaheim—for the first year, then brought in their own cast of costumed characters after that. There was a towering wizard portrayed by a pair of 6-foot-7 twins and a family of trolls named Bleep, Bloop, and King Blop.

The shift to a roller-coaster park began in 1976, thanks largely to the addition of the Great American Revolution, the first roller coaster to feature a vertical loop. Its debut in the spring of that year was timed to coincide with the American bicentennial, and the coaster was center stage in the climactic scene of the following year's suspense film *Rollercoaster*, which had an all-star cast headlined by George Segal, Henry Fonda, and Timothy Bottoms

Magic Mountain unveiled the Revolution, the world's first vertical loop, in 1976 and gave it a name cleverly tied to the nation's bicentennial.
Velorian/public domain, 2008.

as a psychopath who gets his kicks by blowing up (you guessed it) roller coasters.

The Revolution also featured prominently both in *KISS Meets the Phantom of the Park* and the two-part episode of *Wonder Woman* filmed at the park, the similarly titled "Phantom of the Rollercoaster."

And just three years after the Revolution opened, the park's history as Magic Mountain was concluded. The Newhall Land and Farming Company had no interest in continuing to operate the park, which it sold to the Six Flags group for $51 million.

FOR THE KIDS

Not every attraction along 99 has been as big as Magic Mountain (many of us who grew up with the park still refuse to call it Six Flags), or even Pollardville. There are, and have been, a number of other attractions along the highway ranging from quaint to quirky to quietly impressive.

By the 1950s, the postwar baby boom was well under way, and the nation turned its attention to the younger generation. Television shows that celebrated the innocence of growing up like *Leave It to Beaver* and *Father Knows Best* were hits in prime time, and others such as *Howdy Doody* and *Romper Room* were made specifically for the younger set. In 1954, Walt Disney signed a contract with ABC to produce an anthology show for television called *Disneyland*, with the goal of helping to finance a theme park in Anaheim that would use the same name. The show (later known as *The Wonderful World of Disney*) introduced audiences to Davy Crockett, the "king of the wild frontier," along with other historical and magical figures.

Disneyland, the amusement park, opened a year later, but it was merely the most elaborate among a number of such parks geared toward young children and their parents, some of which served travelers along Old 99. These were destinations for parents in nearby communi-

ties who wanted to treat their children to a day of fun, but they could also serve as convenient pit stops for those on longer trips up the highway: temporary antidotes to "Are we there yet?"

Many such parks featured storybook themes that brought to life characters from fairy tales and, in the process, encouraged young children to read. Pixie Woods in Stockton opened in 1955, charging 10 cents for admission and offering attractions that included animal exhibits, such as horses, monkeys, and even seals at Neptune's Lunar Landing. Fairytale Town in Sacramento and Playland in Fresno both opened in the 1950s and took a slightly different approach: each was located right next to the city zoo.

Humpty Dumpty greeted some 5.3 million visitors at the gates to Fairytale Town during its first two decades

Storyland at Fresno's Roeding Park, just west of old U.S. 99—and east of the current freeway alignment—opened a fairy-tale attraction called Storyland geared toward younger children in 1962.

in operation, and it remained open as of 2014, inviting kids to see such attractions as the Old Woman in the Shoe, Hickory Dickory Clock, and Jack's Candlesticks for a "nominal admission charge." (The latest admission prices were between $2.25 and $3.50, compared with nearly $100 for Disneyland.)

In Fresno, an amusement park geared toward younger kids called Playland opened in 1955 at Roeding Park, across from the entrance to the zoo just off Old 99. Parents were known to drive from Tulare, Merced, and other towns within a radius of 50 miles or more for an outing at the park. Seven years later, a companion story-book-themed park called Storyland opened at the same site, featuring 25 exhibits based on children's fairy tales. Little Red Riding Hood, Goldilocks, Little Miss Muffett, and others were all in residence. There was even a live Peter Rabbit and a Jack-and-the-Beanstalk slide, with an angry giant's face staring down from above.

Parents and their kids could spend a full day at the park, wandering through Storyland, taking a train ride through Playland, and, of course, visiting Nosey the elephant and her friends at the Fresno Zoo.

ANIMAL MAGNETISM

In 1939, the federal Works Progress Administration put out a guide to California that gave travelers an idea of what to look for as the side of the road went whizzing by. You might even hear a roar or two as you were passing through El Monte on the southern stretch of Old 99. Any day except Monday, you could pay a couple of quarters to check out a place described on the signs as "Internationally Famous Gay's Lion Farm—The Farm Extraordinary."

Jackie the lion gets playful with his trainer in this photo taken around 1927. Jackie succeeded Slats as the official MGM Studios lion mascot. Both were raised and trained at Gay's Lion Farm in El Monte. *Public domain.*

Circus performers Charles and Muriel Gay had opened the farm in 1925, and it was home to some famous film lions, including original MGM mascot Slats and his successor, Jackie. The five-acre property housed more than 200 African lions in nine enclosures, nestled among various flowers and shrubs. You could see some big cats who had appeared in motion pictures, like *The Circus* with Charlie Chaplin, and you could have an "awwww" moment watching the cubs be fed from nursing bottles. Advertising for the attraction declared that "to visit the great Southwest and not visit Gay's Lion Farm is like visiting India without visiting the Taj Mahal."

The farm was popular with everyone from Lions clubs (for obvious reasons) to schoolchildren to movie stars. The Gays held a special "Lion Banquet" one weekend a year, during which the tamest of the lions was allowed to wander the grounds while guests feasted on, yes, lion meat. Walt Disney, a guest at one of these affairs, was said to have been so taken with the idea that he used it as the inspiration for Adventureland, a jungle-themed attraction at Disneyland.

Actress Avonne Taylor had publicity shots taken with the lions in 1927, the same year her film *My Best Girl* was released.

She was in good company.

Greta Garbo had done a photo shoot at Gay's a couple of years earlier, cuddling with a cub and posing with MGM's Jackie. She had just arrived from Sweden two days earlier when a studio photographer whisked her away to the lion farm for some publicity stills and brief film clips. Garbo,

MGM records Jackie's roar on a sound stage in 1928 for use in the new medium of "talkies." *Public domain.*

who wasn't fluent in English at that point, didn't realize what "lions" were. Once she found out, she was immediately anxious. In a photo with Jackie, she's shown peering over at the lion from the corner of one eye as she leans away from him toward the far edge of the chair, apparently poised to make a run for it should the need arise. (The lion, his front paws resting on a tree stump, appears bemused as he gazes casually over at the starlet.)

Garbo had reason to be nervous: Running a lion farm could be a dangerous business. In the fall of 1928, three large lions broke loose while they were being loaded onto a tram that was to transport them to a film location. Farm manager John Roonan was alerted and tried to help corral the animals, but one of them leaped at him and threw him to the ground, clawing at his chest and mauling him. Others went after the three big cats, stalking them through the jungle-like undergrowth of the lion farm. They caught sight of one, but he turned on them and charged, forced them to retreat quickly into an open cage and shut the door behind them. Gunmen targeted the lion but were unable to subdue him, and his powerful jaws clamped down on the cage. It wasn't until then that a second hail of bullets brought him down.

Gunfire also felled the lion that had mauled Roonan, and the third animal was caught and caged. Roonan's wound required 100 stitches, and he later died.

The lion farm, however, survived the incident and continued to be a popular stop along the highway. El Monte High School even adopted the nickname Lions the same year Gays' farm opened and kept it long after the attraction closed in 1942. It was shut down in the midst of meat rationing for World War II, which made it impossible for the Gays to keep pace with the lions' voracious appetite, and they were forced to loan the animals out to zoos and circuses. Many no doubt hoped the attraction would reopen when the war was over, but the closure turned out to be permanent. In 1949, Charles Gay announced he was selling the land: "We decided it takes youth and agility to handle lions, so the farm will be placed on the market."

Up the road from the lion farm were some other animal-related attractions: the Los Angeles Ostrich and Alligator farms, both of them across from East Lake Park in the Lincoln Heights neighborhood (the name of the

The lion statue that once guarded Gay's Lion Farm now stands sentinel in front of El Monte High School, a mile or so off the highway. The school drew its inspiration from the famed attraction in adopting the nickname "Lions."

park itself was later changed to Lincoln Park), where Old 99 curved north after ending its westward swing into L.A.

Route 99 didn't actually exist when the two farms were founded, in 1906 and 1907, respectively. But the twin attractions remained fixtures in the area for nearly half a century, and an early alignment of the highway (now known as Valley Boulevard) passed directly through their neighborhood, channeling thousands upon thousands of motorists past their front gates.

Visitors to the ostrich park—billed as the nation's largest ostrich farm—could see more than 100 of the birds on exhibit, some of which had been trained to pull chariots or even be ridden astride. People could view ostrich races or, if they were lucky, see babies hatching. The birds were safe enough that they were allowed to pull wagons full of children.

Somewhat more dangerous were the alligators next door, but they, too, were trained to perform stunts that delighted visitors out for a day of fun. One popular attraction, called "shooting the chutes," was an alligator water slide: Trained reptiles would crawl up a ramp, then go sliding down the other side into a waiting pool of water.

Another exhibit showed alligators supposedly being hypnotized, and their eggs were on display in incubators. The park claimed to have more than a thousand alligators of all ages, "from little babies, hardly the size of a lizard, up to huge monsters up to 500 years old or more," a brochure proclaimed. It was more than a slight exaggeration: Alligators don't generally live to be more than about 50 years old. But what could one expect from a pamphlet that displayed, on its cover, a photo of a very young girl on the back of an alligator? (Without the requisite warning, "Don't try this at home.")

A pair of entrepreneurs, Francis Earnest and Joe Campbell, built the farm, and Earnest bought out his partner a couple of years later. He charged an admission fee of 25 cents,

Lincoln Park, once home to the Selig Zoo alongside U.S. 99, as it appears today.

augmenting their gate receipts by selling such keepsakes as alligator handbags and alligator shoes. Sometimes, however, people tried to make off with the saw-toothed reptiles themselves—particularly fraternity pledges trying to get through hazing during "hell week."

In 1953, the park staged an odd "race" between its oldest gator, Billy, and a 250-year-old Galápagos tortoise named Humpy. The owners' children did the honors as "jockeys," and Billy's snappers were strapped shut for the safety of his rider. Humpy didn't seem too interested in following the course and had to be rerouted more than once, but he still managed to cross the finish line ahead of Billy, covering the 75-foot distance in 20 minutes. That same year, the park pulled up stakes and moved south to Buena Park, where it remained until it finally closed

its doors for good in 1984, a victim of flagging attendance.

THE SELIG ZOO

A different set of problems beset the biggest animal attraction in Lincoln Heights, a full-fledged zoo that operated on the grounds of East Gate (Lincoln) Park itself. Had things gone according to plan, it would have become a proto-Disneyland decades before the Anaheim theme park was even conceived, but World War I and a downturn in the film industry conspired to undermine the plans of L.A.'s first movie mogul, William Selig.

Selig was a magician from Chicago who, inspired by one of Thomas Edison's Kinetoscopes, founded the first major motion picture studio in the City of Big Shoulders. Unable to duplicate the contraption, he instead hired someone to copy a French camera, made a few modifications, and dubbed it the Selig Standard Camera. He also came up with a projector, which he called the Selig Polyscope, whereupon he began making and screening movies.

Thomas Edison didn't take kindly to any of this, charging that Selig's "polyscope" was a mere knockoff of his own patented projector. He sued and nearly put Selig out of business, but Selig found a supporter in the Armour meat company, for whom he had made some promotional films a short time earlier. With the release of Upton Sinclair's landmark book *The Jungle*, which exposed unsanitary conditions in the meatpacking industry, Armour found itself in need of some damage control. So it re-released Selig's films and, in exchange, provided him with the financial support he needed to weather the storm. The producer struck a deal with Edison that eventually led to the formation of the Motion Picture Patents Company, giving the nine signatories a built-in advantage—and a near monopoly. Participants in the Patents Company included all the major studios of the day as well as Eastman Kodak, the top supplier of raw film stock, and No. 1 distributor George Kleine.

Selig proceeded to reel off a number of ground-breaking film projects. Among them were an early version of *The Wizard of Oz*; a project documenting the 1913 World Series on film; the first cliffhanger serial, *The Adventures of Kathlyn*; and a film depicting President Teddy Roosevelt killing a lion on an African safari. Selig had wanted to join Roosevelt on his expedition and document the event live, but the president had turned him down. Undaunted, he anticipated T.R.'s success and shot footage of a lion actually being killed in his Chicago studio by a stand-in for the president.

When Roosevelt actually did bring down a lion, the footage was ready to go and Selig released it to theaters across the country. It was convincing enough that many in the audience believed they were seeing actual footage of the president's kill.

William Selig founded the first major movie studio in Southern California, the Selig Polyscope Company studio in Edendale, just south of Griffith Park. It's seen here around 1910. *Public domain.*

It was 1909, a watershed year for Colonel Selig, as he called himself. In the spring, he traveled to the 101 Ranch in Oklahoma, a huge spread covering 101,000 acres that seemed like a good place to shoot a movie. The 101 operated a touring Wild West show that featured an expert horse handler and sure shot named Tom Mix. Selig liked what he saw and featured Mix in *The Cowboy Millionaire*, the first of several dozen short films he would make for the company over the next eight years.

But 1909 was perhaps even more important for another reason: It was then that Selig established a studio in Los Angeles, effectively jump-starting the Hollywood film industry. He had made *The Count of Monte Cristo*, the first commercial film ever shot in California, a year earlier, and he wanted a more permanent West Coast base. Initially, he set up shop behind a Chinese laundry business downtown but soon shifted his operations to Edendale, a neighborhood north of downtown Los Angeles later known as Echo Park. He built his studio at Allesandro and Clifford streets, at a spot that now marks the southern terminus of the Glendale Freeway.

The lion he had used in the Teddy Roosevelt film was just one animal in a growing menagerie Selig had acquired as he filmed a succession of jungle-themed pictures with titles such as *A Wise Old Elephant* and *Wamba, a Child of the Jungle*. He needed a place to house this growing collection, so he did the logical thing: He created a zoo. In 1913, he spent $1 million on the 32-acre plot of land that would become Lincoln Park.

One of the zoo's most impressive features was its entrance, adorned with sculptures created by Carlo Romanelli, a sixth-generation sculptor from Italy. A collection of life-size concrete Asian elephants stood proudly on a pedestal between the two main gates, many of them trumpeting as if to announce the arrival of new visitors. A pride of lions stood guard nearby, and the sculptures were said to have been modeled on the animals within. Total cost: $60,000.

Selig's collection was indeed impressive. When his zoo opened to the public in 1915, it featured some 700 animals. At a time when there were just nine giraffes in the entire country, Selig had

These lion statues stood guard beside an archway at Selig Zoo, among the many impressive concrete animal figures at the site. By the time this photo was taken in 1955, the gateway had fallen into disrepair. The statues were stored in a steel fabrication factory for decades until 2000, when they were rediscovered and moved to the Los Angeles Zoo. *Public domain.*

operation, the zoo drew 150,000 visitors, an impressive number considering the population of Los Angeles at the time was just over three times that figure. Countless travelers made trips from out of town just to see the zoo, while others stopped to check it out as they passed through.

But Selig had even bigger plans for the location: Adjacent to the zoo, he would build a huge amusement park for $2 million. A drawing of the plans showed swing sets, an arched bridge, a carousel, and a Ferris wheel, along with a huge tower at the center of it all, equipped with a bright spotlight. Selig also planned a pool with "artificial surf," the only one of its kind on the West Coast, complete with a white-sand beach "onto which the waves will break as in the ocean on a calm day."

Unfortunately for those looking forward to visiting this magical land of amusement, only the carousel was ever built. The film industry landscape was changing rapidly, both literally and figuratively. New studios were opening in Hollywood, on the other side of Old 99, and Selig's specialty short films faced competition from longer, more elaborate motion pictures.

two of them: a pair of 3-year-olds, each 14 feet tall. And the Asian elephants who greeted visitors at the entrance had five flesh-and-blood counterparts beyond the gates, including a mother and nursing baby.

Big cats were among the main attractions. The 18 Bengal tigers were reportedly the largest number in captivity, and the zoo also had 32 lions, 14 black leopards, and two clouded leopards—the only pair in the country. Seven bears of various types were residents, along with 14 camels, a zebra, an orangutan, seven llamas, 50 monkeys, and four kangaroos. The list went on and on. Many of the animals made appearances in Selig's short movies. His version of *The Wizard of Oz*, for instance, features several camels parading across the screen toward the end, and scenes from *Tarzan of the Apes*, the very first Tarzan movie, were filmed at the zoo itself.

A wide variety of birds, from peacocks to eagles and cranes to macaws, made their home at the Selig Zoo, as well, and visitors ate it up. During its first six months of

Meanwhile, World War I was eating into profits. Members of the Patents Company relied more heavily on overseas releases than independent filmmakers did, and this source of revenue suddenly all but vanished. The independents, meanwhile, had challenged the Patents Company's stranglehold on the industry in court, charging that it constituted a monopoly in violation of the Sherman Antitrust Act. In 1915, the same year the Selig Zoo opened its doors, the courts agreed. Three years later, the Patents Company lost its final appeal, and that same year Selig sold his studio. Not only was he unable to build his amusement park, but Selig suddenly had little left other than his zoo. He kept it for a time, renting out spots there to other studies in need of fierce creatures and "exotic" locales close to home. His income from the venture, however, was hardly reliable. He made a mere $7,000 from it in 1925, and receipts were as low as the $5 he received from Universal for renting out an owl for one day.

An Asian elephant enjoys some shade at the Selig Zoo around 1920. *Public domain.*

Once the superstar producer in California, Selig found his role in the industry reduced to that of a bit player. Tom Mix signed with the Fox Film Corporation, which had leased Selig's studio in Edendale. Louis B. Mayer of MGM fame moved into the zoo studios about 1920. Meanwhile, Selig stayed semi-active as an independent producer, but the cost of maintaining the zoo ate up all his profits, and he sold it in 1925 for less than half of what he had paid for it: $474,000. As a condition of the sale, Selig stipulated that he be able to keep his production offices on the site.

The Luna Park Zoo, as it was renamed, featured "six wonderful animal acts every afternoon at 3 o'clock," according to one brochure that displayed a photo of a three-piece chimpanzee band and extolled a woman named Olga Celeste, famous for her leopard vaudeville acts. According to one account, Celeste "appeared in hundreds of movies, including the first animal movie ever made" and "was believed to have appeared in virtually every film with a leopard between 1910 and her retirement in 1954."

Admission was 30 cents, or 10 cents for kids, and parking was free.

The Luna Park Zoo lasted eight years until the California Zoological Society purchased it, severed ties with Selig completely, and changed the name, yet again, to Zoopark. Massive floods that came with the rainy season of 1938 proved to be the death knell for the zoo, which was shuttered for good two years later. A small amusement park operated in its place until the mid-1950s, and the site eventually became a public park. The magnificent lion and elephant statues that had stood guard at the front gate were removed and carted away to a junkyard. There they remained, all but forgotten, until after the turn of the 21st century, when they were salvaged and restored to be put on display at the Los Angeles Zoo.

Selig received a special Oscar at the 1947 Academy Awards for his role as an industry pioneer, a year before his death. As for the zoo animals, the leopard trainer Olga Celeste scraped together money to buy five leopards and three lions. Others found a home at the Griffith Park Zoo, just west of Old 99 and a few miles northwest of the old Selig Zoo.

Big cats such as these two lions, seen in 1920 at the Selig Zoo, were among the park's main attractions during its heyday. *Public domain.*

HIGHWAY 99 IN COLOR

THE ROAD

This lion statue and its twin on the other side of the road were put in place to guard the south end of the 7th Street Bridge across the Tuolumne River in Modesto, along an old alignment of U.S. 99. The bridge opened in 1916.

Dead Man's Curve, a dangerous section of concrete south of Lebec that was connected to the original Ridge Route. It was replaced by the Ridge Route Alternate and, later, Interstate 5, which can be seen in the background.

A surviving section of Dead Man's Curve (Highway 99 historian Joel Windmiller pictured).

A view of Dog Creek
Bridge from below
shows the impressive
concrete arch span.
Also known as the
Harlan D. Miller
Bridge. Near Vollmers,
north of Shasta Lake.

A date farm lines
the former U.S. 99
(now State Route 86)
south of Coachella.

A sign on Heffernan
Avenue in Calexico marks
the beginning of U.S. 99.

Tower Bridge across the Sacramento
River marks the western entrance to
the state capital along a section of
99E that ran east and west, sharing
the road with U.S. 40. The vertical
lift steel bridge, completed in 1936,
still makes an impressive sight, day
or night.

Motel Drive in Fresno was one of many motel strips that sprang up at entryways to cities along the highway. The bright neon beckoned nighttime travelers to stop for the night and grab some shut-eye.

This section of Lebec Road, just south of town and west of Interstate 5 (background), was part of the highway's old alignment.

Three wooden posts and a broken crossbar are all that remains of an old guardrail along this section of the original Ridge Route, once lined by a low, protective white picket fence meant to keep vehicles from hurtling over the edge.

The giant "GAS" sign at left greets motorists who pass through Fresno on 99 at Princeton Avenue. This photo was taken from the Clinton Avenue overpass, facing north.

THE SIGHTS

The Beacon tower (below) south of Mount Shasta City still rises beside the only English-Norman-style station Richfield ever built in California. You can find it on Mount Shasta Boulevard, the old 99 alignment through town.

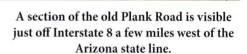

A section of the old Plank Road is visible just off Interstate 8 a few miles west of the Arizona state line.

The Adohr Farms milkmaid statue, along J Street—old U.S. 99—north of Cross Avenue in Tulare, was one of several such statues made to promote the company's products in the 1920s.

Dinny the brontosaurus was the first
of two giant dinosaurs to be built at
Cabazon by Claude Bell, a portrait studio
artist at Knott's Berry Farm. Completed
in 1975, it cost more than $250,000.

This bespectacled dragon greets
children at Fresno's Roeding Park.
At the park's Storyland attraction,
children were invited to learn about
reading from fairy-tale characters
such as Little Red Riding Hood and
Goldilocks.

This
abandoned
trailer is
just one of
many such
decaying
structures
found along
the western
shore of the
Salton Sea.

The moon rises over Mount Shasta on a
summer evening in 2014.

This brick chimney towers over the
Gladding, McBean ceramics plant off
Highway 99W in Lincoln.

The grapevines
that still grow in
Grapevine Canyon,
not the winding
highway, gave
Grapevine at the
northern edge of
the Tehachapis its
name.

Windmills in the San Gorgonio Pass line the highway near Whitewater. The wind farm, which features more than 3,000 such units, is one of three in California.

The Richmaid Restaurant along Cherokee Lane, the former U.S. 99, in Lodi was founded in 1938 as a creamery and ice cream parlor.

The Senator Theatre off Main Street (once U.S. 99) in downtown Chico opened in 1927. The vaudeville and movie house, operated by T&D Jr. Enterprises, has seating for 1,400 theatergoers.

This unique motel and restaurant in Castella, south of Dunsmuir, is built of refurbished rail cars. If offers spectacular views of the stark and jagged mountain rock formation known as Castle Crags.

THE SIGNS

The Pink Motel in Sun Valley was built in 1946 along San Fernando Road.

The Fair Courts Trailer Park along Business 99 in Tulare takes its name from the nearby Tulare County Fairgrounds.

The Fresno Motel's swimsuit-clad diver drew attention to its pool at a time when it was one of the higher-end motels along Motel Drive, north of Roeding Park. Unfortunately, the area later became a haven for drug dealers and prostitutes.

The famed Lodi Arch, or Mission Arch, stands at the entrance to the town center, west of the old highway. Built in 1907, it is a California Historical Landmark and is also listed on the National Register of Historic Places.

The Ontario Ice Center was built in 1957 where the old highway is called Holt Boulevard. It is the second-oldest ice facility in Southern California.

Vince's Spaghetti, founded in 1945, is right across the highway from the Ontario Ice Center.

This Hi-Lo Motel and Café is one of several along U.S. 99 in Weed, where the highway is known as Weed Boulevard.

A sign meant to be seen from Golden State Boulevard, the original U.S. 99 just north of Fresno, marks the site of the Forestiere Underground Gardens. The extensive subterranean estate shielded its creator, Sicilian immigrant Baldassare Forestiere, from the Central Valley heat.

This Las Vegas–style neon cowboy once greeted visitors to Fresno's swanky Hacienda resort inn along 99 at the Clinton Avenue exit. Today, it sits a few blocks to the south outside the Mendes General Store on Olive Avenue, west of Roeding Park.

PART II:
A TOUR OF OLD 99

What will you see if you travel up Highway 99 today? What might you have seen 50 years or a century ago? In some ways, the highway is like a river, changing courses as new bypasses are built and new alignments adopted. Likewise, the cities and towns along its path have changed quite a bit. One-horse towns have grown into thriving cities. Once-bustling communities have all but disappeared. Some spots on the map that began as farm towns have become suburbs of a larger, sprawling metropolis, like Los Angeles or Sacramento.

A trip through California up Old 99 offers a panoramic view of the state's geography, history, and varied cultures. It runs through the nation's film capital (Los Angeles), dairy capital (Tulare County), and farming capital (Fresno County), not to mention the state capital (Sacramento). It passes through sweltering deserts, mountains, eucalyptus groves, and pine forests, crossing bridges that in some cases date back a century and offering views of majestic Mount Shasta and the eerie Salton Sea.

What follows is a brief guide to U.S. 99 as it was and as it is, with a look at each of the communities along the way. The guide proceeds from south to north, starting at the Mexican border and going all the way to Yreka, just south of the Oregon state line.

Included are directions to help you find the old road, with asterisks (*) denoting the presence of concrete pavement from the original alignment.

Calexico

Population (1939)—6,232
Population (2010)—38,572
Elevation—3 feet
Location—Mexican border
Founded—1899
Incorporated—1908

During Prohibition, Calexico was the place to go … in order to get to somewhere else: across the border, to

The old border crossing, seen here at the end of U.S. 99, sits just a few blocks east of the current station in Calexico.

be exact. Its twin city of Mexicali on the other side had plenty of dance halls, saloons, and bright lights to lure refugees from "dry" America to bawdy Baja. Gambling halls such as the Owl beckoned during the 1920s. Many an American tourist drove down Old 99 to (and through) Calexico in search of a good time.

Prohibitionists must have cheered a 1922 fire that destroyed a Mexicali warehouse containing $175,000 in bonded liquors.

For those who wanted to stay on the near side of the border, the Fox Theatre's bright neon tower was a beacon for more wholesome fun.

The town began as a tent city under the supervision of the Imperial Land Company, which also founded Mexicali in hopes of attracting settlement to the area.

Finding the old road: For a few blocks north of the old border station, **Heffernan Street**, east of the current alignment, is signed as Historic U.S. 99. Check near the border for several "Historic U.S. 99" signs.

HEBER (UNINCORPORATED)

Population (1939)—991
Population (2010)—4,275
Elevation—10 feet below sea level
Location—5 miles north-northwest of Calexico
Founded—1901

Originally called Paringa at its founding in 1901, the town was another project of the Imperial Land Company. The company took out a newspaper ad touting Imperial, Paringa, and Calexico as "Three New Prospective Railroad Towns. Each Supported by Thousands of Acres of IRRIGATED LANDS." Prime lots in the three towns, the ad predicted, would become very valuable in just a few years.

The company warned potential buyers not to delay: It intended to double the asking price on the lots within 60 days and without notice. After the Southern Pacific Railroad survey came through, however, the railroad shifted its proposed alignment, forcing the entire fledgling town to pull up stakes and move two years later. It was renamed Heber as a tribute to A.H. Heber, president of the California Development Company. One has to wonder what happened to those who built at the original site.

EL CENTRO

Population (1939)—8,500
Population (2010)—42,598
Elevation—39 feet below sea level
Location—6 miles north-northwest of Heber
Incorporated—1908

Heading north into El Centro just before World War II, travelers on Highway 99 passed fields of alfalfa and stands of eucalyptus. El Centro is the largest U.S. city below sea level, straddling the intersection of two major highways: 99 and U.S. 80 (later decommissioned in favor of Interstate 8), running east and west. Its position at this junction, as well as along the Southern Pacific rail line, helped make it a major shipping center for the produce grown across the Imperial Valley.

To say the city's climate is "hot" would be putting it mildly. El Centro is among the hottest cities in the

This vintage Foster's Freeze neon sign sits beside old 99 in El Centro.

United States, with an average high of 107 degrees in July, when it hit a high of 122 one day in 1995. It's also very dry, getting less than three inches of rain a year. The Algodones Dunes to the east look like something out of the Sahara Desert. Over the years, they became a popular spot for off-road recreation and were used to film scenes set on the desert planet of Tatooine in the *Star Wars* films.

In the early days of the motorcar, however, they were something else entirely.

Because Los Angeles had recently gained prominence as the western terminus of the transcontinental railroad, San Diego civic leaders sought to position their city as the preferred destination for automobile travel. Standing in their way, however, were the shifting sands of the Algodones.

Still, despite this formidable obstacle, San Diego businessman and road builder Ed Fletcher was confident the southern route was superior. So in 1912, when the *Los Angeles Examiner* newspaper challenged him to prove it in a race to Yuma, Arizona, he not only accepted, he even spotted the newspaper's reporter a 24-hour head start.

Fletcher's confidence turned out to be well founded. Even though he needed a team of six horses to pull his car through the sand, he still managed to win the race by completing the trip in under 20 hours.

The federal government furthered Fletcher's cause by greenlighting construction of a bridge across the Colorado River at Yuma. But the sand dunes remained a problem: Travelers could hardly be expected to bring along a six-horse team with them every time they set out down the proposed highway. One suggestion involved laying down a roadway made from an evergreen shrub called arrow weed. It appeared promising, but the sun eventually dried it out and it cracked as the wheels rolled across it, making an awful mess. A mechanic tried a different approach: altering a car to fit the terrain. He took a Model T and raised the drive shaft, then equipped it with a larger set of rear tires. But the car stalled, and it took half a dozen horses to extricate it.

The ultimate solution proved to be a road made entirely from wooden planks—some 13,000 of them on two parallel tracks, spiked to wooden crossbeams laid below. Engineer and auto club consultant Joseph Lippincott dismissed the road as impractical, dubbing it "the most asinine thing" he had ever heard of. But that didn't stop Fletcher from moving ahead with the project. The result was a 6½-mile stretch of roadway, completed in 1915, that was passable but less than permanent: It was worn out and no longer usable within a year's time.

So the state's Highway Commission did what apparently seemed like the most sensible thing, replacing it with a new plank road. It was only 8 feet wide—nowhere near enough room for cars to pass each other heading in opposite directions—so turnouts were built every quarter-mile, marked with old tires hanging from posts.

It was an improvement but still an ordeal for early motorists. In 1919, the *Imperial Valley Press* printed this warning from the El Centro office of the auto club of Southern California: "Parties attempting to travel [the plank road] suffer from thirst and hunger and are sometimes in danger of death as there is little chance of succor arriving unless a call for aid reaches Holtville or Yuma."

The auto club advised travelers to avoid the road altogether.

Maintenance on the road was a never-ending process, as sand drifted onto it and needed to be removed, while the planks themselves often needed replacing. The process of crossing it could be an adventure … if you made it across. One traveler later compared such a trip to getting a chiropractic adjustment, and another suggested bringing along boxing gloves in case a scuffle broke out with one of the other motorists.

Indeed, a trip across the dunes had the tendency to provoke an early form of road rage in drivers navigating the rickety road amid swirling sands and triple-digit temperatures. Heat, sweat, and sand could raise tempers to the boiling point, and stepping on the gas to get across the dunes more quickly was out of the question. The rough nature of the road made even the speed limit of 15 miles per hour a pipe dream, and when the winds kicked up and the sand started swirling, it could take up to two days to make the trip. Drivers learned to come prepared for an overnight stay in the dunes, taking extra boards, shovels, auto jacks, and a supply of food and water.

Traffic jams were horrendous. A line of 20 cars once came face-to-face with a vehicle going the other way. When the driver refused to back up and use the turnout just behind him, the other motorists exited their cars and lifted the vehicle forcibly off the road; their passengers then took the wheel and drove on through. Once they were safely past, they lifted the offending car and driver back on the road and continued toward their destination.

In a sense, it was hard to blame the stubborn driver for refusing to back up. It was all too easy to slip off the road and into the dunes, whereupon it would be almost impossible to extricate one's vehicle from the sand. Many cars wound up stuck there, as one traveler colorfully phrased it, "mutely waiting to disintegrate."

Eventually, the authorities started setting up schedules under which eastbound traffic would proceed in that direction for two hours, after which westbound drivers would get a two-hour window of their own.

But it was becoming increasingly obvious that the plank road would have to go.

A new, 20-foot-wide paved road on a raised grade opened in the spring of 1926, and the plank road was abandoned. Travelers passing through ripped out many of the rotting boards for use as firewood, and another section of road was removed to make way for the All-American Canal; others likely wound up buried beneath the sands. A few remnants are still visible, protected as historical landmarks at the west end of the Interstate 8 frontage road called Grays Well Road.

IMPERIAL

Population (1939)—1,943
Population (2010)—14,758
Elevation—59 feet below sea level
Location—just north of El Centro
Incorporated—1904

Another Imperial Land Company town, Imperial was the first in the Imperial Valley to be incorporated. Originally separated from El Centro, a few miles to the south, it gradually became absorbed into the El Centro metropolitan area. Its location amid an agricultural heartland made it a magnet for Dust Bowl migrants in the 1930s.

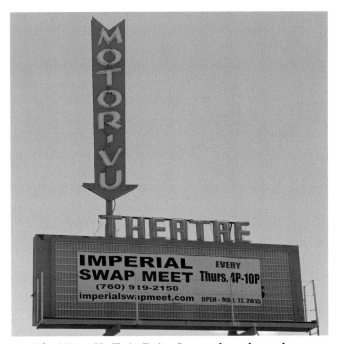

The Motor Vu Twin Drive-In was the only outdoor theater in Imperial County. Built in the mid-1940s, it later added a second screen, remaining open until 2013.

BRAWLEY

Population (1939)—10,439
Population (2010)—24,953
Elevation—112 feet below sea level
Location—13 miles north of El Centro
Founded—1902
Incorporated—1908

The northernmost Imperial Land Company town set up along the railroad (and U.S. 99) was named after a man who wanted nothing to do with the place. Around the turn of the century, an investor from Los Angeles named J.H. Braly had underwritten 4,000 shares of water stock and, in return, the Imperial Land Company had granted him 4,000 acres of land. With Braly's backing, the land company planned to build a city there.

An old Texaco garage sits on Main Street in Brawley, just east of where State Route 86 (former U.S. 99) veers south again after a brief jog eastward into town.

In 1902, however, the U.S. Bureau of Soils came out with a report declaring that the land in the area, with its high alkali content, was unsuitable for agriculture. Braly, alarmed by this turn of events, decided he wanted out of the deal. But at this point, people had already begun to move into the area and were calling the new settlement Braly.

The land company asked Braly to stand by the deal, but even the heat of the Imperial Valley sun couldn't warm his cold feet. He sold the entire contract at a bargain-basement price to a railroad executive, who in turn sold it back to the Imperial Valley Company at a profit of $4.50 an acre. Part of Braly's deal with the railroad man, however, was a stipulation that the new town could not, under any circumstances, be named "Braly." The Los Angeles investor simply had no interest in being associated with a town he believed was destined to fail.

A.H. Heber, for whom the town of Heber was named, came up with the idea to name the town instead after a friend of his in Chicago. The man's name was Brawley, which was sufficiently similar to Braly that it would allow residents already settled there to make a seamless transition.

WESTMORLAND

Population (1939)—1,300
Population (2010)—2,225
Elevation—164 feet below sea level
Location—7 miles northwest of Brawley
Founded—1910
Incorporated—1934

A small community about 14 miles south of the Salton Sea has long been a farm-labor center. The name of the town fluctuated, sometimes being spelled "Westmoreland" and at other times forsaking the second "e" (proving that

A sign advertises date shakes, an Imperial Valley delicacy, along a stretch of former U.S. 99 in Westmorland.

less is sometimes mor). In 1939, its singular feature was the fact that it had the widest main street in the Imperial Valley, U.S. 99 serving that function. It's also known for its bees: A small welcome billboard at the east end of town touts Westmorland as "Home of the Annual Honey Festival."

SALTON CITY (UNINCORPORATED)

Population (1939)—0
Population (2010)—3,762
Elevation—125 feet below sea level
Location—30 miles northwest of Westmorland
Founded—1958

A city with virtually no residents, Salton City is the site of ghostly deserted "ruins" from the heady days of the early 1960s when speculation was the word of the hour. Unfortunately, the investors so badly outnumbered the residents that the town-that-never-was turned into a white elephant. Hopes for the future of Salton City are revived periodically, usually dampened by the fear of flooding, the smell of rotting fish, infernal heat, and the rising salt content of the inland sea's waters.

About 10 miles to the south is the Salton Sea Test Base, where the military practiced dropping dummy atomic bombs onto white rafts floating on the lake in 1944 and '45, in preparation for the attack on Japan. Some of these bombs contained everything except the nuclear component, including triggering devices and a wealth of conventional explosives. During one practice run, a B-29 was carrying a prototype for the "Fat Man" nuclear weapon dropped on Nagasaki, Japan. Its crew accidentally dropped the bomb too soon, and it landed just outside the town of Calipatria, southeast of the Salton Sea.

It created a hole 10 feet deep but, fortunately, failed to detonate and was subsequently covered up with a bulldozer. Everything had to be kept on the QT. It was all very "Area 51."

Tests continued after the war ended, under the auspices of nuclear contractor Sandia Corp. Over the decade following the war, Sandia conducted about 150 tests a year, some of which made use of depleted uranium. There were high-altitude tests, parachute drops to test

One of many abandoned buildings sits on the western edge of the Salton Sea, just north of Salton City a few blocks off old U.S. 99.

space capsules, missile launches—the works. A government report declared that when someone "joked that every bomb shape had been tried at Salton Sea except the kitchen sink, some prankster kicked a kitchen sink out an open bomb-bay during the next test run."

The corporation ended testing at Salton Sea in 1961, moving its program to the Tonopah Test Range in Nevada.

Finding the old road: West of SR 86 (formerly U.S. 99), **Coolidge Springs Road** is a short section of concrete about a mile and a half long that's part of the highway's earliest alignment. It's accessible from the highway via Desert Springs Road, and you can travel the length of it in most any car.

THERMAL (UNINCORPORATED)

Population (2010)—2,865
Elevation—132 feet below sea level
Location—29 miles north-northwest of Salton City

Old Highway 99 runs parallel to the modern freeway as Grapefruit Boulevard through Thermal and Coachella, then as Indio Boulevard to the north. Thermal was the southernmost

of these three towns in date country. Where else could you get one of Russ Nicoll's famous date milkshakes?

Nicoll, a World War I veteran, settled in the Coachella Valley in 1919. Nine years later, he combined his life savings with a $500 bank loan and bought a roadside stand, which he named for his daughter, Valerie Jean. The initial stand was a 12-by-16-foot shack, which Nicoll positioned beside a sharp curve in the road so motorists would have to slow down as they passed by.

Within two years, he had done well enough to replace it with a permanent building. According to a postcard, the new shop was "built from old railroad ties and timbers that were abandoned when the Salton Sea was being formed." It stood among a group of date palms that included "the famous King Solomon tree which was imported from Arabia in 1912 and produced enough pollen for 400 female date palms."

The old Valerie Jean date shop, the first and most famous of the roadside date stands, sits abandoned on the southwest corner of former U.S. 99 and 66th Avenue.

In 1936, the new Indio-Blythe cutoff diverted eastbound traffic away from the shop via what would later become Interstate 10, but Valerie Jean had become so popular that travelers often made a detour just the same.

The business became a landmark along U.S. 99, selling various confections made from the fruit of the palms. In 1944, you could buy 3 pounds of stuffed dates (coconuts, almonds, and walnuts were among the ingredients found inside) or the "gourmet's delight"—a date cake for $3.75. The latter was a special treat, available only in limited quantities thanks to the sugar rationing in effect during World War II.

If you couldn't stop by in person, dates could be delivered via mail order. The king of Morocco and Pope Pius XII were among the shop's long-distance customers. But in a town where high temperatures averaged in the triple digits for one-third of the year, you also needed something cool for the overheated traveler's taste buds. The northern stretches of 99 had Giant Oranges, so why not try something similar with dates?

Nicoll said he got the idea for date milkshakes after learning that some Arabs lived on a diet of nothing but dates and goat milk.

He operated the shop until 1985, less than two years before he died at the age of 90.

Finding the old road: The old highway alignment peels away west of SR 86 at 81st Avenue, then follows **Harrison Avenue** north to Coachella, past the old Oasis travel stop and the long-closed Valerie Jean shop on the southwest corner at Avenue 66. You'll pass by numerous groves of date palms on this old two-lane alignment.

Coachella

Population (1939)—1,100
Population (2010)—40,704
Elevation—66 feet below sea level
Location—4 miles north-northwest of Thermal
Founded—1876
Incorporated—1946

The town was originally called Woodspur after the Southern Pacific built a rail siding there, a distribution center from which founder Jason Rector shipped mesquite lumber to Los Angeles. Residents didn't care for the name and voted on a change in 1901, after Rector graciously declined to have the site named in his honor. They chose the name Conchilla, a Spanish word meaning "little shells," in reference to the white snail shells deposited in the area from a long-vanished lake.

Unfortunately, after developers drew up plans and sent them to the printers, they came back with two letters replaced: The "a" had become an "n," and the "i" had been turned into an "e." Opting against any further delay, Rector and the others decided to adopt the misspelled name.

Indio

Population (1939)—3,500
Population (2010)—76,036
Elevation—13 feet below sea level
Location—6 miles northwest of Coachella
Founded—1876
Incorporated—1930

The "Hub of the Valley" was a highway town, where a line of businesses straddled Old 99 with motels, gas stations, and garages to serve travelers at a bend in the road. It was at Indio that the highway changed direction slightly from a primarily north–south thoroughfare to become a diagonal heading northwest and southeast. At San Bernardino, it would change course again, becoming an east–west highway.

"Twenty-ton diesel trucks rumble through the streets the clock around," the 1939 WPA guide declared.

For those who needed a reason to view Indio as a destination, rather than simply passing through, there were always the dates. The city held its first Date Festival in 1921, and the event soon became the centerpiece of the Riverside County Fair. Other events followed, and Indio eventually became known as the "City of Festivals." One of the biggest has been the Coachella Valley Music and Arts Festival, a three-day event that has drawn major recording artists including the Red Hot Chili Peppers, Madonna, Paul McCartney, and Radiohead since its debut in 1999.

West of Indio, the impressive San Gorgonio Pass wind farm dominates the landscape. Massive turbines that look like airplane propellers rise 80 to 160 feet high and

You can no longer "Roar With Gilmore" gasoline, but you can see this painting that's part of a mural on the side of Clark's Travel Center off the old highway in Indio.

Street, just beyond the northwest edge of town. Clark's Travel Center, just past Monroe Street if you're coming from the south, features historical mural tributes to U.S. 99 on the front and northwest sides of the building.

THOUSAND PALMS (UNINCORPORATED)

Population (2010)—7,715
Elevation—246 feet
Location—11 miles west-northwest of Indio
Founded—1876

Thousand Palms started out as Edom, a railroad depot named for the biblical character Esau's desert homeland. Some residents didn't care for the name, as Esau was hardly a sympathetic Old Testament character. He was, after all, the brother who sold his birthright to his brother Jacob for a bowl of stew. They petitioned the postmaster to change the name to Thousand Palms.

After Interstate 10 was built in 1957, it began the town's transformation from a roadside stop and date-citrus farming community into a small residential and industrial area. Its population grew by more than 50 percent between 2000 and 2010.

***Finding the old road**—Northwest of Indio at Thousand Palms, another old alignment peels off east of the highway as **Varner Road**. It travels a little more than 9 miles, through desert foothills and past a few giant wind turbines, before dead-ending a little beyond Palm Avenue. This last segment is poorly maintained, so four-wheel drive is recommended if you want to travel the last mile or so; then you'll have to turn around and return to Palm.

Varner Road, a segment of old 99, runs east of modern Interstate 10 in the Thousand Palms area.

can be seen in operation on a windy day along both sides of the highway. Wind speeds in the pass average 15 to 20 mph in the narrow gap between the San Jacinto and San Gorgonio mountain ranges, and more than 3,200 windmills loom large over the landscape, twirling like pinwheels in the gusty wind. If you pass through the area and get out of the car to snap a few photos of these impressive machines, be prepared to hold on to your hat.

Finding the old road: Just north of Avenue 50, Harrison Street curves to the left and joins SR 111 for a couple of miles to become **Indio Boulevard**. From Avenue 48 northward, it's signed as Business 10 until it rejoins the interstate of the same number at Jefferson

After returning to I-10 and traveling a little more than 3 miles northwest, turn south at the Indian Canyon Drive off-ramp (exit 120) from I-10, then immediately east on **Garnet Avenue**, where you'll find another old section of concrete road.

WHITEWATER (UNINCORPORATED)

Population (2010)—859
Elevation—1,834 feet
Location—18 miles west-northwest of Thousand Palms
Founded—1862

Whitewater began as the White Water Station, a stagecoach stop between the Arizona border and San Bernardino. It's situated along the Whitewater River, which drains into the Salton Sea.

*Finding the old road: Take the Whitewater exit (114) and turn north of the highway, then curl around eastward on **Whitewater Cutoff**, a short but well-maintained segment of concrete that's part of the earliest alignment. You can cross a 1923 bridge over the Whitewater River on this section, which continues for about a mile before dead-ending. Turning back west, Tamarack Road follows a line of phone poles and appears to be another section of the old road, but it's just gravel for much of the way and four-wheel drive is a must.

CABAZON (UNINCORPORATED)

Population (2010)—2,535
Elevation—1,834 feet
Location—8 miles west-northwest of Whitewater
Founded—1884
Incorporated—1955

A portion of the expressway that was U.S. 99 is still visible in Cabazon, where it is known as Main Street and runs south of the current I-10 freeway.

Dinosaurs still roam the earth in Cabazon. Well, a couple, anyway. And they don't actually roam, they tend to stay in one place. That's how things work when you're a statue.

Those statues—a 150-foot-long brontosaurus and a tyrannosaurus rex measuring 50 feet tall—were the work of Claude Bell, who ran a portrait studio at Knott's Berry Park at Buena Park for three decades. He also liked to create sand sculptures but wanted to make a more lasting impression.

Bell stayed in Buena Park during the week, then drove out to his second home in Cabazon to work on the brontosaurus he called "Dinny" on the weekends. Bell had bought some land in Cabazon in 1945, but it wasn't until nearly two decades later that he started work

Looking off the 1923 bridge over the Whitewater River, part of old 99, toward Interstate 10 in the distance.

on Dinny, using metal rods from a demolished bridge and concrete cast aside by construction crews working on the interstate that would bypass Old 99. He didn't complete the project until 1975, and it cost him more than a quarter of a million dollars.

But he wasn't finished.

"The brontosaurus is just the beginning," he said in 1970. "I've got 62 acres alongside the freeway. In the next 30 years, I'm going to build an entire family of giant dinosaurs here."

He hollowed out the broto's belly for use as a gift shop/museum and predicted he'd have the second dinosaur finished within a year of the first. But it took him a little longer: Bell added the tyrannosaurus, named Mr. Rex, in 1985 and planned to start a third dinosaur after that. Unfortunately, he died three years later at the age of 90.

Finding the old road: A former expressway alignment runs south of the interstate

Mr. Rex, a 100-ton statue of a tyrannosaurus, was the second of the two massive Cabazon dinosaurs to be built.

BANNING

Population (2010)—29,603
Elevation—2,349 feet
Location—6 miles west of Cabazon
Incorporated—1913

"Stagecoach Town, USA" is named for Phineas T. Banning, who operated a stagecoach line between Yuma, Arizona, and the town named in his honor. Banning, who served as a state senator, also built California's first railroad, the Los Angeles & San Pedro, starting in 1968 and sold it to the Southern Pacific five years later. He insisted on being referred to as General Banning based on the honorary title Brigadier General of the California First Brigade, which he earned after donating land for a military base to the Union during the Civil War.

An annual event at Banning called Stagecoach Days, includes a rodeo, parade, and carnival.

Finding the old road: Old U.S. 99 is **Ramsey Street** through Banning, where it passes by the historic Fox Theatre and continues through the heart of downtown.

between exits 111 and 103, the latter of which provides access to the modern Morongo Casino and Cabazon Outlet Center. **Main Street**, as it's called here, offers little of historical interest on a roughly two-mile stretch of road.

The Mountain View Motel is one of the remaining older lodges alongside U.S. 99 in Beaumont, where the old highway is known as Sixth Street.

BEAUMONT

Population (1939)—2,314
Population (2010)—36,877
Elevation—2,612 feet
Location—bordering on Banning
Founded—1884
Incorporated—1912

The gradual climb from the depths of the below-sea-level Salton Sea region ends in Beaumont, at the San Gorgonio Pass, a deep gap in the San Bernardino range flanked by mountains that rise to 9,000 feet on either side. The town itself was originally called San Gorgonio, but the name was changed three years later in tribute to the "beautiful mountain" nearby.

Old 99 is known as Sixth Street during its trek through Beaumont, where it split from the old U.S. 60 before the routes were combined into Interstate 10.

The Highland Springs Resort, about a mile north of the highway, was a well-known destination for recreation and relaxation. Beginning in 1927, it offered alternative health treatments and was known affectionately (or perhaps sarcastically) as the "Last Resort." Visitors could follow a regimen of juice fasting or order a meal from the vegetarian restaurant at the ranch. Over the

years, it drew the likes of Bob Hope, Albert Einstein, Elizabeth Taylor, and Ernest Hemingway.

The resort changed hands in 1948 and began catering specifically to Jewish families, offering an array of activities including horseback riding, tennis, and dancing. The Victorian mansion at the center of the resort, which was built in 1884, burned to the ground in 1970 and was replaced by a modern structure.

*Finding the old road: Through Beaumont, **Sixth Street** is a continuation of the alignment known as Ramsey Street in Banning. You can continue along it before rejoining the interstate just west of Beaumont Avenue. This roughly six-mile segment is worth a detour to get a good sense of what the old highway was like.

Just northwest of Beaumont, you'll find another section of road that represents its earliest alignment. Take the Cherry Valley Boulevard off-ramp and turn southwest of the interstate, then take an immediate right on **Roberts Road** (it's the only way you can turn; the road is blocked in the opposite direction). This old concrete alignment continues for a little more than a mile through a rural setting of softly rolling hills. That concrete is well maintained, and you can see how it sets up a couple of inches from the ground on which it was laid.

YUCAIPA

Population (2010)—51,367
Elevation—2,618 feet
Location—10 miles northwest of Beaumont
Founded—1842
Incorporated—1989

Yucaipa dates from a land grant by the governor of Mexico to Antonio Maria Lugo in 1842. Cattle rancher Diego Sepulveda, a relative of the Lugo family, settled in the area. The Yucaipa Adobe, a state historical landmark at 32183 Kentucky Street, preserves a 19th-century blacksmith's shop, farm implements, and furnishings.

An old sign advertises the Vincent St. George Motel along Outer Highway 10, formerly known as U.S. 99, in Yucaipa.

The name Yucaipa is derived from *yucaipat*, meaning "green valley" in the tongue of the Serrano tribe, which occupied the site for centuries before the arrival of Mexican settlers.

Stater Brothers Markets, which grew to a chain of more than 150 stores, was founded in Yucaipa when the Stater twins, Cleo and Leo, bought the W.A. Davis Market in 1936. The company later moved its headquarters to San Bernardino.

Finding the old road: From Windsor Drive to just west of Yucaipa Boulevard, this old alignment paralleling I-10 to the south is now known as **Outer Highway 10**. It runs for a couple of miles through a neighborhood with an odd assortment of industrial sites, storage units, converted motels, and antique dealers. An aged and dated sign for the Vincent St. George Motel, with a few of its letters missing, stands sentinel over this section of roadway.

REDLANDS

Population (1939)—68,747
Population (2010)—36,877
Elevation—1,357 feet
Location—8 miles north-northwest of Yucaipa
Founded—c. 1865
Incorporated—1888

Redlands took its name from the red soil in the region, but it might just as easily have been Orangelands for all

the citrus produced and shipped from the city. Navel oranges seemed to cover the landscape, and packinghouses were everywhere. In the 1930s, Redlands was the hub for distribution of 15,000 acres of citrus, sent out on as many as 6,500 rail cars each year.

As subdivisions replaced orchards, the city's four-year college, the University of Redlands, took center stage. Opened in 1907 with 39 students and nine faculty members attending what was then a Baptist University, it ended mandatory attendance at religious services in 1972, and its master's program was ranked seventh in the West for 2012. By 2014, its student body had grown to 4,500 and full-time faculty members to 204. Its campus is just a city block from Old 99, which passes through Redlands as Redlands Boulevard.

Royal Truck Stop sits at the west end of old U.S. 99 in Redlands where it's known as Redlands Boulevard.

The old road has begun to show its age in the new millennium. A summer downpour in 2014 created a sinkhole along the venerable highway 10 by 15 feet across and 20 feet deep. The city estimated it would cost as much as $200,000 to repair the damage.

Finding the old road: You can follow **Redlands Boulevard**, an expressway alignment of U.S. 99 that runs through the heart of the city, for just under 10 miles, from the eastern edge of town nearly to the I-10 junction with Interstate 215 in the west. It's a scenic drive that's similar in some ways to segments of the old highway you'll encounter in the San Joaquin Valley.

COLTON

Population (1939)—8,014
Population (2010)—52,154
Elevation—1,004 feet
Location—9 miles west of Redlands
Founded—1875
Incorporated—1885

Virgil Earp was best known for his role in the Gunfight at the O.K. Corral, but he was at the center of a dispute that could have been a whole lot deadlier if he hadn't decided to take his finger off the trigger.

Colton lies a good 500 miles from Tombstone, Arizona, but its connection with the O.K. Corral is a lot closer than one might expect. Earp, the city marshal at the time of the famous gunfight (his brother Wyatt served as his assistant), was also the first city marshal of Colton in 1887—six years after the showdown that would become a legend of the Old West. In the interim, he survived an assassination attempt that shattered his left arm and rendered it useless.

When younger brother Morgan was killed in a billiard hall on Virgil Earp's birthday in 1882, Virgil decided to leave Arizona for Colton, where his parents owned a home. The Earps sent Morgan's body there for burial, and Virgil and wife Allie went along for the ride, as did his older brother James. Virgil spent some time there recovering, but even with just one good arm, he soon found that his skills and reputation were very much in demand.

Colton was at the center of a major railroad war between the Southern Pacific on the one hand and the

Despite being built beside the Sam Sneed Golf Course, business must not have been good enough for The Hub, which has closed its doors.

Atchison, Topeka & Santa Fe on the other. The established Southern Pacific line ran through Colton, but the AT&SF was building a competing line through nearby San Bernardino. The latter, through its California Southern subsidiary, had laid out a course that involved crossing the Southern Pacific tracks at Barstow, which was known as Waterman Junction back then. The rail line was meant to connect San Diego, which was then suffering from a lack of rail service, with the Inland Empire region. But the Southern Pacific, seeking to preserve its monopoly, was having none of it: The railroad parked a locomotive on its line at the very spot of the proposed crossing and refused to move it except when SP trains were passing through. Then it hired a flesh-and-blood, gun-toting insurance policy in the person of Virgil Earp, who stood guard in the cab of the locomotive.

Not surprisingly, residents of Colton and San Bernardino lined up on opposite sides of the issue—and the track. The standoff continued far longer than the showdown in Tombstone: That had lasted some 30 seconds; this one stretched out for a full year. California Southern won a court order that (ostensibly) gave it the right of way to complete its crossing. But the locomotive wasn't budging, and Earp wasn't going anywhere, even as several hundred people carrying guns, shovels, and pickaxes began to converge on the track from both sides one day in mid-September of 1883.

The Colton contingent had Earp on its side, but the San Bernardino partisans had an even more powerful ally: Robert Waterman. Originally from Illinois, Waterman had helped form the Illinois Republican Party in 1854 and was one of two Illinois delegates to the party's national convention two years later, the other being a gentleman named Abraham Lincoln. He moved west to California in 1873 and the following year moved to the San Bernardino area, where he mined for silver and started a ranch in Waterman Canyon. He would serve as governor of California for a single term, beginning in 1887.

Nearby, he founded a town called—that's right—Waterman Junction.

Clearly, Waterman was a force to be reckoned with, and he had a definite stake in the railroad dispute: He wanted the California Southern line to go through. So he deputized a posse to head out and put an end to the standoff once and for all. Riding out at the head of the group himself, he read the court order and threatened to open fire if Earp made a move for his gun. It was the O.K. Corral all over again, but this time, Earp found himself outnumbered. It was his move. Would he raise his gun and open fire, ushering in a bloodbath, or would he back down?

In the end, he chose not to challenge the posse, giving way and allowing the California Southern contingent to build its track. Waterman, exulting in his victory, stood atop the cab of the California Southern locomotive, waving his hat to a crowd of supporters the first time railway's locomotive crossed the former "line in the sand."

None of this reflected badly on the Earp reputation. (How many people, after all, have heard of the "Battle of the Crossing," as it came to be called, in comparison to the Gunfight at the O.K. Corral?) In the years ahead, clan patriarch Nicholas Earp became justice of the peace in Colton and operated a saloon there. Virgil Earp became the town's first marshal, and James Earp opened saloons in Colton, Los Angeles, and San Bernardino.

Virgil Earp served two years as city marshal before resigning his post and turning to other pursuits, running a gambling hall in San Bernardino and promoting prizefights. He died in 1905 and his brother Wyatt, who spent some time in Colton, as well, passed away in 1929. Colton Crossing, meanwhile, became one of most heavily traveled junctions in the country, and more than 110 trains used it each day in 2008.

Finding the old road: Here the old highway is called **Valley Boulevard**. One of several segments to bear this

name in Southern California, it runs parallel to the interstate just to the north, traveling through Colton and the unincorporated community of Bloomington, adjacent and to the west. It's a straight shot of mostly nondescript expressway, though as of 2015, you could still see an interesting old neon sign for a closed bar-restaurant called The Hub just north of Sam Sneed Golf Course. At the west end of this alignment, the old highway morphs into the newer-era Ontario Mills Boulevard west of Fontana.

FONTANA

Population (2010)—203,003
Elevation—1,237 feet
Location—5 miles west of Colton
Founded—1913
Incorporated—1952

Fontana has grown substantially in recent years, from a population of just over 36,000 in 1980 to more than eight times that size three decades later. Both U.S. 99 and Route 66 to the north (Foothill Boulevard) passed through the town, which like many others in the Inland Empire began as a farming community.

Kaiser Steel chose Fontana as the site of the largest steel plant on the West Coast in World War II, and it employed as many as 2,500 workers. The company went bankrupt in the 1980s, and part of the plant was later torn down and paved over to become the California Speedway.

ONTARIO

Population (1939)—13,583
Population (2010)—163,924
Elevation—925 feet
Location—14 miles west of Fontana
Founded—1882
Incorporated—1891

There's a reason this city east of Los Angeles often gets confused with the Canadian province of the same name: It was founded by a Canadian engineer named George Chaffey and his brother William.

For a decade, the city was home to the Ontario Motor Speedway, which opened in 1970 with dreams

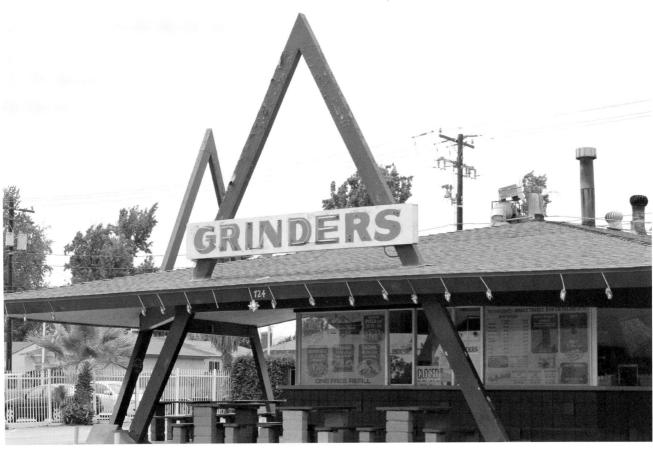

The Grinder Haven sandwich shop has been in business since 1958 along the north side of Valley Boulevard (old Highway 99).

of becoming the Indianapolis Motor Speedway of the West. Indeed, it was patterned as a near-exact replica of that legendary track and even featured 350 bricks from the original Brickyard in Indiana. The racetrack, with its 80,000 aluminum grandstand seats, was built using $25.5 million in bond money. It had a gift shop, a restaurant, and luxury suites for VIPs. Its builders touted it as the only course designed to host races for the IndyCar, NASCAR, and Formula One circuits, as well as NHRA drag races. The Ontario Motor Speedway had something for everyone: Motorcycle daredevil Evel Knievel completed a record jump over 19 cars there a year after it opened, and massive rock concerts—a sort of Woodstock West, with a corporate surfer mentality replacing the hippie vibe—were staged there in 1974 and 1978.

The first of these, California Jam, featured a lineup that included Earth Wind & Fire, the Eagles, Seals and Crofts,

Deep Purple, Black Sabbath, and Emerson Lake & Palmer. It drew as many as 400,000 people, not counting an audience that tuned into ABC for televised portions of the event, and was declared the largest paid concert attendance (tickets were 10 bucks apiece) in history. Traffic on Interstate 10, the successor to Old 99, made rush hour in Los Angeles look like a Sunday drive through the desert: According to one estimate, cars were backed up for 13 miles in both directions. Some concertgoers even left their cars on the shoulders of the freeway and walked to the speedway from as far as four miles away.

Band members had an advantage: They were flown to the venue via helicopter.

The crowd for the 1978 event, Cal Jam II, was almost as large, and the lineup was just as impressive: Aerosmith, Santana, Foreigner, Heart, Stevie Nicks, and Mick Fleetwood were among the performers.

The races drew big names, too. Those who won the track's signature California 500 included Al and Bobby Unser, A.J. Foyt, and Wally Dallenbach. Foyt also won the first two Los Angeles Times 500 NASCAR races, and Bobby Allison and Benny Parsons also won twice. Mario Andretti won the Formula Libre event in '71.

But despite all the big names and big events, the track struggled financially after its successful debut season. By 1973, bondholders were no longer receiving interest payments, and at the end of the decade, the track needed a huge bailout. It came in the form of a bond purchase by Chevron, which paid a total of $49.4 million for the purchase: $35 million for the bonds themselves, $13.4 million to pay off the past-due interest, and $1 million in closing costs. When the deal went through, Chevron said it was undecided whether racing would continue there, but there was little doubt what would happen given the track's history as a financial black hole: The old bricks from Indy were saved, and some memorabilia was sold, but the rest of the racetrack was destined for the scrap heap.

Finding the old road: Through Ontario and neighboring Pomona, the old highway is known as **Holt Boulevard**, which runs a few blocks south of the interstate. Vintage neon for Vince's Spaghetti, a business dating to 1945, and the Ontario Ice Skating Center, built across the highway in 1957, were among the highlights of this section as of 2015. The Grinder Haven, a sandwich shop that opened in 1958, was still open just west of San Antonio Avenue, with a historic neon marker of its own.

POMONA

Population (1939)—20,804
Population (2010)—149,058
Elevation—850 feet
Location—18 miles west of Ontario
Founded—c. 1875
Incorporated—1888

Pomona, like many nearby cities and towns, became an important center for growing citrus before suburban sprawl gobbled up its orchards. Its name was chosen during a contest in 1875, with the winner—a horticulturalist named Solomon Gates—suggesting the name of ancient Rome's goddess of fruit and abundance. (The name Pomona stems from the Latin word for orchard fruit.) The choice showed prescience, as not a single fruit tree had been planted at the time the contest was held.

Pomona is home to California State Polytechnic University, Pomona, or Cal Poly Pomona. It's often confused with its sister campus in San Luis Obispo, which also goes by Cal Poly, and with nearby Pomona College, which isn't in Pomona at all but in neighboring Claremont. It's a private college, while the Cal Poly is part of the public California State University system.

Old Highway 99 in Pomona is called Holt Avenue.

This replica of the original In-N-Out drive-through burger stand sits a few yards away from an actual In-N-Out, so if you get hungry looking at this re-creation, you can drive next door for some real food.

WEST COVINA

Population (2010)—106,098
Elevation—362 feet
Location—24 miles west of Pomona
Incorporated—1923

More people have probably heard of West Covina than Covina, even though the former is an offshoot of the original city. It owes its origins to an initiative by 507 residents to break off and form their own city because they didn't want a sewer plant built within the existing city's boundaries.

West Covina borders Baldwin Park, which is notable as the site of the first In-N-Out Burger. Founders Harry and Esther Snyder opened a small drive-through stand there in 1948 along the highway at Francisquito Avenue. A second location followed three years later in Covina, and the chain had grown to 290 sites across the Southwest by 2014.

The original restaurant with its modest building and canopied drive-through has been gone for years, having been torn down when the new interstate was built. But in early 2014, a replica of the original was unveiled near the original site, a tiny 100-square-foot shack complete with a horseshoe driveway, vintage lights and an old-fashioned neon sign boasting of "NO DELAY" to be served. The one drawback: The vintage site is just for show. If you want burgers and fries, you'll have to try one of the modern-looking In-N-Outs.

EL MONTE

Population (2010)—113,475
Elevation—299 feet
Location—6 miles west of West Covina
Founded—c. 1851
Incorporated—1912

The name El Monte means "the mountain" in Spanish, but there are no mountains in the area. So how did the city get its name? As it turns out, the word is also an archaic term that translates roughly into "scrubland," a description that fit the area well when the first travelers passed through. Some may have come via the Santa Fe Trail, an old Spanish route from Missouri to Santa Fe,

New Mexico, that city leaders claim was later extended to El Monte. The city even adopted the nickname "The End of the Santa Fe Trail." An old welcome sign hanging across Main Street (a portion of Old 99) can be seen in a photo from 1923 bearing the slogan.

There's some dispute about that designation, though. In 1910, the Santa Fe chapter of the Daughters of the American Revolution erected a plaque in Santa Fe declaring that city to be the western terminus of the trail. But the California chapter of that same organization put up a plaque of its own 20 years later in El Monte that marks "the site of the oldest Protestant Evangelical church in Southern California, the erection of the first school house and the end of the Santa Fe Trail."

Whether El Monte was actually at the end of that trail or, as others assert, at the end of a different trail that met up with the Santa Fe in New Mexico, it has a rich history. It was the home of the popular Gay's Lion Farm in the 1920s and '30s, and that park's original lion statue now stands guard at the entrance to the El Monte High School auditorium. The city is also the birthplace of a talking horse—or at least a horse who appeared to talk on television. Bamboo Harvester, a Palomino gelding, was born in El Monte in 1949 and starred in the television series *Mister Ed* during the early 1960s.

Finding the old road: East of Los Angeles, the old highway traveled over a couple of different alignments. The older of the two, another segment called **Valley Boulevard**, continued the Holt Boulevard alignment, dipping south to follow the billboard-lined path of the Southern Pacific Railroad before turning north again into El Monte. It actually crosses the newer alignment, **Garvey Avenue**, which runs straight east and west to Monterey Park. The portion of the Garvey alignment east of this intersection was old Ramona Boulevard, which was paved over by Interstate 10. It's not to be confused with the surface street now known by that name. The sights you'll see along the way include a long line of graceful, almost statuesque eucalyptus trees through Monterey Park and, near the west end of the alignment, a 1934 concrete bridge over Fremont Avenue.

Traffic along Garvey Avenue was backed up at Rosemead Boulevard in this 1952 photograph. The modern Interstate 10 alignment replaced this old city-streets route of U.S. 99 a few years later. © *California Department of Transportation, used with permission.*

ROSEMEAD

Population (2010)—53,764
Elevation—318 feet
Location—adjacent to and west of El Monte
Founded—1861
Incorporated—1959

Rosemead was a contraction of "Rose's Meadow," a ranch owned by early landowner and horse breeder Leonard Rose. He and his wife, Amanda, purchased 600 acres and founded the ranch. A community of chicken and rabbit ranches grew up in the area, which also featured some small truck farms (plots of land that grew garden vegetables intended for sale at markets).

Finding the old road: While the Garvey Avenue alignment of U.S. 99 passes through Monterey Park, the older **Valley Boulevard** route runs through Rosemead and Alhambra just to the north.

A vintage sign along Valley Boulevard, one alignment of U.S. 99, welcomes motorists to Alhambra.

ALHAMBRA

Population (2010)—83,089
Elevation—492 feet
Location—adjacent to and west of Rosemead
Founded—1874
Incorporated—1903

Alhambra, incorporated in 1903, had grown to a city of more than 83,000 by the 2010 census. Early developer Benjamin Wilson named the town at the urging of his 10-year-old daughter, who had been reading Washington Irving's book *Tales of the Alhambra*, about the Alhambra palace in Granada, Spain.

MONTEREY PARK

Population (2010)—60,269
Elevation—384 feet
Location—adjacent to Rosemead
Incorporated—1916

James de Barth Shorb had a daughter named Ramona. What does this have to do with Monterey Park? Quite a bit, as it turns out. When Shorb founded a 500-acre development just east of Los Angeles, he named it after the precocious Ramona, describing it as a "fog- and frost-free neighborhood."

Ramona Acres became just Ramona and then, in 1916, became Monterey Park when residents voted for incorporation by a resounding 455–33 margin. The impetus for this landslide was a sewage treatment plant proposed

This concrete arch bridge was built in 1932 over Freemont Avenue at a three-way split involving Garvey Avenue—an alignment of old 99—Fremont and Monterey Pass Road.

for the area by the nearby cities of Alhambra, Pasadena, and South Pasadena. Rather than raise a stink, Ramona residents simply voted to form a city. The name Monterey Park was chosen for the nearby Monterey Hills.

The Ramona name lived on, however, on Ramona Boulevard—part of Old 99 along with Garvey Avenue, named after another figure from the area's early history. Richard Garvey was a mail carrier for the U.S. Army who rode through the Monterey Pass along a route that later became Garvey Avenue. He began developing land in the area and bringing in water from a dam he built on the Rio Hondo. Unfortunately, he racked up a significant amount of debt and had to sell some of the land he'd begun developing. Shorb was one of the buyers.

Garvey Avenue and Ramona Boulevard formed two adjacent links in the chain of local roads that was Old 99, both of them eventually giving way to a new highway called the Ramona Parkway (or Freeway). The state Highway Commission dropped the Ramona name, along with several other colorful highway monikers, when it decided drivers would find it more helpful if freeway names reflected their destinations.

The Arroyo Seco Parkway became the Pasadena Freeway.

The Olympic Freeway became the Santa Monica Freeway.

The Sepulveda Parkway, originally named for the boulevard whose path it paralleled, became the San Diego Freeway (Interstate 405).

Particularly confusing was the Riverside Freeway, which carried that name because it ran alongside the Los Angeles River, not for any connection to the city of Riverside.

The Ventura Freeway didn't have to change, because it both paralleled Ventura Boulevard in the San Fernando Valley and actually went to the city of Ventura.

The Ramona, for its part, became the San Bernardino Freeway (Interstate 10).

Monterey Park is nowhere near the Monterey Peninsula. Neither should it be confused with the San Diego County town of Ramona. The two Ramonas do, however, share a common thread: Both were named after the same person—if indirectly. It so happens that Ramona Shorb's parents were entertaining author Helen Hunt Jackson one day when the young girl interrupted their gathering—and charmed Jackson to such an extent that she vowed to name the heroine in her next novel Ramona.

The novel of the same name, published in 1884, revolves around an orphaned girl who suffers discrimination because of her mixed heritage: One of her parents was Native American. The book has been through more than 300 printings and four film adaptations, and is performed outdoors each year as part of an annual tradition. It also inspired the name of the San Diego County town, founded two years after the book was first published.

LOS ANGELES

Population (1939)—1,238,048
Population (2010)—3,792,621
Elevation—233 feet
Location—6 miles west of Monterey Park
Founded—1781
Incorporated—1850

Highway 99 wound its way through the oldest areas of Los Angeles, heading west to downtown, then swinging north-by-northwest alongside the base of the Santa Monica Mountains. First, travelers would drive through

This view down Broadway toward Los Angeles City Hall was a common sight for travelers on U.S. 99 when it still followed city streets through the West Coast's largest city.

Lincoln Heights, the first neighborhood in the city to be settled after downtown, then they would pass by Griffith Park on their way to the San Fernando Valley.

On the other side of the highway—opposite the hills that cradle the huge park with its giant carousel, famed observatory, and city zoo—lies what looks like a hollowed-out concrete serpent. Running parallel to the highway for some 10 miles between downtown L.A. and the northern edge of the park, the Los Angeles River looks more like a canal, a cage built to contain a monster that seems to have escaped.

Film buffs saw Arnold Schwarzenegger, the future governor of California, navigate the dry riverbed on two wheels in a chase scene from *Terminator 2: Judgment Day*, and John Travolta race a hot-rod rival on the river

bottom in *Grease*. (Travolta won, of course, when his opponent got bogged down in what little water there was in the river.)

At once sterile-looking and a destination for millions of gallons of treated sewage water every day, the concrete runs more than 50 miles from the San Fernando Valley to the Pacific Ocean at San Pedro.

The river wasn't always like that, though.

In the 1920s, the city commissioned landscape architect and conservationist Frederick Law Olmsted Jr. to create a plan that would have made it one segment of a verdant chain connecting a series of parks and playgrounds across the city. It would have spanned 440 miles of forests, beaches, and schools. Olmsted argued that "with the growth of a great metropolis here, the absence of parks will make living conditions less and less attractive, less and less wholesome." Without such action, he predicted, "the growth of the region will tend to strangle itself."

One look at Los Angeles decades later reveals just how accurate this prediction was. Unfortunately, the city never implemented Olmsted's vision, lacking both the funding (thanks to the Great Depression) and the will to do so. Then, on New Year's Day 1934, torrential rains produced a massive flood that caused the river to leap over its banks. In just 24 hours' time, the downpour deposited a record 7.31 inches of rain on a region that averages just over twice that in an entire year. The riverbed had no way to absorb it.

The Associated Press reported the extent of a cataclysm that affected "persons asleep in houses which were washed away, stranded motorists, some of them New Year's celebrants returning from parties, and travelers riding in machines which fell through weakened bridges across normally dry river beds turned into a maelstrom of mud and water."

Two hundred homes were buried under the muck, and 400 were so badly damaged they were considered uninhabitable. Forty bodies were recovered, but dozens of other people were missing—some of whom were never found. The flood left such a lasting impression that Woody Guthrie wrote a song about it called *The New Year's Flood*: "Down that mountain rolled the wild Los Angeles River, in that fatal New Year's flood."

The disaster convinced Congress of the need to provide the region with the money necessary to contain the rogue river, but the work was slow and hadn't gotten far by the time the next big flood hit four years later. This time, the damage was even worse, because the rain continued over the course of five days: At least 113 people died and more than 5,600 buildings were destroyed. But still the river project, for its sheer scope, took more than two decades to complete. More than 10,000 workers dug channels and poured concrete—3 million barrels of it—by hand, creating that concrete serpent to parallel the asphalt snake of old U.S. 99 along on its journey north toward the San Fernando Valley.

Finding the old road: Valley Boulevard becomes **Main Street** in the Lincoln Park area, then heads west

across Interstate 5 and the Los Angeles River to **Cesar Chavez Boulevard** (formerly called Macy Street). Here, you're within distance of Union Station and Olvera Street, the oldest section of downtown L.A. The iconic City Hall building will be visible a few blocks to the south. At this point, the old alignment jogs three short blocks to the west along Chavez/Macy before turning north along **Broadway** through Chinatown. There you'll pass underneath a pair of golden dragons before heading back across the river to San Fernando Road.

GLENDALE

Population (1939)—62,736
Population (2010)—191,719
Elevation—522 feet
Location—8 miles north of Los Angeles
Founded—1884
Incorporated—1906

The name Glendale was chosen from among several proposals, including Riverdale, Etheldean, and Minneapolis (imagine if basketball's Lakers had relocated there from Minnesota; they wouldn't have had to change their name). The city became a true boomtown in the "Roaring Twenties," adopting the nickname "Fastest Growing City in America" as it grew from fewer than 14,000 residents in 1920 to nearly 63,000 a decade later. The author of the 1939 WPA guide to California wrote that its appearance reflected its recent growth spurt:

> A modern city with wide, well-paved streets and boulevards, its recently erected stucco houses convey an impression of impermanence to visitors from older communities.

Finding the old road: The old alignment runs north through Glendale, Burbank, Sun Valley, and San Fernando along **San Fernando Road** (in places called **San Fernando Boulevard**), which parallels Interstate 5. Much of the area has become industrial, though a few old motels, garages, and liquor stores remained as of 2015. It's about a 30-mile stretch, among the longest for an old 99 alignment, although it's interrupted in Burbank by a three-story mall that was built right on top of the old road.

Bob's Big Boy had a restaurant along old U.S. 99 in West Covina, and another 99 location is still operating just west of the freeway in Bakersfield. The oldest one still in business, however, is this diner in Burbank, which was built in 1949 and is still operating a couple of miles west of the freeway on Riverside Drive. There's even a booth marked by a plaque indicating the Beatles once ate there. It's about halfway between 99's old route and U.S. 101.

A series of concrete overpasses connects Interstate 5 to State Route 14 just north of San Fernando. Four highway alignments meet here: the Sierra Highway (old U.S. 6) and its replacement, SR 14; and I-5, paralleled by San Fernando Road (old U.S. 99), which becomes The Old Road just north of the spot from which this photo was taken.

BURBANK

Population (1939)—16,622
Population (2010)—103,340
Elevation—607 feet
Location—6 miles west of Glendale
Founded—1887
Incorporated—1911

Folks who grew up in the '60s still remember the distinctive voice of deejay and *Laugh-In* personality Gary Owens extolling the praises of "beautiful downtown Burbank" on television every week.

Commercial messages are par for the course in Burbank, which has been hailed as the "Media Capital of the World." The city is home to production facilities for the likes of Warner Bros., Walt Disney, and NBC. As of 2014, Burbank was also the site of the oldest remaining Bob's Big Boy restaurant in the United States, built in 1949 and standing about two miles west of the Old 99 off the Ventura Freeway.

SAN FERNANDO

Population (1939)—7,567
Population (2010)—23,645
Elevation—1,070 feet
Location—12 miles northwest of Burbank
Founded—1874
Incorporated—1911

San Fernando is one of the most historic cities in the region, the San Fernando Mission dating back to 1787.

The San Fernando Valley, in turn, takes its name from the city. But while most of the valley is part of Los Angeles, San Fernando itself remains a separate city. Many other communities in the valley accepted annexation with Los Angeles because the larger city had something they needed: water. L.A. could turn on the faucets, spigots, and sprinklers for them in exchange for a few more tax dollars. San Fernando, on the other hand, had enough groundwater to retain its independence.

As a result, the city became an island, surrounded on all sides by the L.A. city limits. It's the last thing northbound drivers see before they head into the hills for a trip toward a different valley, the San Joaquin.

The Old 99 is called San Fernando Road (or Boulevard) over one of its longest-surviving stretches.

SANTA CLARITA

Population (2010)—209,130
Elevation—1,207 feet
Location—15 miles north-northwest of San Fernando
Founded—c. 1870
Incorporated—1987

Santa Clarita is really a combination of four local towns: Valencia, Saugus, Newhall, and Canyon Country, none of which was incorporated until they combined their territories and became a city. It's perhaps best known as the site of Six Flags Magic Mountain, a roller coaster–heavy amusement park that draws visitors from the San Fernando Valley and beyond.

Though only incorporated in the waning years of the 20th century, the area has a long history of human habitation. In fact, the Saugus Café opened in 1886 at the north end of the newly opened train depot, as Tolefree's Saugus Eating House. Located along the old highway, it served President Teddy Roosevelt a "splendid" New York steak in 1903 and also played host to Charlie Chaplin, Mary Pickford, and Douglas Fairbanks, who ate there in 1919. Later on, Gary Cooper, John Wayne, and Clark Gable grabbed some grub.

The original Saugus Café, on an old alignment of U.S. 99—now called Railroad Avenue—that followed the railroad tracks, first opened its doors in 1886.

Cowboy star Tom Mix, who was supposedly seen in a 1923 film jumping on horseback over nearby Beale's Cut, also stopped by, though it was likely a stuntman, not Mix, who performed the famous leap. Marlene Dietrich even filmed scenes from the movie *Seven Sinners* behind the café, which remains open well into the 21st century as perhaps Los Angeles County's oldest surviving eatery.

With all the star power dropping in for lunch at Saugus, there was little doubt that the foothills were on the cusp of the Hollywood scene. Newhall and Saugus—named, respectively, for land owner Henry Newhall and his hometown of Saugus, Massachusetts—were also the gateway to the Tehachapis, lying just south of where the Ridge Route began its circuitous course across the top of the world. Early attempts to ease the passage of mountains included Beale's Cut and the Newhall Tunnel.

The former dated back to the horse-and-buggy days of the mid-19th century. It actually started out as Banning's cut, created by stagecoach operator Phineas Banning—the same fellow who lent his name to the city of Banning. The Gold Rush had created a sense of urgency among prospectors and fortune hunters heading north, especially when gold turned up on the Kern River, and Banning set out to prove that he could smooth the way for stages to pass across the great north–south divide.

In 1854, Banning cut a slice out of the mountain 30 feet deep, creating a more direct passage north (and south) for horse and buggy. He was just 24 years old, but he already owned the largest stagecoach operation in the region, boasting 15 coaches, 40 wagons and 500 mules. Determined to test-drive his stagecoach through the cut and down the steep incline on the other side, Banning brushed aside warnings that the path wasn't ready, took the reins, and urged his horses forward. The whole mass of mustangs, wagon wheels, and passengers ended up in a pile of chaparral at the bottom of the incline. Banning crowed with delight that it wasn't nearly as bad as he'd anticipated.

Nine years later, General Edward Beale improved that passage by making the cut three times as deep, a full 90 feet. But that improvement came at a cost: Beale set up a toll station at "his" cut and began charging a quarter for every rider on horseback who wished to pass through and a full $2.50 for a team of a dozen horses. On top of that, sheep cost 4 cents apiece. Thereafter, it became known as Beale's Cut.

His slice through the mountain remained the primary passageway from Newhall into the high country for half a century, until the advent of the automobile created the demand for something better: a tunnel.

The Newhall Auto Tunnel, completed in 1910, allowed travelers to go under, rather than over, the steep terrain.

The tunnel was a huge improvement when it opened, but the quickly evolving automobile industry soon made it obsolete. At just 17 feet tall and only a few inches wider, it created a bottleneck of epic proportions as the number of cars on the road doubled, tripled, and multiplied beyond anyone's expectations (except perhaps Henry Ford's). In 1910, California had a little more than 44,000 registered automobiles; that number had increased to nearly 700,000 by 1927.

Two cars could pass abreast through the 434-foot-long portal that was the Newhall Tunnel.

Barely.

But if anything larger tried to make it through, the vehicle on the other end would have to back up and wait for traffic coming the other way to pass. Since the number of trucks increased just as rapidly as automobile traffic, it's no wonder things slowed to a crawl. P.A. McDonald, an assistant engineer for the California Department of Highways and Public Works explained in a 1938 article:

> The existing tunnel is … narrow, dark, and fore-boding looking. It promptly becomes a one-way road on the appearance of limited load vehicles. The speed of all traffic using this route is therefore necessarily reduced to that of the slowest moving vehicle, or, due to heavy trucking on this route, to generally the speed of a truck and trailer negotiating the six plus per cent grade of either approach."

The result, he wrote, caused "traffic on peak days to be jammed for a mile or more from the tunnel portal. The solution was to replace the tunnel with a daylight section of road over the same terrain, a project that required excavating 300,000 cubic yards of material and widening the road at a cost of $900,000. The tunnel was eliminated that same year.

Finding the old road: San Fernando Road becomes **The Old Road**, an expressway alignment dating from 1930. It runs west of Interstate 5 for most of its length and past Six Flags Magic Mountain before coming to an end around Castaic Junction (where the highway crosses SR 126 and not to be confused with Castaic itself, about five miles farther north). Some of this road, however, really isn't so "old" after all. Part of it was put in as a frontage road when I-5 was being built; in those sections, the old highway is actually beneath the interstate's southbound lanes. Before 1930, the highway followed an alignment that took it up the Sierra Highway, an expressway precursor to SR 14, then north through Newhall and Saugus via **Newhall Avenue**, **Railroad Avenue**, and **Magic Mountain Parkway**.

Castaic (unincorporated)

Population (1939)—61
Population (2010)—19,015
Elevation—1,280 feet
Location—6 miles north-northwest of Santa Clarita
Founded—1915

Castaic was, and still is, the last gas(p) for travelers topping off their tanks before the steady climb up toward the Tejon Summit. It sprang up at one end of the Ridge Route when it opened in 1915 and continued to thrive as a way station for travelers after the highway shifted to the west. A few gas stations, inns, and garages were scattered among the curves of the old Ridge Route, but the Ridge Route Alternate and its successor, I-5, offered nothing but wilderness for roughly 30 miles between Castaic and Gorman. Hence, today, you'll see plenty of gas pumps in Castaic, along with a few motels.

Castaic was originally called Kashtuk, a Native American word meaning "eyes." Sam Parsons, anticipating the business that would come with the new Ridge Route, bought an acre of land there and opened up Sam's Place, a gas stop and general store that also housed the first post office. Castaic Lake is a man-made lake to the east of town, which has been described as the de facto replacement for the reservoir behind the failed St. Francis Dam. It shouldn't be confused with Castac Lake (no "i") at the other end of the old Ridge Route, near Lebec.

Finding the old road: Two old alignments exist crossing the Tehachapi Mountains. The oldest is the **Ridge Route**, originally paved in concrete and running from Castaic in the south to SR 138 (the Lancaster Freeway) in the north. It's also accessible by taking the Templin Highway east for a short distance. As of 2015, the road was blocked off by the Forest Service a little

The entrance to Gorman from old U.S. 99, the Ridge Route Alternate, as it appeared on Dec. 15, 1951. © *California Department of Transportation, used with permission.*

more than a mile north of Templin; it was accessible from the north, though portions of the road were rough and prone to rockslides. Four-wheel drive is preferable but not necessary.

The second, newer alignment is accessible by taking the Templin Highway exit and turning west instead of east. Signed as the **Golden State Highway**, it's another segment of the expressway seen farther south as The Old Road and known as the Ridge Route Alternate, which opened in 1933. There isn't much in terms of development here, and you can drive only five of the seven miles between Templin and Pyramid Dam. For the last two miles, you've got to hike (or proceed on bicycle), and

beyond that, the road is submerged beneath man-made Pyramid Lake. The road's a bit bumpy in spots but easily traversable in an automatic transmission vehicle.

GORMAN (UNINCORPORATED)

Population (1939)—68
Population (2010)—about 20

Elevation—3,774 feet
Location—29 miles north-northwest of Castaic
Founded—c. 1877

James Gorman bought a ranch a few miles south of Tejon Pass around 1867 and opened a two-story log building there to the public, offering food, liquor, and a place to lay your head for the night upstairs. The post office, known as Gorman Station, followed about a decade later, and Gorman Post Road—a portion of the old Ridge Route—was named for it. (Post roads were byways designated for postal coaches to deliver the mail, and Gorman Post Road is still the main route through town today.)

In 1898, the Gorman family sold their ranch to Oscar Ralphs, who with his brothers had founded the Ralphs grocery chain. Oscar Ralphs was an equal partner in that business, but after a couple of years, he turned his attention to running the Gorman ranch with his new wife, Mary, whose father owned a neighboring property.

Over the years, the ranch became a town, and the Ralphs family owned almost every business that sprang up there. One exception was the Standard gas station, not only the first to be built in Gorman but also the first in California to be built away from any rail line. This meant fuel had to be delivered by tanker truck instead of by train. The year was 1923, and it was an acknowledgment of the Ridge Route's importance as a corridor connecting the two halves of the state.

Mary Ralphs served on the school board in Gorman for 57 years, and the eldest of her nine children, Lloyd, used a loan from the Greyhound Bus Company to build a hotel and coffee shop in a complex that included the bus depot. Other development followed, almost all of it built by the Ralphses on their land. There was the Caravan Motor Inn, a Carl's Jr. restaurant that opened in 1988, and a few other businesses. But in 1994, they decided to give it all up, putting the entire town up for sale. Asking price: $13.6 million.

*Finding the old road:** North of SR 138, there's a section of concrete from the Ridge Route era that runs a few hundred yards eastward before dead-ending. The road veers northward as **Gorman Post Road**, a five-mile stretch that comes to an end just north of Gorman, where an old three-lane (suicide lane) segment has been paved over in asphalt. Double-back from there and cross under the interstate, then follow **Peace Valley Road**—another segment of the Ridge Route Alternate—north. If you look just to the west, you'll see another section of concrete road that runs a few hundred yards up the hillside.

LEBEC (UNINCORPORATED)

Population (1939)—30
Population (2010)—1,468
Elevation—3,481 feet
Location—5 miles north of Gorman
Founded—1895

Lebec lies just to the north of the Tejon Pass, a sleepy mountain community named for a man named Peter Lebeck, a French trapper immortalized in an epitaph carved into an oak tree a short distance from nearby Fort Tejon:

PETER LEBECK

KILLED

BY

A X BEAR

OCTr. 17

1837

Upon finding the inscription, a group from Bakersfield decided to dig at the base of the tree and found a skeleton—apparently that of Monsieur Lebecque (the proper French spelling). Lebecque had been traveling with two companions when he caught sight of a grizzly and felled it with a shot. Believing the bear to be dead, he approached to claim the pelt. But as it turned out, the bear was still alive and, in a frenzy from its wound, mauled and crushed the startled Frenchman to death. The people of the area, duly impressed, named the town in his honor.

Lebec was once the site of the grandest hotel between Los Angeles and Bakersfield, the Lebec Hotel. For eight years, starting in 1942, it was also home to an impressive

The Emery Whilton Florafaunium was a museum dedicated to plant and animal life that was moved to Lebec piece by piece in 1942 from the 1939 Golden Gate International Exposition in San Francisco. It was damaged in an earthquake and subsequently demolished in 1955.
Ridge Route Communities Historical Society.

museum across from the hotel called the Emery Whilton Florafaunium, a building used at the 1939 World's Fair in San Francisco and moved one brick at a time to Lebec. The building got its name from the fact that its exhibits focused on the state's plant and animal life—including 84 varieties of animals and birds found in the San Joaquin Valley and more than 1,700 varieties of California wildflowers. In fact, it was said to house the world's most complete collection of birds, animals, and flowers.

Whilton, a Los Angeles big-game hunter who had built the Hotel Tulare on Old 99 in 1922, assembled the collection, which included extinct species such as the Wyoming grizzly and the last passenger pigeon. Kern County took possession of the exhibits when Whilton died in 1945.

More than 14,000 people visited the museum in 1949, but its remote location kept attendance figures below what they might have been, and the cost of maintaining the museum there turned out to be prohibitive. None of this was helped by the fact that the humidity and extreme temperature swings in Lebec (elevation 4,000 feet) were damaging the exhibits. So in 1950, the Kern County Board of Supervisors voted to move the museum's contents to Bakersfield, where many of them proceeded to gather dust for years.

The Tehachapi earthquake damaged the vacant building two years later, and it was torn down in 1955.

Today, Lebec is little more than a modest village. Most of its homes cling to the hillside west of the highway, clustered around a few winding roads. A few small businesses and a couple of churches line what passes for the main drag, sleepy Lebec Road, an old alignment of Highway 99, which winds its way north to an off-ramp that leads to nearby Frazier Park. It's there that travelers can find a truck stop, service stations, and a couple of places to catch a bite to eat.

*Finding the old road: Peace Valley Road continues to the Frazier Park I-5 exit, then northward from there as **Lebec Road**, continuing the old alignment. Directly across from the Lebec I-5 entrance/exit, near the site of the old Hotel Lebec, you can see a short segment of concrete road. The road crosses I-5 before heading to Fort Tejon, where two other sections of concrete are clearly visible near the school (one now serves as a bus loading zone). Cross back over to the west side of the interstate and keep heading north about a mile on Digier Road. If you park right past the end of the county-maintained road and look down toward I-5, you'll get a bird's-eye view of the infamous concrete Dead Man's Curve from the original Ridge Route era.

GRAPEVINE (UNINCORPORATED)

Population (1939)—15
Population (2010)—few permanent residents
Elevation—1,499 feet
Location—12 miles north of Lebec
Founded—1923

"The Grapevine" has become synonymous with that stretch of steep, curving highway that descends from Tejon Pass to the base of the Tehachapis at the edge of the San Joaquin Valley. The twists and turns in the road do call to mind a grapevine climbing up the side of a steep natural trellis, and it was a whole lot worse back in the day, before Interstate 5 smoothed out many of the curves and the road consisted of a seemingly endless series of switchbacks.

In fact, however, Grapevine was coined as the name of the canyon between the north- and southbound lanes of the current interstate because grapevines grew wild there. The name dates all the way back to 1806, when a priest dubbed it La Cañada de las Uvas. A small settlement there took the name Grapevine for the same reason. The highway originally went through the canyon, and

The Grapevine Coffee Shop served up refreshments while motorists filled up their tanks at the Union Oil station in the mid-1900s.
Ridge Route Communities Historical Society.

you can still travel the old concrete road there for a mile or two if you exit at the foot of the mountains. Not only is the old road still there, but grapevines are still cultivated alongside it.

Because Grapevine Canyon is … well … a canyon, it's prone to flooding. Even when the Ridge Route was first being laid down, way back in 1914, workers saw their labor get washed away by a major storm and had to rebuild higher up the mountainside. Today's alignment, with southbound lanes rising west of the canyon and northbound traffic descending to the east, rises above the flooding issue altogether.

Although a small Mexican village existed in the canyon during the 1800s, the modern community emerged as a haven for travelers weary from—or preparing for—the long drive over the Ridge Route. A cluster of small businesses popped up, and a post office began operating there in 1923. A couple of auto courts opened there, offering overnight accommodations. When the old Ridge Route gave way to the Alternate, which engineers later widened from three to four lanes, the small service community pulled up stakes and moved up the hill to accommodate the new alignment. This new Grapevine consisted of a Union 76 station with a huge scaffolding sign that was visible for miles, a motor hotel with a dozen cottages, a restaurant and bar, and a scattering of perhaps half a dozen homes.

Before dawn on July 21, 1952, a 7.3-magnitude earthquake struck at nearby Wheeler Ridge, damaging and even toppling buildings throughout the region. The town of Tehachapi took the worst hit from the quake, which left 11 people dead and 35 others hurt. Fifteen homes were leveled. At Grapevine, no one was killed, but a news dispatch reported that "all the buildings at Grapevine Station … were knocked over and described as 'a shambles.'" Another report described a motel and store as "wrecked" and said two people had been injured. (A photo of the motel, where the injuries occurred, showed one section of it reduced to little more than a heap of broken lumber.) The earth beneath the pump island at the gas station shifted and sank, dropping a foot below the level of the building. It was the strongest quake the state had felt in at least half a century.

In a sense, the highway had given life to the town of Grapevine, and the highway brought an end to it. Those few dozen people who lived there, lured to the side of the road by the new business 99 brought with it, were displaced (along with their neighbors to the north in Wheeler Ridge) when the highway was widened in 1960. Today's Grapevine consists of little more than a roadside gas/convenience stop on either side of the interstate and a stretch of the old road still bordered by grapevines in the canyon.

*Finding the old road:** To see a segment of concrete from the Ridge Route era, take the Grapevine exit and head south up **Grapevine Road**, which is between the north- and southbound sections of I-5. A little ways up, you'll see **Lanny W. Reed Drive** to your left: This is a portion of the old concrete alignment, complete with original curbing. It winds its way a short distance before coming to an abrupt end where it's been cut off by the interstate.

GREENFIELD (UNINCORPORATED)

Population (2010)—3,991
Elevation—351 feet
Location—23 miles northwest of Grapevine
Founded—1949

Drivers knew they were getting close to Bakersfield when they passed through this community on Old 99 (now Union Avenue). The Delkern post office opened there in 1949, taking its name from a combination of the terms Kern and delta.

Finding the old road: Take the **Union Avenue** exit and follow that route north to Bakersfield for a view of old U.S. 99, lined with palm and eucalyptus trees on its approach to the San Joaquin Valley's southernmost major city. Through Bakersfield, the highway followed two separate alignments, the earlier path by way of **Chester Avenue** and the later version, which continued on Union farther north before curving onto the **Golden State Avenue** expressway that predated the modern freeway. The two alignments intersect at Garces Circle. Chester continues northward before that alignment turns right onto **Norris Road**, which eventually heads north and runs parallel to modern Highway 99 as the **Golden State Highway**.

BAKERSFIELD

Population (1939)—26,015
Population (2010)—347,483
Elevation—404 feet
Location—8 miles north of Greenfield
Founded—1869
Incorporated—1873, 1898

Bakersfield is oil country, and it has been for decades. If you were to ask what city on the highway was most responsible for keeping cars running along that asphalt ribbon, the answer would have to be Bakersfield. It's the seat of a county (Kern) that produces two-thirds of California's oil, 10 percent of the nation's supply, and 1 percent of the entire world's output. Bakersfield High School's team nickname is the Drillers, and the city is surrounded by productive oil fields.

In the middle of the 20th century, old-fashioned derricks lined city streets, looming like giant, ever-present sentinels against the sky. Gradually, they gave way to less conspicuous pumping devices that bob their heads up and down like giant dinosaurs or grasshoppers by the side of the highway. You don't have to look too hard for them; they're almost everywhere.

This photo from August of 1937 shows U.S. 99, now Union Avenue, south of Bakersfield. Note the solid white lines between the slow and passing lanes on each side of the double-line median. © *California Department of Transportation, used with permission.*

Bakersfield is also known for country music, specifically the "Bakersfield Sound" exemplified by Merle Haggard, Buck Owens, and Dwight Yoakam.

Notables with ties to Bakersfield include former U.S. Chief Justice and California Governor Earl Warren, who grew up there; Edward Beale (the man behind Beale's Cut); pro football player and announcer Frank Gifford, a Bakersfield High graduate; and President George H.W. Bush, who moved to the city in 1949 to sell oil field equipment.

OILDALE (UNINCORPORATED)

Population (2010)—32,684
Elevation—469 feet
Location—4 miles north-northwest of Bakersfield
Founded—1909

Oildale's name makes sense, as it sits right next to three large oil fields. The Kern River and Midway-Sunset oil fields are the state's two largest, boasting some 20,000 active wells between them in the early 2000s. But Oildale could have just as easily been called Spyville—except for the fact that espionage is supposed to be kept hush-hush, and Oildale's role in the intelligence game was very much on the QT.

At the height of the Cold War, Lockheed got the go-ahead to design and build an aircraft that would fly at such a high altitude that it could spy on Soviet bases without being vulnerable to enemy missiles. The USSR, of course, was conducting espionage of its own, and the Lockheed plant in Burbank was deemed too conspicuous a site for the operation. So production was transferred to one of the most inconspicuous sites imaginable: a building disguised as a tire plant on Norris Road in Oildale.

The operation lasted throughout 1956. Parts were shipped to the site, code name Unit 80, on trucks and railroad cars, then assembled and checked before being taken apart again. From there, canvas-covered trucks made night runs with the parts to nearby Meadows Field—now the

The Tower Motel's distinctive oil derrick sign was a perfect fit for the oil-rich area. Located off Golden State Avenue (old 99), just north of the Garces Memorial Circle, it's in Bakersfield near the southern edge of Oildale.

Bakersfield area's primary airport, which also happens to be in Oildale—from which they were flown to Nevada to be assembled once again.

The U-2, as the plane was called, was designed to go above 70,000 feet, an altitude at which it was thought to have been safe from radar detection and interceptor missiles. Unfortunately, on May 1, 1960, a U-2 piloted by Francis Gary Powers was shot down over the Ural region of the Soviet Union. Powers somehow survived the crash, was captured on Soviet soil, and was eventually returned to the United States in early 1962 as part of a prisoner exchange.

FAMOSO (UNINCORPORATED)

Population (1939)—110
Population (2010)—few permanent residents
Elevation—427 feet
Location—19 miles north-northwest of Oildale
Founded—1888

There's not much in Famoso, which amounts to a few buildings at the junction of 99 and State Route 46. Originally known as Spottiswood and dubbed Poso by the railroad, it had its own post office for a while, but even that closed back in 1946. Now there's just an old motel, a service station, and a few other odd structures clustered around the off-ramp. Still, it's hard to miss: A vertical sign with white lettering that bears the town's name is in plain view from both sides of the highway, and there's not much else for miles in either direction.

If you keep going a few miles east on 46, you'll get to the area's main attraction, the Famoso Raceway, a drag strip that began its history as an Army Air Corps training site. A racing club called the Bakersfield Smokers started using it in 1951, and an event eight years later put Famoso on the map with the first U.S. Fuel and Gas Championships, at which the Smokers challenged East Coast driver "Big Daddy" Don Garlits to duplicate his times on their track.

The local racers paid Garlits a substantial sum to come out west and prove his mettle in an event that

The Famoso Inn Motel stands at the junction of Highway 99 and State Route 46. James Dean headed east from here on the ill-fated trip in his Porsche Spyder that ended with his death in a fatal crash.

produced the kind of buzz seldom seen before or since. It was the 1950s, and souped-up hot rods were the perfect fit for a culture built by the likes of James Dean and Elvis Presley, especially in the Bakersfield area, which was becoming a mecca for car lovers even back then. (The city would go on to produce the likes of four-time Indy 500 winner Rick Mears and NASCAR mainstay Kevin Harvick.)

The first time Garlits came to Famoso, somewhere between 25,000 and 30,000 people turned out to see whether he could live up to his billing. That day, he didn't: Garlits was eliminated in the first round. But Garlits would be back, and he eventually silenced his doubters. The March Meet (as it came to be called) turned into an institution, and "Big Daddy" finally won it on his seventh try in 1965. It wouldn't be the last time Garlits won at Famoso, and by the time he retired for good in 2003, he had won 17 series championships awarded by three different hot-rod organizations.

In addition to Garlits, other top names in the sport competed at Famoso, including Don "The Snake" Prudhomme, funny car pioneer Jack Chrisman (whose nephew Art emerged victorious at that first March Meet), and Shirley Muldowney, the first woman to drive a top fuel dragster. The track continued to host events, including the March Meet, as of 2014.

McFarland

Population (1939)—400
Population (2010)—13,745
Elevation—354 feet
Location—6 miles north of Famoso
Founded—1908
Incorporated—1957

Formerly known as Hunt and Lone Pine, this small farm-worker-driven town describes itself as the "Heartbeat of Agriculture." The town is named for co-founder J.B. McFarland, who began farming walnuts, citrus, and grains in 1904 on a plot of land in Anaheim that would eventually become part of Walt Disney's amusement park property. McFarland (the man) was also known for his Percheron draft horses, which he used to plow his fields—and which won several awards for their speed and pulling strength at the California State Fair.

Delano

Population (1939)—2,632
Population (2010)—53,819
Elevation—315 feet
Location—7 miles north of McFarland
Founded—1873
Incorporated—1915

Just south of the Tulare-Kern county line, Delano was the focal point for the farm-labor movement galvanized by Cesar Chavez. In September of 1965, about a thousand workers in and around Kern County's second-largest city went on strike, refusing to work unless growers improved their wages. Filipino and Latino farm laborers joined forces in the strike, which wound up lasting five years, and in 1966, Chavez led a group of farmworkers and their supporters on a 340-mile march up Highway 99 to Sacramento.

That march began in Delano.

The strike and an accompanying table grape boycott finally produced a labor contract between the growers and the workers. When Delano opened its second high school in 2003, it named the campus Cesar E. Chavez High School in his honor.

Finding the old road: The old alignment runs through the heart of town as **High Street**, which parallels what might be stretches of a still older alignment, **Glenwood Street**.

Earlimart (unincorporated)

Population (1939)—225
Population (2010)—8,537
Elevation—282 feet
Location—8 miles north of Delano
Founded—1880

Earlimart got its name from the Earlimart Fruit and Alfalfa Company, which combined the words "early" and "market" to create Earlimart in 1910. The new town, however, wasn't really new at all.

A depot had been built there in the 1880s along the Southern Pacific line, in addition to a post office, a school, a smithy, and a warehouse. The town was named Alila, a Native American word meaning "land of flowers," in reference to the wild poppies that grew there in springtime.

The community, however, suffered during the 1890s as the result of a drought and a series of fires that ravaged local crops, and soon it started to look as though it might become a ghost town. The Earlimart Fruit and Alfalfa Company brought new life to the area, founding a settlement a mile southeast of Alila. The company tried to persuade the Southern Pacific to build a spur line to the new site, but its requests fell on deaf ears, so the recently settled town pulled up stakes and moved to Alila—which itself assumed the name Earlimart.

All this is a nice bit of history, but the town owes its true fame—or, rather, infamy—to an incident that occurred on the rail line there in 1891. About 8 o'clock on the night of February 6, three armed men climbed onto a southbound train from San Francisco and headed for the locomotive, intent on committing a robbery. Brandishing pistols, they forced the engineer and the fireman to stop the train and demanded that the expressman open the door to the express car, where the valuables were kept.

In this case, however, Wells Fargo expressman C.C. Haswell—who was in charge of guarding those valuables—smelled a rat. He got his shotgun, lay down on the floor of the car, and blew out the lights inside. "At a point one mile south of Alila, I was first notified of the fact that something was wrong by the sudden stopping of the train and the firing of several pistol shots in quick succession," he told a reporter the following day. "I stepped to

The White River overflowed its banks north of Delano and just south of Earlimart, making travel a challenge for motorists along U.S. 99 in this photo taken March 18, 1952. © *California Department of Transportation, used with permission.*

the door of my car just in time to see four men get down off the engine and tender. This was enough for me. I did not wait to see any more, but promptly closed the door of my car, put out the lights and prepared for battle."

Then he fired at the door—beyond which stood the masked robbers, the engineer, and the fireman, who had been ordered at gunpoint to smash his way through using a coal pick. The scene was chaos. The intruders answered with gunshots of their own, and amid the hail of bullets, the fireman was mortally wounded by a shot to the abdomen. The expressman suffered a superficial wound to the forehead before escaping out the back. The intruders, unable to lay hold of the loot, abandoned their efforts, leaving the train and apparently escaping on waiting horses.

The suspects were still at large two weeks later, and a grand jury indicted Haswell, whose blind shooting they blamed for the fireman's mortal wound.

He was cleared of the charges within a few days.

As for the robbers, suspicion immediately fell upon the Dalton Gang, whose members were responsible for a series of train robberies in the area. According to one railroad detective, they had a monopoly on rail heists in the region: "There has been nobody holding up trains in the San Joaquin but those Daltons," he declared. That wasn't entirely true, but the Daltons' reputations certainly made them prime suspects in the case.

Lawmen followed Grat Dalton and arrested him in Fresno, but he was released for lack of evidence. Undaunted, they pursued him to San Jose, where he was again arrested and again released before heading south to Paso Robles. His brother Bill—who had served two terms in the State Legislature, representing Merced County—had a ranch there, where he practiced target shooting and sometimes entertained his outlaw siblings.

He soon found himself entertaining sheriff's deputies, as well, when they arrived to arrest Grat and took Bill along for his trouble. This time, neither was released, but instead they were taken to Tulare County and jailed there in connection with the Alila robbery. Both went to trial, and while Bill was acquitted, Grat was convicted and sentenced to 20 years in Folsom Penitentiary—a sentence he never served.

Instead, he escaped from the Visalia jail, possibly with the help of fellow outlaw Chris Evans. Someone used a hacksaw blade to cut one of the bars in Grat Dalton's cell, replacing it with a broom handle smeared with soot to avoid suspicion. According to Sheriff Gene Kay, the horse on which Dalton made his escape belonged to Evans' mother-in-law, and Dalton had some cash on him that was traced to another train robbery in Goshen—one reportedly engineered by Evans and his outlaw partner, John Sontag.

Two other prisoners escaped with Dalton that day, and both were quickly apprehended. Dalton, however, proved more elusive. Believing Dalton had fled to Fresno County, Kay organized a joint operation with the sheriff there to track him down in a hideout at Dalton Mountain in the Sierra foothills east of Centerville. They arrested one man, but Dalton himself wasn't there: He had escaped again and made his way east, eventually rejoining the rest of the gang and returning to the Daltons' hometown of Coffeyville, Kansas. There, the gang launched a brazen endeavor—an attempt to rob two banks at once—that went colossally wrong when armed townsfolk recognized them and surrounded them. Grat Dalton died in the ensuing shootout, and brother Emmett survived only after taking more than 20 bullets.

Grat Dalton died in 1892, and his brother Bill died two years later in similarly violent fashion, gunned down after taking pistol in hand and charging a posse in Oklahoma.

Finding the old road: West of the highway, you can follow an older segment of highway—**Front Street**—for about two miles just west of the freeway. A couple of miles north, also west of the freeway, there's another short section called **Bishop Drive**.

Pixley (unincorporated)

Population (1939)—350
Population (2010)—3,310
Elevation—272 feet
Location—6 miles north of Earlimart
Founded—1872

In its early years, the small town of Pixley (along with Tipton, just up the road), drew some unsavory characters, including Grat Dalton of the Dalton Gang and Chris Evans of the Sontag-Evans Gang, both of whom worked at one point as members of the Grangers Union in Pixley and nearby Tipton.

Evans and John Sontag robbed their first train in 1889 and the following year later got away with $20,000 in a robbery about 25 miles to the north in Goshen. Sontag wasn't in it just for the money; he had taken a job with the Southern Pacific Railroad as a teenager and had been badly injured in an accident while coupling cars in Fresno two years earlier; the railroad had soon fired him, an act the young Sontag never forgave.

Sontag knew the ins and outs of the railroad, knowledge that no doubt helped him in his future endeavors on the wrong side of the law: train holdups in Pixley, Goshen, Ceres, and Kerman (where he and Evans made off with $15,000). In one of the largest manhunts ever conducted, sheriff's deputies from Fresno and Tulare counties joined U.S. marshals, Pinkerton agents, and bounty hunters on the trail of the two wanted men—who, for the record, denied having committed the robberies. They even hired Native American guides to help ferret out the pair.

Sontag and Evans survived a shootout at one of their hideouts in the Sierra foothills and later sought refuge in a vacant cabin in a remote valley. But the posse beat them to it by one day and was waiting in ambush when they arrived. Both men were shot, and Sontag was severely wounded; he died in custody. Evans, meanwhile, lost an eye and was also hit in the arm, but he nonetheless managed to crawl six miles to another cabin, where the occupants took him in and tended to his wounds. Then, when he had fallen asleep, they contacted the sheriff to come and get him.

Evans served 17 years in Folsom Prison before being paroled and banished to Oregon. He died there at the age of 70 in 1917.

Finding the old road: The modern freeway bypassed a roughly mile-long segment of old highway through Pixley known as **Main Street**. It passes directly by town's well-known water tower. As in Earlimart, Delano, and Tipton in this same area, the bypass was built to the east of the older alignment.

and growers, introducing legislation that prohibited the cattle from grazing on neighboring farmland.

(Lindsey died in 1894, and Tipton Lindsey School in Visalia was also named in his honor. The community of Lindsay, in the eastern part of the county, has a different spelling and was named for the Lindsay Land Company.)

Finding the old road: Just up the road from Pixley, this town of similar size is bisected by an old highway alignment of similar length, known as **Burnett Road**. To access it, take the Avenue 152 exit.

Tipton
(unincorporated)

Population (1939)—414
Population (2010)—2,543
Elevation—276 feet
Location—7 miles north of Pixley

The town got its start when the Southern Pacific built a rail stop on the site in 1872 and was, early in its history, dubbed Tip's End. The Tip in question may have been one Tipton Lindsey, a Visalia resident and lawyer who resolved a feud between cattle ranchers and settlers coming in on the railroad. Lindsey himself had raised cattle upon arriving in the area in 1860, but when they died, he ended up studying law and went on to serve for 12 years as receiver of the U.S. land office in Visalia. He also served on the county's board of supervisors and spent four years in the state Senate.

When Tipton sprang up along the rail line, some newly arrived homesteaders began planting crops in the area and complained when cattle from the ranchers' herds began grazing on their land. Lindsey reportedly intervened in the resulting feud between the cattlemen

The Tipton bypass is seen to the left of the old highway (center) and the rail line to the right in this photo from July 16, 1958. © *California Department of Transportation, used with permission.*

TULARE

Population (1939)—6,207
Population (2010)—59,278
Elevation—289 feet
Location—11 miles north of Tipton
Founded—1872
Incorporated—1888

Tulare was named for a lake that no longer exists—at least most of the time.

The lake in question is Tulare Lake, which was the largest freshwater lake west of the Mississippi River from the 17th century until it dried up when the state began to tap its tributaries—the Kings, Tule, Kaweah, and Kern rivers—for irrigation. The lake was never very deep, but it covered a vast area of nearly 700 square miles.

The lake was actually the last remnant of an expansive inland sea that filled California's Central Valley. That sea gradually disappeared as the valley filled with sediment, Tulare Lake lingering as the last vestige of this prehistoric era. Its shallow waters and marshlands were home to the cattails or tules, from which it took its name, as well as migratory birds that used it as a stop on the Pacific Flyway. Sandhill cranes wintered there by the hundreds of thousands, along with ducks, geese, white pelicans, and others.

Even today, a drive up Highway 41 along the phantom lakeshore offers a look at numerous herons and egrets along the banks of a canal: birds that formerly wintered on the lake itself. Charles Nordhoff, author of one of the earliest travel books on California, wrote in 1872 of a camping excursion beside the lake. In the morning, he said, "I was awakened by a noise like the rush of a distant railroad train. I saw a long line of fluttering white in the far distance toward the lake, which represented, I found, an immense body of wild geese, whose wings and cries … caused this kind of roaring noise."

The size of the lake varied, depending on how much rain fell during winter. At times, it extended as far east as the 99 at places such as Goshen and Pixley, though it typically confined itself to an area that stretched only as far as Corcoran. Because it was so shallow, its waters could spill over to cover a large expanse of land within

This 1951 T-29 Corsair was converted for use as a hot-dog joint called Aerodogs, later transformed into a barbecue restaurant, on L Street, just two blocks east of the old 99 alignment (J Street) in Tulare.

a matter of days and recede just as quickly. "In fact," Nordhoff wrote, "probably 15,000 acres on the eastern side of the lake alone have become dry within eighteen months, and are now covered with cattle, grazing on nutritious grasses."

A long dry spell starting in the early 1920s and lasting through the mid-1930s left the lakebed exposed and encouraged cotton farmers, who had begun to plant along the shoreline during the previous decade, to expand their operations into the now-dry lake. Foremost among these was J.G. Boswell, who bought up tens of thousands of acres on the Tulare Lake bed and began to plant cotton there in the '20s. When the nearly forgotten lake sprang to life again, stretching out over 350 square miles thanks to heavy rains and runoff in the winter of 1937–38, it laid much of Boswell's crop to waste.

The catastrophe, followed by further inundations in 1952 and '55, led Boswell to lobby for flood-control projects on the lake's tributaries, spurring the construction of dams on the Kaweah, Tule, and Kings rivers. These projects, however, failed to prevent another huge flood when heavy rains returned in the winter of '69.

Even in flood years, though, the waters of Tulare Lake weren't exactly lapping at doorsteps in the city of Tulare.

It was simply too far away. But the lake and the town that shares its name do hold this in common: Both are rich in history. Olympic champions Bob Mathias and Sim Iness were classmates at Tulare Union High School, where Mathias had starred on the football team. He took up the decathlon in 1948 at the suggestion of his track coach, then went to the London Olympics that same year and won a gold medal, becoming the youngest track and field gold medalist at the age of 17. He repeated his victory four years later in Helsinki, Finland, where Iness added a gold medal of his own in the discus.

Tulare Union honored Mathias, later a four-term member of Congress, by naming its football field in his honor. A replica of the 1960 Winter Olympics cauldron was installed outside the stadium, which stands a few short blocks from the highway, after the Olympic flame relay passed through town that year.

A drive along Highway 99 takes motorists past other landmarks, as well. The International Agri-Center, south of town, hosts the world's biggest farm equipment show, the World Ag Expo, each year. Even though it's not the county seat (that honor belongs to Visalia, a few miles east of the highway to the north), Tulare is also home to the county fair, held each year at the fairgrounds along Old 99.

Finding the old road: The old highway veers off to the left and runs through town along **K Street** south of Inyo Avenue, where it curves slightly left and continues northward as **J Street**. Until recent years, the K Street exit from the freeway heading northbound was a rare left exit. That design, however, has been changed to a more conventional right-hand off-ramp. This seven-mile stretch of old highway runs past the fairgrounds, several old motels, and the Adohr Farms milkmaid statue, among other sights.

GOSHEN (UNINCORPORATED)

Population (2010)—3,006
Elevation—285 feet
Location—14 miles north-northwest of Tulare

John Sontag and partner Chris Evans boarded a train in Goshen on the night of January 20, 1890, and proceeded to execute a train robbery similar to their first job in Pixley a year earlier. The robbers forced the engineer and the fireman to take them to the express car, where they ordered the Wells Fargo expressman to throw down the strongbox. The robbery would have gone off without a hitch, so to speak, had it not been for a hobo riding the rails underneath the car. The transient picked the wrong moment to climb down and make a run for it, and the robbers shot him in the back for his trouble.

Wells Fargo, having lost some $20,000 in the heist, ordered that the perpetrators be brought to justice and declared that money was no object.

Until the 20th century, Goshen was an island amid marshland at the edge of the expansive but shallow Tulare Lake. It later became a way station on the highway, with several service stations and a campground just north of the junction with State Route 198, the east–west corridor connecting the Tulare and Kings county seats: Visalia and Hanford. As Visalia grew westward in the late 20th century, much of the farmland between it and Goshen disappeared.

Finding the old road: The old highway, known as **Camp Drive**, parallels the freeway on its eastern flank. Take the Betty Drive exit to access this section of road. It shouldn't be confused with the frontage road that runs alongside the freeway directly to the west.

TRAVER (UNINCORPORATED)

Population (2010)—713
Elevation—289 feet
Location—9 miles north-northwest of Goshen

Traveling up 99 from Los Angeles north of Tulare as a child, I was greeted by a series of roadside signs every few hundred yards or so reminiscent of the old Burma-Shave markers. These, however, were a little larger and advertised a place called The Hitching Post. Each of the signs looked roughly the same: There was hitching post shaped like a horse's head, with a drawing of a rope ringing the outside. The background appeared like knotted wood, and the center of each sign advertised a different confection, things like hot dogs and ice cream and date shakes. They all led up to a little roadside settlement called Traver, which wasn't much more than a couple of gas stations and a few old homes.

Bravo Farms is the centerpiece of the tiny community of Traver, just east of the freeway on a short section of old U.S. 99 called Sixth Street. For many years, its predecessor, a roadside stop called The Hitching Post, lured travelers with a string billboards along northbound 99. It later changed its name to Valley Farms, then Bravo Farms, expanding its operations and opening an even larger highway marketplace in Kettleman City at State Route 41 and Interstate 5.

At some point, The Hitching Post must have changed hands, and the new owners changed the name to Bravo Farms. (The signs are still there, by the way, though they've undergone a makeover and now feature the establishment's new name.)

In addition to a café, the expansive grounds—decked out to look like an Old West main street—came to include a variety of attractions. Kids could visit the petting zoo, home of a couple of miniature donkeys named Pumpkin and Snowflake, along with Poncho the Military Macaw, six flying rats (otherwise known as pigeons), rabbits, goats, and other critters. A nine-hole miniature golf course beckoned, as did a shooting gallery, complete with a heckling fox and talking tow truck. Perhaps most impressive was the seven-story treehouse that earned a place in the Guinness Book of World Records as the tallest in existence. The owners challenged kids to climb all the way to the top of the crooked multistory marvel and sign their name to prove they'd been there.

For highway buffs, a collection of old road markers and gas station signs could be found throughout the establishment.

The primary commodity of Bravo Farms, however, was cheese, and kids could take a tour to see how it was made. Or, if they preferred, they could grab some ice cream at the ice cream shop. Those date shakes that The Hitching Post used to serve? They were available at Bravo Farms, as well. As of 2014, the place was still going strong and was, in fact, so successful that a second Old West–themed roadside stop was being built on Highway 41 at Kettleman City.

Finding the old road: A short stretch of the old alignment runs east of the highway near Bravo Farms and is known as **Sixth Street**.

KINGSBURG

Population (1939)—1,321
Population (2010)—11,382
Elevation—302 feet
Location—6 miles north-northwest of Traver
Founded—1873
Incorporated—1908

If you visit Kingsburg in May, you might think you've wandered into Stockholm. Except for the weather, of course. You're not likely to encounter Kingsburg's dry desert air or 90-degree days in Scandinavia.

For many of the city's residents, the Swedish Festival isn't just an event, it's part of their heritage. Swedish Americans from Michigan settled in the area back in the 1870s, and their descendants stuck around. One generation followed another, and 19 out of 20 people living within three miles of the town in 1921 were of Swedish descent. (When Rafer Johnson, who would win a gold medal in the 1960 Olympic decathlon, moved to town at age 5 two decades earlier, his family was the only black family in Kingsburg.)

The Swedish Festival takes place for one weekend in May, but signs of the town's Scandinavian roots are visible year-round. There's the water tower, which is painted to look like an old-style Swedish coffeepot. The downtown architecture follows a Swedish theme, and travelers along 99 can take a quarter-mile detour off the highway for a "Viking Breakfast" featuring Swedish pancakes at the Dala Horse restaurant in the center of town.

A Dala horse, for the uninitiated, is a carved wooden horse often painted bright red with a harness of white, yellow, green and blue. The carvings, which date back nearly four centuries, are popular in Sweden as children's toys.

Those new to the area might be tempted to get off the freeway and check out the very Swedish-looking windmill by the side of the road. But if you're traveling north and you're looking to visit Kingsburg, you've gone too far. That windmill belongs not to the Swedish Village, but to a former Pea Soup Andersen's restaurant about five miles up the road in Selma. It still serves pea soup, but Andersen's sold that location several years ago to a steakhouse called the Spike & Rail.

Finding the old road: After crossing over the Kings River and the Fresno County line, you can take the 10th Avenue exit and veer east of the freeway to **Simpson Street**, which runs past the historic Kingsburg train depot. North of town, it becomes **Golden State Boulevard**, a stretch of highway that seems to have been frozen in time during the 1950s, before the freeway bypassed the rural cities of southern Fresno County. The route continues northward, where it's known as **Whitson Street** through Selma, which is itself an earlier bypass of the original **Front Street** along the rail line. Through Fowler, it's called **Eighth Street**, but it's still the same, continuous stretch of asphalt until just south of Fresno.

The Kingsburg Depot dates from 1888 and was moved from Monson in Tulare County in 1902. It sits on California Street, across the tracks from the southern end of this section of U.S. 99, marked by the line of palm trees.

SELMA

Population (1939)—3,047
Population (2010)—23,219
Elevation—308 feet
Location—6 miles northwest of Kingsburg
Founded—1880
Incorporated—1893

The "Raisin Capital of the World," as Selma calls itself, was named for a woman named Selma. Which woman is a matter of some dispute.

Selma Gruenberg Lewis maintained that her father, San Francisco wine dealer Max Gruenberg, once showed her picture to Leland Stanford; the governor, who was also director of the Central Pacific Railroad at the time, was so impressed that he pledged to name the next town on the rail line in her honor. The story of Selma Lewis, who was buried in the city cemetery, is repeated on her grave marker. A less glamorous, but probably more accurate, tale contends that the city was named for Selma Michelsen, the wife of a railroad employee whose name was selected from a list of nominees.

Like much of Fresno County, Selma has long made agriculture the focus of its economy. Some 90 percent of raisins are produced within a mere eight miles of the city, which earlier in its history relied more heavily on wheat, peaches, and plums. At one point, it adopted the nickname "A Peach of a City."

But raisins have long reigned supreme.

Sun-Maid Raisins, which long had its huge plant up the road in Fresno, relocated in the early 1960s to a spot just south of Selma. More than 1,500 growers deliver 100,000 tons of raisins each year to the plant, where more than 600 Sun-Maid employees work. The plant also boasts the world's largest box of raisins, featuring a picture of the famous Sun-Maid Girl. The original model for the iconic image was Lorraine Collett Petersen, a Fresno teenager who was still in high school in 1915 when she posed for

This auto dealership on the west side of the old U.S. 99 alignment in Selma has seen better days.

the portrait. You can see the big box for yourself outside a gift shop at the plant.

(Technically, the site is in Kingsburg, just south of Selma, but don't mention that to Selma residents. There's no reason to spoil their city's rep as "Raisin Capital of the World.")

Finding the old road: The old highway sweeps through town as **Whitson Street**, which veers slightly westward as it changes to (or from) **Golden State Boulevard** on either end of town. You don't have to veer west with it, though. Instead, you can continue straight along **Front Street**, the original main drag alignment that parallels the railroad tracks. When you get to McCall Avenue, you'll see Wilkins Drive In, "serving Selma since 1963," with its distinctive Papa Burger statue on the roof, an iconic feature of A&W during that era.

FOWLER

Population (1939)—1,166
Population (2010)—5,570
Elevation—308 feet
Location—7 miles northwest of Selma
Founded—1882
Incorporated—1908

Fowler was named for Thomas Fowler, a rancher who emigrated from Ireland and served in the state Senate. Unfortunately, Fowler didn't live long to enjoy the honor: He died at the age of 55 in 1884, two years after the town post office opened. The town's most visible symbol from Highway 99 is a giant neon hand that marks the site of Madam Sophia's, a psychic and palm reading business that dates back four decades.

This neon sign points the way to Fowler from old U.S. 99.

MALAGA (UNINCORPORATED)

Population (1939)—125
Population (2010)—947
Elevation—295 feet
Location—6 miles northwest of Fowler
Founded—1886

Malaga was originally named Tokay after a variety of grape used in winemaking. The choice made sense, considering the adjacent community of Calwa took its name from the California Wine Association. Residents apparently had second thoughts about which variety of grape they preferred, however, and changed the name to Malaga (for a different grape variety) shortly after the post office opened.

FRESNO

Population (1939)—52,513
Population (2010)—509,039
Elevation—308 feet
Location—5 miles northwest of Malaga
Founded—1872
Incorporated—1885

It can be a challenge to find portions of Old 99 in the Fresno area. As it did in the Los Angeles area, the old road has followed more than one alignment over the years—some of which no longer exist. The original road ran along Railroad Avenue south of town, but the highway was moved just to the east with the construction of the Fresno-Calwa Freeway in the 1940s, the first stretch of true freeway in the valley.

Drivers used to follow Old 99 through the heart of downtown on Broadway, but if you try to do that today, you'll run headlong into a 12,500-seat baseball stadium that's home to the Triple-A Fresno Grizzlies.

Change is happening all the time along the old road. Some drivers used Fulton just a block northeast of Broadway to avoid the traffic through town until the early 1960s, when it was paved over and transformed into a pedestrian mall. That mall, once hailed as a cutting-edge, modern innovation, lost its luster over the years, and the city council recently voted to open it back up to limited traffic.

Another change destined to affect the old highway is coming down the tracks. In perhaps the biggest dose of irony you'll find along the old road, sections of it were being ripped up to make way for the very mode of transportation they once superseded: a rail line. The state staked out a course for its multibillion-dollar bullet train project right through the heart of Old 99 in Fresno. Demolition crews started work in the summer of '14 when they knocked down a 66-year-old closed bar called Annie's Hollywood Inn on the stretch of the old highway called Motel Drive. Angelo's Drive-In, a burger joint with a *Happy Days* feel, was next. It had opened in 1954 just off the highway but closed for the last time in August after six decades in business, its distinctive neon carted away to a "sign graveyard" on the north end of town.

Traffic is jammed up on H Street, part of the former 99 route through Fresno, at Fresno Street in this photo taken December 12, 1966. Even after the new freeway opened west of here, the old highway still got clogged up on occasion. © *California Department of Transportation, used with permission.*

Whatever happens to the old highway through Fresno, this city in the heart of the San Joaquin Valley can always claim to have affected the highway up and down the state perhaps more than any other town. It owes that distinction to the county's preeminence in agriculture and the inventiveness of a man named James Porteus.

A blacksmith who came to the United States from Scotland in 1873, Porteus settled in Fresno and opened a business there called Fresno Agricultural Works, catering to the area's biggest industry. The business not only survived, it prospered, changing its name to Fresno Ag Hardware and continuing to operate into the 21st century as Fresno's oldest business. As impressive as that is, though, it wasn't Porteus' signature achievement. That came in the form of U.S. Patent No. 261,759, which he received for a tool he dubbed a "Dirt Scraper." Before the

scraper came along, the primary means of moving dirt was by hand, one shovelful at a time. The new tool's main purpose was to dig ditches for irrigation in the naturally arid Central Valley, and Porteus pursued this goal over the next few years by purchasing the rights to two competing models and incorporating their best features into a new device.

He called it the "Fresno Scraper."

Two to four horses or mules pulled the scraper, which featured a steel cutting edge that dug into the soil while the operator used a handle to control how deep the blade would go. The device featured a C-shaped catch bowl, and it enabled the operator to redistribute the dirt to low-lying areas, leveling out the land. It became the basis for the modern bulldozer, and it was so effective that engineers soon found other uses for it beyond irrigation. The Fresnos, as they were called, were used to pave the way for rail lines and even on the Panama Canal. With the advent of the automobile, work crews began using them to build first roads, then highways—like Highway 99.

Workers used Fresno Scrapers to carve out the Ridge Route over the Tehachapis and on many other sections of the road, as well. It wasn't until the 1930s that motorized equipment replaced them as the primary means of road building.

The scrapers also were instrumental in the construction of a Fresno marvel: the Forestiere Underground Gardens. A Sicilian immigrant named Baldasarre Forestiere created this series of subterranean passages and chambers to serve as his living quarters shortly after coming to California at the turn of the 20th century.

Forestiere might have preferred to stay in Sicily, but his father—a wealthy grower of citrus and olives—was from the old school: Only the eldest son could inherit his estate, and Baldasarre's name was a notch below the top of the list. So, like many others, he sought his fortune in America, traveling to Boston and getting work there digging subway tunnels. It was a living, as they say, but it wasn't his passion. He longed to start an orchard of his own, and Boston's climate was hardly conducive to his dreams, so he pulled up stakes and moved out to California.

Forestiere's first stop was Orange County, but land there was selling at a premium, even back then, so he looked farther north and found what appeared to be the perfect spot a few miles beyond what were then the Fresno city limits. The price of land there was a lot more reasonable, and Forestiere knew a deal when he saw one, so he bought up 700 acres. Unfortunately, he soon found that the property he had purchased to plant his orchard was covered with a layer of hardpan just beneath the surface. Compounding the problem, he discovered that it was difficult to find refuge from the sweltering Fresno summers. There was no air conditioning in those days, and that water park just up the road? It wouldn't be built for nearly a century.

So Forestiere combined the two things he knew: growing citrus and digging tunnels. Using a Fresno Scraper, a wheelbarrow, and other tools, he conquered the hardpan and kept right on going: down into the ground, first 10 feet, then 20. Without blueprints or even a written plan, he carved out a series of chambers and tunnels beneath the surface of the earth that he said would "connect up into one of the most involved and yet delightful labyrinths of modern ages."

This labyrinth was filled with Roman arches, and the earthen "roof" yielded every few steps to a skylight that allowed beams of light to infiltrate the darkness. If it happened to rain? No problem. Forestiere dug out the floors at slight angles, so the water ran downhill and into a sump at the caverns' lowest point. But the skylights didn't just let sunlight in, they also allowed tree branches to rise up. Forestiere hadn't given up his dream of creating a citrus garden, he had merely shifted the location—downward several feet.

Indeed, "Gardens" isn't an empty name: Forestiere planted all manner of fruit trees on the property: oranges, lemons, strawberries, figs (a Fresno staple), dates, grapefruit, quince, and others, including several varieties of grape. He even grafted one tree to produce seven varieties of citrus. The tree was still there in 2014, though one variety of fruit, the cedron, had ceased to grow on its branches, perhaps because it was so heavy. In fact, several of his trees have survived for a century, extending their twisted branches and green shoots up toward those skylights.

Forestiere completed the main work on his refuge in eight years, having carved out a living room, a kitchen, a bedroom, and a small chapel. One idiosyncrasy is a peephole through the fireplace, its line of sight aimed toward the floor at one of the entryways. It enabled him to see what kind of shoes would-be visitors were wearing and determine whether they belonged to friendly visitors.

By 1923, Forestiere had expanded his unique domicile to cover some 10 acres in the ultimate exercise in sweat equity (or perhaps more accurately, a labor of love). "All that I have done … required very little money: perhaps $300," he told a reporter in 1924. "What do I want with money? If I had a million dollars, I couldn't spend it. Neither could you. Nobody could. I am broke, but the cavern and all the work it represents are worth more than a million dollars to me."

Still, he wasn't finished, not by a long shot. After completing work on his living quarters, Forestiere labored on for 23 years more. "The Human Mole" died in 1946 at the age of 67, his project still under construction, having contracted pneumonia after being hospitalized for a hernia. He had started work on a 5,000-square-foot ballroom, which his brother Giuseppe completed after his death and used for parties, receptions, and even weddings. Forestiere even had dreams of opening a Mediterranean restaurant, having excavated a 700-foot-long tunnel for cars before he passed away.

After Forestiere's death, his underground creation seven miles north of downtown Fresno became a tourist attraction, bringing in as many as 50,000 visitors a year in the late 1950s. It remained open into the 21st century, drawing smaller but no less impressed crowds just off the highway those Fresno scrapers helped build.

Finding the old road: Earlier versions of the highway veers off in two parallel alignments just south of town: The older known as **Railroad Avenue**, which runs just east of the newer route, **Golden State Boulevard** (which in turn is just east of the modern freeway). The oldest alignment entered Fresno off Railroad Avenue via the city's southern gateway arch at **Van Ness Avenue**, then followed **Broadway** through town to **H Street** and north from there to Roeding Park, where vehicles were funneled via a traffic circle onto a section called **Motel Drive**. During the second half of the 20th century, the Broadway route was cut off, first by a pedestrian mall and then by a new Triple-A baseball stadium. As of this writing, many of the old motels, diners, and other landmarks along the northern section of the road were being removed to make way for the state's high-speed rail project.

MADERA

Population (1939)—4,655
Population (2010)—61,416
Elevation—271 feet
Location—23 miles northwest of Fresno
Founded—1876
Incorporated—1907

Madera, or a point just south of it, can lay claim to being at the exact geographical center of California. The truth of that claim is another matter, but a couple of trees—one a pine, the other a palm—are clearly visible to testify in its behalf.

It's not clear exactly when the trees were planted, but it was long before the advent of GPS technology, so instead, Highway 99 was used as a benchmark. Some unnamed soul with a very long measuring tape or some other now-antiquated device determined that a spot near Avenue 11, just south of Madera, was the exact center of the state. The person, or people, in question then planted a palm tree and, immediately to the north, a pine tree to mark the spot.

No one knows exactly who did the deed. One version of the tale attributes it to students at California State University, Fresno (then Fresno Normal School), and puts the date at 1915, but there's nothing on paper to substantiate that legend. Whoever it was, they wound up about 11 miles too far north, as the actual midpoint of the highway was in Fresno, near Ashlan Avenue.

When more accurate tools became available, scientists determined that the palm-pine site was more than a little off the mark. The Madera County Engineering Department declared in 1972 that the actual geographic center of the state lay east-northeast in the Sierra Nevada mountains at North Fork. A couple of decades later, another group of surveyors used satellite technology to pinpoint the site even more precisely.

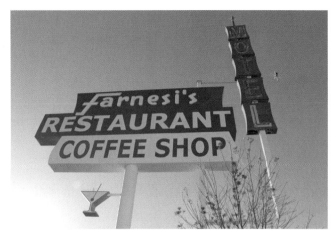

Farnesi's Restaurant has been a roadside staple in Madera for decades.

The Chowchilla arch was built over Robertson Boulevard, just west of Old 99, in 1912. The hollow stucco structure was destroyed by fire in 1937. *From the collection of Michael J. Semas.*

By that time, however, the two trees had become rooted not only in the ground but in tradition. The California Department of Transportation wanted to rip them out for a road improvement project along 99 in the 1980s but ran into fierce opposition from local residents who cherished the twin trees. The state backed off its plans and decided to work around the pair. Caltrans warmed to the trees so much that when a strong storm uprooted the pine (actually a deodar cedar) in 2005, its workers planted a replacement. The original palm, a Canary Islands date palm, still stands beside it, welcoming travelers to the mythical halfway point in their journey along Old 99.

Finding the old road: Bypassed **Gateway Drive** is a pleasant detour from the freeway, sending traffic through a small-town undivided highway lined with trees, businesses, and a smattering of old motels. These days, it's signed as State Route 145.

CHOWCHILLA

Population (1939)—847
Population (2010)—18,720
Elevation—240 feet
Location—17 miles northwest of Madera
Founded—1912
Incorporated—1923

Many towns along 99 carry names of Spanish origin; others, like Chowchilla, are borrowed from Native American nations such as the Yokut. Chowchilla stems from the tribal name Chaushila, which means "marauders."

For many years, Chowchilla had a gateway arch similar to those marking the entrances to Fresno, Modesto, and other towns along the route. Built in 1912 over Robertson Boulevard, the town's main drag just west of Old 99, the hollow structure was built of stucco and less sturdy than some of its contemporaries. It advertised 108,000 acres of land in the Chowchilla area (the town revised the figure to 134,000 five years later when O.A. Robertson, the boulevard's namesake developer, bought a ranch in the area).

By 1936, however, many in the town were worried that the arch had fallen into disrepair and become a safety hazard. The town had paid $300 for maintenance three years earlier, and a significantly larger sum was likely to be needed in the near future. Some members of the Lions Club argued for its removal in March of that year, but no action was taken. The following year, in August, however, a large crowd turned out to watch the venerable arch burn to the ground in what one news report termed "a spectacular fire" that started near one foot of the arch. No one ever figured out how it started, but speculation centered on the possibility that a discarded cigarette or match might have ignited the structure.

Despite the arguments for tearing the arch down, arson was not suspected.

Another fire destroyed a different Chowchilla landmark: the first custom grain elevator to be built in the state, which was constructed in 1916.

But Chowchilla's primary claim to fame (or infamy) was a bizarre and harrowing 1976 incident in which three men hijacked a school bus with 26 children aboard. It was the day before summer school let out, and the kids were on their way back from an excursion to the fairgrounds swimming pool when it happened about 4 p.m.

The kidnappers herded the kids and the driver into two vans, leaving the bus in a drainage ditch west of the city. Then they drove their captives for 11 hours to Livermore, intending to demand $5 million in ransom. They buried them all, still alive, in a moving van at a quarry owned by the father of one of the kidnappers, covering it with 3 feet of dirt. It was the largest kidnapping for ransom in U.S. history, but it didn't work out quite the way the kidnappers had planned. When they tried to call in the ransom demand, the line was busy, so they decided to take a nap. Meanwhile, some of the children helped bus driver Ed Ray stack 14 mattresses in the van in a pile that enabled them to reach the top of the truck. From there, they wedged open a metal lid covering the top of the van and dug their way through the dirt and debris to daylight.

The victims all escaped safe and sound, and the kidnappers were arrested and sent to prison. A TV movie based on the incident starring Karl Malden aired on ABC in 1993. And as for the bus, the school district gave it to Ray, who eventually sold it to a neighbor. As of 2011, it was still in Chowchilla, housed at a nursery.

Finding the old road: Chowchilla Boulevard, west of the freeway, is a short, largely rural stretch of road accessible via the SR 233 exit. To head north, you'll have to take a right on Front Street, then another right on King Avenue to reach it; to go south, just turn left immediately after exiting the freeway.

The Merced Theatre opened in 1931 and continues to operate at 301 Main Street, a block from the 16th Street alignment of U.S. 99 at the center of town.

MERCED

Population (1939)—7,006
Population (2010)—80,793
Elevation—171 feet
Location—19 miles northwest of Chowchilla
Founded—1870
Incorporated—1889

Merced is home to the only University of California campus between Davis and Los Angeles, but it's a relatively recent addition to the landscape, having opened in 2005. The name Merced dates back almost two full centuries before that, when Gabriel Moraga and a contingent of Spanish soldiers stumbled upon a river they named Rio de Nuestra Señora de la Merced (River of Our Lady of Mercy). The name stuck.

The city served as a junction for three key highways: The 99, the 140, which headed into Yosemite National Park, and the 59, which branched off northward to the gold country and Sonora. Old 99 runs through town today as 16th Street, which parallels the current alignment two blocks to the east.

The highway has defined Merced, for better or worse. Sometimes, the road made history; other times, it destroyed it. The freeway bypass built in the 1960s exacted a toll on the city's Chinatown, where the first temple was built in 1875. Eighty-five years later, it was demolished because it stood in the freeway's path.

Finding the old road: Take a 3-mile detour through Merced along **16th Street**. It's similar to the segment in Madera, with a few motels, gas stations, a car dealership and trees lining an undivided highway.

ATWATER

Population (1939)—319
Population (2010)—28,168
Elevation—151 feet
Location—9 miles west-northwest of Merced
Founded—1880
Incorporated—1922

Atwater Boulevard was 99 before the freeway wore that designation, bypassed when the new freeway came through in 1955. But neither stretch of asphalt qualifies as the most impressive piece of pavement in Atwater—that distinction belongs to one designed for much larger, winged vehicles, one built to defend the nation during wartime.

The U.S. government built several airfields along Highway 99 during World War II. Among the most notable was Castle Air Force Base east of Atwater. It opened in 1941 as an Army Air Corps flight school and continued to operate until its closure in 1995. (The name was changed to Castle Air Force Base in 1948 to honor Brigadeer General Frederick Castle; the general had perished after choosing to stay at the controls of his B-17 when it was hit in a bombing run over Belgium, allowing his crewmen to parachute to safety.)

The nearby Castle Air Museum, which opened in 1981 on 11 acres, features one of the most extensive displays of vintage aircraft in the United States. The planes on exhibit there include one of only four surviving B-36 Peacemakers, along with a 10-engine bomber manufactured by Convair between 1949 and 1959 that was the largest mass-produced piston engine aircraft ever built. In all, more than 50 restored aircraft from the World War II, Korean War, and Cold War eras are on display there.

Finding the old road: Follow **Atwater Boulevard** for about a mile through Atwater, east of the freeway. It's a flat stretch of roadway with few trees, a couple of gas stations, and an old building or two among some industrial buildings.

LIVINGSTON

Population (1939)—803
Population (2010)—13,058
Elevation—131 feet
Location—7 miles west-northwest of Atwater
Founded—1873
Incorporated—1922

Home of the last stoplight on Highway 99, Livingston was named for Southern Pacific station operator Charles Livingston. It's also home of a grape-pressing center operated by E&J Gallo Winery.

Finding the old road: What remains of the old alignment in Livingston follows **Campbell Avenue** (known in places as Campbell Boulevard) east of the freeway. You can reach it by taking Exit 201 at Hammett Avenue.

Delhi (unincorporated)

Population (2010)—10,755
Elevation—118 feet
Location—5 miles northwest of Livingston
Founded—1911

Delhi wasn't named after the city in India, and it isn't pronounced the same way, either. The name is a drastically shortened version of Delta-Highland Canal and is consequently pronounced as Dell-high.

The community is largely the product of an experiment undertaken by the state of California in the aftermath of the Wheatland Hop Riot of 1913, a clash between farmworkers and landowners in Yuba County. The International Workers of the World (Wobblies) had attempted to unionize farm laborers, who were living and toiling in intolerable conditions. Durst Ranch, for which they were harvesting hops, wasn't allowing them so much as a roof over their heads; they were forced to sleep in the open, without even a blanket to keep them warm. The drinking water was contaminated, and the company paid its field workers less than $2 for a 12-hour day that began before dawn.

When the IWW issued a call to unionize at a speech attended by some 2,000 workers, the company responded by bringing in deputies, who opened fire on the crowd. Four people, including a young boy, were killed, and the governor summoned 200 National Guard troops to restore order and arrest those (on the labor side, of course) who had supposedly instigated the rioting.

Four years after the riots, however, the still-widening gap between landowners and farmworkers led the state to act. The California State Legislature passed the Land Settlement Act and created a board to implement it, overseeing a new kind of agricultural community. The idea was to make farming affordable for individuals, under a system separate from the one that had come to be dominated by large landholders. Durham in Butte County was chosen as the site for the first settlement, followed in 1919 by Delhi.

Settlers could apply to take part in the program, but they weren't automatically accepted, nor were they left to their own devices. The state prepared the land and installed irrigation systems. The Land Settlement Board then questioned the applicants and had to approve them before they could continue. Afterward, the state provided experts from the University of California to teach them various farming methods.

Ultimately, the experiment failed, and taxpayers ended up footing the bill. Still, however, the Land Settlement Act laid a foundation that community members built on in the ensuing years. As of 2014, Delhi was the largest unincorporated community in Merced County.

Turlock

Population (1939)—4,276
Population (2010)—69,733
Elevation—102 feet
Location—7 miles northwest of Delhi
Founded—1871
Incorporated—1908

Most freeway bypasses built along the 99 corridor closely paralleled the road they replaced. Not so in Tracy. There, the old road went directly through the heart of town, while the new freeway (opened in 1973) skirted the city entirely to the west.

The town itself was originally to have been named Sierra, but that led some to conclude, mistakenly but not unreasonably, that it was a mountain community. The choice of the name Turlock as a replacement seems to have been based on the name of a nearby railroad station that was named, in turn, for the village of Turlough/Turlach in County Mayo, Ireland.

Its diverse population led it to claim a singular distinction in the 1930s, when Ripley's Believe It or Not identified it as the U.S. city with the most churches per capita.

Finding the old road: The old highway through Turlock is a little longer than some other San Joaquin Valley segments at nearly 10 miles, and **Golden State Boulevard** is a more direct route than the freeway bypass. The highway is a divided expressway south of town and looks a lot like the segments farther south, near Fresno. It's undivided, with no central median, in the city proper.

State Route 99 looking north from an overpass near Ceres.

KEYES (UNINCORPORATED)

Population (2010)—5,601
Elevation—92 feet
Location—7 miles northwest of Turlock

Keyes was one of the last places on 99 where motorists faced the prospect of stopping at a traffic signal. The stoplight was removed in the 1980s.

*Finding the old road: At Keyes, just north of Turlock, turn from Golden State Boulevard onto Taylor Road, drive under the freeway overpass, and turn north onto Taylor Court. A few hundred feet up and off to your right, looking toward the freeway, you'll see some concrete from the original road.

CERES

Population (1939)—981
Population (2010)—45,417
Elevation—92 feet
Location—3 miles northwest of Keyes
Founded—1870
Incorporated—1918

Because of the prominence of agriculture up and down 99, it shouldn't be surprising that a few cities along the highway were named for Greek agricultural deities. Pomona was one. Ceres was another. Think "cereal," then start looking along the highway north of Ceres: Although grain silos can be seen up and down 99, they're more prevalent in this area and to the north, between Sacramento and Red Bluff.

The first house in Ceres went up in 1870, and a train depot appeared four years later. Rose Maddox of the pioneering country-western group the Maddox Brothers lived in the Modesto area and had a sister in Ceres. The group made some early appearances in the city's 28-acre Smyrna Park, and Rose Maddox eventually became the first woman elected to the Country Music Hall of Fame.

Ceres serves as the southern terminus of the Modesto bypass, which opened in 1965 and extended north to Salida.

MODESTO

Population (1939)—13,842
Population (2010)—201,165
Elevation—89 feet
Location—5 miles northwest of Ceres
Founded—1870
Incorporated—1884

Without Old 99, there might never have been a Luke, a Leia, a Darth Vader, or a "long time ago in a galaxy far, far away."

There certainly wouldn't have been any Happy Days— at least not with a capital H and D. There would have been no Fonzie, no Laverne, no Shirley, no Mindy, and no Mork. If you're too young to remember these fictional characters, think about it this way: Robin Williams and Harrison Ford would have both needed to find a different breakout role to launch them into superstardom. Heck, Ford might well have continued his first career— as a carpenter.

What does any of this have to do with Highway 99, specifically in Modesto?

Quite a bit, it turns out.

Before the freeway bypass opened in 1965, the highway went through Modesto on 9th Street. On the northeast corner of Ninth and O Street, at the north end of downtown, Ed Burge opened Burge's Drive In in 1947. It would remain open for the next two decades, a classic '50s burger joint complete with carhops, a jukebox, and plenty of teenagers congregating in the parking lot, making out and listening to the kind of music their parents wouldn't let them play at home.

Every Thursday, Friday, and Saturday, kids would get in their cars and start "dragging the main," or cruising, around the city center. Most of the cruising took place a block over from 99, so it didn't interfere with highway traffic. The kids would cruise down Tenth Street, take a left on O to Burge's, then turn around and go back the way they came until they hit G Street. The city eventually tried to discourage the cruisers by making Tenth a one-way street, but they just shifted gears and moved

The Modesto arch that parallels old Highway 99 through town was built in 1912. The slogan "Water, Wealth, Contentment, Health" was chosen over the top choice in a contest to pick the town's motto: "Nobody's Got Modesto's Goat."

One of those teenagers was a kid named George Lucas, who went on direct an obscure dystopian science fiction film called *THX 1138*. It featured some big names—Robert Duvall and Donald Pleasence headed the cast, and Francis Ford Coppola was one of the three producers—but it bombed at the box office and quickly vanished without a trace in the spring of 1971.

It would be Lucas' second film that put him—and Modesto—on the map. *American Graffiti*, released in the summer of 1973, hearkened back to the still-not-too-distant past of letterman jackets, greasers, and malt shops. More specifically, it hearkened back to Lucas' own past in Modesto, where Burge's Drive In on Old 99 served as the template for the movie version, called Mel's.

over a block to Eleventh. Sometimes, they'd head northeast to McHenry Avenue and another drive-in, called Al's.

American Graffiti was a huge sleeper hit. Made on a budget of roughly three-quarters of a million dollars, it raked in a staggering $140 million at the box office and gave Lucas the leverage he needed to make an even more successful movie four years later: the one featuring Luke Skywalker, Darth Vader, and Han Solo, the character made famous by Harrison Ford. If it hadn't been for *American Graffiti*, though, Ford probably never would have gotten the part. Although he'd done some acting in the '60s, he had left the business to become a carpenter. One of his jobs: building cabinets at the home of George Lucas.

It was this chance encounter that led Lucas to cast him in the role of street racer Bob Falfa, and Ford took the part only on the condition that he wouldn't be forced to cut his hair. (His character was supposed to wear his hair in a crew cut, and the cowboy hat Ford wears in the film was the result of a compromise that kept his anachronistic long locks under wraps.)

The film's success not only served as a precursor to the *Star Wars* phenomenon, it also inspired an episode of *Love, American Style*, an anthology series that featured different actors and a different story each week during its five-year run on ABC. The episode aired in 1972 and starred Ron Howard, who had also played in *American Graffiti*; it also featured a drive-in called Al's, just like the one in Modesto.

The show was hugely successful, finishing the year among the top three shows on television in its fourth, fifth, and sixth seasons. Its first spinoff, *Laverne & Shirley*, did even better, finishing in the top three for four consecutive seasons and topping the Nielsen ratings twice in a row. Another spinoff, with newcomer Robin Williams as a manic alien from the fictional planet of Ork, checked in at No. 3 in the ratings during its opening season and launched Williams into a career that would establish him as one of the most popular comedic and dramatic actors of his generation.

None of this would have been possible without Lucas.

Or Modesto.

Or Highway 99, where Burge's Drive In finally closed in 1967, when the cruising culture was giving way to flower power and the old highway had yielded to the new freeway bypass.

In 1997, the city honored Lucas by unveiling a statue of a teenage boy and girl sitting on a '57 Chevy a few blocks northeast of 99. "My childhood in Modesto not only inspired me to make *American Graffiti* but also gave me the grounding and confidence to pursue my dreams," Lucas wrote in a letter dedicating the statue. "I will always have fond memories of Modesto and my time cruising."

Finding the old road: In Modesto, highway hunters have a couple of old alignments from which to choose. The earlier route along **7th Street** crossed the Tuolumne River on a 1916 bridge flanked at each end by concrete lion statues. (As of this writing, officials had plans to replace the two-lane span with a modern four-lane structure by 2020.) This alignment continued north through town to I Street, where it turned east two blocks, passing beneath the Modesto arch before heading north again along **9th Street**. The newer of the two bypassed alignments runs along 9th Street the entire way and crosses the Tuolumne River on an impressive span of its own, a four-lane bridge that's lit by distinctive concrete streetlight towers as it curves gently toward the city.

Salida (unincorporated)

Population (2010)—13,722
Elevation—69 feet
Location—7 miles northwest of Modesto
Founded—1870

Salida began its existence as Murphy's Switch—the switch being a railroad switch—and only later adopted the Spanish word for "exit" as its official name. No, it wasn't an exit on Old 99. The name predates the highway: It referred to the area's identity as a distribution hub for wheat that shipped downriver to San Francisco.

The old highway through Salida passed by Texaco and MobilGas stations, along with the Salida Motor Court, in this photo taken May 27, 1940. © *California Department of Transportation, used with permission.*

The Murphy behind the original name was John "One-Arm" Murphy, who ran a ferry crossing on the Stanislaus River and deeded land to the Central Pacific Railroad when it built a line through the area.

Highway 99 originally ran through Salida, as it did through other towns along the route, along Salida Boulevard, but in 1969, plans for a 3.8-mile bypass east of town were announced at a cost of $4.75 million.

Finding the old road: About a mile's worth of divided highway is all that's left of the old alignment in Salida, running west of the freeway as **Salida Boulevard**.

Ripon

Population (1939)—1,100
Population (2010)—14,297
Elevation—69 feet
Location—5 miles northwest of Salida
Founded—1870
Incorporated—1945

Ripon started out as Stanislaus City, a tract of more than 900 acres owned and developed by W.H. Hughes. Its name changed to Stanislaus Station with the arrival of the railroad in 1872 and to Ripon two years later courtesy of a store owner who hailed from Ripon, Wisconsin.

For many years, Ripon hosted the "World's Largest Rummy Game" annually at tables set up on its main street. Six hundred rummy, bridge, and whist enthusiasts showed up for the inaugural event in 1932, and six years later, the field had grown to 900—nearly equal to the town's population at the time.

A sign by the roadside once proclaimed the Schenley Distillery along Old 99 three miles north of town to be the "world's largest exclusive brandy distillery." Schenley purchased the Roma Winery in the late 1930s with an eye toward paying half a million dollars to upgrade the white, peak-roofed plant on two acres of land. The company's regional manager bragged that it would have a capacity for 1.25 million gallons of wine, which Schenley would distill into cognac. The company planned to produce about 10,000 barrels of brandy a year.

But eight years later, in the summer of 1946, all that money went up in smoke: A still exploded with a bang so loud it was heard all the way down the road in Ripon.

The explosion even broke some windows and dislodged plaster from some walls in town. The force of it sent portions of the plant flying out onto the highway, and extra highway patrol officers were called out to handle the resulting traffic tie-up. All phones in the area went down, and the Pacific Telephone and Telegraph manager who rushed to the site declared, "It looked like an earthquake had occurred or a bomb had exploded."

Two people at the plant were injured, and it could have been a lot worse if the explosion hadn't happened during lunch. But the blast itself wasn't the worst of it: A fire quickly spread, destroying the administration building that sat adjacent to the still. A wooden water tower—a source of water needed to fight the blaze—caught fire itself, and several smaller blasts followed the first: the sound of alcohol exploding.

Wine-press machinery and other buildings on the site were damaged, and 10,000 gallons of barreled brandy were lost, along with 10,000 tons of grapes and 2,500 gallons of high-proof alcohol. The eventual loss was pegged at upwards of $700,000, more than it had cost to upgrade the plant in the first place.

Manteca

Population (1939)—1,614
Population (2010)—71,067
Elevation—38 feet
Location—8 miles northwest of Ripon
Founded—1861
Incorporated—1918

Want some lard? You'll find it in Manteca, right?

Not necessarily.

The name Manteca is Spanish for "lard," but please don't assume this city is the pig fat capital of the world. Blame the railroad, which misprinted the town's choice for the name, Monteca, with an "a" instead of an "o." The town did become a hub for shipping dairy products, however, with a reputation for helping travelers keep their cool. For four decades, Manteca was a destination for travelers in the northern San Joaquin Valley and beyond who wanted to make a splash at the city's water slides.

Yosemite Avenue, just west of the intersection with Main Street (Old 99) in Manteca.
From the collection of Michael J. Semas.

The Manteca Waterslides at Oakwood Lake Resort opened in 1974 alongside a campground, RV park, and go-kart racetrack. Manteca was the perfect place for an amusement park, as the city stood at the spot on the map where Highway 99 met Highway 120. The intersection of the two main roads caused such heavy congestion that it was one of the first places where the state built a bypass for the Old 99, in 1952.

Ironically, the Manteca Waterslides came into being as a direct result of 99's successor to the west, Interstate 5. Budge Brown, who owned the land where the park would be built, wanted to excavate earth there and sell it to road builders laying out I-5. Before he could do so, he had to get a permit from the state because the resulting hole in the ground was sure to fill with water. And a condition of that permit was that he build a campground.

Who would want to go camping in Manteca? It was a good question. Manteca was, after all, smack in the middle of a very flat valley far away from the scenic hills and pines that typically drew travelers to stay at camp-grounds. Brown needed another sort of attraction, so he hit on the idea of building a waterslide. The original model, which was the world's longest at the time, took thrill seekers from the top of a man-made hill a distance of 725 feet into the equally manmade lake.

The idea was a hit, and other slides soon followed.

Brown's pioneering business provided a blueprint for other water parks along 99 and I-5: The Island Waterpark in Fresno, the smaller Time Out Pizza & Fun Center in Tulare, and Hurricane Harbor at Six Flags in Valencia.

The Manteca Waterslides were there before any of them, setting the standard with the first fiberglass slides and the towering 80-foot V-Max speed slide, the tallest slide built in California. The park's jingle played on radios down a stretch of 99 and eastward into the Bay Area, from which parents often took their kids for a weekend getaway.

It's time to play
Let's get away
There's something there for everyone
Let's all go to Oakwood Lake
For some Manteca Waterslides fun (Let's go!)

Other slides included the High Tide, the Subway, Turbulence, the Plunge, and the Cyclone. An average of 175,000 water lovers passed through its gates each summer season during its three decades in business, but new water regulations mixed with rising costs for everything from electricity to workers' compensation eventually forced the park to shut down in 2004.

Finding the old road: In Manteca, **Moffat Boulevard** continues the highway's original trajectory west of the freeway and into the heart of the city, where the old alignment veers north on **Main Street** and meets up with the freeway again on the north end of town.

STOCKTON

Population (1939)—47,963
Population (2010)—301,090
Elevation—13 feet
Location—13 miles north of Manteca
Founded—1849
Incorporated—1850

Many of the towns along Old 99 owe their genesis to the railroad, those twin steel rails that follow the highway up and down the state like a stalker envious of its success. But Stockton is not only older than the highway, it's older than the railroad, too. It owes its existence to a different form of transportation, one you wouldn't expect to find nearly 100 miles from the Pacific Ocean: cargo boats.

It's fitting that the city, the first in California with a name neither Spanish nor Native American, should have taken its identity from a naval officer (Robert Stockton was responsible for driving Mexican forces out of California in the 1840s), situated as it was at the head of a navigable channel. The location was so desirable that Stockton quickly became a busy commercial shipping point, its population surpassing 10,000 by 1870. That may not sound like much, but at the time, it was nearly twice the population of Los Angeles, which had filed for incorporation the same year as Stockton.

Situated as they were beside a river channel that overflowed when the Sierra snows began to melt, Stockton's bustling streets could get more than a little muddy. Perhaps for this reason, it earned the nickname Mudville, the kind of place where it was polite to wipe your shoes more than once before entering a neighbor's home … and the kind of place that, some believe, gave rise to a famous poem titled "Casey at the Bat."

Stockton was not only a shipping mecca, it was also a baseball town from way back. As early as 1886,

The St. Francis Motel on a stretch of old U.S. 99 near Stockton offers free local calls and waterbed suites among its amenities.

Stockton had a team in the California State League, where it competed against teams from San Francisco and Oakland. It was two years later that Ernest Thayer, a reporter for the *San Francisco Examiner*, penned the immortal poem about a prodigious batsman named Casey who played baseball for a team called the Mudville Nine.

There's plenty of mystery surrounding the poem. There's no dateline to indicate where the game took place, and Thayer penned it under a pseudonym, Phin. The Mudville nine's opponents? They aren't even named. This was a poem, not your typical account of a baseball game for the Sporting Green, and Thayer himself declared it was purely fanciful. But even fancy can be based on fact, and there are some indications that the Mudville Nine were, in fact, at least partly based on Stockton's long-ago team.

Though "Casey" himself can't be found on any roster of the era, a couple of other players mentioned by name in the poem show up on rosters of 1888 California League teams. Flynn, who "let drive a single, to the wonderment of all," could in fact be Jocko Flynn, who posted a paltry .127 batting average that season. Considering his struggles at the plate, it would have indeed been a wonderment to see him reach base safely.

The name of another player mentioned in the poem, Cooney, also turns up on a league roster that year: that of the San Francisco Pioneers. Could he have been playing for the Stockton side that day instead? Records in those days were far from complete, and players often shifted from team to team with regularity. (Flynn, for example, also played for the Oakland squad during the same season he suited up for Stockton.)

Other names in the poem—Barrows and Jimmy Blake, along with Casey—are nowhere to be found on any of the league rosters that year, but that doesn't mean players with those or similar names didn't play in Stockton, suiting up for a game or two and then moving on. It also doesn't mean that Thayer didn't take some poetic license with the names. A certain Charles Chase appears on the Stockton roster in '88 and again the following year, and it doesn't seem too much of a stretch to imagine he might have had worn the nickname Casey. Could Jimmy Blake have actually been Bob Blakiston, who played three seasons in the majors but whose name would have far too unwieldy to fit into one of Thayer's stanzas as it stood?

The poem's Blake is described as a "cake," which in that day connoted a dandy or a fop, and a surviving picture of Blakiston fits the image: He's a well-groomed man in a collar, with a neatly groomed moustache and every hair in place. Even so, that might be a bit of a stretch (if Blakiston was the inspiration for this particular character, why didn't Thayer call him Bobby Blake instead?). Still, it's intriguing.

As an aside, it's interesting to note that despite the poem's focus on Casey "at the bat," the most accom-plished member of the '88 Stockton club wasn't a hitter at all. Ace pitcher Charlie Sweeney had already spent five seasons in the majors by the time he joined Stockton, having racked up a whopping 41 wins against just 15 losses in one season four years earlier.

Although other towns have insisted that they inspired the Casey legend, none has quite so strong a claim as Stockton—which has asserted that claim with all the gusto of one of the famous slugger's swings. In 1952, the city went so far as to enlist charismatic former heavyweight champ Max Baer to play the part of Casey in a reenactment of Thayer's poem, with former New York Yankees pitcher Monte Pearson doing the honors as the triumphant pitcher.

Stockton's longtime minor-league team, the Ports, even rechristened themselves as the Mudville Nine for the 2000 and 2001 seasons before reverting to their more traditional name.

Finding the old road: Stockton's earlier U.S. 99 alignments—and there are several of them—are well to the west of the current freeway. The longest-used route followed **Mariposa Street** to **Dr. Martin Luther King Junior Boulevard**, then north on **Wilson Way** and back to the current freeway route.

During a brief period from 1929 to 1934, Stockton had two alignments: 99E along the current freeway route and 99W on **French Camp Road** and **El Dorado Street**. It was in Stockton that, from 1913 to 1927, the old Lincoln Highway merged with 99 as it headed north to Sacramento and, from there, eastward across the Sierra.

Lodi

Population (1939)—6,788
Population (2010)—62,134
Elevation—50 feet
Location—15 miles north of Stockton
Founded—1859
Incorporated—1906

"Oh, Lord, stuck in Lodi again," John Fogerty sang on Creedence Clearwater Revival's 1969 album, *Green River*, and suddenly, Lodi was famous for being the last place on earth the singer wanted to be.

The Hollywood Café, built as a storage shed for growers in 1939, was converted into a coffee shop five years later. It sits on the west side of Cherokee Lane, the former U.S. 99, in Lodi.

He supposedly rode in on a Greyhound for a one-night performance, ran out of money, and lost all his friends.

It never happened, though. In fact, Fogerty had never actually been to Lodi. He confessed he just chose the name because he thought it sounded cool. But even though the song was a B-side to the monster hit "Bad Moon Rising," it got its share of airplay from disc jockeys weary of hearing the hit single, and it eventually got covered by artists as diverse as Emmylou Harris, Tesla, Tom Jones, Buck Owens, and Bo Diddley.

Had Fogerty actually visited Lodi before writing that song, he might have wanted to stick around—especially if he liked root beer. In 1919, Roy Allen opened his first root beer stand just a few blocks west of 99 on Pine Street. He used a formula he had purchased from a pharmacist and set up shop initially at a parade to honor returning World War I veterans. Not only did Allen's first root beer stand offer the enticing beverage for just a nickel, it also offered convenience: It's believed to be the first such establishment with drive-up service, provided by "tray boys."

A second location soon followed, in Sacramento, and Allen brought in Frank Wright as a partner in 1922.

Using their initials, they dubbed the fledgling chain A&W. Allen bought out Wright two years later, and rapid expansion followed through franchise agreements as A&W spread across Northern and Central California, then across state lines into Utah and Texas. The original Pine Street location eventually closed in 1955, but there are plenty of other things to like about Lodi.

Finding the old road: The stretch of old U.S. 99 through town, known as **Cherokee Lane**, is one of the most picturesque along the historic highway. Tall trees shade a roadway lined with historic buildings such as the Richmaid Restaurant and Hollywood Café, both of which opened their doors on the eve of World War II. Richmaid got its start in 1938 as a creamery, serving up scoops of ice cream to help travelers cool off during those hot summer drives down 99. Local teens vied with those passing through town for a seat inside the popular diner, whose clock tower and theater-style vertical neon sign out front are landmarks along this section of the road.

The Hollywood Café opened a year later, though it didn't have a name until actor Slim Pickens dropped in for a bite to eat in the 1940s. He mentioned to the owner that the place reminded him of his favorite eatery in Hollywood, and that led to the formal birth of the Hollywood Café. The distinctive neon sign is hard to miss, though slightly altered from earlier years when the word "the" sat atop the current lettering. Photos of Elvis, James Dean, and Marilyn Monroe graced the side of the building in 2014.

GALT

Population (1939)—700
Population (2010)—23,647
Elevation—47 feet
Location—10 miles north of Lodi
Founded—1869
Incorporated—1946

If there's one thing you can count on in the San Joaquin Valley, it's that summers are going to get hot. So, why not build a thermometer as tall as the temperatures are high? That's what brothers Paul and Bill Giddens did, creating a 50-foot-tall working thermometer that weighed 3,000 pounds and featured more than 11,000 LED lightbulbs.

The thermometer at Giddens Heating and Air along 99 isn't as large or as famous as the 134-foot "world's largest thermometer" in the Southern California town of Baker. But it's impressive in its own right, operated by a high-speed computer and featuring cameras to monitor traffic on the highway, along with a complete weather station that records wind speed and rainfall in addition to measuring the temperature.

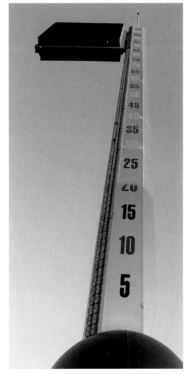

Galt owes its existence (at least in its present location) to the railroad. The original town in the area was Liberty—named for Liberty, Missouri—which stood about a mile to the south and had drawn about 100 people by the 1860s. It had a church, a hotel, a boardinghouse, a saloon, and a smithy. What it didn't have was a train depot, the lack of which proved

The Galt thermometer rises in front of Giddens Heating and Air along Highway 99.

its undoing. Instead, the Central Pacific Railroad chose a course about a mile to the north, and everyone pulled up stakes and moved there: to the site that would eventually be called Galt.

While Ontario, along old U.S. 99 in Southern California, was named for the Canadian province, Galt was named for a city in that province that's now part of the city of Cambridge. One of the town's founders, area rancher John McFarland, had been born in the Canadian city.

Finding the old road: Galt is known not only for its place along Highway 99, but for its location along the original route of the old Lincoln Highway, which passed through the east side of town. The highway (now known as **Lincoln Way** through town and **Lower Sacramento Road** to the south) crossed the Dry Creek Bridge, the longest iron bridge in California, then headed south to Stockton and west through Tracy to the Bay Area.

The route chosen for the Lincoln Highway drew businesses away from the rail line to the west, along Fourth Street, eastward, closer to the course later followed by Highway 99. In fact, Highway 99 followed what was essentially the old Lincoln Highway route south from Sacramento as far as Galt, where the two routes diverged and Lincoln Way split off to the west.

ELK GROVE

Population (2010)—155,937
Elevation—45 feet
Location—14 miles north of Galt
Founded—1850
Incorporated—2000

Although Elk Grove dates back to the middle of the 19th century, when it was established as an important stagecoach crossroads south of Sacramento, it wasn't incorporated until 2000 and has seen is most rapid growth since then, with its population increasing from 75,000 in 2001 to 160,000 just 13 years later.

Sacramento

Population (1939)—93,750
Population (2010)—466,488
Elevation—30 feet
Location—15 miles north-northwest of Elk Grove
Founded—1839
Incorporated—1850

"When you come to a fork in the road, take it."

Yogi Berra probably didn't come up with this little gem driving northbound into Sacramento on Old 99, but if the shoe fits …

The fork, in this case, was at the state capitol building. In one of the earliest alignments, motorists would enter the city from the south via Stockton Boulevard, which deposited them in the heart of downtown. At the capitol, they could either veer northeast via 99E or continue west on the 99W, which was co-signed with U.S. 40 until it hit Davis. Several alignments followed different city streets through Sacramento over the years, the highway south of the capital carrying the name South Sacramento Freeway.

Finding the old road: A 1934 map shows U.S. 99 entering the city from the south via **Stockton Boulevard** and continuing all the way to its terminus at **Alhambra Boulevard**. There, it turned north briefly before heading west along **L Street**. It was at **16th Street** that the two northern alignments parted ways, with 99W splitting off

Looking through the Tower Bridge toward Sacramento and the state Capitol building in May of 1961. © *California Department of Transportation, used with permission.*

northward and 99E continuing on L to **9th Street**, then jogging south a block to **M Street** and thence west across the Tower Bridge.

A decade later, the alignment looked a bit different. As before, the highway followed Stockton Boulevard from the south, then jogged northwest via **5th Avenue** and **Sacramento Boulevard** to **Broadway**. From there, a right turn onto 16th Street brought traffic to **N Street**. Travelers heading to 99E continued on 16th northward out of the city via **Del Paso Boulevard**, while travelers heading to 99W turned west off from 16th onto N Street. They skirted the capitol building to the south, then shifted a block north at 9th Street to **M Street** and across the Tower Bridge.

Don't be fooled by the stretch of highway labeled "California 99" between Sacramento and Yuba City. That road isn't part of the original route and, in fact, bisects the two options that were available to early and mid-20th century travelers. 99 East (99E) followed roughly the same path taken by modern Interstate 80, running northeast from Sacramento to Roseville. 99 West (99W) veered westward from Sacramento to Davis, then hooked north again parallel to modern Interstate 5.

99 West (Interstate 5 corridor)

Davis

Population (1939)—1,243
Population (2010)—65,662
Elevation—52 feet
Location—15 miles west of Sacramento
Founded—1868
Incorporated—1917

The stretch of highway west of Sacramento is the only place outside Southern California that the old 99 conveyed motorists across a true east–west alignment. It even curved back on itself slightly southward before veering off sharply north again at Davis. Today, it's part of Interstate 80, but long ago it was also a realigned segment of the historic coast-to-coast Lincoln Highway.

The Lincoln road's original routing took it south through Galt to Stockton, then west again across the Altamont Pass. It wasn't the most direct route, but there was good reason for the detour: The lowlands between Sacramento and the San Francisco Bay—a marshy expanse that was home to migrating geese, tule rushes, and bright gold baeria blooms—were prone to frequent flooding. They were, however, far less accommodating to rubber tires.

What the Tehachapis were to Southern California, the delta marshes were to the northern state: a daunting obstacle that stood between motorists and their destination. In this case, the obstacle was a huge floodplain that became saturated for six to eight months each year when the Sacramento River spilled over its banks. You could try driving on the only road over the marshland, the Tule Jake Road, but you'd be doing so at your own risk. According to the WPA's 1939 state guide book, "The deeply rutted road that formerly meandered over these swampy acres was impassible in spring when the swollen Sacramento (River) flooded it in a muddy torrent. So yielding was the terrain that the railroad, paralleling the highway on a high embankment, used to sag until the tracks looked like a sway-backed horse."

The solution was to build a bridge, but the marshland was so expansive that it would have to be a very long bridge indeed—more than 3 miles to be precise. The Yolo Causeway, completed in May of 1916, was a two-lane elevated roadway built over the floodplain at a cost of $400,000.

When work on the project was completed, the result was the longest concrete trestle bridge in the world. It cut 30 miles off the driving distance between San Francisco and the state capital, and the day after it opened, more than 2,000 cars traveled across it.

With the passage of time, the number of cars on the road increased, and it became necessary to replace the aging causeway with a more modern structure. Two, in fact. A pair of new bridges, each 46 feet wide and three lanes across in a single direction, were built across the Yolo Bypass marshland in 1962. The combined structure was later renamed the Blecher-Freeman Memorial Causeway in honor of two Highway Patrol officers shot to death nearby.

As convenient as it is, those suffering from chiroptophobia might want to avoid the causeway: 250,000 bats make their home in its rafters during the summer months. If you're an admirer of Batman or Dracula, however, you can take guided tours of the area during the summer and see this huge colony of Mexican free-tailed bats for yourself. They migrate north from their winter quarters in Mexico starting in March, then spend the summer underneath the causeway, finding refuge there in the warm expansion joints that prevent the bridge from cracking.

The bats first arrived in the 1970s and have been there ever since.

Finding the old road: The old highway jogs through Davis over city streets from **Richards Boulevard** north to **First Street**, signed as the Lincoln Highway for a few blocks. Then, turn north on **B Street** to **Russell Boulevard**, which will convey you west to SR 113.

WOODLAND

Population (1939)—5,542
Population (2010)—55,468
Elevation—69 feet
Location—12 miles north of Davis
Founded—1853
Incorporated—1871

The seat of Yolo County, Woodland fashions itself as the "City of Trees." Settlers were drawn to the area by the Gold Rush, among them a Kentucky native named Henry Wyckoff who established a general store called Yolo City in 1853. It was also known, colloquially, as "By Hell," an exclamation frequently heard on the local saloonkeeper's lips. Neither name stuck, though. Four years later, a gentleman named Frank Freeman arrived from Missouri and bought the store, along with 160 acres of land, upon which he then developed a town site. He petitioned the U.S. government for a post office, received approval, and asked his wife what she wanted to call the place. She suggested Woodland, and Woodland it was.

The city became the county seat in 1862, when a massive flood inundated the Sacramento Valley and washed out the city of Washington—which had served as the center of government to that point. (Don't look for Washington on the map these days; it's now called West Sacramento.)

Woodland grew rapidly and prospered. By 1888, it was reportedly the richest town in the nation for its size, and it maintained its wealth for decades to come. In the 1950s, it was said to have had the most millionaires per capita of any city in California.

Finding the old road: Follow **East Street** through Woodland and you'll find yourself on a segment of old 99W. If you take **Sixth Street** west, you'll be on Business 5, which turns north on **Pedrick Road**. This route eventually hooks up with the main Interstate 5 at an interchange. Continue across the freeway via the overpass; then, just before you get to the train tracks, turn left onto **Cacheville Road**, or 99W. This road will continue north, paralleling I-5, all the way to Corning.

DUNNIGAN (UNINCORPORATED)

Population (2010)—1,416
Elevation—69 feet
Location—20 miles northwest of Woodland
Founded—1853

Originally known as Antelope, the town changed its name to Dunnigan in 1876 in honor of A.W. Dunnigan, who had founded an inn there known as Dunnigan's.

ARBUCKLE (UNINCORPORATED)

Population (1939)—1,000
Population (2010)—3,028
Elevation—141 feet
Location—9 miles north-northwest of Dunnigan
Founded—1875

Local rancher Tacitus Arbuckle donated land to the railroad, and the community was named in his honor. He had plenty of land to give: His ranch, established in 1866, consisted of 1,900 acres. Civil War veteran John Canady Ward (who fought for the Confederate side) built the first house in Arbuckle and opened a harness-repair shop there in 1874; he later became the town constable. The first train came through on Independence Day in 1876, and the post office was established that same year.

A schoolhouse opened in 1877, and Annie Linton served as the community's first teacher. By the 1930s, Arbuckle had become known for its almond crop, with some 7,000 acres of the crop planted in the vicinity.

An old gas station that has long since stopped selling fuel sits on the west side of 99W in Arbuckle.

WILLIAMS

Population (1939)—851
Population (2010)—5,123
Elevation—82 feet
Location—11 miles north-northwest of Arbuckle
Founded—1874
Incorporated—1920

Williams was, very briefly, on the front lines of the labor movement when a group of about 50 Wobblies paraded through town. Wobblies were members of the International Workers of the World, a far-left industrial union formed in 1905. Nine years later, they descended upon Williams and threatened to cause a ruckus there. The town leaders, not wanting to stir up trouble, smoothed things over by serving them breakfast and paying them $60 to clean up the cemetery.

The Wobblies reached the height of their influence with some 40,000 members in 1923, but their influence began to decline shortly afterward, and they were increasingly marginalized as anarchists and communist sympathizers.

MAXWELL (UNINCORPORATED)

Population (1939)—506
Population (2010)—1,103
Elevation—92 feet
Location—10 miles north of Williams
Founded—1874

In the days before the automotive era, when America rode the rails, the Big Four ruled California's transportation industry. The Big Four—or "the Associates" as they called themselves—were Charles Crocker, Collis Huntington, Mark Hopkins, and Leland Stanford (the governor, for whom Stanford University is named). Together, they financed the Central Pacific Railway, which gave them the privilege of naming the towns that sprang up along the way.

That's what happened in the case of Maxwell.

The town might have just as easily been named McCoy, in honor of the constable who laid out the original plan. But the constable in question, W.S. McCoy, chose to call it Occident instead.

A nice enough name, but it wouldn't stick.

Spaulding, Lowery & Co., a business based in Winters some 60 miles to the south, announced plans to open a general store there, and George Maxwell built a saloon at the southwest corner of Oak Street and what later became Highway 99W. McCoy then went about circulating a petition to establish a post office in his new town, and one opened there in 1877. One report stated McCoy had been named postmaster, but that turned out to be an error: Instead, he had recommended the saloonkeeper, Maxwell, for the position. Meanwhile, Maxwell had agreed to give the railroad some land for its train depot; gifts of this sort often led the Big Four to name the depot (and therefore the town) for the donor.

In this case, that was Maxwell. Accordingly, four years after McCoy founded the town, the *Colusa Sun* reported that "the Railroad Company had decided to call the town formerly known as Occident, Maxwell, and as the name of the post office is already Maxwell, it will certainly be called by that name." Maxwell celebrated by building a livery stable next door to his saloon, but he didn't get to enjoy the honor for long: He passed away at the age of 51, barely a year after the newspaper announced the town had taken his name.

WILLOWS

Population (1939)—2,024
Population (2010)—6,166
Elevation—138 feet
Location—18 miles north of Maxwell
Founded—1862
Incorporated—1886

Tiny Willows was once home to a pro baseball team, the Cardinals in the Class D Far West League. The circuit included eight teams from Northern California and Oregon, with names like the Eugene Larks, Medford Nuggets, Santa Rosa Cats, Vallejo Chiefs, and Marysville Peaches. It was as low as you could go on the ladder of

An undated photo from the Cal State Chico archives shows a General Gas station in Maxwell.
Meriam Library, CSU Chico.

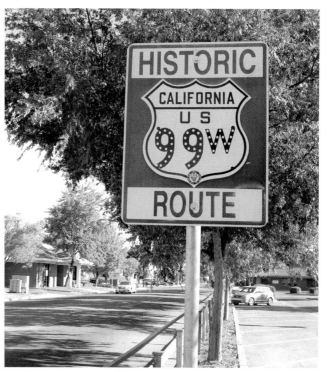

A sign designates the roadway as Historic U.S. 99W in Willows.

organized baseball. Still, they had a major league affiliation (with St. Louis, of course) and played three seasons at 2,200-seat Ajax Field starting in 1948. Built two decades earlier, the stadium was named for Tom Ajax, who managed the amateur Willows Giants to several championships in the early 20th century. Under Ajax's tutelage, the Giants had defeated teams from much larger cities such as San Francisco and Sacramento.

Later results, however, weren't always so stellar. A newspaper account from 1935 made an afternoon ballgame at Ajax Field seem more like a vaudeville comedy act. The principals that day were the Giants and the visiting Woodland Oaks, from just down the road, and reporter Jay Sehorn referred to their encounter that day as "the goofiest baseball game of the season."

"It was such a messed-up ballgame that the official scorers had to call for a half dozen new pencils and rulers to change the scorebook," he declared in his account. "If umpires Bobby Schang and 'Shorty' Griffith had been smart—they would have kicked the 23 players who performed in the game off the field and called it a day in the seventh" inning. Woodland made a total of eight errors in the field yet still managed to prevail in by the absurd score of 20–16.

Thirteen years later, when Willows got a professional (actually semipro) team, it didn't fare much better. The Cardinals finished a game under .500 during their first season and managed a third-place showing in their second year before tumbling into the cellar during their final campaign.

Ajax Field burned to the ground in September of 1962, but the Cardinals' legacy lives on: Willows Intermediate School adopted the Cardinals as their mascot.

ARTOIS

Population (2010)—295
Elevation—167 feet
Location—8 miles north of Willows
Founded—before 1876

Artois was born as Rixville, then subsequently called Germantown for the large number of Germans who had settled in the area. A trading post preceded the arrival of the railroad, and the post office opened its doors in 1877.

There was a lot more to this town in 1891 than there is today: a general store, a millinery, a blacksmith, a hotel, a meat market, a fruit and tobacco store, a shoe store, and no fewer than four saloons.

One of those watering holes had been the scene of a bizarre incident in the spring of 1878, when a blacksmith named Christian Mutschler entered the establishment with two of his supposed friends, John Kelley and Henry Holmes. (They would turn out, in the end, to be not so much friends as finks.) Kelley and Holmes proceeded to become involved in an altercation with the saloon owner and, as often happened in the Old West, things got ugly from there.

Holmes and Kelley decided to have some fun at the barkeep's expense by lighting a sack of wood shavings on fire in the middle of the saloon. Lacking the spine to carry out the plot themselves, however, they instead persuaded Mutschler to do the deed. He obliged and, for his trouble, got a bullet in the leg: A couple of cowboys sitting nearby hadn't taken too kindly to choking on a roomful of smoke while they were having their drinks, so they drew their guns and fired.

Buildings sit abandoned along Highway 99W, the main street through Artois.

No charges were brought against the pair, but Mutschler was arrested and charged with arson. The justice of the peace released him when no one came forward to testify against him, but there seems to have been a reason for this: Certain individuals were out to get Mutschler, but they didn't want him in jail. They wanted him dead. Perhaps it had to do with another fire Mutschler was suspected of starting a year earlier in St. John's. Or perhaps his so-called friend John Kelley just wanted a scapegoat. For whatever reason, no sooner had Mutschler been released than Kelley swore out a complaint that the blacksmith had threatened to kill him.

Mutschler wisely decided to get out of Dodge, or in this case Germantown, while the getting was good, but someone had told the local stage operators not to let him ride. Instead he limped up the road toward Orland—wounded leg and all—and was quickly apprehended by deputies acting on Kelley's complaint. He was taken into custody and locked up in another saloon, of all places, because the town didn't have a proper jail. In the middle of the night, a dozen or more masked men broke down the door to the saloon, laid hold of Mutschler, and took him just beyond the edge of town, where they shot him to death.

Mutschler's brother hired a private detective from San Francisco to look into the matter, and the governor put up a $500 reward for a conviction, but it went unclaimed. Five people, including Mutschler's two "friends," Holmes and Kelley, were arrested in connection with the murder but eventually released for lack of a evidence, and the crime ultimately went unpunished.

The Mutschler affair notwithstanding, Germantown wasn't a bad place. According to one account, the town had "a number of fine residences and a substantial, neat school building." Although "a small town, comparatively," it figured "largely in the total prosperity of the county."

Local lore has it that the townsfolk voted to change the name in 1918, when anti-German sentiment was running high thanks to World War I. The impetus, as the story goes, was this: U.S. troops arriving in town by train took the name as an insult, which led to a brawl and, ultimately, to the name change. (Artois, a region in France, had been the site of three battles during the early years of World War I.)

More than a century has passed since the town's heyday, and time has taken its toll. These days, Artois is almost a ghost town. Perhaps the new I-5 artery drained the town's lifeblood out of it when the interstate bypassed Old 99W. Wooden buildings sit abandoned alongside the old highway in the dusty old downtown—if it can be called that—looking like a set from an old Western. One can almost envision the ghosts of those masked men dragging Christian Mutschler through the front doors of one of those buildings to meet his fate.

ORLAND

Population (1939)—1,195
Population (2010)—7,291
Elevation—259 feet
Location—10 miles north of Artois
Founded—1878
Incorporated—1909

Orland is named for the first irrigation project undertaken in California by the U.S. Bureau of Reclamation: the Orland Project, begun in 1887. Many buildings in the city date back to the time of its incorporation. The town's welcome arch is its distinguishing feature, and Orland is known as the "City of Arches."

The 1939 WPA guide describes Orland as a place "where modern schools and business buildings are shaded by umbrella and black walnut trees."

A car heads north on 99W after passing beneath the Orland Arch.

CORNING

Population (1939)—1,377
Population (2010)—7,663
Elevation—276 feet
Location—14 miles north of Orland
Founded—c. 1882
Incorporated—1907

Corning was named for John Corning, who served as assistant superintendent for the Central Pacific Railroad from 1868 until his death a decade later. He wasn't the only railroad man in his family to have a town named in his honor: Corning, New York, was named for his uncle, Erastus Corning, longtime president of the New York Central Railroad.

During its early years, the town was known as the "Clean Town," but agriculture was always a focus of the local economy. The first olives were planted in the region during the late 19th century, and they soon became the dominant crop in Corning, home to the world's largest ripe olive cannery (Bell Carter Olive Company). In 1923, the city slogan was changed to reflect this emphasis: It's now called the "Olive Town."

Finding the old road: At Corning, 99W turns East at **Solano Street** and continues for about a mile to **3rd Street**. Turn north there, and you'll be on 99W northbound once again, all the way to Red Bluff.

99 EAST

ROSEVILLE

Population (1939)—6,425
Population (2010)—127,323
Elevation—164 feet
Location—20 miles northeast of Sacramento
Founded—1864
Incorporated—1909

A trip up State Route 99 is a straight shot north from Sacramento to Yuba City, with very little in between: a convenience store, a fruit stand or two, and a lot of asphalt. You might want to gas up in Sacramento if you're low on fuel, because you won't see another gas station until you're halfway to Yuba.

You won't pass Roseville on this route, because State Route 99 along this stretch doesn't follow the original path of U.S. 99E, which was co-signed with U.S. 40 as it headed northeast into Roseville as Auburn Boulevard and Roseville Road. It's an old alignment that parallels the modern Interstate 80 over that span, diverging from U.S. 40 at Washington Boulevard, where it veered northward.

Roseville seems to have gotten its name from the abundance of wild roses growing in the region. It was first mentioned in print by that name in November of 1864, when news reports indicated 29 residents had voted for Abraham Lincoln and 17 had cast ballots for his Democratic opponent, George McClellan.

The town started out as a stagecoach stop called Griders and got a boost when the Southern Pacific Railroad moved its regional hub from nearby Rocklin in

The Carnegie Public Library in Roseville, seen here in 1912, is now a museum and sits just off the old highway—Washington Boulevard—on Lincoln Street. *Roseville Historical Society, public domain.*

1909. Twenty years later, nearly 1 in 5 residents worked for the railroad.

The railroad gradually declined in importance as highway travel became more popular, but it was still involved in one of the most memorable—and alarming—events in Roseville's history. On the morning of April 28, 1973, the United Press International reported that "railroad boxcars loaded with nearly two million pounds of bombs and propane gas exploded one after another … in deafening and window-shattering blasts which lasted five hours and were felt 100 miles away."

The 250-pound bombs—more than 7,000 of them housed in 18 boxcars—were part of a military munitions shipment intended for use in Vietnam. Amazingly, no one was killed, but according to one report, the explosions "completely leveled the half-dozen buildings that made up the nearby town of Antelope."

George Manzoli, a Southern Pacific switchman who witnessed the disaster, told reporters, "It was almost like an atom bomb. There was a mushroom of smoke, of fire, that went about 300 yards up into the air, and then there was a loud noise. I went through a war in Europe when I was a kid, but I never could imagine what it would be like to see a lot of bombs go off in a boxcar."

The Highway Patrol found two undetonated bombs embedded in a paved street a half-mile from the disaster site, and shrapnel fell from the sky over a three-mile radius. In Sacramento, 15 miles away, the state capitol building was closed for fear that the concussions might have weakened the dome. "The eye of the disaster looks like a hydrogen bomb might have been dropped on it," Sheriff Duane Lowe said.

Finding the old road: Heading out of Sacramento on **Del Paso Boulevard**, turn east on **El Camino Avenue** a short distance to **Auburn Boulevard**. The Capital City Freeway bisects this alignment at one point, so cross it via Marconi and take an immediate left on the Lincoln Highway. This becomes Auburn again in short order and continues northeast before eventually veering north and becoming **Riverside Avenue**. Riverside will end at **Vernon Street**, which will carry you northwest to **Washington Boulevard** through Roseville.

LINCOLN

Population (1939)—2,094
Population (2010)—42,819
Elevation—167 feet
Location—11 miles north of Roseville
Founded—1859
Incorporated—1890

In the golden age of railroads, Charles Wilson envisioned a rail line east of Sacramento, to be called the California Central. Launching the effort in 1857, he was able to finish grading on the project before running into financial problems, which forced him to halt the project in 1860 with the rails only partially laid.

The ceramics plant of Gladding, McBean, a company founded in 1875, is still visible along the old highway, Lincoln Boulevard, in Lincoln.

Finances proved to be a recurring problem for the company, which cut its workforce by 40 percent and recruited cheap Chinese labor to get the project back off the ground. But more money problems forced another halt in the project a year later, and it was five more years before it could resume. Two years after that, in 1868, foreclosure put the company out of business a little more than a decade after it was formed.

Wilson, however, left a lasting legacy: The town of Lincoln was named in his honor (Lincoln was his middle name), not, as might have been supposed, for the famous president of the same era. His company's money problems were actually a boon to Lincoln, which became for a time the northern terminus of the still-incomplete rail line. But when work resumed in 1866, the town lost some of its luster.

It reinvented itself as a pottery center in the 1870s, when clay deposits were discovered south of town in the Ione formation. The clay sediment in the region dated back 65 million years, to a time when the area was submerged under a shallow inland sea, and it quickly became a new source of income for the region. The Gladding, McBean ceramics company, founded in 1875, became the linchpin of this new prosperity, initially producing clay sewer pipe. Nine years later, the company used terra-cotta trim made at its Lincoln plant to build a two-story office building on San Francisco's Market Street; in the 1890s, it supplied clay roof tile for Stanford University.

You can still see the company's plant, complete with a brick chimney so tall it looks like an obelisk, on the east side of the old highway just north of town.

Finding the old road: Next, leave Washington Boulevard in Roseville and turn left onto **Industrial Avenue**. Just after you make this turn, look out for a power station on the west side of the road. There you'll find a short slab of concrete from the highway's early years. At the north end of the slab, look for a stamp in the concrete that identifies it as the work of Fredrickson Bros. Contractors and bears the date May 6, 1929.

The road becomes **Lincoln Boulevard** through Lincoln a few miles up the road and continues to the small community of Sheridan, where it merges with State Route 65.

There's not much left on Sheridan's main street these days: a couple of dilapidated buildings alongside the post office line a short spur of what used to be the highway. There's also a historical marker at the spot once occupied by a one-story house and a shed built there in 1855 and '57, respectively. Union Shed, as it was known, "became a popular wagon and freight trails crossroads and stop with as many as 60 teams boarded per night," according to the marker. It was renamed Sheridan in the 1860s after Civil War General Philip Sheridan.

Once signed as 99E, this route became SR 65 in 1964. Plans called for it to be part of the proposed Eastside Freeway, a companion project to the Westside Freeway (Interstate 5) that was in development at the same time. Those plans, however, never reached fruition. The state made the west-side project a priority because of its interstate status, and by the time it was complete, there weren't enough funds to finish the east-side freeway along the western edge of the Sierra Nevada. In addition to this northern segment, from Roseville to Marysville, a southern section of the unfinished project stretches north from Highway 99 near Bakersfield to Exeter, where it abruptly ends. The rest of the highway is nothing more than a dotted line indicating a planned route on some old maps.

An old, closed country store along a spur of old highway is one of the few buildings in the tiny hamlet of Sheridan.

Women and children lined up to pick hops in the blistering sun during August of 1913 at the Durst Ranch in Wheatland. Blazing heat and unsanitary conditions helped spark the deadly Wheatland Hop Riot. *Public domain.*

WHEATLAND

Population (1939)—479
Population (2010)—3,456
Elevation—92 feet
Location—11 miles northwest of Lincoln
Founded—1866
Incorporated—1874

Wheatland, described in the 1939 WPA guide as "a village of weather-beaten, tree-shaded houses among hop fields," had an important role to play in California history. In the winter of 1846–47, seven surviving members of the pioneering Donner Party arrived in Wheatland, seeking help for those still stranded in the Sierra snows at Donner Lake. It was one of the most infamous tragedies on record: By the time a rescue party reached them in February, 39 of the pioneers were dead and many of the survivors had eaten their corpses just to stay alive.

The town was even more well known, however, for the Wheatland Hop Riot of 1913, described in the WPA guide as "California's first important strike by field workers."

The 640-acre Durst Ranch produced hops, a flowering cone used in brewing beer. Ralph and Jonathan Durst, the brothers who owned the operation, needed workers for the harvest. So they put out fliers promising a high-wage job to any (white) picker who arrived at the ranch by August 5 for the three-week picking season.

The fliers, however, worked too well, and the number of workers who showed up far exceeded the jobs available—or the money allotted to pay them.

Pay was a major issue.

The Durst brothers had devised an ingenious system of compensation that enabled them to line their pockets while providing an insidious incentive for the pickers to stay on the job. They set wages at $1.90 a day for 100 pounds of picking, but they held $1 of that back to ensure the workers didn't abandon their tasks at some point during the grueling, unusually hot summer season. They'd be paid once the entire crop had been picked, and not before.

This was asking a lot, to say the least, especially in light of the fact that conditions on the ranch were intolerable. Workers could rent a tent for 75 cents a week, but it did little to shield them from the triple-digit heat. Making matters worse, there weren't enough to go around, and many were forced to sleep out in the fields. Toilet facilities consisted of nine outhouses—all without doors and all in the camp, rather than the fields a mile away. Clean water was nearly nonexistent, although the Dursts did *sell* lemonade to the workers for 5 cents a glass.

A union organizer for the militant International Workers of the World (IWW) named Blackie Ford found an eager audience when he spoke to discontented pickers on the second day of the harvest. The next day, he led more than 400 of them to confront Ralph Durst at his office and demand changes. Among them: fresh ice water three times a day in the fields, clean toilets, a flat rate of $1.25 for each 100-pound hopsack they picked, and garbage collection.

Durst agreed to them all except the pay increase, and Ford told him it wasn't enough: The workers would go on strike.

Durst responded by slapping Ford across the face with a work glove, then he told the union man to get off his property.

Ford refused.

Durst responded by heading into town to round up a posse that included the sheriff, the district attorney, and four constables to evict the protesters by force. When Durst and his men confronted the group, one of the strikers threw a rock that hit the sheriff in the head; meanwhile, Durst pointed out Ford and the other officers began pushing their way through the crowd to lay hold of him. The strikers responded by grabbing the sheriff, and one of the deputies fired his shotgun into the air. A striking picker lunged at the constable, and the pair grappled for the gun as shots went off, the striker ultimately grabbing the gun and beating the deputy over the head—for which he himself was shot.

The deputy wound up dead even so, as did the district attorney and two of the pickers. And when the dust cleared, several others emerged badly injured. The sheriff, badly beaten, had been shot in the arm and the head. A wealthy farmer's arm had been shot off, and gunfire had shattered another deputy's right arm. According to a report in the *San Francisco Chronicle*, five others were hurt, as well.

The workers high-tailed it out of town, afraid of more violence and worried that Durst might retaliate against them. Governor Hiram Johnson called out the state militia, while law enforcement rounded up Ford and another IWW organizer, both of whom were convicted of murder (even though neither man was actually present at the riot) and sentenced to life in prison.

After all that, the Durst brothers wound up meeting the strikers' demands for better working conditions and paying them a flat fee of $1 per 100 pounds, not quite

The State Theatre in Marysville opened as the National Theatre in 1927. It's on E Street just north of 5th, both of which serve as sections of the old highway alignment.

what they'd been asking for, but better than what they'd been getting.

Today, a plaque near an electrical substation at Sixth and A streets in Wheatland marks the site of the hop riot. It's less than a mile east of old 99E.

Finding the old road: Highway 65—the former 99E—is a two-lane road called D Street through Wheatland. Just north of town, exit onto **Rancho Road** south of Marysville for a 3-mile side trip across scenic countryside that stays closer to the parallel rail line than the modern alignment. Look for an old bridge, peeling white paint on its wooden railings. A stamp on the southeast end of the concrete dates it to 1935.

MARYSVILLE

Population (1939)—5,763
Population (2010)—12,072
Elevation—62 feet
Location—13 miles northwest of Wheatland
Founded—1851
Incorporated—1851

Yuba City

Population (1939)—3,605
Population (2010)—64,925
Elevation—59 feet
Location—adjacent to Marysville, west of the Feather River
Founded—1849
Incorporated—1908

Yuba City, which straddles the modern alignment of Highway 99, and Marysville just across the river, together form an urban area once envisioned as a great metropolis. A welcome sign placed at the city limits of Marysville proclaimed it the "Gateway to the Gold Fields," and the population surged to nearly 10,000 by the mid-1850s. After more than $10 million in gold had been shipped from Yuba City to the San Francisco mint, the city fathers had visions of the boomtown becoming the "New York of the Pacific."

Marysville and Yuba City enjoyed a friendly rivalry from their earliest days as Gold Rush towns. The two even, for a time, had similar names: Marysville was originally "Yubaville," but to avoid confusion, the city fathers renamed it Marysville in honor of Mary Murphy Covillaud, a survivor from the ill-fated Donner Party. As for Yuba City, it likely took its name from the Spanish word for grape, *uva*.

The twin cities' location at the confluence of two rivers, the Feather and the Yuba, appeared to be perfect for boats traveling downriver, laden with gold. But the hydraulic mining process used to get at the gold also created so much debris that it soon made the Feather River impassible to the boats traveling downriver to Marysville.

The rivers' confluence also created another potential problem: flooding. That potential became a catastrophic reality in 1955, when torrential rains hit in December, swelling the rivers to such an extent that the entire city of Marysville—all 12,500 residents—was ordered evacuated. Highways across the state were closed, and although U.S. 99 remained open to the Oregon border, it was limited to one-way traffic north of Weed.

Thirty-eight people died when a levee failed at Yuba City on Christmas Eve, as the Yuba River washed away one-third of the Fifth Street Bridge. Meanwhile, the manager of the Yuba County airport reported that some

A giant gold miner guards one of the holes at a miniature golf course beside the highway near Yuba City.

600 Sutter County residents had to be rescued via helicopter. "This is, without a doubt, the greatest flood in the records of this river system," said Lloyd Magar, a weather forecaster based in Sacramento.

The aftermath of the flood brought a few rays of sunshine courtesy of Annette Funicello and other members of the Mouseketeers from TV's *Mickey Mouse Club*. The flood had done its best to preempt the holidays, but Walt Disney had seen a newsreel report of the disaster and decided to lend his support by bringing young cast of the show to town for a belated Christmas party on February 25 of the following year.

A video of the event survives, showing Yuba City kids (and their parents) greeting the Mouseketeers at the airport and watching them perform a special show in town. Even Santa showed up for the festivities. It's still remembered around town as the year the Mouseketeers saved Christmas.

Finding the old road: A segment of old 99E parallels the highway just south of Marysville. You can access it by taking the Olivehurst exit, which will dump you onto **Lindhurst Avenue**, a two-lane road that widens to four lanes and is known as **Beale Road** farther on. In all, the segment's about 2½ miles long.

In Marysville itself, you can follow the old alignment by turning left onto **5th Street**, which crosses the Feather River via the Twin Cities Memorial Bridge and turns into **Bridge Street** on the far side in Yuba City. Turn north on **Plumas Street**, west briefly on **Colusa Avenue**, then north again on **Live Oak Boulevard** to continue along the original alignment. Live Oak Boulevard won't get you as far as the town of Live Oak—you'll have to rejoin the modern 99E before you get there.

Live Oak

Population (1939)—800
Population (2010)—8,392
Elevation—79 feet
Location—11 miles north of Yuba City
Incorporated—1947

Live Oak is a relatively small city on the 99W, but it had a big part to play in shaping highway policy. The town was among the first where engineers sought to bypass the business district with a new highway alignment. Road crews completed the bypass, then watched as local merchants pulled up stakes and relocated the entire business section beside the new road. The experience helped spur legislation that restricted the degree to which private operations could encroach on freeway rights of way.

The city is also home to one of just a few dozen bicentennial living-witness trees, believed to have been standing at the signing of the U.S. Constitution. The status of the valley oak tree along 99E was recognized in 1989; as of 2014, it was one of just 35 such trees in the nation.

Hazel Street, looking east, a few blocks west of Highway 99E in central Gridley. *Meriam Library, CSU Chico.*

Gridley

Population (2010)—6,593
Elevation—30 feet
Location—7 miles north of Live Oak
Founded—1874
Incorporated—1905

George W. Gridley turned failure into a legacy. A New York native who later moved to Illinois with his parents, he came up with the notion that he could drive cattle and 600 head of sheep across the central plains to the Golden State. In the process, he lost the animals but ultimately found a new home, buying 25,000 acres of ranch land on what became the town site, where he engaged in wood-cutting and grain production. Some of his descendants continued to live in the area as of 2014.

The Hazel Hotel, a boxy brick-and-masonry building designed in the Italianate style, recalls the town's railroad days and dates to 1888. It has earned a spot on the National Register of Historic Places. The hotel is about a half-mile west of 99E in the center of town.

A historical photo from the Cal State Chico archives shows the highway through downtown Chico.
Meriam Library, CSU Chico.

CHICO

Population (1939)—7,961
Population (2010)—86,186
Elevation—245 feet
Location—30 miles north-northwest of Gridley
Founded—1860
Incorporated—1872

A new stretch of freeway bypassed central Chico in the early 1960s—one of the few segments of the highway north of Sacramento that isn't still a two-lane road. Even here, however, it remains possible to travel back in time … and down a distinctive segment of Old 99.

The forerunner of the original highway in Chico was the Esplanade, a name that comes from an Italian word referring to a level plain and connotes the sort of leisurely drive travelers embarked on before cars were quite so fast and traffic was quite so congested. In fact, the Esplanade predates the advent of the motorcar altogether. It was the brainchild of John Bidwell, Chico's founding father,

who arrived in 1843 on one of the first wagon trains to reach California and shortly afterward struck gold on the Feather River. Bidwell used his newfound wealth to snap up 28,000 acres along both sides of Chico Creek, opening the first store there in what later became the Tres Hombres Restaurant building.

It wasn't long before he had laid out a plan for a city of 50 blocks, offering free lots to anyone who would build on the site. Its centerpiece was his own mansion, a distinctive 26-room Victorian home that rises three stories. Completed in 1868 at a cost of $60,000, it became the place to see and be seen north of Sacramento, as Bidwell and his wife, Annie, entertained the likes of President Rutherford B. Hayes, Susan B. Anthony, Governor Leland Stanford, and John Muir there.

Bidwell built this lavish home on the old Shasta-Tehama Road, which brought trappers, explorers, and prospectors through the area on horseback and stagecoach. Bidwell also built his town around this thoroughfare, which bisected the city. The northern end of it, which served as a sort of driveway to his palatial estate, was the Esplanade, and in 1870, Bidwell lined it with six rows of locust trees. These not only served to provide shade, but also provided wood for fence posts. They were removed in 1914 and replaced two years later by six rows of European sycamores, a welcome site to the growing number of motorists passing through the city on hot summer days. The trees along the Esplanade helped set the tone for the city as an oasis of shade in the Sacramento Valley, and it's no wonder the Arbor Day Foundation designated Chico—which boasts more than 30,000 street trees—as "Tree City USA."

Anyone traveling through Chico will notice the Esplanade's distinct character. It's a broad, four-lane boulevard, separated by a central median. That's not particularly unusual. But on either side, for the space of several blocks, there's also a third lane running in each direction that's separated from the main road by a secondary island. These narrow routes were designed to accommodate neighborhood traffic, leaving the central lanes free for highway travel. Bidwell himself even decreed that no gravel be placed on either side street, and an early county ordinance called for a $25 fine (no small sum in those days) to be assessed against owners of heavy wagons who used them. The east side was dedicated to travelers riding on horseback, while the west side served as a bike lane years before such became fashionable.

Chico remains a bike town to this day, which should come as no surprise considering it's a university town and Chico State predates even U.S. 99E by decades. *Bicycle Magazine* named it "America's Best Bike Town" in 1997.

As for the Esplanade, by 1915, the gravel on the main central roadway had given way to concrete, and the dirt side roads were finally paved around 1924. Still, that didn't mean Chico had any desire to rush travelers through on their way to points north or south. Quite to the contrary. Even today, traffic signals on the Esplanade are timed to preserve a leisurely pace: Drivers can avoid a red light by maintaining a steady rate of 27 miles per hour along the Esplanade.

Through town, the road splits into a pair of one-way routes with the standard names Main and Broadway. South of downtown, old 99 is called Park Avenue, which

veers east toward the freeway on a road known as The Skyway.

Finding the old road: The bypass of Chico is one of the few sections of freeway this far north. You can access the older route from the south via **Park Avenue**, which becomes **Main Street** (a one-way street) through downtown and **the Esplanade** near Bidwell Mansion. Continue north from there until you rejoin the modern highway. Note: If you're going southbound, you'll take **Broadway**—one way in the opposite direction—instead of Main Street.

Los Molinos (unincorporated)

Population (1939)—200
Population (2010)—2,037
Elevation—223 feet
Location—26 miles north-northwest of Chico

Los Molinos traces its history to a Mexican land grant. Albert G. Toomes, a Missouri native who had come to California in 1841, received more than 34 square miles of land in appreciation for his carpentry work in building a house for the Mexican governor in Monterey. Pioneer John Bidwell had dubbed a waterway in the area Mill Creek because it "suggests its value as a water-power" for milling. This gave rise to the Spanish name Rancho Rio de los Molinos, or River Ranch of the Mills.

Toomes built an adobe and stocked his ranch with cattle, later adding a flock of Cashmere goats numbering more than 200.

The community of Los Molinos is much smaller than the original land grant, covering just about 2.2 square miles.

99 West Rejoins 99 East at …

Red Bluff

Population (1939)—3,517
Population (2010)—14,076
Elevation—305 feet
Location—15 miles north-northwest of Los Molinos (99E); 19 miles north of Corning (99W)
Founded—1850
Incorporated—1876

Sometimes confused with Redding to the north, Red Bluff is a much smaller town that derives its name from a red bluff at a bend in the Sacramento River.

The location was notable before the town itself even appeared, thanks to William B. Ide, who owned some land on the riverbank just a couple of miles north of town. In 1846, Ide heard a report that the Mexican government, which ruled California at the time, intended to expel all settlers who weren't Mexican citizens. Outraged, he led a group of about 30 Americans in the Bear Flag Revolt against Mexican rule, capturing the town of Sonoma on the North Coast and proclaiming a new California Republic.

Ide served as president of the republic for a grand total of 25 days, before he joined U.S. forces led by John C. Fremont in wresting control of the entire territory from Mexico. Ide then returned to his home in the Red Bluff area, where he died of smallpox six years later.

Finding the old road: The old 99 disappears here for a while, having been replaced by Interstate 5.

This clock tower along 99W in downtown Red Bluff is a 75-foot replica of the original 100-foot tower that stood atop the Cone & Kimball Building at the same intersection, on Main (99W) and Walnut streets. The building and original tower, built in 1886, burned to the ground in 1984.

Cottonwood (unincorporated)

Population (1939)—150
Population (2010)—3,316
Elevation—420 feet
Location—16 miles north of Red Bluff
Founded—1849

The halfway point between Red Bluff and Redding, Cottonwood centers on Main Street—the bypassed Old 99—where the center divider is home to a parade of two-dimensional figures representing cowboys and cattle.

Producers of the movie *Almost Heroes*, featuring Chris Farley (in his final role before his death) and Matthew Perry, filmed scenes in Cottonwood in 1997. The story focused on a pair of explorers trying to beat Lewis and Clark to the Pacific Ocean.

It wasn't the first time Hollywood had been to town. *Hell Is for Heroes*, which featured an eclectic cast including Steve McQueen, Bobby Darin, Fess Parker and Bob Newhart, filmed there during the summer of '61. Hell was an apt term. It was particularly hot one afternoon when the director set up a scene that was supposed to take place in Germany during 1944, where a squad of Americans had to hold off a full German company for 48 hours while waiting for reinforcements. He had to shoot it four times, and each time the actors were so drenched with perspiration that the makeup crew had to do some serious damage control.

The heat was so stifling that many of the scenes were shot in the evening, after things cooled off. But some of the actors remained hot under the collar. Darin and McQueen—who had a reputation for being surly and difficult to work with—reportedly weren't getting along, and a columnist on the scene commented to Darin, "Steve McQueen is his own worst enemy."

Darin's reply? "Not while I'm still alive."

Sadly, his comment proved ominous. Darin, who had suffered from heart problems since childhood, died in 1973 at the age of 37. McQueen was just 50 when he died of cancer seven years later.

*Finding the old road: Heading north, take the Bowman Road exit. Check first just west of the freeway for a gated entrance marked as **Floyd Road**, a concrete remnant of the earliest alignment. Then go back across to the east side of the freeway, and you'll find yourself on **Main Street**, a bypassed alignment of old U.S. 99 that continues for 2½ miles through Cottonwood. Another segment of the old road runs west of the freeway as **Rhonda Road**, but you'll have to go back to the center of town on Main Street to get there: Turn west on Fourth Street, then north on Rhonda, which will take you up to Anderson.

ANDERSON

Population (1939)—1,445
Population (2010)—9,932
Elevation—430 feet
Location—5 miles north of Cottonwood
Founded—c. 1872
Incorporated—1956

Like many other towns along 99, which for so many miles paralleled older rail lines, Anderson owed its existence to the railroad. In this case, it was ranch owner Elias Anderson who lent the town his name, having donated land for a station to the Oregon and California Railroad.

Finding the old road: The highway that used to be 99 is signed as SR 273 through Anderson and Redding, for a length of some 15 miles. It's known as **Market Street** most of the way through Redding, though it's also **Pine Street** (one way northbound) and **California Street** (one way southbound) for a short distance in that city's downtown area.

REDDING

Population (1939)—4,188
Population (2010)—89,861
Elevation—495 feet
Location—11 miles north of Anderson
Founded—1873
Incorporated—1887

Old 99, renumbered as Route 273, diverges from the modern interstate for 15 miles between Anderson and Redding. Through Redding, it's known as Market Street, itself a bypass of the even-older route through town.

That would be California Street: originally a dirt road fronting the newly installed railroad tracks where a few businesses popped up to serve travelers making their way into town. Redding's population doubled during the 1930s, when men streamed into town to claim jobs on the crews building nearby Shasta Dam. California Street became a bustling, raucous center of nightlife where the workers went to relax and blow off steam.

Construction on the dam began in 1937, and the following year, World War I flying ace Jack Young—recognizing an opportunity when it presented itself—leased the lower floor of a secondhand shop for use as a bar and grill called Jack's. Young had owned a bar of the same name in Indio, but business had slowed there with the completion of the All American Canal. In Redding, Young had plenty of competition. His establishment was one of as many as 20 in an area that was rapidly becoming

Gene's Hamburgers (left) and Jack's Grill (right) are two longtime favorite spots to grab a bite along the old highway in Redding.

Redding's red light district (the upper floor even housed a brothel for a time), but it thrived even after the dam was completed in 1945.

Young sold the bar in the 1940s, and it has gone through a series of ownership changes over the years, but otherwise time seems to have stood still. All the other bars from the district's brassy, brawling heyday have vanished, but Jack's remained at its original location—which still looks more like a thrift store than an eatery—more than 75 years later.

Perhaps Redding's most distinctive landmark, however, is its Sundial Bridge, a pedestrian walkway across the Sacramento River supported by cables running from a single tower. The bridge's modern design resembles a sailboat or something out of a science fiction movie. Designed by Santiago Calatrava, the Spanish architect who designed the Olympic stadium for the 2004 Games in Athens, Greece, the bridge opened on Independence Day of that same year.

Finding the old road: There's a piece of old highway dating from 1926 north of town. To get there, continue on Market Street north from downtown across the Sacramento River and turn east on Lake Boulevard toward Interstate 5. Before you get to the freeway, then north again on **Boulder Drive**, a short segment of the old highway continues for just a half-mile.

Farther north, yet another section of old highway survives as **Wonderland Boulevard** through the small community of Mountain Gate. From northbound I-5, take Exit 687, cross over the freeway to and drive up Wonderland, which parallels the interstate on its western flank.

The highway once continued under what is now Shasta Lake, and you can find it on the other (north) side as **Lakeshore Drive**. Take the Lakeshore exit from I-5 and double back south on the west side of the freeway. You'll cross a couple of vintage, 1920s-era concrete arch bridges over Doney and Charlie creeks. During drought years, pieces of the old highway will be visible from dried-up sections of Shasta Lake.

Farther north, take the Vollmers exit and turn west, back under the freeway, toward Dog Creek Road. Take a left on Fenders Ferry Road and head back toward the interstate. Shortly after you pass beneath it, you'll be looking up at a 1927 concrete arch span that was part

of old U.S. You can also see the bridge from the top by turning right off the freeway and traveling about a half-mile to the end of the road, then hiking down a U.S. Forest Service road and turning left on a path that once carried U.S. 99. It's about another half-mile from there to the bridge, which is equipped with four benches for travelers to rest along their journey. It was a different time.

Another old highway bridge, this one from 1927, can be accessed by taking the La Moine exit a few miles up. Go back over the freeway on Slate Creek Road, then take your first left to see the bridge, which was part of an old highway alignment.

Still another stretch of old highway, which runs between Pollard Gulch to the south and Gibson as **Eagles Roost Road** and **Gibson Road**. Along the way, you'll see concrete bridges from the old highway, dating from 1915 and 1928.

But we're not done yet. You can see another bridge, a 60-foot concrete T-beam span dating from 1929, along **Mears Ridge Road**, a segment of old highway that's known as **Shotgun Road** farther south and is accessible from the Sims exit north of Gibson.

Other segments of old highway are accessible at Conant (**Conant Road** west of the freeway), Sweetbriar (**Sweetbriar Avenue** east of I-5), Castella at the Soda Creek Road exit (a road known as both **Main Street** and **Frontage Road**, also east of the freeway), and just south of Dunsmuir (along Crag View Drive, which runs east of the interstate).

DUNSMUIR

Population (1939)—2,610
Population (2010)—1,650
Elevation—2,280 feet
Location—53 miles north of Redding
Founded—1887
Incorporated—1909

One of the few towns along the highway in sparsely populated Northern California, Dunsmuir touts itself as "Home of the best water on earth" and retains much of its 1920s-era charm. Early on, the town was known by such names as Poverty Flats and Pusher, which may explain why residents were only too happy to honor Alexander

An old-fashioned clock and the historical California Theatre lend an air of timeless charm to downtown Dunsmuir along the old highway.

Dunsmuir by naming the town after him in exchange for his donation of a fountain to the town. The fountain still stands, though it has been moved to the baseball field at the city park, a site where Babe Ruth once played exhibitions.

A section of Old 99 runs through the heart of Dunsmuir, away from the modern I-5 bypass. The lofty vertical neon sign outside the California Theatre rises high beside Dunsmuir Avenue, as the historic highway is known there, at the center of town. Opened in 1926, the 800-seat theater played host to such stars (in person, not just on the screen) as Clark Gable, Carole Lombard, and the Marx Brothers.

The theater opened and closed at various points over the years and, as of 2014, was open again, showing films from the Golden Age of cinema.

Dunsmuir was also notable as the site of the last public lynching in California. The chain of events that led up to it began in the summer of 1935, when Robert "Half Ear" Miller Barr and Clyde Johnson, both in their 20s, robbed a roadhouse and made a run for it, with Dunsmuir Police Chief Jack Daw and Deputy George Malone in pursuit. The robbers abandoned their car, hid in the bushes, and ambushed the lawmen when they arrived, opening fire and hitting both men. Daw was mortally wounded, and Malone was hit, as well, but he was still able to chase Johnson down and capture him in the woods.

The prisoner was taken to Yreka and jailed there, but friends of the popular Daw were far from satisfied. At his funeral, said to have been the largest ever in the region, they began hatching a plot to take vengeance on Johnson. Then, on a Saturday in August, they donned masks and all piled into 25 cars for the trip to Yreka, where they broke down the doors of the jail and laid hold of Johnson. Martin Lange, a deputy on duty, tried to stop them, but they only grabbed him, too. They drove for 15 miles before they threw Lange out of the car, then took Johnson into the woods, where they strung him up from a tall tree and executed him by hanging.

The vigilantes then went in search of Barr. Law officers, however, found him first, arresting him under the alias Donald Bouchey in San Pedro. Authorities made sure the vigilantes wouldn't repeat their earlier break-in at Yreka by holding him at Folsom Prison. Though tests showed that Johnson had been the one who pulled the trigger, Barr ultimately pleaded guilty to his role in Daw's murder and was transferred to San Quentin.

No one was ever arrested in the lynching of Johnson.

In an ironic turn of events, however, Lange—the deputy at the Yreka jail who had refused to turn Johnson over to the mob—was himself killed a year later while seeking to arrest a pair of brothers for disturbing the peace with their gold-mining operations. The brothers killed two other men, as well, and once again a mob of vigilantes began talking about bringing a pair of murderers to justice. As with Miller, however, lawmen found the brothers first and took them into custody; they were later convicted of murder and sentenced to be hanged, but those sentences were subsequently commuted to life in prison.

Finding the old road: The bypassed section of old 99 that passes through Dunsmuir along **Dunsmuir Avenue** is one of the most picturesque you'll find. It runs through downtown and under the freeway, continuing to the now-vanished town of Mott (though Dunsmuir Avenue does become **Mott Road** at its northern end). Along the way, just south of Upper Soda Road, you'll pass an old concrete arch bridge that once carried U.S. 99 and now bears the northbound lanes of I-5.

CITY OF MOUNT SHASTA

Population (1939)—1,009
Population (2010)—3,394
Elevation—3,394 feet
Location—9 miles north-northwest of Dunsmuir
Founded—1870
Incorporated—1905

The City of Mount Shasta took the name of the nearby peak in 1924. Before that, the town had been known as Strawberry Valley, Berryvale, and Sisson, after the man who donated land to the Central Pacific for a railroad station in 1886, Justin Hinckley Sisson. Mount Shasta was built on old lava flows and is the site of one of just two remaining Richfield Beacon gas stations. The station itself is no longer in business, but the tower still loomed over the highway and the building that once housed the business as of 2014.

The volcanic mountain for which the town takes its name is the fifth-highest peak in California. The mountain's singular character—it rises solitary, apart from any mountain range, from the valley below to more than 14,000 feet in elevation—has given rise to any number of speculative stories about its supposedly mystical nature. Strange lights have reportedly been seen emanating from it, and cloud formations that look suspiciously like spaceships have been witnessed hovering nearby. Explorer and conservationist John Muir was so entranced by his first sight of it that he wrote in 1874: "I was fifty miles away, afoot, alone and weary, yet all of my blood turned to wine and I have not been weary since."

A Yreka teenager named Frederick Spencer Oliver upped the ante in the 1880s when he put forth a claim that he had written a manuscript under the guidance of an ancient inhabitant of the lost continent Lemuria. This supposedly "channeled" manuscript revealed the existence of a city beneath the mountain with walls "polished as by jewelers, though excavated by giants." A professor named Edgar Larkin, director of the Mount Lowe observatory north of Los Angeles, chimed in with a story of his own. He undertook an expedition toward the mountain and, with the help of a long-distance telescope, made out what he reported to be a mystic village at its base. About 1,000 people lived there, he said, and they were engaged in peaceful agrarian activity, "contented to live as their ancient forebears had lived before Lemuria was swallowed by the sea." In the midst of the settlement, he said, was a magnificent temple, "a marvelous work of carved marble and onyx, rivaling the beauty of the temples of the Yucatan."

Whatever Professor Larkin saw or thought he saw, no evidence to corroborate the existence of such a city has been found. Still, that hasn't stopped self-proclaimed mystics and opportunistic businesses from capitalizing on the story. Later stories of alleged Bigfoot sightings only added to the region's allure for seekers of the supernatural and fantastic, and plenty of opportunists remain eager to cash in on decades of stories concerning what might be in or on the great mountain.

Finding the old road: The Mt. Shasta City exit will funnel you directly onto **Mt. Shasta Boulevard**, the old 99 alignment through town. Within a quarter-mile, you'll come across the old Richfield Beacon station on your right, the only one in California to have been built in the English-Norman style. As of 2015, its tower was one of only two still standing in the state. In town, you can take the newer alignment by veering at a 45-degree angle with Mt. Shasta Boulevard, or you can follow the older alignment, **Chestnut Street**, which veers left one block farther north. In all, the segment covers just under 5 miles.

North of the city, near Black Butte, two other segments of the old road survive on opposite sides of the interstate as **Summit Drive** and **Truck Village Drive**.

A souvenir shop at the south end of town welcomes visitors to Weed.

WEED

Population (1939)—4,000
Population (2010)—2,967
Elevation—3,425 feet
Location—10 miles north-northwest of Mount Shasta
Founded—1897
Incorporated—1961

Weed, not to be confused with Weed Patch in Kern County, had nothing to do with invasive plants but was named in honor of Abner Weed, who purchased the Siskiyou Lumber and Mercantile Mill and 280 acres of land at the site for $400 in 1897. He obviously saw something in the place: specifically, that the wind currents in the area were useful in drying green lumber. The writer of *The WPA Guide to the Golden State* in 1939, however, was much less enamored of the little town, which the volume described as "a lumber town, bleak and raw looking, in a hill-rimmed hollow."

The author continued: "Along the railroad sidings behind the business district, spread great lumber mills with vast rows of stacked pine boards. In clearings at the edge of the brush huddle desolate, unpainted company shacks, barracklike rooming houses and company stores."

The *Redding Free Press* echoed this view of Weed as a dingy, dangerous town, describing it as the "Sodom and Gomorrah of Siskiyou County." This shouldn't have been surprising: The population was predominantly male, consisting of mill workers and a few supporting businesses, so things could get rough. There were shootings, barroom brawls, and the like.

Not all the mishaps were fueled by testosterone, however. One in 1963 was the result of one honey of an accident. A pair of trucks collided on the highway, whereupon 150 beehives were shattered and the insects let loose, prompting residents to flee for their homes as they tried to avoid being stung. The city's firefighters doused the crazed insects with chemical foam and cleared the roadway, sweeping up the hives with power shovels. Four men on the trucks suffered minor injuries.

Despite its rough reputation, the city also had an undeniable charm, with its clean air, pine-covered vistas, and views of snow-covered Shasta looming on the horizon.

The Hi-Lo Motel and Café had been around for decades into the second decade of the new millennium, the letters of its vintage neon sign still lighting up in sequence. And the growth of the marijuana trade provided the town with a catchy if quirky new motto for T-shirts, caps, and bumper stickers: "I'm high on Weed."

Finding the old road: The old highway, now signed as Business 5, goes through Weed as **Weed Boulevard**, then continues north of town as **Edgewood Road**. At the northern end of Edgewood Road, cross under the freeway overpass westward and continue on **Stewart Springs Road**, another piece of the old 99 route that will take you all the way to Yreka, a distance of about 24 miles on the west side of Interstate 5. There's also a short section of old 99 on the eastern side of the freeway just south of Yreka that's known, for part of the way, as **Shamrock Road**. A vintage neon sign for a closed restaurant called Shamrock Dinners is a landmark at the southern end.

Yreka

Population (1939)—2,126
Population (2010)—7,765
Elevation—2,582 feet
Location—29 miles north-northwest of Weed
Founded—1851
Incorporated—1857

Yreka got its start as a Gold Rush town but didn't get its name from the Gold Rush—even though it sounds suspiciously like Eureka, the name of another Northern California city that means "I have found it!" in Greek. Eureka is also the state motto, but again, it has no rele-

The relocated Yreka sign, with statue of prospector and burro.

vance whatsoever here. Yreka, for its part, isn't Greek or even European. It's a convoluted form of the Native American word *wáik'a*, meaning "white mountain" or "north mountain."

The mountain in question is the imposing 14,000-foot Mount Shasta, which was part of the town's name (Shasta Butte City) before it was changed to Yreka in 1852. Apparently, however, that was a mistake: The name was actually supposed to be Ieka, but it was mistakenly transcribed as Wyreka, with the "W" later being dropped.

Mark Twain had a different, albeit fictional, explanation: "There was a bakeshop," he wrote in his autobiography, "with a canvas sign which had not yet been put up but had been painted and stretched to dry in such a way that the word BAKERY, all but the B, showed through and was reversed. The stranger read it wrong end first, YREKA, and supposed that that was the name of the camp. The campers were satisfied with it and adopted it."

Finding the old road: The old highway is **Main Street** through the heart of Yreka and is signed as SR 263 farther north. Up the road a little ways, another section of old highway runs through the small community of Hornbrook east of the freeway as **Hornbrook Road**. Your next glimpse of old U.S. 99 is visible if you take Exit 793 onto **Bailey Hill Road**, also east of the freeway. At the Oregon State line, a very narrow segment of poorly maintained road veers away from the freeway off the Hilt exit as **Jefferson Road**.

TIMELINE

1850—Sacramento incorporated.

Los Angelese incorporated.

1851—Marysville incorporated.

1857—Yreka incorporated.

1864—Beale's Cut excavated; the narrow cut through the mountains separates the San Fernando and Santa Clarita valleys, opening the way for stagecoach traffic.

1869—San Bernardino incorporated.

1871—Woodland incorporated.

1872—Chico incorporated.

1874—Wheatland incorporated.

1876—Red Bluff incorporated.

1884—Modesto incorporated.

1885—Fresno incorporated.

1886—Willows incorporated.

Karl Benz introduces the first modern automobile, the Benz-Patent Motorwagen.

1887—Redding incorporated.

1888—Tulare incorporated.

Redlands incorporated.

Pomona incorporated.

1889—Merced incorporated.

1891—Ontario incorporated.

1895—California State Legislature creates state Bureau of Highways.

1896—Griffith J. Griffith donates more than 3,000 acres of land to the city of Los Angeles, marking the creation of Griffith Park.

1898—Bakersfield incorporated.

1905—City of Mount Shasta incorporated.

1905–07—Colorado River floods Salton Sink, creating the Salton Sea.

1906—Glendale incorporated.

Lodi incorporated.

Los Angeles Ostrich Farm opens in Lincoln Heights.

1907—Madera incorporated.

California Alligator Farm opens in Lincoln Heights.

Corning incorporated.

Lodi Arch built.

1908—Model T introduced.

El Centro incorporated.

Brawley incorporated.

Fowler incorporated.

Calexico incorporated.

Turlock incorporated.

Yuba City incorporated.

1909—Orland incorporated.

1910—Newhall Tunnel opens, replacing Beale's Cut as primary means of passage between San Fernando and Santa Clarita valleys.

1910—Voters approve the $18 million State Highway Bond Act to establish 3,052 miles of highways.

1911—Three-member California Highway Commission formed.

San Fernando incorporated.

Burbank incorporated.

1912—El Monte incorporated.

Ground broken on first section of state highway funded under 1910 bond.

Beaumont incorporated.

Surveys begin for future construction of Ridge Route.

1913—Banning incorporated.

Filmmaker William Selig purchases 32 acres in Lincoln Heights, a site that will become the Selig Zoo.

1915—Second bond passed, allocating $15 million to complete work authorized under initial bond and $3 million for an additional 680 miles of roadway.

Delano incorporated.

Ridge Route between Castaic and Grapevine opens.

1917—June McCarroll paints white line down the center of the highway in Indio.

Concrete installation begins on the Ridge Route.

1918—Ceres incorporated.

Manteca incorporated.

1920—Williams incorporated.

Ridge Route fully paved with concrete.

1922—Snowstorm strands scores of motorists on Ridge Route.

Atwater incorporated.

1922—Livingston incorporated.

1923—Chowchilla incorporated.

1924—California State Legislature approves project to paint lines down the center of highways.

1925—Gay's Lion Farm opens in El Monte.

Selig Zoo renamed Luna Park Zoo.

1926—State Legislative Route 4 becomes part of U.S 99 under the new federal highway system.

St. Francis Dam opens.

Frank Pohl opens first Giant Orange stand, in Tracy

1928—First six Richfield Beacons light up.

Surveying begins for Ridge Route Alternate.

St. Francis Dam collapses.

1929—Fresno Zoo opens at Roeding Park.

Construction begins on Ridge Route Alternate.

1930—Greek Theatre completed at Griffith Park.

1933—Ridge Route Alternate opens as U.S. 99 through Piru Canyon.

Traffic circle opens in Bakersfield.

U.S. 99 split into eastern and western alignments from Sacramento to Red Bluff.

1935—Griffith Observatory completed.

1937—Construction begins on Shasta Dam.

1939—Statue of Father Francisco Garcés unveiled in Bakersfield traffic circle (Garcés Circle).

1940—Arroyo Seco Parkway (Pasadena Freeway) opens as the nation's first freeway.

1944—Shasta Lake fills with water.

1945—Ripon incorporated.

1946—Pollard's Chicken Kitchen opens along Highway 99 in Stockton.

1947—Work begins to widen the Ridge Route Alternate portion of U.S. 99 from a three-lane road into a four-lane highway.

1948—Fresno-Calwa Freeway, the first stretch of freeway opened in the San Joaquin Valley, completed, bypassing Railroad Avenue alignment.

1952—Manteca bypass completed.

1953—Tulare bypass completed.

Four Level Interchange, or "the Stack," opens in Los Angeles.

1954—Chowchilla, Delano bypasses completed.

1955—Atwater bypass completed.

James Dean dies after driving up 99, eating at Tip's Coffee Shop and receiving a speeding ticket at Mettler.

Playland amusement park opens at Fresno's Roeding Park.

1956—Runaway truck ramp added on Five Mile Grade north of Castaic.

1957—North end of Fresno bypass completed.

1958—Salton City development sales begin.

1959—Pixley bypass completed.

Fairytale Town storybook park opens in Sacramento.

1961—Weed incorporated.

1962—Storyland amusement park opens at Fresno's Roeding Park.

North Shore development at Salton Sea opens with yacht club, motel.

1963—Selma Freeway completed, bypassing Golden State Boulevard (old U.S. 99) between Fresno and the Tulare County line.

Merced bypass completed.

Bakersfield bypass completed.

1965—Modesto bypass completed.

1967—Burbank converts a section of old U.S. 99/San Fernando Road into a pedestrian mall.

1968—Federal highway decommissioned; last U.S. 99 road signs removed.

1970—Four CHP officers shot to death by two gunmen along Highway 99 in what would become known as the Newhall Incident.

1971—San Feranando (Saugus) earthquake strikes; the magnitude-6.6 quake damages or destroys several freeway overpasses.

Magic Mountain amusement park opens in Valencia.

1973—Turlock bypass completed.

Pyramid Lake completed, submerging a portion of the old U.S. 99 through Piru Gorge.

1974—Manteca Waterslides open.

1984—North Shore Yacht Club closes at Salton Sea.

1987—Santa Clarita incorporated.

1994—Northridge earthquake, measuring 6.7, kills 57 people in northern San Fernando Valley.

1996—Livingston Bypass eliminates last stoplight on 99.

Buck Owens opens his Crystal Palace in Bakersfield.

2000—Elk Grove incorporated.

2004—Manteca Waterslides close.

2007—Mammoth Orange in Chowchilla closes, is eventually moved to Fossil Discovery Center.

Pollardville closes.

REFERENCES, PART I

"50 Cars Were Held in Snow; Hurry Rescue," San Bernardino Daily Sun, p. 1, Jan. 10, 1930.

"40 Autoists Trapped in Snow," San Francisco Chronicle, p. 1, Jan. 31, 1922.

"$400,000 Fire Hits Bakersfield Inn," The Fresno Bee, p. 1, Feb. 20, 1964.

"150 Motorists Are Still Caught in Snow on Ridge Near Bakersfield," Santa Cruz Evening News, p. 1, Feb. 1, 1922.

"176 Guests at Opening of Ballroom," The Bakersfield Californian, p. 14, May 9, 1940.

"1000 Fighting Forest, Brush Fire on Ridge," Oxnard Press-Courier, p. 1, Sept. 22, 1928.

"25-Vehicle Pileup Caused by Fog Causes Snarls, Closes California Highway," The Boca Raton News, p. 3A, Dec. 24, 1993.

"2 Children Die Daily in Tulare," The Bakersfield Californian, Jan. 26, 1938.

"2 Lions Slain, Man Clawed in El Monte Jungle Hunt," Modesto News-Herald, p. 1, Sept. 27, 1928.

"$2,000,000 Mine Plant Brings $97,000 as Junk," Woodland Daily Democrat, p. 3, Feb. 3, 1931.

"A Projected Ostrich Farm," Daily Alta California, March 14, 1888.

"A 60-Minute Ceremony That Took a Year to Prepare," The Disney History, April 26, 2011, thehistoryofdisney.blogspot.com.

"About Us—History," CAT Certified Scales. Catscale.com.

"Accident Kills Young Woman," Santa Cruz Sentinel, p. 7, Dec. 27, 1978.

"Accidental Blast Closes Ridge Route," The Bakersfield Californian, p. 1, Feb. 9, 1951.

Air Commerce Bulletin, v. 2, 1931, pp. 507, 508

"Alternate Ridge Route Great Engineering Project," Van Nuys News, p. 1, Dec. 21, 1931.

Amelinckx, Andrew. "Old Time Farm Crime: Fleecing Feathers," Modern Farmer, July 15, 2013. modernfarmer.com.

"America Rides the Gypsy Lanes," Santa Cruz News, p. 9, July 11, 1936.

"Americans Only Are Welcomed at Lodi," San Francisco Chronicle, p. 3, April 18, 1918.

"An Interview with Doris Stiggins," kvie.org.

"Anaheim Ostrich Farm," San Francisco Bulletin, Oct. 13, 1983.

"Arroyo Highway Fete Is Planned," The Fresno Bee, p. 7, Oct. 23, 1940.

Ashworth, Phyllis. "Ruth Alexander Collection," International Women's Air and Space Museum, Cleveland, April, 2002.

"Attachments, Liens, Etc.," Los Angeles Herald, p. 7, Jan. 23, 1887.

"Auto Camp Booklet Is Aid to Motorists," Ukiah Dispatch Democrat, p. 4, July 7, 1928.

"Axelrod: The Flying A Dog," www.retroplanet.com.

Ayers, B. Drummond Jr. "In a City of Motorcycle-Cop Mystique, an Officer, and Quake Victim, Is Laid to Rest," The New York Times, Jan. 25, 1994. www.nytimes.com.

"Bakersfield Inn c. 1949," Bakersfield Magazine, www.bakersfield-magazine.net.

Bayles, Fred. "Time, Costs Conspired Against Quake Proofing," p. 26, Hazelton (Pa.) Standard-Speaker, Jan. 19, 1994.

"Beach Development And County Harbor Will Require Another Route To San Joaquin Valley," Oxnard Press-Courier, p. 1, April 30, 1927.

Beath, Warren. The Death of James Dean, p. 35-36, Grove Press, New York, 1986.

"Beauties and Resources of County Related in Pamphlet," The Bakersfield Californian, p. 9, Aug. 8, 1924.

Benston, Liz. "Herbst family looks south," Las Vegas Sun, April 16, 2007, www.lasvegassun.com.

Blaisdell, George. "Great Selig Enterprise," The Moving Picture World, July 10, 1915. www.movielocationsplus.com.

"Blasting of L.A. Aqueduct Continues," Oxnard Daily Courier, p. 1, July 16, 1927.

"Blaze Destroys Inn, Starts Forest Fire," The San Bernardino County Sun, p. 1, Oct. 15, 1932.

" 'Bloody 99' Title Arouses Safety Council," The Bakersfield Californian, June 22, 1948.

"Boats Now Run Regularly Over What Was Once A Barren Desert," El Paso Herald, p. 1, July 23, 1906.

Bowen, Jerry. "Giant Orange squeezed slice of Americana," Historical Articles of Solano County, Jan. 16, 2005, solanoar-ticles.com.

"Brown Denies Gaming Bribe," San Mateo Times, p. 12, July 11, 1956.

Browning, William. "U.S. Gas Price History: From 25 Cents to Nearly $5 a Gallon," Yahoo! News, April 25, 2011.

"Cadillac Jack's and Pink Motel," Los Angeles Conservancy, www. laconservancy.org.

"The California Alligator Farm," www.lincolnheightsla.com.

"California Copper Properties," San Francisco Chronicle, p. 6, April 13, 1901.

Caltrafficsigns.com.

"Canada to Mexico by Auto," The Washington Post, p. 4, Oct. 16, 1910.

"Car Hurtles Ridge Route; Man Leaps," Santa Cruz Evening News, p. 1, April 24, 1928.

Cathro, Morton. "Bon Appetit!" Oct. 4, 2005, www.bloodhorse.com.

"City Isolated by Heavy Rainstorm," The Bakersfield California, p. 2, Jan. 23, 1943.

"City of Roseville: History," www.roseville.ca.us/visit_roseville.

"Central Valley Volcano of Unrest as Strike Goes on," The Piqua Daily Call, p. 1, Oct. 11, 1933.

"Claim Eclipse Triggered Earthquake," Lebanon (Pa.) Daily News, Feb. 10, 1971.

Clifford, Frank. "Curry Co. Turns Over Yosemite Concessions," Los Angeles Times, Oct. 2, 1993. www.latimes.com.

"Coast, Inland Valleys Feel Flood's Force," San Bernardino Daily Sun, p. 14, March 4, 1938.

"Coffee for Nickle [sic] Still Served Here," The Bakersfield Californian, p. 49, Jan. 14, 1977.

"Coffee Shop Opens," The Modesto Bee, p. B-7, Dec. 17, 1965.

Cole, D.L. The Beacon Story, 2010, Olive Press Publications, Los Osos, Calif.

"Colorado River On a Rampage," Tombstone (Ariz.) Weekly Epitaph, p. 3, July 15, 1906.

Colvin, Richard Lee. "Dust Bowl Legacy," Los Angeles Times, March 26, 1989, http://articles.latimes.com.

"Conscript Many To Fight Worst Fire In State," Oxnard Daily News, p. 1, July 14, 1924.

"Cop-Killer Manhunt Ends With Suicide," Abilene Reporter-News, p. 2-A, April 7, 1970.

Crawford, Richard W. The Way We Were in San Diego, The History Press, Oct. 25, 2011.

"Curry Acquires Lebec Resort On Ridge," Modesto Evening News, p. 9, Oct. 27, 1922.

"Curse of the Felizes," Glendale News-Press, Oct. 31, 1993, english. glendale.cc.ca.us.

Darr, Alan. "The Gilmore Oil Company," Sept. 27, 1995, http:// mlsandy.home.tsixroads.com/.

"Decline of the 'little guy,'" The Bakersfield Californian, p. 17, Feb. 13, 1974.

DiMento, Joseph F.C. and Ellis, Cliff. Changing Lanes: Visions and Histories of Urban Freeways, 2013, Massachusetts Institute of Technology, Cambridge, Mass., p. 47.

"Disastrous Break in the Los Angeles Aqueduct," The San Francisco Chronicle, p. 1, May 21, 1913.

Dunlap, John W. "Health Authorities of San Joaquin Deny Transients' Problem Critical," San Bernardino County Sun, p. 2, Feb. 6, 1938.

"Durant Files Suit For Insurance Money," Oakland Tribune, p. 7, Dec. 18, 1923.

Dyrud, Marilyn A. "The Limits of Professional Autonomy: William Mulholland and the St. Francis Dam," Oregon Institute of Technology.

"East Highway Travel Body To Erect 30 20-Foot Signs," Woodland Daily Democrat, p. 1, Aug. 24, 1927.

"The Eisenhower Interstate Highway System," Federal Highway Administration, www.fhwa.dot.gov/interstate.

Erish, Andrew A. Col. William N. Selig, the Man Who Invented Hollywood, University of Texas Press, Austin, Texas, 2012, p. 129.

Evans, Kenneth W. "Tiny's Waffle Shops Gain Great Impetus," San Jose Evening News, p. 8, April 3, 1939.

"Everest: The Death Zone," NOVA, PBS, Feb. 24, 1998.

"Ex-Motel Operator Guilty of Bribe Try," San Bernardino County Sun, p. 6, Dec. 4, 1954.

Fairytaletown.org.

Farrell Aidem, Patricia. "Heroic Civilian Vet Honored for Role in Police Gunbattle," Los Angeles Daily News, 2005.

"Fear Disaster From Quake-Damaged Dam," Lebanon (Pa.) Daily News, Feb. 10, 1971.

Ferris, Steve. "Gun Fights Erupt Hourly In This Town," The Modesto Bee, p. D-2, July 28, 1965.

Fimrite, Peter. "Central Valley fog disappears, fruit, nut crops decline," May 22, 2014. www.sfgate.com.

"Final Talk Between CHP, Murder Suspects Related," Van Nuys News, p. 9-B, Oct. 23, 1970.

"Find 140 Torrent Victims; Hundreds More Are Sought," Woodland Daily Democrat, p. 1, March 13, 1928.

"Find Dam Badly Built," Oxnard Daily Courier, p. 1, March 15, 1928.

Fitzgerald, Michael. Column. The Stockton Record, June 10, 2012.

Fitzgerald, Michael. "Rustigian was staple of shtick on stage," The Stockton Record, Dec. 1, 2013. www.recordnet.com.

"The Floods in Southern California. Great Washouts on All the Railroads," The San Francisco Chronicle, p. 6, Dec. 27, 1889.

Flying A ad, p. 24, The Fresno Bee, May 26, 1952.

Flying A ad, p. 20, The Fresno Bee, Sept. 12, 1952

"Fokker Air Corporation Bought For Four Million," The Modesto News-Herald, p. 1, Oct. 25, 1928.

"Former Campers Slept With 6-Gun," Long Beach Independent, p. 91, June 15, 1972.

"Foster Curry Buys Hotel At Lebec," Mariposa Gazette, Aug. 26, 1922.

"Freeway Extension: State to Pull Plug on the Last Traffic Light on Route 99," Los Angeles Times, July 26, 1987, latimes.com.

"Fresno Gasoline Price War End Provides Puzzle," The Fresno Bee, p. 1-C, Feb. 18, 1966.

FSA Prepares To Spend $150,000 To Safeguard Health Among Migrants," The Fresno Bee, p. 3-B, Feb. 2, 1938.

Galvan, Louis, Sheehan, Tim and Matlosz, Felicia. "108-Vehicle Pileup Kills at Least Two On Fresno Highway," The Fresno Bee, Nov. 5, 2007.

"Gas Price War Raging in U.S. 99 Service Stations," The Bakersfield Californian, p. 19, Feb. 8, 1955.

"Gay's Lion Farm Will Not Reopen" San Bernardino Daily Sun, p. 4, Oct. 30, 1949.

"George Woolf, Great Jockey, Dies as Result of Spill in Santa Anita Race," The Berkshire Evening Eagle, p. 4, Jan. 4, 1946.

Gia, Gilbert. "The Crystal Inn and El Adobe Nightclubs," Kern County Historical Society Quarterly Bulletin, Vol. 57, No. 3, Fall 2007.

"Gilmore Station History," gilmorestation.com.

"Goes To Sleep At Wheel; Plunges To Death," Santa Cruz Evening News, p. 9, Aug. 4, 1922.

" 'Golden State Highway' Title Selected To Replace 'Valley Route,' " The Modesto Bee, p. 1, July 10, 1927.

"The Great Flood," Greetings From The Salton Sea, www.greetings-fromsaltonsea.com.

"The Great White Way: Richfield Beacons," richfieldbeacons.weebly.com.

"Griffith J. Griffith: LA's Original Celebrity Wife-Murderer," The Native Angelino, Sept. 21, 2012. www.thenativeangeleno.com.

"Griffith Park Tunnel Conference Subject," Van Nuys News, p. 7, Oct. 17, 1930.

"Griffith Park's Unique Donor," http://english.glendale.cc.ca.us.

"Group of Armed Men Blow Up Aqueduct Carrying L.A. Supply," Santa Cruz News, p. 1, May 27, 1927.

"Guard asked For Tulare Peach Area," Santa Cruz Evening News, p. 1, Aug. 14, 1933.

Guzowski, Kenneth J. "Columbia River Highway Bridges," p. 7, National Park Service.

"Hacienda Readies New Supper Club," The Fresno Bee, p. 81, Nov. 17, 1963.

Hall, Carla. "Zoo to display lion statues from early L.A. menagerie," Los Angeles Times, May 14, 2009. articles.latimes.com

Hamlin, David and Arena, Brett, Los Angeles's Original Farmers Market, p. 41-56. Arcadia Publishing, San Francisco, 2009.

Herskowitz, Mickey and Perkins, Steve. "Sports Hot Line," Traverse City (Mich.) Record-Eagle, p. 12, Nov. 11, 1977.

"Highway Traffic Circle Urged By C.C.A. Leaders During Conclave," The Bakersfield Californian, p. 7, Sept. 10, 1932.

"Historic Kennett Quits As a Town," Santa Cruz Evening News, p. 2, April 15, 1930.

Hong, WookSun. "Oppression and Poverty Persists in the Central Valley," Feb. 9, 2014, http://lawprofessors.typepad.com.

"Hotel Man Accused of Bribe Attempt," The Bakersfield Californian, p. 37, June 23, 1954.

Imlay, Michael. "Col. Griffith's Brush With the Cursed Grim Reaper," Cryptic L.A., Oct. 28, 2008. http://mimlay.com.

"Increase In Traffic Real Highway Problem," Van Nuys News, p. 6, May 9, 1924.

"Insiders Explain The Gas War," The Modesto Bee, p. C-1, June 27, 1971.

"Interregional, Regional, Metropolitan Parkways in the Los Angeles Metropolitan Area," March 30, 1946.

"Involves Largest Deposit of Soda," San Francisco Chronicle, p. 3, Nov. 8, 1913.

Japenga, Ann. "Man Who Had a Heart for the Okies," Los Angeles Times, Jan. 18, 1987. http://articles.latimes.com.

Jonathan H. "Inundated Underwater Cities." www.terrastories.com.

"June McCarroll's Lasting Legacy," American Countryside, Oct. 18, 2010, http://americancountryside.com.

"Jury Fails Fix Cause of Death," Lincoln Sunday Star, Sept. 21, 1930.

Kane, Bonnie Ketterl, "A View From the Ridge: The Roadways," p. 177, 217, 236, Bonnie's Books, Visalia, Calif., 2014.

"Kennett Machinists Go Out on Strike," San Francisco Chronicle, p. 4, May 13, 1919.

"Kidnapper Arrested after Long Pursuit," Los Angeles Police Department blog, Jan. 28, 2008. http://lapdblog.typepad.com.

"Klein's Truck Stop," reviews, yelp.com.

"Labor Activism," Digital History ID 587, www.digitalhistory.uh.edu/

Laflin, P. "The Salton Sea: California's Overlooked Treasure," The Periscope, Indio, Calif., 1995. www.sci.sdsu.edu.

Landphair, Ted. "The Incredible Saga of the Salton Sea," Voice of America, June 5, 2012. blogs.voanews.com.

"Last stoplight on its last legs," Lodi News-Sentinel, p. 5, Jan. 11, 1992.

Laughnan, Woody. "Hoot Has The Recipe—Experience," p. 4-B, The Fresno Bee, Aug. 28, 1970.

Laughnan, Woody. "Voice Behind The Thrill In Café On A Hill," The Fresno Bee, p. J2, Sept. 13, 1973.

"Leopard Lady," Long Beach Independent, p. 2, Sept. 4, 1969.

Lester, Paul. "Two Sexy 'Urban Cowgirls' - One Called Debra Winger—Give Travolta a Run for His Movie," People, Aug. 18, 1980. www.people.com.

"Let the 'Gas' Wars Continue," The New York Times, April 22, 1985.

Livingston, Jill. "That Ribbon of Highway I," Living Gold Press, Klamath River, Calif, 2000.

Livingston, Jill. "That Ribbon of Highway II," Living Gold Press, Klamath River, Calif, 1998, 2010.

"Local Nursery Is Growing Thousands of Young Trees for Beautifying Boulevard," Bakersfield Californian, p. 9, May 8, 1936.

"Looking for a motel in 1933," Historic Highways, historichighways.wordpress.com.

"Los Angeles Ostrich Farm," www.lincolnheightsla.com.

Lynch, George Gilbert. "Bakersfield's entertainment hot spots of the 1950s," bakersfield.com, March 23, 2009.

Lynch, George Gilbert. "Made in the shade," people.bakersfield.com, Sept. 4, 2007.

Lynch, George Gilbert. "The evolution of the Garces Circle," Feb. 26, 2009, http://people.bakersfield.com.

"Magic Mountain Adds to the Fun of Living in Valencia," The Van Nuys News, p. 33, Sept. 20, 1970.

Maharidge, Dale. "Can we all get along?" Mother Jones, November-December, 1993. www.motherjones.com.

Manuel D. Martin Claimed by Death," The Bakersfield Californian, p. 11, Jan 25, 1937.

"Many Men Thrown Out Of Work at Plants," San Francisco Chronicle, p. 4, June 1, 1919.

Marcum, Diana. "Mammoth Orange food stand suddenly a hot commodity," Los Angeles Times, June 3, 2012. latimes.com.

Marelius, John. "Spring Completion Slated for 'Magic Mountain' Park," The Van Nuys News, p. 7-A, June 26, 1970.

Master, Shannon. "St. Francis Dam disaster: Mulholland's tragic mistake," signalscv.com, March 22, 2009.

McCarthy, Charles. "Valley landmark gets new juice," The Fresno Bee, April 11, 2008.

McClurg, Sue. "The Salton Sea," Western Water, March/April 1994, p. 3-11. www.sci.sdsu.edu/.

McKenna, Brian. "Officer Down: The Newhall Incident," police-marksman.com.

Meares, Hadley. "Phantom Fast Lanes: Whitnall Highway and the Footprint of Best Laid Plans," www.kcet.org.

Miller, Bill. "The lost light of the Siskiyous," Mail Tribune, June 13, 2012, www.mailtribune.com.

"Minute Men of Owens Valley Await Call," Santa Cruz Evening News, p. 3, June 7, 1927.

Modesto Visitors Destination Downtown, www.visitmodesto.com/visitors/downtown.

Montanez, Farin. "Paleontology Foundation buys Mammoth Orange shell," Madera Tribune, June 14, 2012.

Morgan, Lindsey. "El Monte, California," www.localpages.com.

Motorboating, the Yachtsman's Magazine, January 1948.

"Mrs. Griffith Has A Fainting Spell," Los Angeles Herald, Feb. 18, 1904.

"Mrs. Griffith's Terrible Story," San Bernardino Weekly Sun, p. 2, Feb. 19, 1904.

"Mulholland, Builder of Ill-Fated St. Francis Dam, Resigns Office," San Bernardino Sun, Nov. 14, 1928.

Murphy, Thos. D. On Sunset Highways, p. 336-337, 342, L.C. Page & Co, 1921.

Myers, R.C. "Ramona Boulevard a 6-Mile 'Airline' Urban Route Without Grade Crossings," California Highways and Public Works, p. 6, February 1935.

Nelson, Lauren. "Pixie Woods: Stockton's magical forest still enchanting after all these years," Lodi News-Sentinel, July 6, 2012. www.lodinews.com.

Nichols, Chris. "Sun sets on Pollardville," Lodi News-Sentinel, March 29, 2007, lodinews.com.

"No Lion," Long Beach Independent, p. 1, Oct. 3, 1969.

"November 20 letter to Leo Hart," www.docstoc.com.

O'Clifford, James. "Freeway Squeezes Giant Oranges dry," p. A-28, Long Beach Press-Telegram, Oct. 18, 1973.

"Oil Firm Calls Gasoline Wars 'Cannibalism,'" The Fresno Bee, p. 18, May 4, 1965.

"One Killed, Four Injured in Mad Plunge of Truck," The Bakersfield Californian, p. 5, July 27, 1946.

"Orland Arch," Waymarking. www.waymarking.com.

"Overlooked Something,' Says Builder of Fatal Dam," San Mateo Times, March 21, 1928.

Owens, Buck. Buck 'Em!, 2013, Backbeat Books, Milwaukee, Wis.

"Owens Rescues Damaged Sign," The Kokomo Tribune, p. 24, April 23, 1999.

"Owens Valley Banks Closed; L.A. is Blamed," Santa Cruz Evening News, p. 7, Aug. 5, 1927.

"Owens Valley Ranchers Halt Siege," San Bernardino County Sun, p. 1, Nov. 21, 1924.

"Owner of Giant Orange Protected by Injunction," Bakersfield Californian, p. 19, May 1, 1941.

Palace Showboat at Pollardville, http://www.palaceshowboat.com.

"Pass Fire Raging," Woodland Daily Democrat, p. 2, Aug. 23, 1927.

"Plotters Dynamite L.A. Aqueduct," The Bakersfield Californian, p. 1, May 21, 1924.

Pollack, Alan. "St. Francis Dam Disaster: An Extended Timeline," scvhistory.com, March 13, 2014.

"Pollardville Chicken Kitchen," www.uer.ca.

Poole, Bob. "CHP honors slain officers," Los Angeles Times, April 5, 2008, articles.latimes.com.

"Purifying Smelter Fumes," Oakland Tribune, p. 6, Oct. 23, 1909.

Rasmussen, Cecilia. " 'Doc June' Drew the Line on Safety' " Los Angeles Times, Oct. 12, 2003.

"Recalling 'Grapes of Wrath' Furor," The Fresno Bee, p. 14, Dec. 24, 1968.

Reich, Kenneth. " '71 Valley Quake a Brush With Catastrophe," Los Angeles Times, Feb. 4, 1996. articles.latimes.com.

Reiring, Ron. "Whitnall Parkway—The Freeway That Never Was," whitnallparkway.blogspot.com.

"Rescue Many Motorists On Ridge Route," The Oxnard Press-Courier, p. 1, Jan. 31, 1922.

"Retired Newhall CHP officer to speak on 1970 'Newhall Incident,' Santa Clarita Valley Historical Society, www.signalscv.com.

"Richfield Buys Airport Near Merced," Santa Cruz Evening News, p. 8, Aug. 24, 1928.

"The Ridge Route," Bakersfield Californian, p. 12, Nov. 10, 1915.

"Ridge Route Survey For Traffic Ordered," San Bernardino Daily Sun, p. 19, Oct. 6, 1927.

Robinson, John. "Sandberg's Hotel on the Old Ridge Route," Los Angeles Corral, Summer 2002.

"Roscoe Tanner," National Aviation Hall of Fame, http://nationala-viation.org.

Sahagun, Louis. "There It Is—Take It," http://graphics.latimes.com/me-aqueduct/.

"San Franciscan Admires Belmont Traffic Circle," The Fresno Bee, p. 28, Jan. 3, 1933.

Saunders, Mae. "Migratory Camp Gives Haven for Wanderers," The Bakersfield Californian, p. 9, Aug. 18, 1939.

Saunders, Mae. "National Problem of Migratory Worker Centers in California," The Bakersfield Californian, p. 13, Aug. 3, 1939.

Scott, Harrison Irving. "Ridge Route: The Road That United California," Torrance, Calif., 2006.

"Scores die in Flood Disaster," Van Nuys News, p. 1, March 13, 1928.

"Selig Polyscope Company," The Wonderful Wiki of Oz, oz.wikia.com.

"Selig Zoo and Movie Studio," www.lincolnheightsla.com.

Semmes, Ben. "Former chicken farm, popular restaurant, landmark buys the ranch," Tri-Valley Herald, July 19, 2006, www.inside-bayarea.com.

"Several Decisions," Los Angeles Herald, p. 3, Aug. 22, 1891.

"Shasta County Farmers Object to Coram Smelter," San Francisco Chronicle, p. 41, April 28, 1912.

"Shot From Behind," Los Angeles Herald, p. 3, Oct. 29, 1891.

"Sinatra Admits Plans For New Salton Sea Development Fail," The Modesto Bee, p. 13, Nov. 10, 1948.

"Sinatra to Open New Salton Sea Resort," San Mateo Times, p. 2, Nov. 4, 1948.

Slothower, Laurie. "Fresno was their home," Santa Cruz Sentinel, p. 58, Nov. 21, 1986.

"Small Award for Damage by Smelter Smoke," San Francisco Chronicle, p. 31, Nov. 17, 1907.

"Smallest City In California Wants To Disincorporate," Santa Cruz Evening News, p. 2, April 2, 1930.

"Smelter Smoke Kills Live Stock," San Francisco Chronicle, p. 19, May 21, 1905.

"Smelter's Shutdown Cripples Whole Town," San Francisco Chronicle, p. 4, June 8, 1919.

Smith, Dottie. "Copper mining and the toxic copper smelters," ShastaCountyHistory.com.

Sonnichsen, Donna-Marie. "Reunion, documentary preserve memory of hardscrabble life that was Tagus Ranch," Tulare Voice, http://tularevoice.com. June 19, 2013.

"Spirit of Fair Play Needed in Outdoors," San Bernardino Daily Sun, p. 24, March 27, 1926.

Stahlmann, Jenni. "You're Gonna Wish Your Kid Could Go To THIS School!" Parenting On Purpose, http://www.jenniandjody.com.

Stanley, Gerald and McColgan, Susan. "Educating Farm Labor Children," interview with Leo Hart, Feb. 2, 1977.

Stanley, Jerry. " 'Grapes of Wrath' Grads," Chicago Tribune, March 14, 1989, http://articles.chicagotribune.com.

Stargel, Cory and Stargel, Sarah. "Vanishing Los Angeles County," p. 58, Arcadia Publishing, Charleston, S.C., 2010.

"The Start of Something Big," Palm Springs Life magazine, www.palmspringslife.com.

"Stopping Distances for Big Rigs," HG.org Legal Resources.

Strei, W.E. "Auto Camp Kit is Comfort to Road Tourists," San Bernardino Daily Sun, p. 17, Aug. 21, 1921.

Sweeney, James. "Quake safety a low priority for California's highways," Santa Cruz Sentinel, p. A-8, Oct. 30, 1989.

"Three Lions Hold Police At Bay After Breaking From Captivity At Farm," St. Petersburg Independent, p. 6, Sept. 27, 1928.

"Three Meet Death When Auto Plunges 1000 Feet," Oxnard Press-Courier, p. 1, Sept. 9, 1928.

"Tips Restaurants Opens New Unit at Market Town," Van Nuys News, p. 6, March 2, 1950.

Timeline, 1925-1929, www.garboforever.com.

"Tolan's Bill For Federal Aid To Migrants Scored," The Fresno Bee, p. 18, Jan. 14, 1940.

"Touring Autos from the South," Bakersfield Californian, p. 6, Aug. 29, 1907.

"Treatment of Fumes from Smelters," San Francisco Chronicle, p. 23, Jan. 12, 1916.

"Truck Checking Station Opened on Ridge Route," California Highways and Public Works, p. 24, March 1938.

"Truck Has Good Test For Year," Oakland Tribune, p. 40, Jan. 22, 1922.

"Tule fog causes severe problems in Central Valley," Dec. 10, 2012. www.kcra.com.

"Twinning frees hostage, takes his own life," Redlands Daily Facts, p. 1, April 7, 1970.

"Two Leading Inyo Bankers Face Arrest," San Bernardino County Sun, p. 1, Aug. 14, 1927.

"Two Men Killed When Car Plunges 215 Feet Off Ridge Route Road," Oxnard Press-Courier, p. 1, Dec. 24, 1927.

U.S. Reclamation Service, p. 15, 1904.

"Valley Auto Road the Best," Bakersfield Californian, p. 6, Sept. 4, 1907.

"Van Nuys Motorists Caught in Forest Fire Area, Effect Escape," Van Nuys News, p. 1, Aug. 23, 1927.

Van Rhyn, Art. "The Ridge Route" (thesis).

Vaught, Steve. "Lighting Up the Coast—The Beacon Tavern and the 'Richfield Lane of Lights,' March 16, 20111, paradiseleased. wordpress.com.

"Vibrating Mattresses," The Connellsville Daily Courier, p. 16, June 11, 1973.

"Victory Ball Guest," The Bakersfield Californian, June 22, 1944.

Walker, John. "Historical Perspective: Fresno's Van Ness Arch," June 2, 2013, fresnobee.com.

Wallis, Michael. "The Real Wild West," p. 342, St. Martin's Press, N.Y., 1999.

"Washington Good Roads Association," www.historylink.org.

"Water Spreads Over Highway Near Madera," The Fresno Bee, p. 22, March 2, 1938.

Wharton, David. "Maestro of Drink Has Free Hand," Los Angeles Times, April 12, 1985, articles.latimes.com.

Wharton, David. "The Motel of Make-Believe," Los Angeles Times, Aug. 2, 1990, articles.latimes.com.

Weber, Devra. "Dark Sweat, White Gold," p. 169, University of California Press, Berkeley, 1994.

"Welcome to Clark's Travel Center!" www.clarkstravelcenter.com.

"Where are the Burma Shave Signs?" Legendary Route 66. www. legendsofamerica.com.

"Who's Faster? … an old alligator races a young tortoise," Long Beach Independent, p. 114, Feb. 22, 1953.

Wilkerson, Lyn. "Slow Travels–California," 2009.

"William Mulholland," New Perspectives on the West, www.pbs.org.

"Woman falls 100 feet to death from Magic Mountain Colossus," San Bernardino County Sun, p. 5, Dec. 27, 1978.

Worden, Lee. Magic Mountain. http://www.scvhistory.com.

"Work is Started on Key Unit of Valleys Project," The Modesto Bee, p. 6, March 15, 1936.

Wyatt, Virgil. "New Queen of Girl Pilots Toiled in Beauty Shop To Earn Money for Her Course in Flying," Santa Cruz News, p. 5, Aug. 21, 1930.

REFERENCES, PART II

"30 Dead, Hundreds Evacuate Homes As Flood Sweeps L.A.," The Modesto Bee, p. 1, Jan. 1, 1934.

"1913: Wheatland hop riot," libcom.org.

"A Brief History of the City of Alhambra," City of Alhambra, www.cityofalhambra.org.

"A Brief History of Woodland," Stroll Through History. www.strollthroughhistory.com.

"A River Runs Through It; the (Un)Natural History of the Los Angeles River," www.dailykos.com.

Abbott, William W. "A Historic Tale of Two Towns," March 26, 2010. www.californialandsettlements.com.

"About Us," Percheron McFarland. www.percheron-mcfarland.com.

"Admits Part In Killing Of Daw, Dunsmuir Chief," Santa Cruz Sentinel, p. 1, Sept. 5, 1936.

Alexander, Kyle W., "Yesterday Today & Tomorrow," The San Bernardino County Sun, p. B-4, May 1, 1960.

Allen, David. "California Jam festival rocked Ontario in 1974," Inland Valley Daily Bulletin, April 4, 2014. www.dailybulletin.com.

"American Graffiti–1973," www.historicmodesto.com.

"Bakersfield, Oil Capitol of California, Breadbasket of the West," www.sjvgeology.org.

Baseball-Reference.com.

Bates, James B. "The Plank Road," The Journal of San Diego History, Spring 1970, Vol. 16, No. 2.

Benziger, Jeff. "Ceres: Images of America," Arcadia Publishing, San Francisco, 2010.

"Bees Close Highway 99 In North," The Fresno Bee, p. 8-C, Nov. 1, 1963.

Bieser, Dick. "11 dead in Tehachapi Quake," Santa Cruz Sentinel, p. 1, July 21, 1952.

"Blast, Flames Hit Distillery Near Ripon," The Modesto Bee, p. 1, July 11, 1946.

"Bobby Darin: Hell Breaks Loose on Location," TV Radio Mirror Magazine, December 1961. www.bobbydarin.net.

Brightwell, Eric. "Welcome to friendly El Monte, the end of the Santa Fe Trail (or at least some trails)," Jan. 23, 2013. www.amoeba.com

"Cabazon dinosaur builder dies of pneumonia at 91," The San Bernardino County Sun, p. 12, Sept. 12, 1988.

"Cabazon dinosaurs," Weirdca.com.

"California Theatre," Cinemat Treasures. cinematreasures.org.

Campbell, Will. "Songs About Los Angeles: 'The New Year's Flood' by Woody Guthrie," April 23, 2009, blogging.la.

Carter, Lloyd. "Landmark of bygone era burned," Long Beach Independent, p. 18, April 29, 1971.

"Chico." localwiki.net/chico.

"Chowchilla's History," www.ci.chowchilla.ca.us.

"City of Marysville Ordered Evacuated," San Mateo Times, p. 1, Dec. 23, 1955.

"Club Hears Pleas For Removal Of Chowchilla Arch," The Fresno Bee, p. 14, March 15, 1936.

"Colton Crossing: A Model for Public-Private Partnerships," inlandempirecenter.org.

"Community of Arbuckle," Colusa County, California. www.countyofcolusa.org.

"Concrete Causeway Across the Yolo By-Pass, California," Concrete Highway Magazine, p. 56, January, 1919.

"County Will Move Lebec Florafaunium," The Bakersfield Californian, p. 21, April 27, 1950.

Crawford, Richard. "Wooden plank road cut through dunes to Yuma," San Diego Union-Tribune, Oct. 22, 2009. www.utsandiego.com.

Crosby, Sherry Joe. "Gorman CA: For Sale: Family Prices: Hometown to Move," Los Angeles Daily News, 1997.

Crowson, Garrell Glenn. "Almost Eleven: The Murder of Brenda Sue Sayers," p. 12, 2013, Friesen Press, Victoria, BC, Canada.

Dalton, Eva. "The Dalton Gang and Their Family Ties," p. 32, Ohnick Enterprises, Meade, Kansas, 2005.

"The Dalton Gang," www.eshomvalley.com.

"A Dinosaur Shapes Up On A Desert Roadside," The Fresno Bee, p. 44, March 25, 1970.

"Delhi State Land Settlement," Community of Delhi, www.delhicalifornia.net.

"Dead or Alive," Arkansas City Daily Traveler, p. 4, May 15, 1891.

"Delano Farm Strikers Seek Student Support," The Fresno Bee, p. 7-B, Nov. 14, 1965.

"Destruction, Courage, Aid To Stricken Mark Quake," The Fresno Bee, p. 10, July 23, 1952.

Drago, Henry Sinclair. "Outlaws on Horseback," p. 205

Duff, Brian. "North of Sacramento US 99 Develops Split Personality," Santa Cruz Sentinel, p. 5, Sept. 17, 1956.

"Earlimart History," Earlimart School District, www.earlimart.org.

"El Monte Legion Stadium," www.elmontelegionstadium.com.

"Elk Grove Community," www.elkgrovecity.org.

Emerson, Sandra. "Redlands declares emergency to obtain sinkhole funds." Redlands Daily Facts, Aug. 12, 2014. www.redlandsdaily-facts.com.

Farrow, Ross. "Residents are proud to be 'Stuck in Lodi,'" Lodi News-Sentinel, web.archive.org.

"Fire Destroys Business Section of Mining Town," Los Angeles Herald, p. 11, July 10, 1910.

"Fire Razes Arch, Old Landmark At Chowchilla," The Fresno Bee, p. 9, Aug. 28. 1937.

"Flaming Brandy Burns 3 After Still Blast," The Pittsburgh Press, p. 10, July 12, 1946.

"Florafaunium Creation of One Man," The Bakersfield Californian, p. 9, March 11, 1942.

"Florafaunium in Lebec Will Be Demolished," The Bakersfield Californian, p. 21, July 6, 1955.

"Forestiere Underground Gardens," www.undergroundgardens.com.

"Fresno Scraper," www.asme.org.

"From Brawley By Way Of Mecca," San Bernardino Daily Sun, p. 2, Jan. 20, 1912.

"Frontier Lawman Virgil Earp," www.historynet.com.

Garone, Philip. "The Fall and Rise of the Wetlands of California's Great Central Valley," p. 194, University of California Press, Berkeley and Los Angeles, 2011.

"Gidden Brothers create giant road side wonder," The Galt Herald, May 19, 2010. www.galtheraldonline.

"Gladding, McBean: About Us," www.gladdingmcbean.com/aboutus.html.

"Glendale History - A Brief Look," The Glendale Historical Society, glendalehistorical.org.

"Good Detective Work," Santa Cruz Sentinel, p. 2, March 18, 1891.

Good, Kay. "The exact center of California Monument," Sierra Star, Sept. 16, 2010. www.sierrastar.com.

Hall, Duane. "Where the Palm Meets the Pine," A Geographer's Scrapbook, Feb. 27, 2010. duanehallca.blogspot.com.

"Hazel Hotel," NoeHill Travels In California, www.noehill.com.

"Hi-Lo Motel Café–Weed, CA" Walterworld, Oct. 7, 2010. freetv-airconditioned.blogspot.com.

"History," Auto Club Famoso Raceway, famosoraceway.com.

"History," City of Coachella, www.coachella.org.

"History," Highland Springs Resort, www.hsresort.com.

"History," Salida Chamber of Commerce. salidachamber.com.

"History of Yreka," City of Yreka, ci.yreka.ca.us.

"Huge Booze Supply Is Lost In Blaze," Santa Ana Register, p. 2, June 26, 1922.

"Imperial Sand Dunes: Old Plank Road," DesertUSA, www.desertusa.com.

"Improvement of Weston Brandy Plant is Slated," The Modesto Bee, p. 11, June 20, 1938.

"Jack's Grill: The Legend," www.jacksgrillredding.com.

Justice, Stephen. "50 Years of Fuel Dragsters at the March Meet," wediditforlove.com.

"Kaiser Steel Plant Site," The Center for Land Use Interpretation, clui.org.

Kane, Bonnie Ketterl. "The Grapevine," The Ridge Route Communities Museum & Historical Society. www.rrchs.org.

Kane, Michael. "Losing his cool," New York Post, Oct. 23, 2011. nypost.com.

"Keep Border Closed," San Bernardino Daily Sun, p. 12, Dec. 22, 1924.

"Kern to Receive Florafaunium Sunday," The Bakersfield California, p. 1, March 14, 1942.

Ketterl Kane, Bonnie. "Welcome to Lebec," The Ridge Route Communities Museum & Historical Society, rrchs.org.

Kulczyk, David. "Assassination in Germantown," Where the losers write history. www.dkulczyk.com.

Kulczyk, David. "Hops of wrath." www.newsreview.com.

Lanser, Edward. "A People of Mystery," Los Angeles Times, May 22, 1932.

"Learn about the wild history of Redding's California Street at Shasta Historical Society lecture," Redding Record Searchlight, Oct. 14, 2013. www.redding.com.

"Lebec Shares in Kern Growth," The Bakersfield Californian, p. 24, Jan. 2, 1950.

Lindelof, Bill. "40 years later, witnesses recall dramatic explosions," The Sacramento Bee, www.sacbee.com.

"Looking Back to the Past," Brawley, California, www.villageprofile.com.

Lowry, Sam. "The Wheatland hop riot," lib.com/history/1913-wheatland-hop-riot.

Luna, Nancy. "SoCal institution In-N-Out opens replica 1948 burger stand," Orange County Register, Feb. 26, 2014. www.ocregister.com.

Lynch, George Gilbert. "Oildale's secret military history," The Bakersfield Californian, Nov. 11, 2009. www.bakersfieldcalifornian.com.

"Lynchers Seek Second Suspect," Reading (Pa.) Times, p. 1, Aug. 5, 1935.

Malnic, Eric. "Pilot launched Atomic Age over Hiroshima," Los Angeles Times, Nov. 2, 2007. articles.latimes.com.

"Manteca Waterslides—The Lost Parks of Northern California," youtube.com.

"Many Are Hurt In Bakersfield; Oil Refinery Burns," The Fresno Bee, p. 2, July 21, 1952.

Marcum, Diana. "Decades after school bus kidnapping, strong feelings in Chowchilla," April 3, 2011, Los Angeles Times articles.latimes.com.

Martin, Bill. "Underground World of Builder," Long Beach Press-Telegram, p. C-7, July 24, 1970.

"Maxwell," www.countyofcolusa.org.

May, Tina. "OMS sale completion today," The San Bernardino County Sun, p. 1, Dec. 17, 1980.

May, Tina. "Speedway's destruction racing along," The San Bernardino County Sun, p. B1, May 29, 1981.

McDonald, P.A. "Elimination of Newhall Tunnel Bottleneck Soon to Be Realized," California Highways and Public Works, p. 10, January 1938.

McKenney, J. Wilson. "Roadside Date Shop on the Desert," The Desert Magazine, p. 12, August 1938.

"Modesto honors George Lucas with sculpture," Lodi News-Sentinel, p. 8, July 12, 1997.

Moon, Debra. *Chico: Life and Times of a City of Fortune*, p. 52, Arcadia Publishing, San Francisco, 2003.

Moore, Sam. "History of the Fresno Scaper," Farm Collector, January 2002. www.farmcollector.com.

Morton, Ella. "Pee-Wee's Big, Adventurous, 6,000-Year-Old Dinousaurs," www.slate.com.

"Mudville Re-enacts Casey at the Bat," San Mateo Times, p. 10, Aug. 29, 1952.

Mulcahy, Gilbert. "Chico Esplanade," California Highways and Public Works, May-June 1949, pp. 11-13.

"Munitions blast shatters Roseville," Long Beach Independent Press-Telegram, p. 1, April 29, 1973.

Nordhoff, Charles. "California: For Health, Pleasure, and Residence," p. 208, Harper & Brothers, 1872.

"Officers Slain in Riot at Wheatland," San Francisco Chronicle, p. 1, Aug. 4, 1913.

Patterson, Richard M. *Historical Atlas of the Outlaw West*, p. 19, 23, 30, Johnson Publishing Co., Boulder, Colo., 1985, 2000.

"Rancho Rio de los Molinos," Southwest Shasta Historical Group, historyandhappenings.squarespace.com

Rasmussen, Cecilia. "Monterey Park History," Los Angeles Times, Jan. 17, 1994. articles.latimes.com.

Red Bluff-Tehama County Chamber of Commerce, redbluff-chamber.com

Reitman, Valerie. "Bid to Annex Gorman to Kern County Denied," Los Angeles Times, Jan. 21, 2006. articles.latimes.com.

Reynolds, Jerry. "Breaching the Pass," scvhistory.com.

"River Breaks Through Levee, Floods Yuba City; 8000 Flee," San Mateo Times, p. 1, Dec. 24, 1955.

"Rixville," History & Happenings, Southwest Shasta Historical Group. historyandhappenings.squarespace.com.

Romney, Lee. "Old accounts and strange tales orbit around Shasta," Los Angeles Times, Jan. 23, 2012. articles.latimes.com.

"Rosemead City History," Rosemead Chamber of Commerce, www.rosemeadchamber.org.

"Russell Nicoll; Inventor of the Date Shake," The Los Angeles Times, Jan. 29, 1987. articles.latimes.com.

Sacramento History Online. www.sacramentohistory.org.

"Salida Bypass," The Modesto Bee, p. 1, June 29, 1969.

"Salton Sea Test Base," Greetings from the Salton Sea, www.greetingsfromsaltonsea.com.

Santiago, Denise-Marie. "Wagons Ho: El Monte Insists Trail Didn't End in Santa Fe," Los Angeles Times, June 21, 1987. articles.latimes.com.

Sehorn, Jay. "Merkley Shows 'em as Oaks Beat Giants," Woodland Daily Democrat, p. 4, May 13, 1935.

"Shasta Cascade on the Silver Screen," shastacascade.hubpages.com.

Sheehan, Tim. "Demolition continues in Fresno for state high-speed rail project," The Fresno Bee, Political Notebook, July 16, 2014. www.fresnobee.com.

Simon, Rich. "Sightseeing on the Phantom Freeways of the Southland," Los Angeles Times, Nov. 28, 1994. articles.latimes.com.

"SP blames military in rail blast," The Bakersfield Californian, p. 6, Aug. 29, 1977.

"Story of the Alila Stoppage Recounted," San Francisco Chronicle, p. 13, Feb. 8, 1891.

"Sun-Maid Raisins," Online Highways, www.ohwy.com.

Taylor, Constance. "A Highway, a wetland and 250,000 bats," BayNature, July 25, 2013. www.baynature.org.

"The Olmsted Vision," The City Project, www.cityprojectca.org.

"The Plank Road," San Diego Yesterday, Dec. 1, 2011. www.sandiegoyesterday.com.

"The Story of Lincoln Way," www.galthistory.org.

"The Story of the Great Yolo Basin Concrete Trestle," California Highway Bulletin, p. 6, July 1, 1916.

"Thousand Palms: The Yesteryears," thousandpalmscc.com.

"Tipton Lindsey," ancestry.com.

"Train Robberies," Encyclopedia of Robberies, Heists and Capers, www.fofweb.com.

"The Tree Committee of the Bidwell Park and Playground Commission (BPPC) is currently working on a draft Urban Forest Management Plan," City of Chico. www.chico.ca.us.

TulareCountyAudubon.org.

"Weed Now and Then," www.snowcrest.net.

Yniguez, Rudy. "Nuke lab used Salton Sea base," Imperial Valley Press, Oct. 22, 2005. articles.ivpressonline.com.

Yucaipa Adobe," www.sbcounty.gov/Museum/branches.

INDEX

Stephen H. Provost is a journalist and author. He has worked as an editor, reporter, and columnist at newspapers throughout California. His previous books include *Fresno Growing Up: A City Comes of Age 1945–1985*, a history of his hometown, and *Memortality*, a contemporary fantasy adventure. Provost lives with his wife on California's Central Coast, where he is the editor of *The Cambrian* newspaper. Provost frequently blogs on writing and current events at his website, stephenhprovost.com.

Explore California with more great Craven Street Books

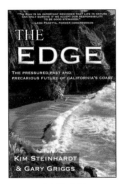
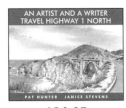

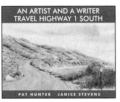